CW01337249

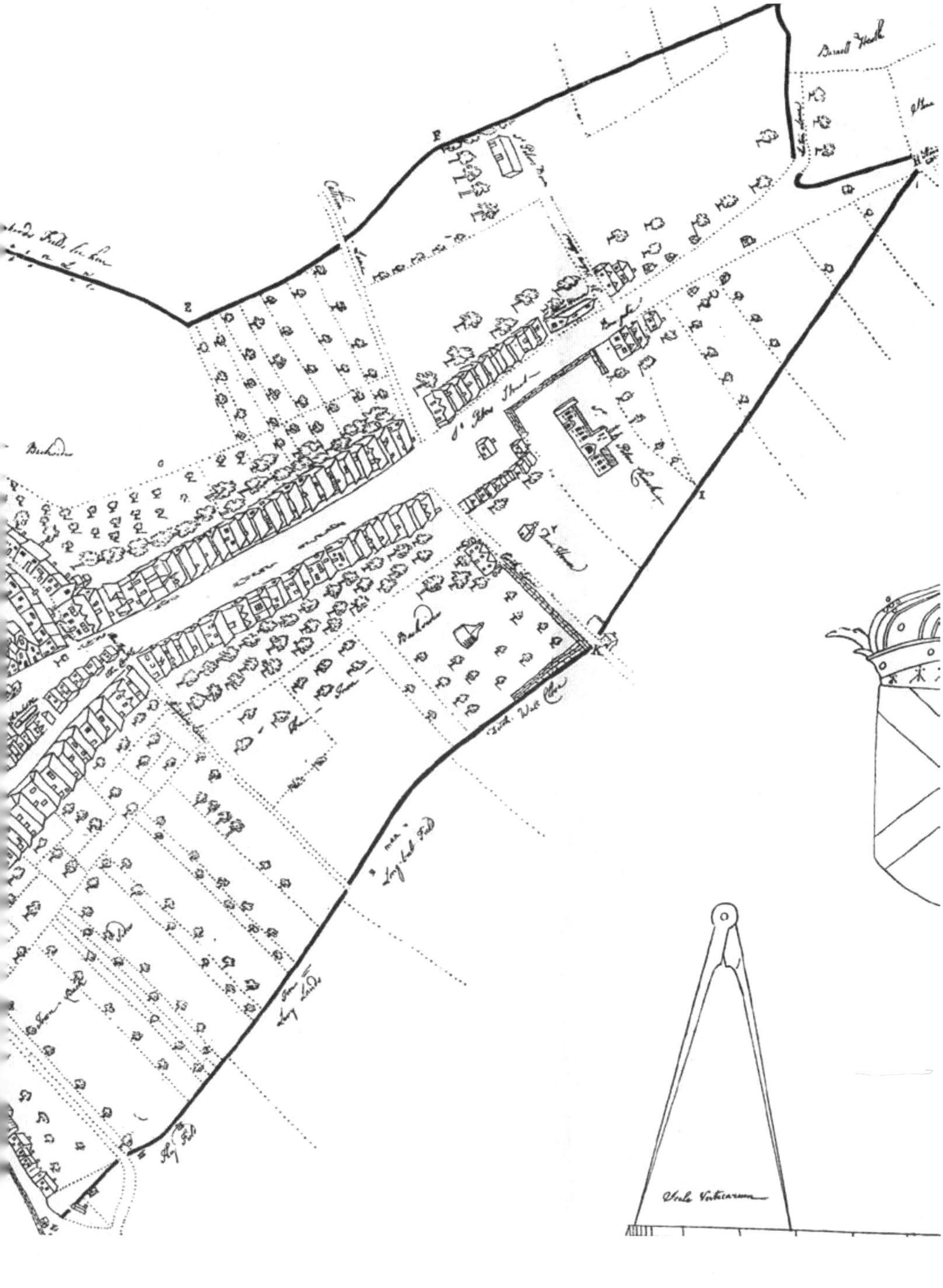

Noble Sr.

Wee received yors of the 26th of this instant, wherein wee perceive that you have called in the horsses, listed for you out of the division of Hartf: & that you are ready to advance for the defence of this County & Kingdome. Wee desire you to send to the Committee, & Rec: at St Albons for ther pay, for wee conceive that a Troope, to be pd some from Hartf: & some from St Albons, will make much trouble & difference, & yet bothe yors & the Maiors must be so, if wee should pay them as you mention, because the Maior have some in your division also: besides our treasure is very thin at this tyme & the more for the want of the 200li. besides, wch was ordered to be pd from yr Rec: to Hartf: & that other mony wch ye standing committee was ordered to pay to our Rec: out of the Earle of Manchester [illegible] mony, due to him, to pay his souldiers [illegible] quarter on this side of the County, wch makes them unable to pay any more mony, for want of that wch is ther due wch they have long expected, therfore wee desire you to expedite the suddain pay of those somes for us, as you can; although you pay more souldiers then yor share cometh unto, yet wee will assure you that wee shall pay our part, whatsoever it be. & desire that the some as may be an accompte may be taken, & see more even what is due to you, or to us, & so continewe for after times: & wee desire you to send for us, as well as for yor owne side of the County wch wee have [illegible], & wee shall strive as close to you, in any friendly maner. & doe reste

yor friends assuredly

[illegible]

Wm. Carter

Geo: Banastre

William Plomer

*Undated letter from Hertford committee to Col Alban Coxe, [HALS: 70538 see No 51 p41]*

Hertfordshire Record Publications Volume 23

# THE IMPACT OF THE FIRST CIVIL WAR ON HERTFORDSHIRE 1642-1647

Edited by Alan Thomson

Hertfordshire Record Society

2007

Hertfordshire Record Society

The publication of this volume has
been assisted by generous grants from
The Marc Fitch Fund
Isobel Thornley Bequest Fund
The Scouloudi Foundation
in association with The Institute of Historical Research



ISBN 978-0-9547561-5-4

Printed by
Biddles Ltd, King's Lynn

# Contents

# Illustrations

# Acknowledgements

My thanks are due to the following individuals and institutions for their assistance in the preparation of this volume: Firstly to Sue Flood and her colleagues at Hertfordshire Archives and Local Studies for all their help in providing a variety of documentary sources and particularly in the deciphering of obscure texts; to the staff of the National Archives at Kew for their patience, good humour and help in providing the bulk of the documentary sources; and to those who agreed to read the text and comment on it, particularly Professor John Miller, Professor Steve Hindle and Mr Alan Greening.

# General editorial method

- The original folio number has been included for sources which have been numbered in the original. This is in italics. The document number is in bold type and enclosed in square brackets. Otherwise the editor has imposed his own pagination which is in italic
- Original spellings have been retained. Some punctuation has been inserted to make the text accessible. Christian names, surnames and place-names have been left as they were written in the text but have been standardized in the footnotes.
- Standard early modern abbreviations such as $w^{ch}$ (which) and $w^{th}$ (with) have been silently extended, and others which become standard in context $q^{td}$ (quartered) have been likewise extended
- Words inserted above the line by the original writer are written thus <armies>.
- Words crossed through ~~thus~~ were deleted by the original writer.
- Illegible deletions have been rendered thus : ~~*illeg*~~
- A question mark after a word signifies the most likely reading of a barely legible word eg since?
- Editorial notes are given in bold Italic text in round brackets eg ***(On reverse)***
- (Round brackets) used in the original text have been reproduced
- Headings in <u>underlined text</u> appear for clarity, where they were not usually underlined
- Single Latin words or short phrases have been italicised eg *in primis*
- Underlining has been included where it is part of an arithmetical account where there is an added total but otherwise omitted
- Latin numerals have been retained where used and put in *italic* and Arabic numerals standardized in format where they form part of an account with an added total
- As the old-style calendar was in use, the modernized year has been shown for dates from 1 January to 24 March eg 3 February 1643 as 1643/4. In the footnotes, dates have been modernized where necessary
- Money: 12 pennies (12d) = 1 shilling (1s); 20 shillings =1 pound (£1) However in the text of accounts the Latin li for *libri* (pounds) has been retained where appropriate
- Measures of volume for grains: 4 pecks = 1 Bushel; 1 Bushel = 36.4 litres

# Abbreviations used in the text and footnotes

| | |
|---|---|
| *Al Cant* | Venn J & J A, *Alumni Cantabrigienses to 1900* Part 1, 4 vols, (Cambridge, 1922-7) |
| *Al Ox* | Foster J, (ed) *Alumni Oxonienses; The members of the University of Oxford 1500-1714,* 4 vols, (Oxford, 1891-2) |
| Beaven, | Beaven, A B, *The Aldermen of the City of London,* 2 vols (1908-13) |
| BL | British Library |
| *CCC* | Green, M A E (ed) *Calendar of the Proceedings of the Committee of Compounding 1643-1660,* 5 vols (1889) |
| Cecil | Dyfnallt Owen, G (ed) *HMC Salisbury (Cecil) Mss,* Vols XXII (1971), XXII (1976) |
| Chauncy | Henry Chauncy, *Historical Antiquities of Hertfordshire*, 2 vols (2nd ed, Bishops Stortford, 1826) |
| *CJ* | *The Journals of the House of Commons 1625-1666,* Vols II-VIII of series (1803) |
| Clutterbuck | Robert Clutterbuck, *The History and Antiquities of the County of Hertford,* 3 vols (London, 1815-27) |
| DP | Deposited Parish Documents (HALS) |
| *EHR* | *English Historical Review* |
| F&R | Firth, C H, & Rait, R S, (eds) *Acts and Ordinances of the Interregnum 1642-1660*, 3 vols (1911) |
| HALS | Hertfordshire Archives and Local Studies |
| *Herts Vis* | Metcalfe, W C, (ed) *The Visitations of Hertfordshire*, (1886) |
| HBR | Hertford Borough Records (HALS) |
| HMC | Historical Manuscripts Commission (now part of the National Archives) |
| *LJ* | *The Journals of the House of Lords 1628-1666*, Vols IV-XI of series, nd |
| *NewDNB* | *New Dictionary of National Biography* (Online) |
| QSB | Quarter Sessions Book (HALS) |
| QSR | Quarter Sessions Roll (HALS) |
| TNA | The National Archives (formerly the Public Record Office) |
| *VCH Herts* | William Page, (ed) *The Victoria History of the Counties of England: A History of Hertfordshire*, 4 vols, (London, 1902-14) |

# INTRODUCTION

## The Historiographical Context

Alfred Kingston wrote his book on the civil wars and Hertfordshire in 1894 and made three significant points. These were: firstly that the county acted as outpost and outlet for the civil protection of London; secondly it saw more of the organization and movement of Parliamentary armies than any other county; and thirdly that it suffered more of the effects of the presence of Parliamentary troops within its borders than any other county in the Eastern Association. These three themes are brought out in the documents included in this volume. He also saw Hertfordshire as an overwhelmingly Puritan county that was divided early on between Royalists and Parliamentarians, but later split between the more radical Independents and more conservative Presbyterians. Many histories of counties in this period have identified the changes in the Parliamentary war effort as being related to the emergence of these differences of religious and political viewpoint.[1] For many years in the mid 20th century historians were more concerned about the causes of the civil wars than how they were fought. However a number of county studies were made of the conflict including those in: Cornwall, Nottinghamshire, Suffolk, Kent, Norfolk, Cheshire and Sussex, and later Warwickshire.[2] In the mid 1990s authors studied London, Stratford upon Avon and Worcestershire.[3] Two stood out, that by D H Pennington and I A Roots on the Committee at Stafford and that by Clive Holmes on the Eastern Association, the former being a study of wartime administration in one county, the latter in one region.[4] In 1992 Charles Carlton produced the first edition of his work on the

---

[1] Kingston A, *Hertfordshire during the Civil War and Long Parliament,* (1894)

[2] Coate, M, *Cornwall in the Great Civil War and Interregnum 1642-1660: A social and political study*, (Oxford 1933); Wood, A C, *Nottinghamshire in the Civil War,* (Oxford, 1937); Everitt, A, *Suffolk & the Great Rebellion*, (Ipswich, 1961); Everitt, A, *The Community of Kent and the Great Rebellion, 1640-1660*, (Leicester, 1966); Ketton-Cremer, R W, *Norfolk in the Civil War,* (1969); Morrill, J S, *Cheshire 1630-1660: County Government and Society during the English Revolution*, (Oxford, 1974); Fletcher, A, *A County Community in Peace and War: Sussex 1600-1660*, (Harlow, 1975); Hughes, A, *Politics, Society & Civil War in Warwickshire 1620-60*, (Cambridge, 1987)

[3] Porter, S, (ed.) *London and the Civil War,* (Basingstoke, 1996); Tennant, P, *The Civil War in Stratford-upon-Avon: Conflict and Community in South Warwickshire, 1642-1646,* (Stroud, 1995); Atkin, M, *The Civil War in Worcestershire*, (Stroud, 1995)

[4] Pennington D H, & Roots, I., *The Committee at Stafford 1643-5*, (Manchester, 1957); Holmes, C, *The Eastern Association in the English Civil War*, (Cambridge, 1974)

general impact of the British Civil Wars, and this has been followed by others such as that by Martyn Bennett, both of which have given the broader perspective on how the wars were fought across the British Isles as a whole and their overall impact[5].

Alongside these histories, various county record societies have published primary sources relating to the period, notably *The Letters of Sir Samuel Luke* by the Bedfordshire Record Society[6] and a number of parts of volumes in the Buckinghamshire Record Society. The Hertfordshire Record Society has published volumes on the aristocratic and gentry accounts pre- war, mid 17th century parish registers and post war wills and inventories, but none have specifically touched on the war itself.[7] No record society seems to have fully exploited the rich resources in the State Papers (SP 28 Series) which are now in the National Archives at Kew. These are the series known as the Commonwealth Exchequer Papers.

## The sources

The majority of the documents in this volume are taken from what had been the papers deposited by a local sub-committee of the Committee for Taking the Accounts of the Kingdom, which had been set up to audit income and expenditure by local wartime committees in each county controlled by Parliament. They include a mass of material, which still remains largely un-calendared, in a range of volumes and boxes. Some of the records are in booklet form, while others are either collections of bills and receipts held together by pins or laces, or loose individual documents and, in one case, a roll of inventories sewn together. A useful guide to these and other records for local historians was produced by Aylmer and Morrill in 1980.[8] They

---

[5] Carlton, C, *Going to the Wars: the Experience of the British Civil Wars1638-1651,* (1992); Bennett, M, *The Civil Wars experienced: Britain & Ireland 1635-1661*, (2000)

[6] Tibbutt, H G (ed) *The Letter Book of Sir Samuel Luke 1644-1645,* Bedfordshire Record Society XLII (Bedford, 1963) *passim.* Sir Samuel Luke was a Parliamentary army officer and MP who captained a troop of horse at Edgehill and raised a regiment of dragoons in Bedfordshire for Essex's army in 1643. He became scoutmaster -general, assisted in the recovery of Newport Pagnell in October 1643 and became its governor. It was then garrisoned by Hertfordshire and Bedfordshire troops. He later cooperated with Cromwell with these troops to seize Hillesden House and surprised Fortescue's Royalist cavalry at Islip in May 1644. He was removed by the Self-Denying Ordinance. [Sean Kelsey, 'Luke, Sir Samuel (*bap.* 1603, *d.* 1670)', *NewDNB*]

[7] See previous works published by the Society

[8] Aylmer, G E & Morrill, J S, *The Civil Wars and Interregnum,* (1980)

identified Volumes 1-119 as being orders and warrants by the Committee of the Army, commanders etc. which are organized chronologically rather than geographically, which include a number relating to Hertfordshire notably Volumes 11 and 17. Volumes 126-139 they identified as military accounts arranged by county, including Hertfordshire material in volumes 129-30. Other outline and some more detailed calendars exist at The National Archives.

The bulk of the manuscripts in the SP28 Series are in boxes which Aylmer and Morrill and the outline calendars in the National Archives identify as follows: SP28/11 includes orders and warrants issued by the Army Committee acting on behalf of Parliament, and by military commanders, to pay troops and commanders for the period November to December 1643. SP28/17 is the same for July-August 1644. SP28/129 are army accounts of military officers and garrisons for various counties, Part 11 being for March 1644/5 and relating to payments for quartering the Earl of Manchester's Army[9]. The material in SP28/154 consists of accounts and schedules for assessments, loans and contributions for counties, including Hertfordshire, and 155 just for the shire, much of the latter being in a poor condition.

The contents of the box for SP28/209B, includes books, booklets, and single accounts and papers of County Sequestration Committees from various counties including Hertfordshire. SP28/217A includes inventories of goods and chattels of papists and delinquents in various counties (including

---

[9] Montagu, Edward, second Earl of Manchester (1602-71) Politician & Parliamentary army officer, with a house at Totteridge, then in Hertfordshire, was an opposition peer who had fought at Edgehill and replaced Lord Grey of Wark as the commander of the Eastern Association armies. He conscripted up to 20,000 men including those from Hertfordshire, defeated the Royalists at King's Lynn and with Cromwell at Winceby in Lincolnshire. He was also given power to sequester the 'malignant' clergy in the counties, including a number of key Arminians and others in Hertfordshire. 8000 men under Manchester including levies from Hertfordshire, helped defeat the Royalists at Marston Moor in June 1644, but many died either in battle, of wounds or disease and many of the conscripted infantry deserted. By the autumn, with the Cambridge treasury empty, the remaining soldiers were in arrears with their pay and near starvation. Manchester was supposed to move westwards to join up with the Earl of Essex but did not reach Reading until the end of September. He failed both to pursue the Royalists after the second battle of Newbury and to take Donnington Castle and Basing House. The subsequent Parliamentary attack on Manchester by Cromwell and others led to his removal from power under the Self-Denying Ordinance and the replacement of the aristocratic led armies by the New Model Army. [Ian J Gentles, 'Montagu, Edward, second Earl of Manchester (1602-1671) *NewDNB*]

Hertfordshire) on parchment and paper. Sources in SP28/230 are the County Committee orders, accounts and papers for various counties including Hertfordshire, and 231-3, the same just for Hertfordshire, which include particularly, the papers of the more radical Militia Committee, which effectively took over the running of the war from the older County Committee. SP28/255 includes general papers, letters, orders, certificates and petitions from 1642-5 for various counties.

Dealing with the sheer volume of material in the SP28 series is difficult. As Ann Hughes states for Warwickshire, much of the material is random rather than systematic, and the impression given by the surviving material from the County Committee is of an improvised hand-to-mouth organization, preoccupied by the immediate needs of the military situation. This is certainly true of Hertfordshire. However as Hughes also warns the evidence is largely the result of the activities of the Committee for Taking the Accounts of the Kingdom and its local sub-committee and is therefore predominantly financial. The evidence for the administrative work of the committee is biased towards money and goods provided, rather than on how the troops were actually raised or their length of service. As in Warwickshire, the membership of the Sub-Committee of Accounts in Hertfordshire was more moderate than that of the Militia Committee, which took over the running of the war, and therefore rather different views are provided on how the war was being run.[10]

This volume aims at providing, both for the local historian and the general reader, a transcript of a selection of the original primary source manuscripts from a range of volumes and boxes in this series, most of which have remained un-calendared. In addition, two sources from the SP23 series, SP23/82 *ff* 775-782, are included, which relate to the charges against Sir John Boteler,[11] and Box 77 *ff* 83-4 which relates to a letter to the committee of compounding on Sir Thomas Coningsby's estate. The first has been included as it is seen as important in showing the dividing line between the activists on both sides and those quiescent royalists who tried to remain neutral for as long as possible, despite pressure on them from opposing sides. The second shows the impact on an estate where a Royalist was imprisoned. One source from the SP16 State Papers, general series, is a petition of the Militia Committee to

---

[10] Hughes, *Warwickshire,* pp169-70
[11] For Boteler and Coningsby see Appendix

the Committee of Both Kingdoms which shows the division in the county by mid 1644 between the more radical Militia Committee and the more conservative elements in the shire.

The structure is designed to provide a general introduction to the background and to the outbreak of war, referring to available printed material, followed by introductions to the three main sections of the documents, how the county organized and ran the war, how the war was financed, and what the effects were on communities and individuals. In order to allow an understanding of what sources are available locally, a number of relevant manuscripts from various collections held by Hertfordshire Archives and Local Studies (HALS) at County Hall, Hertford, have also been included. These have been integrated with the national material in the three broad sections, but obviously their use as sources for a variety of evidence is not exclusive to the theme of that particular section and cross references have been made between documents in the different sections. These include deposited official and family papers (HALS: DE/Lw/O3) relating to Sir John Wittewronge,[12] as a commander of a local volunteer regiment, and extracts from his diary and accounts (HALS: DE/Lw/F18 *f*17), extracts from the Little Munden Account Book (HALS: DP/71/5/2) indicate how a local parish rated itself to pay for the costs of war. Sequestration papers relating to Lord Capel from the Malden manuscripts are included as well as those relating to the minister of Hunsdon, Edward Jude. The letters in the Coxe papers indicate the relationships between both the local gentry and between Colonel Alban Coxe of the St Albans Standing Committee and Silius Titus,[13] a local militia captain. He was later to defect to the royalists after his contact with the king at Holmby House and Carisbrooke Castle. Individual documents from Quarter Sessions Rolls (QSR) show a number of effects of the war and those from the St Albans City Muniments (Off Acc 1162) indicate the measures taken to modify the rating of income from charities. One account has been included from the Hertford Borough Records (HBR) which gives a vivid account of a night-time encounter in the war.

A set of brief biographies have been included for reference purposes, including those men of local importance not in the new online Oxford Dictionary of National Biography. The indices, both the subject and place, and the personal name index, refer to the document number, rather than the

[12] For Wittewrong see Appendix
[13] For Capel, Coxe and Titus see Appendix

page, largely to avoid repetition and following the style of previous volumes in this series. The maps, portraits etc. are provided to give information which is best appreciated in visual form, and are cross-referenced to the text. Footnotes in the text are designed to either illuminate obscurities, or point the reader to references elsewhere in the documents, or to external sources, whether primary or secondary.

One of the principles of selection has been to provide a range of different historical voices. Many of the voices heard in general accounts of the period are those of the aristocratic commanders, of gentry turned soldiers such as Oliver Cromwell, of the King and his courtiers, of the leading Parliamentarians such as John Pym, of those grappling with political ideas such as John Lilburne or Gerard Winstanley, plus a host of would-be journalists in the mass of news sheets, a phalanx of clerics through their sermons and any crackpot who could get him or her-self into print. I am thinking here of Lady Eleanor Davies, the notorious soothsayer who latterly had an estate at Pirton near Hitchin. Even the Putney debates do not really reflect the views and attitudes, hopes and fears of the mass of not very political, tradesmen, townsmen and Hertfordshire minor gentry.

In these documents I hope a range of voices will be heard: from the self-important new gentleman, Sir John Wittewronge, dressing himself up in his finest to go into battle; to the wealthy merchant, former mayor of Hertford and property developer, Gabriel Barbor[14], chairman of the local Hertford Committee. Then there are the lesser gentry, either trying to avoid making commitments about their horses, or complaining about the range of exactions imposed upon them. There are also over-worked local officers, trying to get recompense and the alehouse-keeper solemnly listing the expenses of the committeemen's dinners. In contrast to this are the semi-literate collectors struggling with various taxes and contributions, and the High Collector Toby Combe Esq so concerned to get his sums right that he repeats the phrase "I say", as if to emphasise that his arithmetic must be correct, whereas the Treasurer William Hickman,[15] when questioned, would say no more than he had to. Local constables reveal themselves reluctant to confirm evidence that would convict the local cleric, while the local landowner, Sir John Boteler,

[14] For Barbor see Appendix
[15] For Combe and Hickman see Appendix

finds himself faced with testimony from villagers and tenants providing damning evidence against him.

# I Background to the Civil War

## Hertfordshire on the eve of the Civil War

Hertfordshire in the seventeenth century was larger in area than today, as it included parishes such as Studham, Caddington and Kensworth later lost to Bedfordshire, and Totteridge, lost to Middlesex in 1965, though it had gained the Cambridgeshire part of Royston in 1889. It was the seventh smallest English county, the population being c73,000.[16] The most significant influence on it was the expansion of London, from which roads went North and Northwest through the county, notably the Old North Road through Ware and Royston to York and the Chester Road, which went via Barnet and St Albans and Hitchin. It contained about 20 market towns, the most significant being Hertford, St Albans, Hemel Hempstead, Watford and Royston. Other towns of significance were Ware and Bishops Stortford where innkeepers provided services one day's journey out of London. By 1637 there were 17 carrier services in the county and the mass of alehouses and inns meant it proved attractive for quartering troops throughout the war.[17]

It was closely connected to both London and Cambridge through the educational ties of the Inns of Court and the Colleges, many of the sons of gentry attending both institutions. Those from the middling sort also found their way into London as apprentices to the London companies and guilds, and those who made their money in London, often purchased estates in Hertfordshire. There was more geographical mobility than might be thought, some Hertfordshire men making their fortunes in London, then Virginia and then back again in London. The malting trade flourished notably down the Lea Valley and particularly at Ware, where malted barley was shipped down the river to the London brewers. London corn chandlers also frequented Hertfordshire markets buying grain to feed the capital's population and tanners supplied the metropolitan leather trades. Agriculture was relatively advanced, most arable farmers practising convertible husbandry as well as

---

[16] Munby, L M, H*ertfordshire Population Statistics 1563-1801*, (Hitchin, 1964) p46

[17] For this and subsequent paragraphs see Thomson, A, 'Hertfordshire communities and central-local relations c1625-1665' Unpublished PhD Thesis University of London, 1988

some floating water meadows and developing soft fruit. It was thus a prosperous county and one which was reckoned rich enough to be heavily taxed during the war.

Prosperous merchants and business men in the main towns of Hertford and St Albans liked to style themselves 'Gent', over 40 doing so in Hertford in 1641 as did professional men, doctors, lawyers, former civil servants and servants of the crown. Some of the wealthiest landed gentry and aristocracy, the Capels, Cecils, Careys and Egertons had property in a number of counties and other senior gentry like the Lyttons had family connections across the south east, northern home counties and East Anglia, particularly with other puritan gentry who came to sit in the Long Parliament in 1640. Others like the Fanshawes and Sir John Harrison were tied in with the royal bureaucracy, while the leading magistrates such as Sir Richard Lucy and Sir Thomas Dacres[18] were part of a network of clients of the Earl of Salisbury. These connections and those with London linked the county closely to the metropolis, and it is not surprising that when the leaders of the opposition to King Charles remained in London and he left for York, that the majority of the county sided with Parliament.

## The Militia Ordinance and the lieutenancy

Although King Charles I had failed to arrest the Parliamentary opposition leaders in January 1642, and failed to agree who should command an army to suppress the Irish rebellion, the civil war was not officially declared until he raised his standard at Nottingham on 22 August. The king had decided to leave London, fearing for his own and his wife's lives, and went to York, where he called all loyal peers to attend him. Meanwhile Parliament had passed a militia bill in March, which the king had refused to sign, and Parliament had then passed it into law as if he had. As it could not be called an Act of Parliament without his signature, instead it was called an ordinance.[19] If you were named in a militia commission and attempted to implement the Militia Ordinance and organize defences for the county, you were identified as a Parliamentarian. The king, fearing he would lose the military initiative, issued his own Commissions of Array, to named commissioners in each county, who were to raise troops by a royal

---

[18] For Lucy and Dacres see Appendix

[19] For a list of relevant ordinances see Firth C H & Rait R S, (eds.) *Acts and Ordinances of the Interregnum 1642-1660,* 3 Vols, (1911) (*henceforth* F&R)

proclamation on 4 July. If you attempted to implement this commission, you were seen as a Royalist.[20] Through the Militia Ordinance, Parliament was able to replace the lords-lieutenant and their deputies and put in men loyal to their cause. The Earl of Salisbury[21] was regarded as untrustworthy, as he had briefly joined the king at York, following a proclamation in May summoning the aristocracy and gentry there. Even though he returned to Hatfield, he was replaced as lord-lieutenant of Hertfordshire by his son, Charles, Lord Cranborne.[22]

The importance of appointing to the lieutenancy was that it was the official organization that controlled the local trained bands of the militia, the only trained military force besides those who had taken part in continental wars. To prepare for a war, which by June seemed almost inevitable, a Parliamentary committee, the Committee of Safety, was created, to which the Hertfordshire MP, Sir Thomas Dacres, was appointed. This decided who was to be added or removed as deputy-lieutenants, on the advice of local MPs. John Brograve, Sir John Gore and William Presley had been nominated as deputies in June, and on 23rd August, Robert Cecil, younger son of the Earl of Salisbury, Sir John Garrard, Sir John Reade, Sir John Wittewronge and William Leman[23] were all approved to be deputy-lieutenants. It is clear from Toby Combe's account **[98]** that it was the deputies that were actually carrying out any requests from the centre. Later in the month Richard

---

[20] For the controversy over the Commission and Sir John Boteler see sources [**142-3**]. For how the Commission of Array was received in other counties see Hutton, R, *The Royalist War Effort 1642-1646*, (2nd ed, 1999) pp10-12

[21] Larkin, J (ed) *Stuart Royal Proclamations Vol. II: Royal proclamations of King Charles I 1625-1646,* (Oxford, 1983) pp765-6, 777-81; For a biography of Salisbury see Appendix A

[22] *CJ* II, p660. For Cranborne see Appendix& for his role see [**1**]

[23] For biographies of Presley, Cecil, Garrard, Reade, Wittewronge and Leman see Appendix A. There were two Sir John Gores in Hertfordshire, one from Gilston, the other from Sacombe, the latter fighting for the king. The former Sir John was the son of the Lord Mayor of London of the same name, his first wife was Hester, the sister of William Presley and he was elected to the second Protectorate Parliament, though excluded from sitting. John Brograve (1596-1670) was the eldest of 14 children of Simeon Brograve of Hamels, Braughing and Dorothy Leventhorpe of Albury, who had been to Sidney Sussex Cambridge in 1612. He married Hannah the daughter of Sir Thomas Barnadiston of Suffolk, but kept a low profile until 1649, when he was subsequently appointed to a number of local committees in the 1650s. [*CJ* II, pp 602, 625; Rowe, A, *Garden Making and the Freman Family: A memoir of Hamels 1713-1733*, Hertfordshire Record Society Publications XVII, (Hertford 2001) pxii; F&R II, pp300, 468, 665, 1070, 1432]

Jennings[24] was also added and in October, James Maine. Subsequently, when the more conservative group of deputies proved inactive, some of the more radical men from the main towns were appointed deputies, to carry out the ordinances, including John Heydon,[25] John Robotham, Gabriel Barbor, and Dr John King[26]. These were later to be key Parliamentarians running committees which replaced the lieutenancy and financed the war, raising a new force of volunteers and organizing the militia and trained bands.[27]

## The trained bands of the militia

The county had had, since the 16th century, a militia organized on a hundredal basis, usually two hundreds being grouped together to raise a militia company. This is shown in the late 16th century and early 17th century in Anne King's twelfth volume in this series *Muster Books for North and East Hertfordshire*,[28] though one parish from Broadwater and three from Braughing hundreds were added to get some equality of numbers for taxation purposes. The structure of lords-lieutenant, deputies, captains and muster-masters had been established from Mary's reign onwards, though their authority had lapsed in James' reign. It is clear from the 1602 and 1605 musters, transcribed by King, that, at the start of his reign, there was a sub-structure within this division of captain, a lieutenant, an ensign bearer, three sergeants and 2 drummers for the trained bands of the militia. These were the men, who in theory, were regularly trained each year in the use of their weapons. Various parishes, depending roughly on their population, provided a mixture of corslets and pikes, muskets and calivers, with the men trained to use them. Some were armed by the parish or town, others by individuals or sometimes two or three inhabitants.[29]

---

[24] For Jennings see Appendix

[25]Heydon, a lawyer at Lincoln's Inn, had purchased the Oxhey estate in Watford in 1638 along with three mills. He was a JP in the County and Liberty from 1641, but was removed by the king in July 1642. Committed to parliament, he provided a horse worth £18 and then sat on numerous local committees throughout the 1640s. [TNA C231/5 *ff*468, 485, 530-1; SP28/130 Pt II, Commissary book for horses; F&R I & II *passim*]

[26] For Robotham and King see Appendix

[27] *CJ* II, pp609, 625, 673, 733, 736, 795; III, p223; Bennett M, *Historical dictionary of the British & Irish Wars 1637-1660*, (London 2000) pp60, 153-4

[28] King, A J, (ed) *Muster Books for North and East Hertfordshire 1508-1605,* Hertfordshire Record Society XII, (Hertford, 1996)

[29] King, *Muster Books,* pp175-208

The main weapons used by the infantry were the pike and the musket. The pike was a pole up to 16 feet long, though often shortened for ease of carrying, with a metal spike for repelling cavalry and opposing infantry. Pikemen usually wore corslets or defensive body armour, though corslets also came to mean pikemen, when they wore the armour. They helped defend those carrying the two types of firearm, the musket, which required a forked rest for firing, and a caliver which was a 17 bore gun without a rest[30]. In the early 1620s the serviceable weapons were specified as either a four-foot long musket, or a bastard (light musket) or a petronel (carbine used by horsemen).[31] Though the musket had been improved over the previous century, most musketeers by 1640 still had matchlock firing mechanisms, carried leather bags with shot and wadding, and individual wooden cartridges of powder on a bandoleer. By then muskets might be up to 6 feet long with a range of about 250 yards.[32] By the civil war, the caliver seems to have been largely replaced by the carbine, which was used by the dragoons or mounted infantry, though one or two still had calivers in 1642. The cavalry usually had a brace of pistols with a flint or wheel lock mechanism. **[16-20]**

It is clear from the 1605 muster that the pikemen were also expected to carry a sword and dagger to protect themselves in close combat as well as some armour to protect the body and limbs, thought this was not always provided. They also sometimes wore a burgonet, a head piece or light steel helmet, and poldrons on the shoulders. The former are mentioned in bills for the 1640s, but not the latter directly. They were also supplied with murions by 1638, which were helmets with a visor. They also required a girdle, or sword belt, with hanger to hold the sword. From the numbers, it looks as if about 150 pikes, 50 muskets and 100 calivers had been supplied for a trained band for the division of Edwinstree and Odsey in 1605 of 300 men. There were four divisions in the county, the others being Hertford and Braughing, Cashio and Dacorum, Broadwater and Hitchin. In a report to the Privy Council in February 1638, the county militia foot were listed as 750 each of muskets and corslets (pikemen) and the cavalry as 53 light horse and 27 lancers or heavier horse. The total in the trained bands for the county before the Civil War would have been c1580 men, roughly the 1500 militia mentioned by Sir John Boteler. **[142]** As late as 1638-9, the militia in Hertford Borough were

---

[30] King, *Muster Books*, pp224-7

[31] Boynton, L, *The Elizabethan militia 1558-1638*, (1967) p239

[32] Melia S S, *The Battle of Newburn Ford 1640*, (Newcastle, undated) p16

provided with new equipment including new murions, bandoleers, swords, muskets and gunpowder. Local craftsmen were also repairing the old equipment and constructing new butts for target practice.[33]

During the 1620s and 1630s, Charles I had tried to achieve a 'more perfect militia', by having them trained more regularly. Attempts were made to standardize the weapons by replacing the older versions, and a variety of training manuals were replaced by a new book of training orders modelled on recent practice in the Netherlands in the 30 Years' War.[34] This required the services of a muster-master, an experienced soldier who was employed and paid for by the local aristocracy and gentry in their capacities as deputies or captains. This had caused particular problems between the Privy Council, William, second Earl of Salisbury and his deputies, when the latter refused to pay a muster master and queried under what authority they were operating, given the lack of legislative clarity on the matter.[35] William Love[36] was at one point in the early 1640s the Muster Master for the Hertfordshire regiments though there is no indication he had been trained.

The position of the militia had been complicated by the issue of whether they could be forced into 'foreign service' i.e. used against the Scots in the late 1630s or whether separate levies of conscripts had to be made for these expeditions. At various points in the 1620s and 1630s Salisbury had been required to raise 100 or more men for overseas expeditions and these tended to be the usual collection of ex-gaol-birds, paupers, drunks and the less stalwart of the community. This was a form of impressment. If and when they returned from their expeditions, they were another source of trained men. It is not clear, before the war, what groups there were in the militia apart from the trained bands, and how many formerly pressed men were available to fight. However there was still resistance by the part-time men of the militia to spending much time out of the county in the civil war, particularly at harvest time, **[139]** and this type of parochialism survived within the county throughout the Bishops' Wars and into the Civil War.[37]

---

[33] TNA SP16/381 *f*66; HALS: HBR20 *ff*170v, 175, 195v; King, *Muster Books*, pp208, 224-7
[34] Boynton, *Elizabethan Militia,* p240
[35] *Cecil*, XXIV, pp266-74
[36] For Love see Appendix
[37] HALS: QSB2A *f*134; *Cecil* XXII, pp266-73

The month before the Scottish Covenanters met in November 1638 the militia horse were being reorganized. Those with estates worth £200 p.a. were ordered to provide a light horse, and those with estates worth £300, a heavy horse for the lancers. In February 1639 with the start of the First Bishops' War with Scotland, the county was expected to pay for training 500 of the militia and 40 horses. However the militia said they were only for the defence of the county, so Salisbury ordered 110 pressed men to Selby, in Yorkshire instead, with sufficient funds for 15 days travel. At the start of the Second Bishops' War he was required to levy 650 foot soldiers, 50 strong horses and 17 able carters for the artillery and get them to Harwich for embarkation for the north by ship. However opposition by the militia and the local taxpayers meant that only 100 men were sent in July, 34 deserting en route, a worse record than any other county. Those still billeted in the shire before departure then attacked 'Popish remnants' in local churches, smashing windows and breaking up altar rails in 15 cases of iconoclasm. This continued into August 1640 until they were disbanded. Thus there were a number of men, who had been trained, but many were alienated from the King's government and his political and religious policies and some were no doubt inclined later to join the local volunteers in the civil war.

The officer corps was largely provided by the aristocracy, the gentry and their sons. Some of these such as John Watts[38] of Mardocks near Ware, or Sir Thomas Dacres of Cheshunt, had gained experience fighting on the continent in Mansfeld's, the Cadiz or other expeditions. These senior magistrates and others like Sir William Lytton[39], Sir Arthur, later Baron Capel, Sir John Boteler and Sir Richard Lucy[40] were the deputies who had to supervise the musters, but the situation of the deputies changed dramatically between 1640 and 1642. As Royalists such as Capel and Fanshawe left the county to join the king, or were removed from their positions by Parliament, so others were appointed as above. However few of the gentry, not involved at Westminster, seem to have been keen to implement the Militia Ordinance, which required them to put the county in a posture of defence and to secure the magazines.

---

[38] John Watts was a senior magistrate and deputy-lieutenant, son of a former mayor of London, who continued to serve as a JP until his death in 1648, but was not included on any major wartime committees. He and his son had been active in 1638-9 ensuring that the militia in Hertford were inspected and supplied with new equipment. He was buried in Ware on 1 December 1649. [HALS: HBR20 *ff*170v, 175r, 195v; DP/116/1/1 Ware Parish Register]

[39] For Lytton see Appendix

[40] For Lucy see Alan Thomson, 'Sir Richard Lucy, Baronet, (1592-1667)', *NewDNB*

## The financial background - Pre-War Taxation

Before the war had started many men were already paying higher than normal levels of taxation as a result of both Ship Money payments up to 1640 and legislation signed by Charles I between 1640 and 1642. Money had to be raised to pay those who had loaned money to fight the Scots and to pay off the Scots army that had occupied Newcastle during the Bishops' War of 1639-40, and other monies were required to pay for the army to be sent to suppress the Irish Rebellion. Thus listed in some of the parish returns are sums for the traditional subsidies, six of which were raised in 1640, mainly to pay off city merchants who had lent sums on the security of a future subsidy. Then there was a revived Poll Tax of 1641 and the tax of £400,000. The Poll Tax, which received royal assent on 3 July 1641, was graduated and levied on men over 16, who were thought to be able to spend a certain sum of money. Higher rates were graded by rank, dukes paying £100, esquires and others £10 and most wage earners 6d. A proclamation was passed to enforce its collection and it was specifically raised to pay off the Scots army and to tax non-landed wealth.[41] The £400,000 was resolved upon in May 1641 by the Commons, and passed in March 1642. It was levied on the counties and taxation districts according to their traditional subsidy allocations, local JPs and gentry acting as commissioners, and appointing local men of some standing as high collectors of hundreds. Between them they then allocated the sums that were to be collected within each parish. Each parish then allocated who was to pay what, probably using the recent re-evaluations of the Ship Money returns. Papists and aliens paid double amounts. The commissioners in effect became the first county committee.[42]

### Events in Hertfordshire May-September 1642: The rise of the volunteers

However the radical citizens of Hertford had already taken the initiative in May to drill and train under the terms of the Militia Ordinance as a volunteer company[43], but opposition had arisen to their activities. On 1 June, Captain William Turner, a grocer of Hertford, complained to the Commons of the

[41] Larkin, *Proclamations,* pp745-6; Braddick, M J, *The nerves of state: Taxation and financing of the English State, 1558-1714,* (Manchester, 1996) pp103-4

[42] Pennington & Roots, *Committee at Stafford,* pp xxviii-xxix

[43] They may have trained as volunteers, as the proclamation issued by the king in May had specifically forbidden his subjects belonging to the trained bands or militia to exercise by virtue of the Militia Ordinance. [Larkin, *Proclamations*, pp767-9]

activities of Mr Keeling,[44] the Recorder, and Mr Andrew Palmer[45] the Mayor of Hertford, who had tried to use the local quarter sessions to intimidate those who had been carrying out military exercises. It so happened that Turner was the foreman of the grand jury, who had to decide whether there was a case to be heard before sessions, and he persuaded the jury that there was no case to present. Keeling and Palmer were then ordered to appear before the Commons, and the volunteers obtained an indemnity order against their being prosecuted for carrying out training. On 18 June a royal proclamation forbade all levies of forces not authorized by the King, so they then obtained authority directly from Parliament to form a volunteer company in July and trained under Mr Isaac Puller, the son of the radical puritan town lecturer, Abraham Puller.[46]

The radicals at Watford drew up their own petition in June, which was presented on 1 July by the vicar of Watford, Doctor Cornelius Burges,[47] by then a favourite preacher of the Commons. In this they explained that they had raised 50 horses, horsemen and arms as well as £1270 in money and plate, but needed authority to enlarge this troop. They wanted acceptance of John Leonard and Zachary King[48] as treasurers, and recommended John Bird as captain, also requesting pay for a lieutenant and corporal. They sought permission to train and exercise at Watford until required by Parliament

---

[44] For Turner and Keeling see Appendix

[45] Andrew Palmer Esq, on the resignation of Gabriel Barbor as a chief burgess in September 1639, had been appointed a borough assistant and chief burgess on the same day. He had paid £1 in the Ship Money tax of 1637 and was one of the wealthiest inhabitants in 1641, being reckoned able to spend £100 p.a. in the Poll Tax Assessment. Mayor the same year, he put into his annual accounts the charges for his imprisonment in London, which came to £13-6-8d. He attended the months court meeting in April 1643 and appears to have been rehabilitated in December 1644, when he agreed to repay £11-2-8 ½d on the understanding he had been overpaid when mayor. The clerk noted "*Et sic quietus est*" (And thus all is quiet/settled) [HALS: HBR20 *ff*181, 211r, 223; 46 *ff*908, 933; Chauncy I, pp491, 492]

[46] Larkin, *Proclamations,* pp770-5; *CJ* II, pp597, 679; For Isaac Puller see Appendix. Abraham had been appointed a lecturer at All Saints in Hertford on 19 March 1642 [*CJ* II, pp488, 607]

[47] For Burges see Marjorie Bray, 'The Watford lecturer and his house', *Hertfordshire's Past*, No 6 (Spring 1979) pp 9-19; Tai Liu, 'Burges, Cornelius (*d.* 1665)', *NewDNB*

[48] Zachary King, a mercer from Watford from at least 1633, was treasurer of the Watford Volunteers in November 1642 and was put on the Volunteers and Militia Committees in 1643. He was Treasurer of the Militia funds in the western part of the county, 1643-4 and treasurer for the towns in the south west of the county, paying sums into the St Albans treasury, including those for the poor clergy of Ireland. He later served as the High Constable of Cashio Hundred in 1648. [HALS QSB2B *ff*92d-93; *LJ* V, p441; F&R I, pp289-91, 356-8]

elsewhere.[49] The inhabitants of St Albans followed suit in August and volunteers were given authority by Parliament to be trained under Alban Cox[50] and John Marsh[51], and these three urban companies later became the basis for the first Hertfordshire volunteer regiment.[52]

## The defeat of the Royalists

On 12th July Hertfordshire MPs and JPs were ordered to implement the Militia Ordinance and the county MPs, Sir William Lytton and Sir Thomas Dacres, went to the July quarter sessions at Hertford specifically to raise money, plate, arms, armour and horses under *The Propositions,* the Parliamentary legislation for loans and gifts to fund the war.[53] On 4 July the king issued a proclamation forbidding the removal of county magazines. The county ordinance was stored in both St Albans and Hertford, and possibly also in other towns such as Buntingford.[54] In order for it not to fall into the hands of Royalist sympathizers, Parliamentary loyalists were ordered to take it into their care. In St Albans, Dr John King, John Robotham and Ralph Pemberton secured it[55] and in Hertford, Gabriel Barbour, Isaac Puller, Humphrey Packer[56] and Joseph Dalton[57] were ordered to put the magazine in a safe place.[58] These men all became the Parliamentary leaders in the shire and on

---

[49] BL 669 *f*5, *Humble Petition of the inhabitants of Watford*, (1 July 1642)
[50] For Cox(e) see Appendix
[51] John Marsh, Esq of Shenley, owner of an inn in St Albans, was put on the Hertfordshire Volunteer Committee when a Captain in September 1643 and by the December he had been promoted to Lieutenant-Colonel. He served on numerous committees in the 1640s, was a JP in the Liberty in 1651-9, latterly being of the quorum, a puisine judge in 1653 and a commissioner for treason trials in 1656. He sent his son Richard to Gray's Inn in 1657. [TNA C193/13/3 *ff*30-1; HALS: DP/3/12/1; DP/93/5/2 *ff*73d, 96; *LJ* VI, p76; F&R I & II, *passim*; Smith & North, *St Albans,* p98; Foster, J, (ed.) *Register of Admissions to Gray's Inn, 1521-1889* (1889) p284]
[52] *CJ* II, p712
[53] *CJ* II, p667
[54] Larkin, *Proclamations*, pp781-4; Falvey, H & Hindle, S (eds.) '*This little commonwealth': Layston parish memorandum book, 1607-c1650 & 1704-c1747*, Hertfordshire Record Society Vol XIX, (Hertford, 2003) p60
[55] *CJ* II, p714; For John Robotham and Ralph Pemberton see Appendix
[56] For Puller and Packer see Appendix
[57] Joseph Dalton of Hertford, tanner, was a chief burgess in 1632, Mayor of Hertford 1636, 1642-5, 1655, and on Hertford Committees from November 1642 until January 1660. He had been in dispute with the Ship Money sheriff, Thomas Coningsby, before the war, when as mayor he had withheld Ship Money for the town claiming he had loaned it out. [TNA SP16 /387 *f*46; Chauncy I, pp491, 492; F&R I&II Passim; *CJ* II, p853]
[58] *CJ* II, p721

the committees that were set up to run the war. At the end of July, the mayor of St Albans, William New[59] and the mayor of Hertford, Andrew Palmer, were put in gaol in London, for allowing the King's proclamation on the commission of array, to be read in the market place.[60]

Other confrontations also took place in Hertford between July and September. At the quarter sessions, Sir John Boteler was named by the king as the *Custos Rotulorum* on a new commission of the peace of 15 July and Charles Cecil, Lord Cranborne,[61] Dacres and others were to be displaced. Boteler had been involved in persecuting the Hertford Volunteers and in early August received a copy of the Commission of Array and it was alleged he summoned a group of local gentry to meet at Hertford on 18th to carry out the Commission. On examination, different versions of these events by different witnesses reveal the turmoil in the county at the time, the suspicions that abounded and give a vivid feel for the clash of loyalties experienced. **[142]** [62]

In mid August it was reported that soldiers under Captain Ansell of the Duke of Bedford's regiment and other Londoners had been sent out to search Lord Capel's house at Little Hadham, where they found arms sufficient to arm a thousand men with horses, pistols and carbines. They also were reported as visiting Ware Park, the home of Sir Thomas Fanshawe, where they found two cannon, barrels of powder, muskets and pikes.[63] They remained in Hertford and in late August managed to prevent both Boteler and John Watts Esq.[64] the

---

[59] William New, gent, pewterer, a borough assistant 1619, alderman, 1627, Mayor 1630 and 1641, revived his reputation to be elected again in 1649 and renew the town charter under the Commonwealth. He had at least two sons by his first marriage, John and Robert, both later Mayors of St Albans, the former thrice, and another son John by his second marriage to Ellen Choppin(g). [Chauncy II, p304; Smith & North, *St Albans*, pp47, 64, 161, 206-7, 216 n37, 242]
[60] *CJ* II, pp694, 743
[61] For Cranborne see Appendix
[62] TNA SP23/82 *ff* 775 - 782
[63] BL: E115 (7) *A Perfect Diurnall of the proceedings in the county of Hartford from Tuesday the 15 of August to the 29* (London, 1642)
[64] John Watts Junior, had been a captain of the local militia in the 1630s and possibly in the Bishops' War, and made a reputation as an anti-puritan cavalier. In August 1640 in the Green Dragon tavern in Bishopsgate he drew his sword after telling those present that 'he had that day seen the king and kissed his hand', accusing the less respectful diners of being 'puritans', following a dispute with two Essex clothiers over whether the Scots were rebels or good Christians. He lived in Ware parish and, with his wife Frances, had at least 5 children: Sarah in 1636, John 1639, George 1640, Thomas 1641 and James 1642. He was to fight for the Royalists and was knighted for his defence of Chirk Castle. He later lived at Tewin where he

son of the deputy-lieutenant and senior magistrate, from putting the commission of array into execution. However on 14 September Watts raised a force in east Hertfordshire and attempted to take Hertford, seize the magazine and again put the King's commission of array into effect, while Ansell's troop were moving up the Old North Road to Puckeridge to search a Catholic's house. Watts was defeated by the combined efforts of the local militia and Ansell's troop and he was detained at the Bell Inn, reports of the action appearing in the early newssheets.[65] Despite later attempts by Boteler in January 1643, to get an accommodation petition delivered to the king in Oxford, and the obtaining of a pardon for all Hertfordshire men, and despite the attempt to read out proclamations against the activities of Parliamentarians in St Albans by Thomas Coningsby[66] the same month, the Royalists were effectively excluded from any control in the shire by the end of September. As a result the Parliamentarians could fully prepare for war.[67]

## Hertfordshire in Wartime

### Leadership[68]

In any one county local leadership fell on the shoulders of certain men. The two chairmen of the key committees behind the war effort were Gabriel Barbor of Hertford and Dr John King of St Albans. Barbor became Chairman of the Standing (executive) Committee for most of the Hertford wartime committees, being particularly associated with the Committee for the Volunteers that became the radical Militia Committee. His son John became an officer in the local volunteers and militia, and his son Joseph a cornet in the

---

paid £10 Decimation Tax in 1656. [TNA SP28/197 Pt II *f*16; HALS: D/P116/1/1 Ware Parish Register; Cressy, D, *England on edge: Crisis and Revolution 1640-1642*, (Oxford, 2006) pp107, 326]

[65] BL: E118/13 *Exceeding joyfull news from Derby. Also the taking of Sir John Watson neer Hertford, f3* (London, 20 September 1642)

[66] For Coningsby see Appendix A. For this incident in St Albans see BL E85 (15) *Kingdom's Weekly Intelligencer*, No. 3; For the petition see BL: E 84 (39), 7 January 1643, *The Humble Petition of the Inhabitants of the County of Hertford to His Majesty.*

[67] TNA: SP23/82 *f* 775; Holmes, C, *The Eastern Association* p53; Kingston, *Herts,* p30

[68] Biographies of all the key figures mentioned here appear in Appendix

regiment of Colonel Norwich. One of his daughters married Isaac Puller, son of the local Puritan preacher Abraham Puller and a colonel in the local militia. Barbor was thus the most significant supporter of the war throughout the period and was important both for his local and London connections and his commitment to politically active Puritanism, as a member of the Feoffees for Impropriations.

Barbor's counterpart in St Albans was Dr. John King. He was one of the four men into whose care the magazine at St Albans was given in August 1642, and, with the capture of the local MP, Edward Wingate[69] by the Royalists, and the imprisonment of the mayor, William New, he became a key political figure in St Albans, sometimes acting as a link between the borough and the county, and sometimes between the St Albans Committee and Parliament. He became the chairman of the St Albans Standing Committee, being nominated to numerous local committees from 1643 to 1660, as well as serving as a borough burgess and as a JP in the Liberty of St Albans from 1645-60 and in the county from 1652. He was thus the key civilian player in St Albans on behalf of Parliament.

The key commanders in the field of the Hertfordshire regiments and troopers were Sir John Wittewrong, Sir John Garrard, and Colonels Adam Washington, Alban Cox, and Thomas Nicholls. Wittewronge in August 1642 became a deputy-lieutenant for Hertfordshire and a captain of the trained bands of the Hundreds of Cashio and Dacorum. Appointed Colonel of the first Hertfordshire volunteer regiment in 1643, he was sent first to Uxbridge and then to run the garrison at Aylesbury. He later served on the St Albans Standing Committee. Garrard also became a deputy lieutenant in August 1642 and commanded a militia regiment at the start of the war, and was appointed Parliamentary sheriff of the county 1643-5 following the removal

[69] Edward Wingate of Lockleys, Welwyn, was married to Mary, daughter of Ralph Allway of Cannons, Shenley, whose other daughter, Frances, was the wife of Eustace Nedham Esq of Wymondly. Both Wingate and Nedham had been captains in the militia in the 1630s and Wingate had raised a troop of cavalry at the start of the war but had been captured by the Royalists by November, imprisoned in Oxford, and threatened with a charge of treason. Mary Wingate had presented a petition to Parliament in person on the last day of 1642, and arrangements were put in motion for an exchange of prisoners with Sir William Fleming, a Royalist. However this was refused on 5 April and on 7th this petition was presented to the Commons. It was not until 8 June that Wingate, as the MP for Hertford replacing Fanshawe, returned to the Commons and Fleming was released a week later [*CJ* II, pp842, 891-2, 909, 935, 965; *CJ* III, pp33, 120, 130]

of Sir Thomas Coningsby the Royalist. Kingston claimed that Garrard's regiment was disbanded for lack of pay, but he seems to have led his regiment into Newport Pagnell Garrison in November 1643 and under Major-General Browne in 1644. He was appointed to most local Parliamentary committees in the 1640s, but was not a regular attendee, presumably because of his military duties.[70]

Washington was the commander of another regiment of Hertfordshire volunteers and militia and was put on the assessment committee in February 1643. Colonel Alban Cox(e) had been a Colonel in the local militia and was ordered by Parliament to train the St Albans volunteer troop of horse in August 1642. He became an active committee man, using the buildings in the Great Court of the Abbey as his HQ, when he commanded the county volunteer horse, which was used to prevent incursions by Royalists. He helped round them up after Naseby, then sided with the New Model Army against Parliament in 1647. One outsider was Colonel Thomas Nicholls Esq. whose estate in Shropshire was plundered by the Royalists in October 1642, and he moved to Hertford, obtained the lease of the Balls Park estate from the Hertford Sequestrations Committee, got onto the local Militia Committee and commanded a local militia regiment. When Shrewsbury fell to the Parliamentarians, Nicholls returned to rescue his property and was re-instated as an alderman there in 1645. Though many other men came on to committees or commanded troops at different levels, the above were key leaders in the civilian and military establishments in the 1642-7 period in Hertfordshire. It is their names who frequently appear in the records discussed below.

## The local committees and the Eastern Association

The traditional way of organizing the county for war was through the Lieutenancy. However the 21 year old Charles Viscount Cranborne proved slow in implementing the requests of Parliament and the lieutenancy was not an effective body for raising large numbers of troops, money and supplies. The deputies had been asked to send money and plate up to London in mid-October but it was not until 17th November, with the Royalist threat from Buckinghamshire imminent, that local subscription commissioners were

[70] HALS: Garrard Mss 27235-7; DE/B2102/T14; GEC *Complete Baronetage,* I, pp188-9; Henning, B, (ed.) *The History of Parliament: The House of Commons 1660-1690*, 3 vols. (1983) II, p373; Kingston, *Herts*, p52; F&R, I, passim

appointed. These were the more radical urban gentry, active within the volunteers including Joseph Dalton, the new mayor of Hertford, Charles Michell,[71] Thomas Mead[72] and Humphrey Packer from Ware. As a temporary expedient they raised 200 dragoons to patrol the county border and prevent incursions, and by December the trained bands were moving into Buckinghamshire. At Tring a company was formed under Captain Field, which went to the Aylesbury garrison, and money collected in the town for *The Propositions* was ordered to be paid to them for their wages.[73]

It was becoming clear that the lieutenancy and ad hoc commissioners were incapable of both running and financing the war, which was now going to be much longer that originally anticipated. On 10 December 1642 the Commons' decision to unite the six eastern counties (Cambridge, Norfolk, Suffolk, Essex, Hertfordshire and Huntingdonshire) was sent to the House of Lords. On the 15th they discussed an Eastern Association army, but in early January the Hertfordshire volunteer forces were also required to join those from Buckinghamshire in Aylesbury[74] garrison, because of Royalist activities around Brill. As a result, county committees were set up for the implementation of individual ordinances, relating to armies and finance including that for the Eastern Association. However this meant that Hertfordshire had already committed forces within a county that was never in the Association, a decision which was to place additional burdens on it in the future.

The most significant publication on the work of county committees remains that of Pennington and Roots on the committee at Stafford.[75] They showed that the powers of the county committee there grew out of a series of ad hoc measures, starting with the raising of £400,000, an act to which the king had

---

[71] Charles Michell of Watton at Stone was a commissioner for the Propositions in 1642 and his house was assessed for 7 hearths in 1663. He may have been related to the Michell brothers in the volunteers [TNA E179/248/23 *f*48; *CJ* II, p 53]

[72] For Thomas Mead(e) see Appendix

[73] *CJ* II, p887

[74] According to Lamb, Henry Bulstrode's regiment was already in Aylesbury, which had batteries to the north and west to deter Royalist attack. Joint forces made an unsuccessful attack on Brill at the end of January and there were frequent alarms throughout 1643. By mid April £200 weekly had been voted for the garrison which sum was increased to £600 in September [*LJ* VI, p216; Lamb, G, 'Aylesbury in the Civil War', *Records of Buckinghamshire,* Vol 41, (Aylesbury, 2001) pp183-9]

[75] Pennington D H, & Roots, I A, *The Committee at Stafford 1643-5*, (Manchester, 1957) p2

given his consent in March 1642, before the quarrel over the Militia Bill severed agreement between the King and Parliament. They argued that this and the subsequent ordinances for *Weekly Assessments* of 24 February 1643, and that for *Sequestrations* of 27 March 1643, resulted in each appointing county committees to which were delegated authority to collect finances. Although new county committees continued to be appointed for specific purposes, in fact new functions were absorbed automatically by existing committees. In Hertfordshire the situation was rather different from Stafford, partly because of the need to organize early subscriptions under *The Propositions*, and partly because of its link with the Eastern Association. The situation was also affected by disputes between the more conservative county gentry and more radical townsmen.

The major work on the Eastern Association remains that written by Clive Holmes.[76] In this and other sources, it is clear that Hertfordshire was rather different from other areas, as it effectively had local forces operating before the Association was established, and that these militia and volunteer troops were already defending the northern and north western approaches to London. However another ordinance was passed authorizing those in Hertfordshire to assist Buckinghamshire, without being directly associated with it in another grouping of counties.[77] In order to raise money for the war, committees were established on 27 March 1643 for *Weekly Assessments* for the defence of the county. Known as the 'Defence' Committee, it still included Cranborne, his younger brother Robert, who was serving as a captain in a London regiment, and the old and newly appointed deputies, as well as some of the traditional gentry and citizens of the boroughs. Four days later the committee was given power over the sequestration of Royalists,[78] and five weeks later the Defence Committee was extended to include a number of townsmen and other supporters of the volunteers.[79] Early on, this committee split its jurisdiction over parts of the county into two, with an executive group or standing committee at Hertford and another subordinate one at St Albans. Everitt[80] stated that in Kent there was a gradual change from control by the lieutenancy to control by the committees. Fletcher argued that in Sussex and in most

---

[76] Holmes, *Eastern Association*, *passim*

[77] *CJ* II, p910; Holmes, *Eastern Association*, pp63-65, 254 n139

[78] F&R I, p113

[79] F&R I, pp85-6, 117-123

[80] Everitt, A, *The Community of Kent and the Great Rebellion 1640-1660*, (Leicester, 1966) p129

counties, the development of the county committees out of the lieutenancy was gradual and experimental, but that in some, a single committee, sometimes with a permanent headquarters, usually with its own secretariat and a routine of daily and weekly business, engrossed power. Hertfordshire seems to have fitted neither model, the development of committees partly relating to disputes between the more conservative and more radical local groups.[81]

The eastern counties had been slow to implement the December ordinance setting up their association, and it was not until a conference at Bury St Edmunds in February 1643 agreed to implement the instructions for the Eastern Association, that the troops came to be organized.[82] Even though strategy was coordinated in London by the Parliament and its committees, and once the Scots had entered the war, by the Committee of Both Kingdoms, another centre of power was Cambridge, where representatives of the counties, that were part of the Eastern Association, met and supported the Earl of Manchester's army, following the replacement of Lord Gray of Warke as commander. The first Hertfordshire delegates to the Cambridge Committee were Henry Meautys[83] and Ralph Freeman.[84] The Hertford committee was

---

[81] Fletcher, A, *A county community in peace and war: Sussex 1600-1660*, (1975) pp325-6
[82] Holmes, *Eastern Association,* pp76-7
[83] Henry Meautys Esq (b. 1585) of St Jermyns in St Michael's parish, was the son of Thomas Meautys, and had married Elizabeth, daughter of Sir William Glover, alderman of London. His brother Thomas (1590-1649) was the more famous clerk to the Privy Council 1622-41, who had been in Francis Bacon's service and married his niece. The brothers' maternal first cousins were the daughters of the Ship Money sheriff Thomas Coningsby. Thomas Meautys, following a severe illness in January 1642, had retired to Bacon's house at Gorhambury, the rights to which he had acquired, but within three years of his death in 1652, Thomas sold off the estate at Gorhambury and other properties inherited by his brother, to Sir Harbottle Grimston [Aylmer, G, *The King's Servants: The civil service of Charles I, 1624-1642*, (1961) pp156-8, 291-4; Foster, *Marriage Licences*, p911]
[84] Ralph Freeman (c1606-1665) was the son of William (died 1623) and Elizabeth Freeman (died 1633) and the nephew of Ralph Freeman, Lord Mayor of London (died 1634) all of Aspenden Hall, which he thus inherited. He had been High Sheriff in 1636 and the king attempted to put him on the commission of the peace for the county on 15 July 1642. He was nominated to numerous committees from 1643-48 including the Sub-Committee of Accounts for the county, but does not appear to have been active on these, preferring, as Chauncy suggested, that he 'made his house neat, his gardens pleasant, his grove delicious …' He had at least three sons and sent the third, Thomas, to the Middle Temple in 1651 [TNA C231/5 *ff*330-1; HALS: DE/Cd/F46 Diary of Ralph Freeman; *VCH Herts* IV, pp17-9; F& R, I, *passim; Middle Temple Admissions,* p150; Falvey & Hindle, "*This little Commonwealth*", p90; Rowe, *Freman Family,* pp xvii-xxi]

the senior one within the county, the St Albans standing committee having to follow its orders on some occasions.

The other duties of these committees were those of the commissioners for *The Propositions*, as the money was clearly not coming in to the centre at a fast enough rate. On 3 May Sir Thomas Dacres MP and John Heydon Esq were appointed accountants for the weekly assessment, and four days later an ordinance was passed to raise money from those who had *not* contributed or loaned money, plate or horses under *The Propositions*. In order to provide flexibility, on the 18th a further ordinance allowed money raised in this way to be spent on the armies of the Eastern Association. By June 1643 it was clear that to really make the legislation effective, a number of the more active supporters of Parliament had to be added to these committees and they included a number of men of lesser rank.[85] Kingston argued that the extension of the membership was because it was necessary that all parts of the county were represented. This would mean that the fullest possible local knowledge could be utilized and it would make the avoidance of taxation more difficult. In practice however only a minority of those nominated actually sat on the committee and signed its orders and warrants on a regular basis.[86]

Thus over the period from December 1642 to May 1643 the committees were established with a variety of functions and responsibilities, but gradually the higher ranking, large landowners and deputy-lieutenants, were being replaced by the lower status townsmen and lesser gentry. Despite the multiplication of members put on these committees, it is clear that they largely merged and became effectively two standing committees of about 6-8 members at any one time. Those who did most of the work at St Albans under the chairman, Dr John King, included Alban Cox, Ralph Pemberton, John Rotheram and Tobie Combe, and at Hertford, under Chairman Gabriel Barbour, were Thomas Meade, William Carter,[87] William Love, Thomas Nicholls and the Michell

---

[85] *LJ* VI, pp29, 76; F&R, I, pp139-41, 145-55, 160, 168-171

[86] Kingston, *Herts,* p42

[87] This was either William Carter of Offley, gent or William Carter of Hatfield Woodside, Esq, a Counsellor at Law of the Middle Temple, and JP for the County and Liberty, "a man of admirable piety and integrity". He married Mary daughter of John Darnall of Hertingfordbury. One was added to the Hertford Committee in March 1643. It is possible that both served at different times though as the one appointed to the Sequestration Committee in June 1643 was the former from Offley [F&R I, p 19, 117-23, 168-71; Chauncy II, p19]

brothers, with Adam Washington when he was not in command of a regiment. Later other members became more active. These standing committees, generally known either as 'the committee at Hertford' and 'the committee at St Albans', virtually took over the day-to-day running of the war from the lieutenancy, which still had nominal authority, in some cases. Occasionally a joint county committee met at Hatfield or Hertford, which *did* include some of the more established county gentry, presumably meeting under the auspices of previous legislation, but the war was being run in 1644 by the new Militia Committee made up largely of 10-20 men drawn from the towns of Hertford, St Albans, Watford, Hemel Hempstead, Stevenage, Ware and other minor gentry from the rural areas. This appears to be the opposite case to Warwickshire where only one committee operated with occasional meetings in Warwick and Coventry.[88] Everitt noticed that in Suffolk there were a considerable number of floating members of committees who might be appointed for a month or a year. As Morrill warned, appointees to a committee might never be active, and it was the committee men who actually signed the bills and warrants that can be identified as the active Parliamentarians. Both of these observations apply to Hertfordshire, though clearly the local Sub-Committee of Accounts was an entirely different body, with different purposes. Also, as in Warwickshire, ad hoc appointments seem to have been made of men who became active and some nominees never seem to have got involved in committee work.[89]

## The Military Commitments of the Committees

According to Holmes, from April to July 1643 Lord Grey's[90] forces served as a brigade in Essex's Army, joining him at the siege of Reading, whilst Cromwell[91] led a separate group to defend the northern boundaries of the

---

[88] Hughes, *Warwickshire*, p172

[89] This can be seen by the signatures on a variety of documents issued by these standing committees [Morrill, *Cheshire,* p185]; Everitt A, *Suffolk and the Great Rebellion1640-1660,* Suffolk Record Society Publications, 3 (Ipswich, 1960) p25; Hughes, *Warwickshire*, p173

[90] William, first baron Grey of Warke, was appointed commander of the Eastern Association forces in December 1642 [Sean Kelsey, 'Grey, William, first baron Grey of Warke (1593/4-1674)', *NewDNB*]

[91] Oliver Cromwell, Parliamentary military commander, later Lord Protector, he raised troops in west Hertfordshire, in January 1643, arresting the Royalist Sheriff, Thomas Coningsby in St Albans. He was appointed as Colonel under Lord Grey of Warke in the army of the Eastern Association, in which Hertfordshire troops served. Appointed Lieutenant-General and overall cavalry commander under Manchester, many of his troops wintered in the county 1643-4. In February 1644, with troops from Hertfordshire, he took Hillesdon House, Buckinghamshire,

Association. The exception was the Hertfordshire Orange Regiment which garrisoned Aylesbury.[92] **[4-6]** Given that Cromwell had been recruiting in Hertfordshire earlier in the year, it is likely that a number of his regiment also came from Hertfordshire. At this stage, although the volunteers were technically part of the associated forces, they seemed largely independent. In October 1643, though this arrangement still applied, a new ordinance allowed a much broader committee to be established, which only applied to Hertfordshire, to raise up to £200 a week for the support of the volunteers. Whilst they remained in the county, the volunteers were under the control of the committee, but if they were sent elsewhere, they were under the Earl of Manchester's authority. This 'Volunteers Committee' came later to be referred to as the 'Militia Committee', and on 18 December 1643 they were expanded yet again, having already raised three regiments, the Black, the Orange and the Green.[93] This 'new Militia Committee' was resented by the old guard who had been excluded from it and a petition from the west of the county was presented against its activities. **[46]**

It is not easy to determine how many of the volunteer regiments existed at any one time, and how they were differentiated from the militia, except that in theory the militia did not normally serve out of the county, a defence they had used in the late 1630s against being sent north against the Scots in the Bishops' Wars. It was claimed in mid June 1643 that the Earl of Essex was advancing into Oxfordshire with troops from Hertfordshire, Buckinghamshire and Bedfordshire, and in late October, when the royalists seized Newport Pagnell, Hertfordshire volunteer foot and horse went to Hitchin to prevent incursions there, and the Hertfordshire trained bands stayed to defend St Albans while the three London regiments went to Dunstable.[94] By late November, Sir John Garrard's regiment of militia foot were destined for Newport to replace a London regiment.[95]

---

then Lincoln and York. The left wing of the cavalry at Marston Moor outside York contained the Eastern Association cavalry, including some of his Ironsides from Hertfordshire, and they were also involved in the mopping up of Royalist garrisons in the Northern Home Counties [John Morrill, 'Cromwell, Oliver (1599-1658)', *NewDNB*]

[92] Holmes, *Eastern Association,* pp69-70

[93] *LJ* VI, pp244, 342-3; F&R, I, pp289-91, 356-8

[94] BL: E73 [8] *The Parliament Scout* 18; E249 [17] *Perfect Diurnall*, p54

[95] BL: E77 [23] *The Parliament Scout* 23, *f*101

As well as the three local regiments of foot, there appear to be one or two troops of horse attached to each. Redbourn had to supply scout horses to Lieutenant Colonel Marsh and to Captain Titus "belonging to the Green regiment." The relationship is seen in the Redbourn accounts, **[5]** which refer to money paid to the "volunteers of Captain Ayleward's company, one of the Captains of the militia of the county". Those in Captain Bellfield's[96] company were referred to just as 'volunteers', but it is clear that in any one parish, between one and three individuals also hired men to serve as a soldier for them at a month at a time. Whether this soldier could be easily defined as volunteer, a member of the militia or a conscript is problematic.

Under the early ordinances passed by Parliament, including that for raising men under the Militia Ordinance and under *The Propositions* of 9 June 1642, men were provided by traditional methods used by the lieutenancy in the past. These were extended after February so that individuals, like Mr Lane of Sarratt, had to provide the equivalent of a musketeer and a half and also provide the maintenance for the soldiers whilst they were in service **[6]** At Redbourn, **[5]** the wealthy William Beaumont provided a complete set of armour, a musket and pay for two soldiers. Other men volunteered, either for specific companies, or as part of existing militia regiments.

Sir Samuel Luke wrote in his journal on the last day of 1643 that there was a regiment of foot and 150 horse of the Hertfordshire trained band in Uxbridge garrison and they had given the French ambassador three or four volleys of shot as he passed through. Given that Garrard's was in Newport, this must have been Adam Washington's.[97] It is also clear in a letter from Waller[98] in July 1644, that some of the forces sent with Major-General Browne[99] were

[96] Anthony Belfield was the third generation of the family in Studham. He had married Joane the daughter of Henry Lodges of Bedford by whom he had four sons: Henry, John, William and Anthony. It is not clear which of these men was the captain referred to [*Herts Vis,* 28]

[97] Philip, I G, (ed.) *Journal of Sir Samuel Luke, III,* Oxfordshire Record Society, XXXIII (Banbury, 1953) p226.

[98] Sir William Waller, successful in the south early on in 1642, was Parliamentary commander in the west from February 1643, where his success was marred by lack of supplies and money and his army was defeated at Roundaway Down in July. He commanded the siege of Basing House later in the year which involved some Hertfordshire troops. Many of his own troops were from London, one of his Colonels being George Thompson, whose troops quartered in the shire. [Barbara Donagan, 'Waller, Sir William (*bap.* 1598?, *d.* 1668)', *NewDNB*]

[99] Major-General, later Sir Richard Browne, was a Parliamentary army officer and London politician who later became Lord Mayor of London. He was the senior captain in the Orange

mainly from the trained bands of the militia, who were deserting and returning to the county. The forces sent with Browne were these same two militia regiments, Garrard's and Washington's, which had gone to Towcester in early July.[100] Presumably some of those, originally in the trained bands, left the militia to take up a more permanent role in the regiments which had joined with Essex or the Association forces under Manchester.[101] However Hughes assumed in Warwickshire that Parliamentary regiments there were a mixture of volunteers and the militia, and this may well have been the case in Hertfordshire. Some of these locally recruited forces were later merged with other troops to form regiments in the New Model Army, whilst others were used to man the East Anglian and northern home counties garrisons.[102]

From other sources and contemporary newssheets, it is clear that Hertfordshire regiments or part-regiments were sent to Uxbridge, Aylesbury, Abingdon, Reading and Newport Pagnell garrisons and were used in attacks, on Boarstall, Hillesdon, and Greenlands, all fortified Royalist manor houses. They were also deployed across Buckinghamshire, Bedfordshire and Northamptonshire to prevent royalist incursions into the Eastern Association. Levies by the latter meant that other Hertfordshire men, as well as volunteers, ended up in Eastern Association regiments, some of which fought at Marston Moor, and, after the regrouping for the New Model Army, others were deployed across the country against royalist armies. By late 1645 many were in the garrisons that surrounded Hertfordshire and protected London and some later also went to Ireland and Scotland. The cost of keeping these troops escalated, wherever they were, and this meant that Hertfordshire committees were perennially short of hard cash, and frequently resorted to borrowing.

---

Regiment of the city trained bands by spring 1642 and served under Waller in the capture of Winchester. In June 1644 he was appointed major- general of the forces sent to seize Oxford and commander in chief of the forces of the associated counties of Berkshire, Buckinghamshire and Oxfordshire, that Hertfordshire forces joined. These combined troops plundered Royalist supplies, captured garrisons and took prisoners. However Browne and Waller quarrelled over the overlap between their authority and he was left with unpaid and hungry troops who, despite this, skilfully defended the garrison at Abingdon against Royalist attack. [Keith Lindley, 'Browne, Sir Richard, first baronet (c.1602-1669)', *NewDNB*]

[100] BL: E 53 [21] *Mercurius Civicus* 18; [24] *The True Informer*, 37 *f* 272; E54 [21] *Mercurius Civicus*, 19.

[101] Kingston, *Herts*, pp52-4

[102] Hughes, *Warwickshire,* p173

## The financial commitments of the Committees

Once the civil war had started, it was assumed by many that it would be over in a few months, and possibly even by Christmas 1642, after one big battle had decided the issue. However the Battle of Edgehill in October was not decisive, and even though the royalists gained some advantage and advanced on London, they were held up at Brentford and then turned back at Turnham Green, never again getting any closer to the capital. Initially therefore, under the system of loans set up on *The Propositions* of 9 June 1642, people were expected to lend money, horses and plate to Parliament. It required the inhabitants of each county to gather arms to defend the 'King and Parliament' against 'Papists' and those who were planning to bring in an arbitrary government. As an incentive 8% interest was promised, the money to be repaid once the peace of the kingdom had been restored.[103] The two county MPs, Dacres and Lytton, were requested by Parliament on 5 July, to go to the assizes in Hertford to "advance the propositions for bringing in of plate and monies and horse". On the 12th, Sir John Harrison and Edward Wingate, the MP for St Albans[104] were requested to join them at the assizes on 14th, and on that day Lord Cranborne and Robert Cecil were also requested to join them on 15th. The process was still very slow to implement in some areas, so on 13 October, the Commons requested the first accounts on *The Propositions* to be sent up from Hertfordshire, and on 27 January 1643, Dacres was asked to inquire into the money which had come in under them and discover the problems connected with it.[105] Sums were initially paid into treasurers at the Guildhall in London. These were the aldermen Sir John Wollaston, Towse, Warner and Andrewes, who were merchants and financiers, well used to dealing with large sums of money and commercial transactions.[106] Those within an 80 mile radius of London were expected to deliver the money and goods in person. It is clear from the Hemel Hempstead claims that many had done this, as the individual treasurers are named in their returns.

As the cost of war escalated in 1643 and attempts at peace failed, an ordinance of 24 February required additional regular sums of money for Essex's main army and a system of *Weekly Assessments* 'for the Lord General's Army' as it was called, to be instituted, Hertfordshire initially

---

[103] Morrill, J, *Cheshire*, p95
[104] For Wingate see Appendix
[105] *CJ* II, pp654, 667, 671, 806, 945
[106] F&R I, pp8-9

having to contribute £450 per week, which was extended on 31 March.[107] These assessments were based on the £400,000 tax and were designed to tap the real wealth of the inhabitants, except servants on yearly wages. According to Cannan the local committees appointed the assessors in each parish, who then estimated the annual value of all kinds of real and personal property, the income from the latter being assessed to amount to 5% of its capital value. The committees then added up the returns from all the assessors within the county and calculated what number of pence in the pound would be necessary to obtain the sum required. The rate was then collected, in the case of rents, from the tenants, who could then deduct it when paying rent to their landlord. By May each county had appointed two treasurers to receive the payments for *Weekly Assessment*, those for Hertfordshire being Sir Thomas Dacres MP and John Heydon Esq. of Watford.[108]

The *Weekly Assessment* was a radical departure from traditional taxation as it was based on the Ship Money assessments. In Tudor and early Stuart England Parliamentary taxation had been sporadic, intermittent and light, largely affecting the landowning groups. With the attempted annual collection of Ship Money between 1635 and 1640, a wider group, including the middling sort, were affected. Others, apart from the poorest, had to pay, as Ship Money was based on 'common payments'. These included, particularly in Hertfordshire, payments for purveyance and cartage, which had been progressively extended under James I, as he often visited Theobalds Palace at Cheshunt and his hunting lodge at Royston. Composition for purveyance required payment by parishes for the difference between the higher 'market price' and the lower 'King's price' for a range of commodities. Cartage involved taxation to pay for the carriage of these and other goods of the King. In order to fund this and other common payments, such as those for the poor rate, which increased as a result of the bad harvests and the implementation of the Book of Orders to cope with them in the 1630s, parishes had reassessed themselves and included more in the lower orders of society in the payments. This, along with militia rates and Coat and Conduct money for the Scots Wars, had produced opposition within the county, and by 1640 the vast majority of tax payers were refusing to pay Ship Money. It is

---

[107] F&R I, pp85-100, 117-123

[108] F&R I, pp139-41; Cannan E, *The History of local rates in England in relation to the proper distribution of the burden of taxation*, (2nd ed 1912)

not surprising then that the regular *Weekly Assessments* and subsequent exactions, such as the Excise tax, provoked local hostility.

The pay of the forces in the Eastern Association was to be raised by voluntary subscription from those who had met the initial cost of setting them out, but this, according to Holmes, did not apply to Hertfordshire, as Parliament passed a special ordinance allowing the county committee to raise a weekly assessment and to use the remainder of *The Proposition* money. He was unsure why Hertfordshire was given, what he called 'preferential treatment', but this may relate to the fact that the Hertfordshire volunteer troops in Aylesbury were already being treated as a separate unit from the rest of Grey's forces. The committee managing finances became known as the Assessment Committee, and as the deputy-lieutenants had been involved in the war effort, they, former subsidy commissioners and a few of the activists were named to this newly enlarged county committee.[109]

*The Propositions* did not bring in as much as was hoped for, so an ordinance was passed in late November 1642 to carry out a review of who had, or had not loaned sufficient sums. A Parliamentary committee, the Committee for the Advance of Money, was set up to raise loans and impose assessment on those who had not subscribed voluntarily. This started in London and was extended on 7 May to all those who had not contributed to the Parliamentary war chest. This enabled the activists to assess everyone in the county worth more than £10 income *per annum* in land or holding a personal estate valued at £100 or more, and require money of up to a fifth of the annual income or a twentieth of the total value of their personal property. This tax became known as *The Fifth and Twentieth Part* or some variation of the phrase.[110]

Assessments for the Association, once the command had changed from Lord Grey of Warke to Edward Montague, Earl of Manchester, were often referred to as being for 'the Earl of Manchester's Army'. When Lincoln was added to the Eastern Association, a further rate for £450 per week was demanded from the county.[111] The central authorities in Cambridge allocated so much per county to be collected each month or week, and the two treasurers appointed

[109] Holmes, *Eastern Association*, pp78, 257 n40; Pennington & Roots, *The committee at Stafford*, p xxix
[110] F&R, I, pp38-9, 145-55; Holmes, *Eastern Association*, p 80
[111] F&R I, pp291-8

in Hertford and St Albans were William Turner and William Hickman respectively. They split the burden imposed on the county between them, the hundreds of Hertford, Braughing, Broadwater, Odsey, Edwinstree and the half-hundred of Hitchin paying roughly 3/5 of the amount, and the western hundreds of Cashio and Dacorum paying roughly 2/5 [**104**]. Hickman thus became known either as the St Albans treasurer or, more officially as the treasurer for the two hundreds of Cashio and Dacorum. He was clearly in receipt of frequent payments from the collectors in each parish [**78, 93, 95**]. In 1645 Parliament levied a *Monthly Assessment* rather than the previous *Weekly Assessment* for the New Model Army. It was not levied on a monthly basis but was continuously collected in order to raise a monthly income of the sum decided upon for each county or sub-division. This lasted into the 1650s.[112]

As well as assessments for the Association, Hertfordshire inhabitants found themselves paying for their own militia. This was authorized under an ordinance of 19 September 1643 following an earlier ordinance for the Watford area, which had raised a volunteer force the previous November. The new Volunteer (later called Militia) Committee was allowed to levy up to £200 a week across the county to support the local forces. Local people also had to pay for the excise, originally a Dutch invention, which was a new form of indirect taxation on commodities purchased rather than a direct tax on landed property or wealth. Hostility to the excise was seen particularly in relation to those commodities seen as essentials rather than as luxuries, such as beer, meat and salt. Ordinances for excise duty on tobacco were passed in September 1643, on beer and wine in October, meat in January 1644 and a whole host of goods including hats, hops and starch in July, herring in August and spirits in September.[113] The hostility was similar to that shown in the earlier seventeenth century towards monopolies which had pushed up the prices of ordinary goods. Both the new Assessments and the Excise were disliked because they proved effective and were levied on a much wider range of social groups, the excise including the poorest. It is not surprising therefore that there are echoes of popular royalism or anti-committee feeling among local people.

---

[112] Kennedy, W, *English Taxation 1640-1799: An essay on policy and opinion,* (1913 Reprint 1964) pp39-40
[113] F&R I, pp305-6, 315-6, 361-2, 496-7, 511-2

Over 1643-4 a wide range of taxes and contributions were expected of them, which were far greater than the Ship Money, Coat and Conduct money and common payments for purveyance which they had objected to so much at the end of the 1630s and had led many to oppose Charles 1 in 1640-2. Hertfordshire became tied in more and more with the activities and demands of the Eastern Association. These demands required more active men to be involved, as the attitude of some of the older gentry families and traditional supporters of the crown cooled. Thus on 1 June a lot of new names were added to the various local committees to help raise money across the county.[114] The following month further sums were levied to raise more horse for the Association, specifically in Hertfordshire for Sir John Norwich's Brigade, which ventured out of the Association in Bedfordshire, Buckinghamshire and Northamptonshire.[115] This was referred to in various parish accounts as 'horses for Sir John Norwich'. However Parliamentary forces found it difficult to defeat the royalists in 1643 and needed assistance from the Presbyterian Scots. Initially payments for the Scots army were voluntary, but later became compulsory, and a similar situation also applied for the problems, both religious and military, in Ireland. Other local assessments were made for fortifications, special units and levies of horses, so, to many local people, constant demands were made on their purses, which are reflected in the parish returns. This resulted in criticisms of the local committees who had responsibility for levying taxation.

How secure both militarily and financially, the committees were, depended on the immediate military threat and the extent of exactions at any one time. Hughes argued that the Committee in Warwickshire was not in a strong position until the middle of 1643, and although it could be argued that Hertfordshire was never seriously threatened militarily, the burden of both taxation and free quarter and other exactions made it periodically financially insecure, the committeemen borrowing and using their own money to pay troops, as in Warwickshire. By the middle of 1643 it was therefore clear to all that the war would last longer than anticipated, that Hertfordshire would remain under Parliamentary control for the foreseeable future and that the committee structures and financial measures would have to be expanded as the demands of war increased.

---

[114] F&R I, pp168-171
[115] F&R I, pp215-55

## II Organizing the county for war (Section A)

### Part 1: Raising and equipping the troops

The first part relates to the appointment of officers, and the raising of the troops including the volunteers, the militia and impressed men. Sir John Wittewronge of Rothamsted [**1**] was appointed as captain of a foot company of the trained bands for the western parishes of the county on 25 August by the Lord Lieutenant, now Charles Lord Cranborne, who replaced his father William Cecil, second Earl of Salisbury. Officers had their servants or troopers to accompany them, for whom they had to provide equipment. **[2]** Supplies for the soldiers came from the local committee **[3]** but orders initially came from Lord General Essex **[4]**. Soldiers provided by individual parishes needed approximately a shilling a day to survive, sometimes a monthly rate of between 28 and 32 shillings being provided by one or two parishioners **[5]**. William Beaumont[116] not only paid for the soldier, his musket and armour, but also for his upkeep and the repair of the musket when it was damaged. Lord Grey was able to use all three types of soldiers in the Association forces, the volunteers, the militia, and those paid for by local parishioners.[117] It is clear from Mr Lane's accounts **[6]** that some local men were involved with Essex's army, while others, who were either volunteers or men from the militia, served under Wittewronge in Aylesbury. Initially individual colonels like Hawes bought their own equipment, to be later reimbursed by the committee. **[7]** Some of the local militia were used for raising impressed men by 1644, and were paid for the days they trained **[8, 10]**. Others were recruited specifically to be scouts under Captain Thomas Marsh, each scout being paid a guinea a week **[9]**.

When all the armies began to run out of volunteers, paid troops and militia, then impressments took place. Throughout the 16th century and in the early years of Charles I's reign, impressments had been used for foreign expeditions. The records of impressments are scattered in different documents and as a practice it probably took place earlier than officially recorded. There were clearly increasing numbers of impressments in 1645 for the New Model Army **[11]** but we also know from Adlord Bowd's[118] first bill

[116] For Beaumont see Appendix

[117] Holmes, *Eastern Association*, p77

[118] Adlord Bowd had been apprenticed as a draper for seven years to William Gardiner of Hertford and his wife Marie in March 1643, with the consent of his mother Joane, and would

of August 44 that the 600 men to be raised for the Eastern Association were likely to be impressed, as his second bill of October referred to impressed soldiers running away, as did that of John Andrewes **[59-60]**. Captain Newman Humphreys of the local militia was given the job of impressing men from East Hertfordshire villages as early as May 1644, including 50 from Sawbridgeworth **[8]**. The parishioners of Redbourn seem to have been responsible for pressing their own men, clothing, guarding and conducting them to Berkhamsted in the same period, and may possibly have had to provide some for the Earl of Manchester in the summer of 1643, as did those at Bushey **[82]**. Those at Little Munden made a special constable's rate in October 1645 to pay for the recruitment of the impressed soldiers **[92]**. It is clear from other sources that impressed men were often the causes of considerable trouble, as the St Albans Committee found to their cost when New Model recruits in April 1645 were found to have committed various robberies and felonies on their march through the shire and had to be gaoled, one, William Hawkins, being executed for his offences.[119]

Officers usually had to supply their own uniform and equipment. Wittewronge, having been a captain of a militia company in 1642, and then Colonel of a volunteer regiment in 1643 and in charge of the Aylesbury garrison, was also made a deputy-lieutenant for the county, and in order to show off his new status, he dressed himself up in an expensive outfit which included a great red velvet saddle and gilt stirrups, **[2]** but not so the ordinary ranks. The Watford Volunteers purchased their own buff coats through Mr Vaughan as early as the 20 July 1642, **[12]** and through their purchase we are able to learn the names of those who first volunteered. William Gardiner, draper of Hertford, already a captain in the militia, provided many uniforms for the troops[120] **[13]** which Wittewronge was to command in the Aylesbury garrison. He and his workmen probably made the coats, shirts and hose required, and would have obtained the shoes from one or more of the many

probably have been no more than 17 at the time. He acted as a secretary to the local committee and later became a freeman draper and a borough assistant in 1656. He refused to take the oath under the Corporations Act of 1662 and was assessed for 9, later 7, hearths in All Saints Hertford in 1663. This property was probably "Treasuries" in Honey Lane, later the Old Coffee House Tavern. My thanks are due to Alan Greening for this information [TNA: E179/248/23 *f*121; HALS: HBR20 *ff*422d-3; 26 *f*40; Chauncy, p493]

[119] JPs of St Albans to Speaker Lenthall 18 April 1645 [Bodleian Library, Oxford, Microfilm of Tanner Mss 60 *ff*101, 138, 140]

[120] For Gardiner see Appendix

cobblers, or cordwainers as they were called, in Hertford. He also supplied the snapsacks or haversacks for the soldiers in which to keep their food and drink, and he and Thomas Barnes bagged up the uniforms in sacks and carried them to Aylesbury, having stored them in Hertford Castle. It is clear from these bills that the Hertfordshire volunteers' uniform was a blue coat with grey hose or breeches [**14**]. The cavalry troops and dragoons also required saddles and other horse furniture. The Watford Volunteers purchased saddles for their troop in mid July 1642 from Thomas Harrison, who may well have been a specialist London saddler. Other saddles were later made and supplied by John Pennyfather,[121] a cordwainer from Hertford, and by Thomas Finch, who made the other leather items for horses. In St Albans Thomas Reddman and William Jones[122] provided large and small saddles for the light horse and the dragoons that the county had to raise in 1644 [**21-23**].

From a number of documents, including the Watford receipt for buff coats, the names of some of the junior officers and ordinary soldiers in the volunteers and militia can be identified. Those sources include the records of wages paid by the Militia Committee to the captains and colonels, both in the Aylesbury garrison and as part of Sir John Norwich's brigade. The latter contains a list of 'gentlemen' as well as soldiers and some can probably be identified as coming from the families of established gentry, urban businessmen and active committeemen, including members of the Barbor, Fairclough, Gardiner, Goodyere, Dixon, Hale, King, Eteridge, Nicholls, Rutt, Heydon, Arris, Thoroughgood, and Hickman families and local craftsmen such as John Almond and Henry Beech from Hertford **[12, 107-8].** Other key figures, such as Mr Ayres, the surgeon, were appointed at the rate of 10/- a week, whereas in full-time armies they might expect 5/- a day.[123] **[15]**

---

[121] For Pennyfather see Appendix

[122] There were at least six saddlers in St Albans in the mid 17th century. Jones kept a saddlery at the Swan Inn in Holywell Street at his death in 1673-4, when he was the inn holder. Reddman had a shop, but at his death, the stocks were not great and his assessment for the poor rate did not indicate that he was very prosperous [Smith & North, *St Albans*, pp39-40, 48, 179-80, 186]

[123] This may be a young Thomas Arris (c1622-85) who graduated from Cambridge in 1643 and became a fellow of the College of Physicians in 1644. His father Edward had been sergeant-surgeon to Charles I and lived at Great Munden. Thomas was a churchwarden and auditor of the accounts at St Peters church and was on the assessment committee for the county in the 1650s. He became a leading doctor in St Albans, latterly residing at Hall Place to the north of St Peters Church, and becoming the MP for the town from 1661-79 [Smith & North, *St Albans*, pp3, 103, 165; Henning, *Commons* I, p 548; Melia, *Newburn Ford*, p22]

## Part 2: Arming the troops

Sources in this section show how weapons, ammunition and other supplies were provided. Whatever soldiers were raised, they had to be armed, and provided with ammunition. Before the war started the Watford Volunteers raised enough money to buy their own weapons and equipment, spending £75 with Stephen Estwick and purchasing pistols and carbines from Werner Pin **[16].** The active committee men in the Parliamentary cause, who had secured the magazines at Hertford and St Albans, had responsibility for providing the other volunteers with weapons and ammunition.[124] In November 1642, following the return of the soldiers from Edgehill,[125] the deputies handed over the pikes they had abandoned, to the Watford Volunteers. The Hertford master cutler, John Almond, was employed to mend and scour calivers and muskets for the infantry, as well as serving himself in Captain Moulson's troop **[19, 108].** Thomas Crowch, the Hertford locksmith, also used his skills with metal to dress and repair muskets, pistols and 'horse arms' **[18].** The cases of pistols for the troopers and the armour, muskets and bandoliers for the infantry were brought up from London by the local carrier John Pritchard **[17].** Powder and ammunition had to be sent up from London, once the initial supply in the castle had been exhausted. Also when the troops were in the field, the barrels of powder and bullets, as well as large quantities of match to fire the muskets, had to be sent up to them by wagon **[24-26].** William Turner, the Hertford Treasurer had the responsibility for purchasing the powder and match in London with local funds, thus being away from his business for 2 days. Some of the bullets were manufactured locally using lead from other sources, and wagons had to be constructed to carry materials when regiments either went on exercise or on campaign **[28-9].** Musket balls varied in size from ½ to ¾ inch and could be made of other metals or even stone.[126]

---

[124] *CJ* II, pp714, 721

[125] Before Edgehill the Countess of Sussex wrote to Sir Ralph Verney that large numbers of soldiers and carts of ammunition had arrived at St Albans on 8 September 1642 and 10 cannon as well as gentlemen of the Inns of Court to guard Essex. On 7 November she reported that Essex had marched from St Albans the previous Sunday, and on 19th that the county was supplying 200 dragoons to defend borders of the county and on 1 December that all the trained bands and others had gone out of the county to Buckinghamshire. [*HMC 7th Report* Appendix Verney Papers, pp440, 442, 443]

[126] Melia, *Newburn Ford,* p16

The militia regiment under Colonel Adam Washington had some artillery in the form of drakes[127], and two teams of horses had to be employed to carry the ammunition for them from London to Hertford. In emergencies, such as that when it was feared Hitchin was being attacked by royalists from Bedford, Washington had to pay the gunners 1s 4d a day out of his own pocket and get himself reimbursed through the committee in Hertford **[27].** The committeeman from Hitchin, Robert Draper,[128] had the drakes repaired during the emergency of summer 1645 **[27, 33].** The county appointed a gunner, William Parr, in May 1645, who was given the responsibility of preparing the guns for action, for which he was paid 14/- a week **[31-2].** He seems to have replaced Captain Pegg[129], who had previously used Hertford Castle as a workshop for repairing the drakes as well as other weapons for the infantry **[20].**

## Part 3: Supplying the horses

This part includes sources where some of the horses were raised within the county, though others seized can be seen in Section C, when their losses were claimed for by local people. A large number of horses had to be found, as they were used as mounts for the cavalry and dragoons, as draft animals for the artillery, ammunition and baggage trains, for pulling carts and supply wagons, for post and communications, for the scouts and intelligence service.[130] This meant that under *The Propositions,* one of the essential elements was the lending of horses along with cash and plate. Horses also required riders, for all purposes, and these may not have been trained cavalry troops, but those capable of riding a horse to a particular destination and taking part in whatever duties were assigned. [**34-37**]

Horses were obtained either legally, being loaned through *The Propositions*, given for particular purposes, sometimes paid for directly, or requested by

---

[127] Drakes were light guns with short barrels with an approximate range of 746 yards. They varied in size from 3, 6, 9 or 12 pounders, firing canisters which contained bags of lead musket balls at short range. They were fast to reload and were for supporting front-line infantry and had been used in the Bishops' Wars [Melia, *Newburn*, pp18-19]

[128] For Draper see Appendix

[129] Pegg was a copyhold tenant of Brickendonbury manor, whose name survives in Peg's Lane Hertford. My thanks are due to Alan Greening for this information.

[130] A useful article on the whole subject is P R Edwards, 'The supply of horses to the Parliamentarian and Royalist armies in the English Civil War', *Historical Research*, LXVIII, 165, (Feb. 1995) pp49-66

local committees.[131] In other cases horses were taken, with or without a receipt, by the commanders of local, regional or national armies. The value of these could, and sometimes were, claimed back in the parish petitions presented later to the Sub-Committee of Accounts. According to Pennington, on paper there were detailed arrangements for horses to be valued and paid for: the permission from two deputy-lieutenants to take it; the duplicate recording of all details about it; and its branding with a mark to indicate it was now the property of the state. Horses were easy to steal and some officers allowed those seized to be sold. Many complaints were put into the authorities about the unjust seizure of horses as can be seen from the Hertfordshire sources **[120-2]**. In May 1643 the Commons ordered the release of Captain Andrewes, who had used such strong armed methods to raise horse in Hertfordshire that he had been arrested by the local committee.[132]

Initially under *The Propositions*, named commissaries of horses had the job of raising the required number from the county or its divisions. Three specific parish accounts from Standon **[34]**, Barkway **[36]**, and Tewin **[38]** provide evidence for the above as does the letter from Roland Lytton[133] to Alban Coxe **[43]**. That from Tewin shows that Essex's army, forces under Middleton[134] and the local troops under Puller and others unidentified, all took or commandeered horses in the parish, and some went to cavalry troopers, others to dragoons. The Standon accounts show how the process started in 1642 with men lending horses, which were valued by the central commissioners Smith and Richardson, but that also local men Humphrey Packer and Edward

[131] Edwards calculated that 6,704 horses were raised in London and the South East under the Propositions from 21 June 1642 to 6 July 1643 [Edwards, 'Supply of horses', p58]

[132] Pennington, D, 'The War and the People', in Morrill, J, (ed) *Reactions to the English Civil War*, London 1982) pp118-9; Holmes, *Eastern Association*, p83. Andrews led a company of Randall Mainwaring's regiment of London redcoats made up mainly of zealous puritan apprentices who had come into conflict earlier in 1643 with the traditionalist rector of St Mary's, Lambeth, by allowing his men to smoke in church and interrupt sermons. This culminated in the soldiers tearing the rector's prayer book in half and taking the surplice off his back [Lindley K, *Popular Politics and Religion in Civil War London,* (Aldershot, 1997) pp261-2]

[133] For Lytton see Appendix

[134] Sir Thomas Myddleton was a commander of Eastern Association forces, whose troops later, as part of the New Model Army, melted down Wrexham church organ pipes to make musket bullets and gained a reputation for trickery, shooting six Royalists while pretending to be friends [Charles Carlton, *Going to the wars: The experience of the British Civil Wars, 1638-1651*, (1994) p277]

Wood also assessed the value of horses for Captain Robotham[135] of the local militia. Eustace Nedham,[136] underwrote a horse at Welwyn valued by Sir John Read and Captain Hale in November 1642. If the horse was provided 'complete' i.e. with complete saddle, bridle, reins, stirrups, and possibly some horse armour, it was worth more than one without this horse 'furniture' as it was called **[127].**

Horses were required for each new military unit that was commissioned.[137] In April 1643 Lord Grey of Warke's Eastern Association regiments, which had probably been wintering in the county, needed fresh horses for the spring campaigns, and Eustace Nedham found himself having to supply them from Little Wymondley, both to a quarter-master under Captain Salkins and a corporal under Captain Cromwell **[127].** The local militia, volunteer regiments, the various troopers employed by the Eastern Association commanders under Manchester, including Colonel Middleton, and the special brigades or groups such a those under Colonel Norwich (Norris) in 1643 or under Silius Titus in 1644-5 all required new levies of horses **[30, 34, 36, 60].** In some cases riders had to be provided for some of these special units and the parish, as at Barkway, had to provide cash for the upkeep of both man and horse by the month **[36].** By 1645 it was not always easy to find the right rider and Rowland Lytton requested the return of his servant who had had to accompany the horse **[43].**

---

[135] For Robotham see Appendix

[136] Eustace was the first son of George Nedham of Little Wymondley and Margaret Stile of Kent. He married firstly Anne daughter of Luke Norton and secondly Frances, the daughter of Edward Wingate. In 1634 he had two sons, George and Luke and a daughter Lettice [*Herts Vis,* p78]

[137] Doctor John King wrote to the Speaker, William Lenthall, on 19 September 1643 that he had received a warrant for 100 horses for a troop of arquebusiers from Essex. The Committee asked for deferment of the warrant as they were raising 300 light horses for Manchester, and the county had recruited Colonel Middleton's regiment twice and other companies under Essex and Waller had been provided with horse. The Earl of Denbigh's officers had 'swept away' many horses when they went through the county, which meant in total that they had provided at least 1,000 or possibly 1200 horse, mainly at their own cost and now had to provide 120 dragoons for Manchester [*HMC Portland Mss* I, p131]

Horses were sometimes provided following a warrant, though these were sometimes considered bogus as at Tewin **[38]**. Sometimes the warrant required the parish or individuals to provide them, presumably the individuals being paid for them by the parish, which recouped the sum later through local rates. Those requests for horses at Barkway are described as being imposed on individuals, some at Wymondley as being 'commanded by the Committee at Hertford' while others were seized without any authority. Some men provided horses privately, in other words as a private donation, while others were sent to a specific place such as Wendover.

The type of horses required varied depending on the duties for which they were needed. Cavalry horses had to be strong and relatively young. Horses of scouts or messengers needed to be light and fast, most of those being supplied from Barkway being light **[36]**. Any old nag could be provided for pulling carts for supplies. Horses were variously described by their status, stoned (a stallion or un-castrated), gelding (castrated), or by colour, black, white or bay (chestnut coloured). This then gave some description which might mean they were recoverable if only on a relatively short loan. Horses could be bought in the local market and some of the pressure was probably taken off the local farmers when the Eastern Association employed its own agent for buying horses and London dealers sold as many as a hundred at a time. According to Pennington there was no dramatic increase in prices paid for horses until the re-equipping of the New Model Army in 1645. However Edwards estimates that during the war the value of horses did rise, increasing by a third or half of their pre-war levels. [138]

Evidence from Hertfordshire, which seems to have supplied horses for many forces and duties outside the shire, supports Edwards' view about an increase in prices. In November and December 1642, Mr Gale and Thomas Garrett of Bushey listed one horse each which were valued at £6, and in the November following, Michael Warren and William Weedon also listed horses for the same amount. Sir Peter Saltonstall of Barkway paid composition in money of £10 instead of actually providing a light horse and harness in kind **[36]**. Sir Edward Chester[139] from the same parish actually provided one in kind valued

[138] Pennington, 'The war and the people' p 109; Edwards, 'Supply of horses' pp49, 53

[139] Sir Edward Chester (1590-1666), son of Sir Robert Chester of Royston and Barkway, educated at Christ's College Cambridge and the Middle Temple, had married Katherine Stone, daughter of John Stone Esq, Sergeant at Law of London, but being widowed, married in 1642 Anne, the daughter of Sir Peter Saltonstall of Barkway, who at 22 was less than half his age.

at £9/8/6d. John Rowley[140] gent provided a light horse and complete horse furniture valued at £14 as well as £3-10/- for a month's pay for the horse and rider. The parish of Barkway provided another light horse valued at £12. These however are well above £6-£8 cited by Edwards, and this may reflect the constant demand on the county.[141]

These sums give us an idea of the range of initial values of nags and horses, with or without accoutrements at the start of the conflict and the estimates for what a volunteer cavalryman would have cost the Parliament each month. However, as supply could not meet demand, the price a good horse fetched rose. By 1643 a horse taken from Francis Rowley of Brent Pelham by Captain Andrewes was valued at £16, though we have to be careful not to assume this was the real, rather than a deliberately inflated, value to get higher compensation for loss of the value of its use over the period. Other horses were seized outright. John Caesar[142] of Sandon had two bay horses taken out of his stable at night which were valued by neighbours at £30 the pair in July 1643, and the following month, 9 horses valued at £100, were actually taken out of the carts when they were bringing in the harvest **[126].** Six days later, a Major Battersby took two of his coach horses valued at £40 the pair on the authority of Sir William Waller. Clearly the type, size, age etc. of a horse would help determine its value. Those who were listing horses at a low value may well have been getting rid of old, weak or un-biddable horses. Thus horses varied enormously in value from £5 for an old nag to £20 for a strong coach horse in peak condition. However even before 1645 some horses appear to have been valued at up to £20 each.

---

He was subsequently put on the county Commission of the Peace by the King in July 1642 and knighted in 1643, possibly to try and win him over to the Royalist side, but he appears to have remained neutral. He inherited the manors of Royston, Berewyk, Cokenhach and Nuthampstead [TNA: C231/5 *ff*330-1; Foster, *Marriage Licences*, p272; *VCH Herts* IV, pp31, 35; *Al Cant* Pt I Vol I; Chauncy I, pp158, 182, 203, 204, 207, 211, 212; *VCH Herts* III, pp260-1, IV, p31]

140 John (*d.* 1668) was the son and heir of Thomas Rowley, of Barkway, gent. He had been at Halstead School, Essex, Gonville & Caius College, Cambridge, from 1621 and was admitted to Grays Inn in 1622. He had refused to pay Ship Money on land in Reed on the grounds that he was unjustly rated. He was made sheriff in 1650 and was assessed for 11 hearths in 1663 [TNA: E 179/248/23 *f*89; SP16/376/106; *Al Cant* Pt I Vol 3; Foster, *Gray's Inn Admissions,* p167]

141 Edwards, 'Supply of horses', p53

142 Sir John Caesar, (1593-1647) youngest son of the former Chancellor of the Exchequer, Sir Julius Caesar, lived at Hyde Hall. He had been admitted to the Inner Temple in 1612 and had been an active JP 1633-6. He appears to have tried to stay neutral during the civil war [HALS: QSB2A Passim*;* Anon., *Students admitted to the Inner Temple 1547-1660*, (1877) p205]

The major requisitioning of horses took place in the county around Hemel Hempstead immediately after the battle of Edgehill. Tobie Combe accounted for 101 horses and harness which were used for supplying ammunition and arms to defend the City of London from the advancing royalist forces. Henry King and Timothy Weedon acted as the commissaries to value the horses. King then went to Dunstable with the horses and their riders and delivered them to the Wagon-Master General. Some of the horses requisitioned early on from other parishes may have been part of this consignment. Other horses were provided by special forms of levy across the county **[98].** By July 1643 the inhabitants of Bushey provided £46/11/- in horse and arms for the Eastern Association cavalry and by September 1644 were paying £11/16/- towards a general county rate for 50 dragoons and 50 light horse **[82].** Hertfordshire therefore provided horses for local forces and for duties outside the county. It was the committees in Hertford and St Albans that had to coordinate all the demands for men, ammunition and horses and try and respond to the demands of the centre in London as efficiently as possible

## Part 4: Running the war

This part includes sources related to the operations of specific committeemen, and how the committee attempted to manage some of their troops. Captain Kensey had to ensure that the right sums of money were raised from the parishes for which he was responsible, as he had a percentage from them as collector **[44].** Barbor and King as chairmen of standing committees, were able to claim an attendance allowance of 5s (25p) a day and living expenses of the same amount when they or other committee members visited London on committee business **[45, 47].** The treasurer paid this out of the sequestrations account. Apart from these and military expenses they also paid for celebrations after the victory at Naseby and the costs of the local administration and secretariat **[50].**[143] When meeting in the King's Arms at Hertford or the Christopher at St Albans the committee could also claim for a meal and everything else that went with it **[49].**

The local regiments of volunteers and trained bands had to be supplied directly by the county wherever they were sent. This sometimes meant that both committees attempted to control Colonel Alban Cox's forces on the same day in August 1645. Even after the war was over, the Committee at Hertford

[143] Hughes, *Warwickshire,* pp180-1.

kept in touch with Cox as the county representative at Bury, and Silius Titus corresponded with Cox on the demeanour of the King **[51-7].** Gabriel Barbor the chairman, with one of his sons in the Orange regiment in Aylesbury, had a particular concern to see that the Hertfordshire troops there received enough supplies as well as some moral support **[3].** Committees or their agents tried to put pressure on Parliament to ensure that their particular soldiers received enough money to survive, or to get them released from service. To administer the demands of the centre the committees employed secretaries and agents for communications.

## Part 5: The secretariat and communications

The committees employed a number of men as clerks and messengers, as well as calling on the services of local tradesmen for fortifications, mending weapons, carrying supplies etc. The Hertford Committee met in the King's Arms and employed Anthony Mowry as secretary in 1643, Adlord Bowde in 1644, and Gabriel Barbor's own clerk, Thomas Bevis, in 1645. Mowry was paid £1 for 50 warrants, just under 5d a warrant, **[58]** whereas Bowde was paid between 1d and 4d per warrant depending on their length and 16d a day writing letters **[59-60].** Ordinary warrants were usually charged 1d. Bevis understood that latterly the committee clerk had a salary of £13 per quarter or £1 a week. Assuming a six day week, this would have worked out at 3s 4d a day, a lot more than Bowde was paid. However, according to Bevis, the clerk latterly employed only worked on Fridays. It is clear from his petition that at times of crisis he was up half the night writing out warrants and was only relieved of some of the burden when printed blanks were invented for raising the militia rates **[62].** The tools of his trade are seen in his bill for stationery supplies which required the purchase of quills and ink, wax, and laces to seal and tie together papers as well as paying for the cost of sending letters. **[61]**

John Andrews and others were employed by the Hertford committee as messengers who delivered letters frequently to St Albans and London but also to the Earl of Manchester, whether he was at Lincoln, or Reading, being paid 3s a day expenses. John Andrews had to go to the High Constables to get hold of runaway soldiers and take horses to where they were needed **[64].** John Clarke and Maurice Dalton also were sent to fetch runaway soldiers from Northampton and took horses to Bedford **[65].** Thus ordinary local townsmen, who might otherwise have not travelled far, found themselves riding across the South East and East Midlands on committee business and benefiting financially from the war effort. For sequestration activities the Hertford Committee employed a solicitor, Gabriel Odingsells[144], and a number of agents and collectors including Edward Heath and Edward Chandler. Similar arrangements appear to have been made at St Albans for the western half of the county and muster masters and paymasters were also employed for the regiments that were recruited. Jeremiah Fitch was also employed as a commissary for the supply of horses, and the widow Faireman kept horses stabled for the committee's use **[63].** The committee also had to raise more local taxes for fortifications.

## Part 6: Fortifying the garrisons and towns

The fortifications of some towns in the civil war were extensive and elaborate, particularly if they were likely to be besieged or were in a relatively indefensible position, but those in Hertfordshire were probably of a simpler design.[145] As Lord General Essex and his army spent a number of weeks in the early years of the war camped in and around St Albans, in late 1643 the town was fortified with a series of defence works to prevent any successful royalist attack from Buckinghamshire or Bedfordshire getting into the town. London newssheets reported that fortifications had begun in early November and that the town was well fortified by the end of the month.[146] The men employed to supervise this work on behalf of the army were Adjutant-General English (or Inglis) and a Dutch engineer, Jacob Culenbourg, who probably had siege experience from the 30 Years' War in Europe. They, with the help of local workmen, constructed a series of breast-high ramparts and redoubts[147] or additional defensive extensions on the edge of the town **[67-72].** Inglis and Culenbourg were paid in three instalments, presumably as each section was completed. A special local rate had to be raised to pay for this. The borough authorities also helped in the construction of a guard house and two turnpikes, one at Holywell Hill and the other at Cock Lane. Once constructed, the local

---

[144] Gabriel Odingsells was either the father or grandfather of the Gabriel Odingsells (*b. c*1690-1734) a dramatic writer, who having been to Oxford became mentally unstable and hanged himself in 1734 [*Al Ox* 3, p1085]

[145] See the diagrams in Porter, S, *Destruction in the English Civil Wars* (Stroud, 1994) p19; and in Haythornthwaite, P J, *The English Civil War 1642-1651: An illustrated military history* (1994) p104

[146] BL: E74 [21] *The True Informer*, 7; [16] *The Scottish Dove*; E75 [3] *Certain Informations*; E77 [8] *The Compleate Intelligencer & Resolver*, 5

[147] Redoubts projected from the walls so that there was no dead ground and defenders could cover all the area in front of the walls with cross-fire [Porter, *Destruction,* p17]

inhabitants were expected to provide wood and candles for the soldiers on guard in the guard house. Dr Toms claimed that the earthworks were particularly strong near St Peter's Church and at the St Stephens end of town, citing the Mayor's accounts for 1642-3.[148]

Hertford also decided to build defensive works in and around the town, perhaps fearing a repetition of the incidents in July 1642 when royalists under John Watts Junior had tried to seize the magazine. They established three turnpikes outside the houses of Mr Bull the attorney, John Fulches and John Keeling, the borough steward. They employed John Holland, a local carpenter, to supervise the work. This involved boarding up the Old Cross, by which one turnpike and a turnstile were built, and also constructing a second turnstile against the tower of the castle. A series of bulwarks or fortifications were also built around the town and Mr Keeling's barn was used as a guard house and a second one constructed next to Mr Barbor's, the local committee chairman. Four carpenters were employed in this work and other local craftsmen provided the iron and brick work and labourers were employed to fill in the defence works with earth **[73-5**].

Not only did Hertfordshire have to pay for these relatively small defence works, but when Newport Pagnell was captured from the royalists, they and three other counties, Bedfordshire, Buckinghamshire and Northamptonshire had to share the cost of extensively fortifying the town, the Hertfordshire levy being £200.[149] Later they also had to help support the other garrisons within the Eastern Association as well as paying for their soldiers in Aylesbury, Abingdon, Bedford, and Reading, which were all garrison towns at various stages of the war [**66**].

# III Paying for the war (Section B)

## Part 1: The Propositions, loans and contributions

Wartime measures to raise money included initially *The Propositions,* which was then extended to the *Weekly Assessments* and a range of other

[148] Toms, E, *The Story of St Albans* (Rev ed Luton, 1975) p102

[149] A plan of the fortifications at Newport Pagnell in 1644 still exists. These were constructed by another Dutch engineer Captain Cornelius Vanderboone [Porter, *Destruction,* p7]

contributions. Details of donations under *The Propositions* appear in many parish accounts, and in the accounts of the collectors and High Collectors. There is also frequent mention of the *Weekly* or *Monthly Assessments*, and the tax known as *The Fifth and Twentieth Part* that arose out of the review of the inhabitants' contributions. There was also a second review of those whose wealth was thought to be such that they should have paid more tax. Committed Parliamentarians however, such as those from Hemel Hempstead, John Besouth and Tobie Combe, brother to the late Francis Combe, were prepared to loan £50 as early as 5th and 19th August 1642 respectively. Mary King, widow, and Samuel Southen also lent £20 in August and a number of other Hemel Hempstead inhabitants were prepared to lend £10, which would be in the region of £3000 today, if a multiplier of 300 were used. [**78**]

The horses that were lent under *The Propositions* were valued by commissaries at between £10 and £16 and the silver plate was weighed and around 5s 4d was paid per ounce of silver. Even gold rings were loaned [**77**]. However the regulations were relaxed and many local people, unable to get a day or two off to go up to London and back, paid their money into two local treasurers, Joseph Dalton, the mayor of Hertford, and Mr Humphrey Packer [**79**]. Under the process of review, at Hemel Hempstead, John Binn of Eastbrookhaye paid £5-10/-, and Henry Turner £1. Even Adam Washington paid a further £5 at Brent Pelham. Mr Turpin became one of the treasurers for the review. A year later on 11 October 1643 an additional ordinance allowed the Earl of Manchester to carry out a second review of payments and contributions in the eastern counties so that it was more effective.[150] [**78**]

The committee had to raise a local tax for the local militia and volunteers **[91].** Eventually they raised enough to support three local regiments, the Black, the Orange and the Green, presumably named after the distinguishing scarves or sashes they wore. At Redbourn, and therefore presumably across the county as a whole, seven rates were made between October 1643 and November 1644, Redbourn's share doubling to over £21, the total for the period coming to over £128. These were firstly paid to Zachary King of Watford and then to Thomas Tanner of St Albans, as did the collectors from Kensworth, Northchurch and Little Gaddesden. However by November 1644 these appear to have fallen into arrears. Who received the rates as pay can be seen in the militia payments to troops **[93, 95, 96, 97, 108-9, 113]**.

---

[150] F&R I, p309; Pennington & Roots, *The committee at Stafford*, p xxxiv

Apart from these regular taxes and levies, there were other voluntary contributions that local people were expected to make. As the war continued and more casualties took place, an additional ordinance of 6 March 1643, building on previous Tudor legislation, required assessments to be made for the widows and orphans of those killed, and for maimed or injured soldiers. These did not seem to prove very effective, so that a second ordinance had to be passed in October under which Hertfordshire was expected to raise £120.[151] However one device of the Hertford committee was to get poor widows to look after maimed soldiers, and to help out sick soldiers, so that they got well and returned to their units **[136-7].** Horror stories of the Catholic rebellion in Ireland in 1641 and the massacre of Protestants, led to an ordinance for the poor Protestants in Ireland on 30 January 1643 and one specifically for the clergy in Ireland on 18th September 1643, which required all churchwardens and overseers of the poor in the county to receive gifts from all inhabitants in their parish by 26 November, and those within a 10 mile radius of London were to pay these directly into the London treasurers.[152] Both of these measures come to be seen reflected in the parish accounts **[80, 82, 87, 91, 95]**.

A new stage in the war was reached when, following a number of defeats of Parliamentarian forces by the royalists in England, the Scots decided to join in to oppose Charles I's armies, and an ordinance of 27 October 1643 authorized the raising of a loan of one third of £100,000 or £33,333 6s 8d 'for the better enabling our brethren of Scotland for our assistance and defence, in this common cause of our religion'. Hertfordshire had to raise £3000, and in theory, no one was going to be forced to lend money 'unless his ability and means of livelihood in lands, leases, money and other personal estate exceed the sum of £1,000'.[153] In practice many with far less income seem to have contributed, perhaps for religious reasons, or possibly through pressure from neighbours. Others disliked paying the Scots **[80, 81, 102]**.

Local taxes were also raised to pay for the fortification of St Albans, but a major commitment developed for the county when it was decided on 18 December to erect and maintain a garrison at Newport Pagnell, Buckinghamshire, which had just been captured from the royalists. To do this

---

[151] F&R I, pp328-30
[152] F&R I, pp285-7
[153] F&R I, pp322-7

the county had to contribute £125 towards the initial fortification, provide 150 soldiers and £500 a month to maintain the garrison. In order to ensure this happened, and again to widen the net of active participants within the local committees, a special ordinance was passed for 'further addition of power to the committee of the county of Hertfordshire'. It was designed to compel: officers to do their duty; persons assessed to pay their taxes; and both towns and people to perform their proportional part of the burden, both in personal services and rateable taxes.[154]

Whilst paying all these additional taxes, local people had the burden of free quarter imposed on them (see section C). They also found that their contributions to the Eastern Association were also increasing, the monthly sum to be sent to Cambridge rising in January 1644 to £675. This was then renewed every few months.[155] They had to provide an additional 500 foot, 50 cavalry and 50 dragoons in July[156] and additional funds for Cromwell's cavalry in October, which is reflected in the Hemel Hempstead accounts [**78**]. Thomas Dacres MP was again the specific treasurer for this.[157] In October the Parliamentary 'British Army in Ireland' was in difficulties keeping the supporters of the Irish Catholic Confederation at bay, and a special ordinance was passed by which Hertfordshire had to supply £65 a week for 12 months.[158] With the Self- Denying Ordinance, and the reorganization of many of the national and regional armies into the New Model Army under General Sir Thomas Fairfax, many of these assessments came to be consolidated over the early part of 1645. From February, £2,432 a month had to be raised in the county for the New Model and £651 for the Scottish Army.[159] This was a vast sum to raise on a regular basis and proved not to be sufficient to defeat the King in 1645, despite his setback at Naseby in June.

Hertfordshire had to pay for specific garrisons or campaigns outside the county, but later could claim some money back from the excise. However, when another special tax which was levied in August 1645 for the reducing of Newark, Notts, still a royalist stronghold, Hertfordshire had to raise a further £752 for this, but the following month their contribution to the Newport

[154] F&R I, pp356-8
[155] F&R I, pp368-71, 515-6
[156] F&R I, pp472-5
[157] F&R I, p530
[158] F&R I, p531
[159] F&R I, pp614-26, 630-46

Pagnell garrison was lowered to £245.[160] Some of the money for all of these taxes could be recouped by pursuing the sequestration of royalists and Catholics, and using their estate income, and the sale of their property to finance the Parliamentary war effort (see Section C). In July 1644 a further indirect tax was introduced with the excise, borrowed from the Dutch. This was not just on alcohol but also on necessities such as meat and salt, so everyone virtually had to pay some excise duty. There is evidence both of opposition to this and that men did pay it **[83, 99, 101,102]** until that on meat and salt was dropped in 1647 and by then it was being paid back to the county to pay off military debts [**103**].[161] However, a major problem of organization throughout the war was how to collect the bewildering variety of taxes, levies rates and assessments.

## Part 2: Assessment and local rating

The traditional way of assessing and collecting taxes was through the vestries, the local JPs, parish constables and high constables of the hundreds. However when the sheriff, Thomas Coningsby, had found difficulty collecting Ship Money in the county in the late 1630s, he had appointed his own collectors for the purpose. The Ship Money evaluation was based on that for the common payments of purveyance and cartage, which had been extended under the Stuarts and Ship Money assessments hit a wider proportion of the population than previous forms of taxation.[162] *Weekly Assessments* for the Parliamentary armies largely used either the Ship Money, or individual parochial assessments, which were devised for the purpose. They were largely based on the number of acres held, and the value of goods owned, but could include other items. For example those living in Little Munden found themselves paying a shilling for every £20 of value in goods and a penny an acre for their landed property **[88, 92]**.

In order to assess and collect the different sums, high collectors for the hundreds were appointed by the committees and sub-collectors and parish assessors were appointed within the parish. This had already been used for the collection of the subsidy of £400,000 and the Poll Tax before the war started **[78, 86, 96]**. The assessors tended to be the wealthier and higher status

[160] F&R I, pp742-3, 762-6
[161] Braddick, *The nerves of state,* p99
[162] For a discussion of this whole issue see A Thomson, 'Hertfordshire Communities'

parishioners. The sum to be provided by the parish was decided by the committee at Hertford or St Albans, who allocated them, via the divisions, to each community. The collectors then paid them to a high collector, Toby Combe Esq in the case of the Dacorum division **[98]**.

## Part 3: The collection of rates, loans, taxes and contributions

The high collector, depending on the tax and the warrant received from the appropriate committee, either paid it to one of the county treasurers or directly to central treasurers at the Guildhall in London. In other counties, such as Cheshire, committees went on using the constables and high constables for collecting the new assessments, whereas in Hertfordshire, new collectors were often appointed for each levy.[163] In order to keep track of who had lent or given what, tickets or receipts were sometimes given, or lists provided of those who had not received receipts. Toby Combe was both a high collector for one set of taxes and a treasurer for the local militia, to whom sums were paid directly. In larger parishes there were different men acting as collectors, in smaller ones the same men tended to find themselves collecting a number of assessments. This bound more and more local people into the tax collecting system, and therefore into the war effort **[84, 94-8]**.

The initial gifts and loans on *The Propositions* can be seen in individual parishes where separate returns were sometimes made for this one form of payment as well as the overall amounts. Hemel Hempstead, a market town in the west of the county, made a return for *The Propositions* in which the two wealthiest men, Tobie Combe Esq and John Besouth[164] lent £50 each to the Guildhall treasury in August 1642, before Charles raised his standard at Nottingham to proclaim the supporters of Parliament to be rebels. They were thus anticipating events and can be seen to be ardent supporters of the Parliamentary cause. Mary King, widow, not only gave £20 at the same time but also freely gave towards the buying of horses for Cromwell who was recruiting troopers in the area in early 1643. One of those who probably became a captain-lieutenant in the Ironsides was John Gladman,[165] who paid

---

[163] Morrill, *Cheshire,* pp95-105.

[164] John Besouth held the Manor of Agnells in Hemel Hempstead until his death in 1643. His daughters Hester Martyn and Mary King held the manor jointly until 1650. Mary was already a widow [*VCH Herts* II, pp215-30]

[165] Gladman succeeded James Berry as captain-lieutenant in Cromwell's regiment of 'Ironsides' in 1644 and was promoted to captain when his troop became part of Fairfax's horse

£7 for his 5th and 20th part. Thomas and Nathaniel Axtell were members of the extensive Axtell family with lands and property in Hemel Hempstead, Berkhamsted and the adjacent parts of Buckinghamshire. One of the Axtell family, Daniel, became a captain and then a lieutenant-colonel, in the New Model Army.[166] Those giving or lending money early on also included Samuel Sowthen who gave £20 in August and John Nashe, John Gaze, Joseph Marston,[167] Samuel Baker, John Gate and Jonathan King gave £10 each. These were the lesser landowners and wealthier traders of the area **[78]**.

## Part 4: Allocation of, opposition to and repayment of money raised

Issues that arose from the assessment and collection process included the allocation of financial responsibility between the Hertford and St Albans committees where Hertford contributed 3/5 and St Albans 2/5 of any tax. Also conversely when the income from the excise was to be distributed, Hickman was told by the St Albans Committee to get their proportion from the Hertford Committee **[99]**. This was needed as St Albans had already been spending money for cavalry for the Eastern Association, and Hickman, as treasurer, had to juggle any income between various expenditure accounts many of which were periodically in the red. A related issue was the allocation within a taxation division of sums to be raised from different towns and parishes. Within the Cashio division, St Albans and other towns, such as Watford, were in dispute, which required a letter from the two county MPs **[100]**.

---

regiment in 1645, when he commanded Fairfax's own troop. In April 1648 he and William Packer helped to break up Leveller agitation in the ranks, when they were stationed at St Albans and he later investigated the Diggers and decided they were harmless. Imprisoned as a precaution in 1662 he continued to be seen as a potential threat to the Stuarts until 1685 [Robert Zaller, 'Gladman, John (*fl.* 1644-1685)' *NewDNB*]

[166] Daniel Axtell of Berkhamsted became a captain in Pickering's foot regiment, then major and Lieutenant-Colonel under Hewson, at Pride's Purge, and the trial and execution of Charles I. His troops were quartered in Hertfordshire in 1644 (*see* **119** below). At the siege of Drogheda, he was later governor of Kilkenny and in charge of a regiment that attacked Royalist strongholds, but was suspended by Ireton for killing prisoners. Captured in 1660 he suffered the full penalties of treason as a regicide. [Alan Thomson, 'Axtell, Daniel (*bap.* 1622, *d.* 1660)', *NewDNB*]

[167] Joseph Marston of Hemel Hempstead had married Mary, daughter of Thomas Porter of Ayot St Lawrence, and in 1634 had three sons, William, Joseph and Henry. He held the manor of Woodhall in 1637 [*VCH Herts* II, pp 215-30; *Herts Vis*, p74]

There was considerable opposition to the excise particularly at Ware, which was not a borough and had a history of resentment against its neighbour Hertford, and the excise men felt threatened **[101]**. Resentment was also aimed at both the local committees, who were accused of drinking the proceeds, and at the Scots, being referred to as 'rogues and rascals' **[102]**. The committee however was often in desperate need of funds and borrowed £400 from its chairman, Gabriel Barbor, **[103]** the St Albans Committee owing a similar sum to the Eastern Association **[104]**. Hickman was frequently in arrears to the Association both for the *Weekly Assessments* and *The 5th and 20th Part*. **[105]**

## Part 5: Paying the Troops

As well as providing regular funds for the Association, the committees had to keep their own funds for paying their own volunteer regiments and militia **[106]**. Sources reveal which officers received pay directly or on behalf of their men. Sir John Wittewronge's regiment, which was out of the county for 77 days, were paid over £2,874, or over £37 a day. Humphrey Packer's account for Sir John Norwich's cavalry not only reveals that the troopers received 17s 6d a week pay but that there was a wide variation in pay among the commissioned and non-commissioned officers. The Colonel, who was both Major-General and Captain received £24 a week, his captain 8 guineas and lesser sums for the other officers. As well as a cornet, a clerk and scout-master he also had with him a marshal, a master of arms, and a quarter-master as well as 3 corporals, 2 trumpeters and a saddler **[107]**. Each troop also varied in number, Norwich's troop containing 105, and Captain Moulson's 61 **[108]**.

When the infantry in the militia were mustered under Colonel Nicholls he had with him a captain-lieutenant (first-lieutenant) and an ensign (second-lieutenant), as well as 4 sergeants, 4 corporals, a marshal and 2 drummers **[109]**. Differences in the number and type of non-commissioned officers was presumably the result of the varying needs and requirements of infantry and cavalry. The numbers of soldiers allocated from the North-east of the county to the militia regiments do not vary dramatically from the numbers allocated in the 1605 muster, recorded by King. Layston provided 13 (compared with 12 in 1605), Therfield 17 (16) and Barley 12 (10) though others did not provide any to this particular militia group.[168]

---

[168] King, *Militia*, pp193-208

Infantry in the militia received 8d a day, compared with the trooper 2s 6d, but then the latter had to pay for the food and upkeep of his horse as well as himself. The captain-lieutenant received 4s a day, the ensign 2s, the drummers and sergeants 2s and the corporals 1/4d, twice the ordinary infantryman **[109]**. The militia were paid for when they mustered but also for when they went out of the county to defend the perimeter around London, while the volunteers and other Association troops went further a field, and had to be paid via travelling paymasters.

Paymasters were appointed by the committees to ensure that the cash got into the soldiers' hands. William Love became the paymaster for both the Black and Orange regiments and he also had to pay Hertfordshire's share of Sir John Norwich's horse brigade **[106-8]**. This involved him not only collecting money from William Turner, the treasurer at Hertford, and William Hickman, the treasurer at St Albans, but also taking the Hertfordshire share of the Eastern Association money to William Leman[169], the treasurer at Cambridge **[113-14]**. He also had to ensure that Hertfordshire troops elsewhere were paid. These included those under Colonel Mitchell, that were sent to help in the siege of Greenland House, a royalist stronghold near Henley on Thames, which was finally captured in the summer of 1644 after the walls were flattened by cannon fire **[112]**.[170] His St Albans equivalent was a committeeman, Fromabove Dove,[171] who latterly took over some of the paymaster's roles for the western hundreds **[103]**. Dove, as quartermaster, was required to pay Sir John Norwich's cavalry at Ware, having received over £800 from the two standing committees. He then had to go to pay them at Moreton in Buckinghamshire and on to Cambridge to pay William Leman the Association Treasurer £1,000 **[110]**. Love was also helped by a messenger, Henry Peach,[172] who had responsibility for carrying £300 to the London treasury, **[105]** and in July 1644 was sent to pay the Orange regiment whilst Love had to pay at least part of the arrears to the Captains **[111]**. Humphrey Packer Junior was specifically appointed paymaster for Sir John Norwich's regiment, **[107]** and Captain Andrew Sherlock of the local dragoon company was paid directly from the committee via the treasurer, William Turner. His account book reveals numerous casual payments to poor or maimed soldiers,

---

[169] For Leman see Appendix

[170] Porter S, *Destruction,* pp30, 45.

[171] For Dove see Appendix A

[172] By 1675, Henry Peach was a maltster, being appointed constable of Ware. [Hunt, E M, *The History of Ware*, (2nd ed, Ware, 1986) p122

individual officers for drums and colours, and for horses lost in service, as well as officers in the militia for their days' service. Thus, with an increasing number of local troops scattered over a wide area and different treasurers to pay for different forces in different armies, the structure of payment was far from simple.

William Love was also involved in training the troops. At one time he was the Muster Master, but then Mr John Kinge,[173] from Hertford, took on that role, which involved reviewing, checking, mustering and training the troops in basic weapons drill **[110]**. The ways in which this was done can be seen in the payments given to Captain Thomas Bowles[174] when he trained his troops in north Hertfordshire around Hitchin and Stevenage for up to 10 days. Captains were paid at the rate of 7s 6d a day, lieutenants at 4s, ensigns (second lieutenants) at 3s, sergeants at 1s d and drummers at 1s **[10]**. Similarly Captain Newman Humphreys prepared for the intense activity of the summer months by exercising and training his militia troops for 10 days in May 1644, and travelling round south-east Hertfordshire villages impressing soldiers **[8]**.

With the formation of the New Model Army in 1645, Love became responsible for paying the Hertfordshire troops in the various garrison towns surrounding the county. In March 1646, with the war near its end, he stated the desperate financial situation in a letter to the Hertford Committee **[114]**. He had had to borrow over £1,200 to pay the local troops and would have to borrow more until the taxes came in. He had had to travel around the eastern counties to collect the arrears for the garrison towns and then go to Newport Pagnell and Newark to pay the Association troops stationed there. He feared he was being accused of fraud and embezzlement. In fact he was put in charge of an inquiry into the loss of funds, and eventually his assistant, Captain James Pinckney, was found guilty of embezzlement.[175]

---

[173] John King, grocer of All Saints, became a borough assistant in Hertford in 1648 [HALS: HBR25 *f*6 , Chauncy II, p493]
[174] Bowles (*d.* 1669) was from Wallington, the son of Lewis Bowles, whose family had been in Hertfordshire since the reign of Henry VII. In 1644 he was made a Captain of a foot company in the Hertfordshire militia. He was assessed for 7 hearths in 1663 [TNA: E179/248/23 *f*69; *Herts Vis*, p112; Chauncy I, p97]
[175] Tibbutt, *Luke's Letter Book, passim*

Thus any analysis of the cost of the war reveals four significant features: firstly that many showed support by early subscription to the propositions; secondly that Hertfordshire was heavily burdened with national, regional and local taxes and contributions; thirdly that the measures adopted to assess and collect these were varied, increasingly sophisticated but different from other counties and fourthly that the committees often struggled to meet their financial obligations, were often in arrears, borrowing money from the richer sort and trying to pay their own troops before they deserted. They also had a major problem paying their troops who were scattered over a wide area. However communities and individuals also suffered because of the cost of free quarter and plunder taken by Parliamentary soldiers, meant to protect them.

## IV The impact of the war on communities and individuals (Section C)

### Part 1: The effects of free quarter and depredations by soldiers

The documents in Section C help the historian identify the impact of the war on individuals and communities. Apart from what were seen as non-Parliamentary forms of taxation, free quarter, or billeting, was one of the issues that Parliament had objected to in the Petition of Right in 1629. However by 1643 both Royalists and Parliamentarians engaged in it. As Royalists never controlled Hertfordshire, all the free quarter that was taken in the county was by Parliamentary armies. On 15 November 1643 it was reported that Essex's army was billeted at St Albans, Redbourn and places round about.[176] In theory quartermaster-sergeants or their agents negotiated billeting with the local authorities, whether the mayor of the town or the village constable. Both individuals and communities, particularly those around St Albans, suffered from the imposition of free quarter on a regular basis. Householders were expected to house men and sometimes their horses from overnight to nearly three months at a time. Billeting might be in the main house, outhouses or barns. Sometimes local gentry had senior officers billeted on them, but at other times they had ordinary soldiers. The most congenial might be the local volunteers who were billeted overnight, as they

---

[176] BL: E76 [22] *Kingdom's Weekly Post*, 3, *f*18

moved westwards into Buckinghamshire, simply because they were local. Those apparently disliked most were the Scottish soldiers, particularly some of the former mercenaries employed by Colonel Meldrum,[177] who wintered in Hertfordshire in 1643-4.

John Hall of Colney Street had George Anderson billeted on him for 13 weeks, **[115]** and John Beech of St Stephens had two soldiers taking free quarter from 14 February to 6 May a total of 11 weeks, 5 days **[116]**. An officer in Essex's Lifeguard stayed 3 weeks and his men 10 weeks in the winter of 1643-4 with John Hart of Park Ward in St Stephens parish, the men being charged 2s 6d a day for their bed and board, and the horses 2s 8d a day for their stabling and fodder **[117]**. In some cases large numbers of soldiers stayed in a parish for a few days, and any one parish could be burdened on a number of occasions. In Bushey, 150 men and their horses stayed 8 days in August 1643 and in October two of Essex's regiments stayed one night. In May 1644 500 foot soldiers stayed 2 days in the same parish **[118]**. In theory tickets or receipts had to be issued by the army authorities, or sometimes the soldiers themselves, which indicated how many soldiers and their horses had been billeted and for how many nights. However, many soldiers left without these being provided, hence the later claims via the local committees.

The various regiments that were billeted in the county, apart from Essex's soldiers and Colonel George Thompson's[178] and Colonel Hudson's London Trained Bands in and around St Albans, included at various times, Lord Denbeigh's, Colonel Hammond's foot, Colonel Meldrum's dragoons, Colonel Barclay's artillery, Major Bofa' troopers and Colonel Bluers' men as well as most of the Earl of Manchester's forces, who were allowed to take free quarter across the county in the winter of 1644. The extent of Manchester's free quarter repayments indicate both the disposition and command structure of his forces before the formation of the New Model Army and the earlier commands of those who became prominent later such as Cromwell, Ireton, Disborowe, Crawford, Whaley and Harrison. They also indicate which towns

---

[177] Colonel Sir John Meldrum, a Scottish mercenary soldier, who had fought in Ireland, the Low Countries and for Sweden, then for Parliament at Edgehill, was active clearing Royalists from the East Midlands, Lincolnshire and Yorkshire but lost Newark to the Royalists in March 1644. He died of wounds received at the siege of Scarborough in May 1645 [Charles Carlton, 'Meldrum, Sir John (*b.* before 1584?, *d.* 1645)' *NewDNB*]

[178] George Thom(p)son originally from Watton at Stone. See [Alan Thomson, 'Thomson, George, (*bap.* 1607, *d.* 1691)' *NewDNB*]

took a heavy burden of free quarter in that period notably: Hitchin (£245), Ashwell (£179), Baldock (£141), Ware (£137) Stevenage (£135) and Hatfield (£134) **[123]**.

By July 1644 the burden of free quarter on the county and the absence of three Hertfordshire regiments out of the county created a double problem of paying for the militia forces out of local funds, while at the same time providing free quarter for out-of-county troops. As a result the grand jury petitioned quarter sessions to present their grievances to Parliament **[139]**. The Hertfordshire Militia Committee, criticized in the petition, responded with its own petition to the Committee of Both Kingdoms, **[140]** in which it was claimed that the three county regiments were costing £1,000 a week to finance and that loans had had to be borrowed to pay them. This reflected a political clash between the more conservative local groups whose allies in Parliament had pushed through an ordinance transferring power over the militia back to the lieutenancy.[179] The context to this clash went back to February when a petition to the Lords had complained of the great burden of free quarter, which had lasted 17 weeks, and asked for the removal of Essex's forces, the suspension of taxes and the repaying of debts.[180] On 3 July an ordinance for putting the Associated Counties into a posture of defence involved the raising of forces under a revived lieutenancy, not under the militia committee, it being only mentioned in a supportive role to punish mutineers. This was part of a struggle between the more conservative 'Political Presbyterians' in Parliament and their 'War Party' opponents, sometimes referred to by historians as the 'Political Independents'. The latter's local allies on the Militia Committee in a counter attack on the 27 July, presented their own petition and it was referred to the Commons committee for reforming the army, along with the petition attacking the committee, particularly its chairman Gabriel Barbor. In August a compromise solution was worked out whereby the Militia Committee was continued in power indefinitely, but the treasurers had to provide quarterly accounts to the lieutenancy, and local committee men and commanders had to take The Covenant. This retained the local Independents, like Barbor, in power, but restricted the committee membership by excluding radical sectaries, who would not have taken The

[179] On 16 April, the Militia Committee's power had been extended for 4 months, which ran out in mid August [*CJ* III, pp 460-1; *LJ* VI, pp521-3]
[180] *LJ* VI, pp440-1

Covenant, from local influence.[181] By April 1645, with the lead up to the formation of the New Model Army and the victory of the Independents with the Self Denying Ordinance, the focus shifted to the activities of royalists who were still troubling the county borders **[141]**.

By the end of 1644 parishes and individuals had been given an opportunity to claim for, not only the repayment of free quarter taken, but not paid for, but also all the depredations and losses suffered, including thefts, spoliation of cereals and consumption of hay by horses. The losses, depredations and plain stealing that soldiers carried out included weapons and ammunition **[116, 117, 120, 122],** horses, saddles and other equipment, **[120, 121, 122]** beds, bolsters and blankets, **[119]** bibles, money and other valuables. Sheep, **[117, 118, 120,121]** poultry **[116, 118, 121]** and other animals were seized and taken away for human consumption, fodder for horses [**120, 122]** and wood taken or cut down for fuel **[120, 121].** Free quarter was particularly burdensome on farmers and estate owners when cavalry or dragoons were billeted on them as horses consumed large amounts of fodder, or horse 'meat' as it was called, including oats, peas and sometimes other grains if they could get them. However individuals suffered a series of burdens and losses throughout the period. Later in the early 1650s William Hickman, as part of an auditing process, had to produce a schedule of payments made by him for free quarter claimed by parishes in the western hundreds and this reveals the overall burdens, which in many cases ran into over £100. Over £3,000 had been paid out for this schedule alone, besides previous piecemeal payments **[124]**.

Clearly the depredations of the soldiers, many of them from outside the county, were an unfortunate side effect of the war and one which provoked local hostility as at East Barnet. Here as elsewhere there is evidence that the harvest and agriculture in general was disrupted by the lack of available manpower and by the commandeering of horses. This can be seen in the effect on individuals and parishes in different parts of the county.

## Part 2: General effects on individuals and parishes

Some people were generously compensated for their losses, whether of liberty, income or property. The widow of Captain Wingate, MP for St Albans, who had been imprisoned by the royalists in the Worcester campaign,

[181] *CJ* III, pp575, 579-84; *LJ* VI, pp440-1, 664-6

received £80 of his arrears **[125]**. John Caesar of Sandon, son of the former Chancellor of the Exchequer, Sir Julius Caesar, had however been roughly treated by soldiers who took away his carts at harvest time and six days later his coach horses **[126]**. Eustace Nedham of Little Wymondley, having supported the war with taxes etc. found soldiers had seized arms, armour and ammunition to the value of £127 **[127]**. Mr Lane of Sarratt, having provided a soldier and for his maintenance, paid taxes, and given free quarter, also had to give money for the fortifications of St Albans and supply Essex's troops with wood for fuel when they were wintering there **[128]**.

The effects of free quarter on an individual parish can be seen in the accounts for Redbourn **[120]** and in the individual claims from St Stephen's parish in St Albans.[182] On the road leading out of St Albans towards the midlands, the parish of Redbourn was particularly vulnerable to both casual free quartering by passing soldiers going north, as well as the more long-term free quarter taken by the winter garrison of St Albans. This took place in the first two years of the war when Lord-General Essex made the city his winter base defending the approaches to London from royalist attack and when major field campaigns were seldom implemented, largely because of the weather and the logistical difficulties. With armies on the move, communities in this area were also vulnerable to demands for horses and carts to be commandeered to move supplies or the artillery train. The inhabitants of St Stephens in St Albans returned a number of claims, **[130-133]** for the various sums they felt were owed to them, many written in the same hand. Being largely a rural parish, a number of farmers not only provided the statutory taxes but also claimed for free quarter taken particularly by cavalry regiments. John Marshall had provided hay for the horses and lost sheep and other goods. Mr Nicholas Rolfe quartered Colonel Sir William Constable, his officers and about 60 soldiers as well as losing wood, poultry and weapons. His relative William Rolfe lost five sheep and his neighbour John Edwards a gelding taken out of the plough.

Some of the soldiers were local, being members of the militia or volunteers, and may have been known to the inhabitants, by name, if not personally.

---

[182] In a report to Manchester about free quarter in St Albans on 14 September 1644 'touching the difficulty of finding provisions and pay for the regiments' it was reported that the inhabitants were unwilling or unable to accommodate the soldiers 'with victuals upon trust.' [*HMC 8$^{th}$ Report Duke of Manchester Mss*, p61]

Others came from far a-field, and sometimes refused to give their name to avoid payment or responsibility. Some even came from Scotland, **[131]** and there appears to have been some hostility towards them, particularly if they helped themselves to the contents of barns into which they had broken. The experiences of Eustace Nedham and John Caesar are significant in this respect **[126-7]**. It is clear from the East Barnet account **[119]** that it was almost impossible to recover goods once they had been commandeered or stolen, and it was equally difficult in some cases to decide who were real or feigned soldiers. Also revealed in this account were the difficulties in gathering rents when so many men were away fighting and few tenants could be found. An interesting statement of the longer term economic effects of the war can be seen in the pamphlet, *A Husbandman's Plea against Tithes* of 1646 which echoes the Barnet account, where because of a change of minister an attempt was made to raise tithes twice in one year. *The Husbandman's Plea* was signed by many in the West of the County where economic problems seemed greater.[183]

However there were some positive effects of the war for some individuals. Those who provided uniforms, coats, stockings, saddles, arms etc. benefited from the wartime taxation that paid for them, and thus some of the taxation, as in London, was recycled within the local economy. The craftsmen who built the fortifications and the carriers who took the supplies to the troops or fetched them from London did well, as did those who were employed by the local committees. However there were some that can be seen as the victims of war.[184]

[183] The original is in the House of Lords Record Office, and it was published as a pamphlet as part of a campaign by radical sects against the Anglican Church tithes

[184] Porter, *London*, p195

## Part 3: The victims of war

Some individuals were the victims of war in other ways than free quarter or loss of property. Edward Wood, an ensign to Captain Dawges[185] in scouting out the enemy and disarming malignants, was in straitened circumstances as he had not been paid for a year, but was granted £2 as a free gift **[134]**. The widow of Captain Field was generously given £80 of his arrears, **[135]** whilst other widows had to look after injured soldiers, who were likewise compensated for their injuries **[136, 137]**. Other sick soldiers, who had fought at Marston Moor, were also paid small sums to help them on their way to join the Earl of Manchester at Reading **[138]**. Others, who were dramatically affected, were the wives of imprisoned royalists, such as Mrs Coningsby of North Mimms, who suffered loss of poultry as well as ten acres of wood cut down for winter fuel for Essex's troops **[121]**. However, those who lost most were the royalists and Catholics who were sequestered by the local committees.

## Part 4: The political effects of the war and the sequestration of royalists

Compared to other counties where local people had had to work with Royalists, there was no punishment of the whole population in Hertfordshire as those who were declared to be 'delinquents' were a relatively small number of prominent landowners. The county also escaped the fate of paying double taxation as, like London, it was only ever occupied by one side.[186] However there were growing differences between the more moderate gentry and the more radical committeemen. These differences were related to war aims, property rights and who held the real power. The radicals were associated with Cromwell and the Political Independents or War Party MPs, who increasingly wanted complete victory against the royalists. The moderates however, associated with the Earl of Manchester and the Political Presbyterians or Peace Party MPs, wanted firstly to avoid defeat, but progressively after Marston Moor, to negotiate with the King. Gabriel Barbor, Dr John King and the Militia Committee were associated with the former, and those who came to oppose them locally with the latter.

---

[185] William Dawges gent, of Hatfield, was a captain in the militia and the Hertfordshire solicitor for sequestrations, later Parliamentary surveyor. He was on the Hertford Committee until 1649 then again in 1659 being a JP 1656-9. He was assessed for 23 Hearths in 1663 [F&R I & II, passim; TNA: C139/13/6 *f*41d; E170/248/23 *f*24]

[186] Porter, *London*, p194

Those who ran the war had the real power over taxation and resources, and the Militia Committee, dominated by townsmen and lesser gentry, came to be challenged by the established Deputy Lieutenants, who came to represent the more conservative elements among the country gentry. The third issue arose over the sequestration of Royalist estates, the processes being managed by a committee rather than going through the courts. Established legal procedures were seen to be ignored as were the property rights of landowners, when land was confiscated, tenants changed and income from rents used for the war effort. Radical townsmen made decisions in committee about the property of gentry and aristocracy who had, until 1642, been colleagues or friends of many moderate parliamentarians and conservative gentry. The imprisonment of Royalists as 'delinquents' or for non-payment of fines, without going through traditional court procedure could be seen as 'Roundhead tyranny'. These differences arose in a Grand Jury petition and over the position of Sir John Boteler.[187]

The petition from the Grand Jury of July 1644 **[139]** brought to a head a number of political issues that had been simmering since the start of the war. It was particularly concerned about what was perceived to be an excessive financial burden on the county compared with others in the Eastern Association, and the activities of the Militia Committee, which were seen by the more conservative elements as going beyond its remit. It was also concerned about the economic effects of not having enough men to get in the harvest. In response, the Militia committee proffered a petition of its own **[140]** bemoaning the shortage of money to pay the soldiers as a result of the 5th July Ordinance, which seemed to restrict their money-raising activities by restoring the power of the Lieutenancy. They accused a few disaffected people of fomenting the Grand Jury petition and reiterated what the Committee had achieved so far. They identified those opposing them as being linked to Sir John Boteler, who had sought a pardon from the King in early 1643 and claimed malignants were stirring up opposition within the county. The Militia Committee, however, managed to keep their position and continued to work through Sir Thomas Dacres, the county MP **[141]**.

The position of Sir John Boteler of Watton Woodhall had been ambivalent since before the start of the war. He was named by the King as *Custos*

---

[187] Ashton, R, 'From Cavalier to Roundhead Tyranny, 1642-5' in Morrill, J, (ed.) *Reactions to the English Civil War 1642-9*, (1982) pp195-7

*Rotulorum* in a new Commission of the Peace issued on 15 July, and carried out a half-hearted attempt to implement the Royalist Commission of Array in August 1642. However he continued as a local JP until July 1643, his conduct being investigated the following month and six charges against him being made [**142-3**]. This followed the setting up a Commons Committee for Sequestrations in March 1643, and subsequent local sequestration committees in both Hertford and St Albans. The witness statements in Boteler's examination give a vivid picture of the turmoil at the time and the extent to which passions ran high against those considered extremists on both sides. It was also quite thorough in its examination both of local people and of Sir John's servants.

The sources for the account of Sir John Boteler come from the State Papers 23, the Committee for Examinations. They show the difficult situation pro-royalist traditional gentry, who had served the King, were in, if they were stuck in a Parliamentary controlled county, and did not want to commit early on. Sir John had been a JP in the county since 1635 and in the Liberty since 1641, actually chairing the county bench in 1643. He was alleged to have supported John Watts junior and John Keeling in July 1642 in their attempt to stop the Hertford volunteers exercising and to have spoken disparagingly of the local militia. He was further alleged to have attempted to have carried out the royalist commission of array in the county and to have carried an accommodation petition to the King at Oxford at the end of the year, and have come back with a pardon for the county[188] [**142**].

It is difficult at this distance to judge whether or not he obtained a fair hearing before the committee of examinations. There were a number of hostile witnesses against him, who alleged he had spoken against Parliament and threatened those who opposed him in Watton at Stone. However their evidence was not consistent and they were not always prepared to back up the

---

[188] It had been reported on 13 January 1643 that horse from Aylesbury intercepted Dr Seaton and Mr Francis Goodere on their return from Oxford on 12 January, who had gone with the Hertfordshire petition to the King. Thomas Tyrill and others in Aylesbury garrison sent the speaker the petition and the King's answer and got hold of 20 books attacking parliament, "which were to be dispersed in that county and whereof you will finde (by the examinations herewith sent you) Sir John Butler to be partly guilty". Francis Goodere Esq of Hatfield, was the son of Sir Henry Goodere, married Catherine daughter of George Onslow, and had at least one son, Henry, born c1629 [Bodleian Library, Oxford: Microfilm of Tanner Mss 64 *f*121; *Herts Vis*, p58]

detail of the allegations. However he did not deny all of the detail charged against him, and one can only judge that all the local people knew he was a royalist sympathizer, and that he had used certain phrases at key points either publicly or privately which seemed to condemn him. It appears that not long after his examination he was imprisoned, first in the Peter House, and latterly in The Tower, and that despite agreeing to pay a composition fine, his failure to complete payments led to his further sequestration. By about 1645-6 he had been in prison for 2 years and was seeking redress from the Commons on what he saw as unjust treatment, given what he claimed were contributions he had made to the Parliamentary war effort **[143]**.

From an early point in 1642 it became clear who in the county was going to join the king and become an active royalist. However it is not so clear how many quiescent royalist supporters and conservative neutrals remained in the shire, and how many were under suspicion of being secret royalists. Two of the prominent royalists were Arthur Capel, the former county MP, recently ennobled as Lord Capel of Hadham, owner of the Hadham Hall and Cassiobury estates, **[149-51]** and the MP for Hertford, Sir Thomas Fanshawe, the Exchequer official and owner of Ware Park, near Hertford **[145, 148]**. They were more conservative in outlook, Fanshawe being an active promoter of Arminianism, and Capel, although more puritan, became a constitutional royalist.

Other known royalists included the mayors of Hertford and St Albans, Andrew Palmer and William New, as well as the steward of Hertford, John Keeling, and the Ship Money sheriff, Sir Thomas Coningsby, who was reappointed by the king, and later attempted to implement the commission of array in St Albans. Both mayors ended up in gaol, Coningsby in The Tower **[146]**. By the end of August, Fanshawe's and Capel's houses had been raided by troops of the Earl of Bedford and large quantities of arms, ammunition and gun-making equipment found. Fanshawe was disabled from sitting in the Commons in September and went to join the king, fighting for him at Edgehill. Capel raised 800 horses for Charles, and advanced him £12,000 in money and plate, also fought for him at Edgehill, but failed to obtain the plate from the University of Cambridge. As a consequence, a Parliamentary committee sat to consider how best to sequester Capel estates, he being one of the wealthiest men in England with properties in at least ten counties, and a reputed income of £7,000 p.a. making him a multi-millionaire by modern standards.[189][**149-51**]

Other royalists, or suspected royalists, were also subject to the process of sequestration. Later Henry Carey, Lord Dover of Hunsdon, was sequestered, although his son John, Viscount Rochford, served in the Parliamentary army. Sir John Harrison, the customs farmer, who had built the Balls Park mansion at Hertford by 1640, having initially cooperated with Parliament, joined the King at Oxford, where his daughter Anne married Thomas Fanshawe's brother Richard. Both Richard and the third brother, Simon, were also to have their Hertfordshire properties sequestered.[190] **[156-61]** Those gentry arrested for forwarding the king's interest, supporting the commission of array, or under suspicion of doing so, were sequestered before the general ordinance of 27 March 1643, including Coningsby, Boteler and Keeling. The list of Royalist and Catholic delinquents within the county **[144]** was probably drawn up in late 1643 and illustrates the wide range of aristocracy, gentry, clergy and others who were identified as active Royalists, and recusants. Under the later ordinance in August, their personal property was valued, fines levied, real property let to tenants and the income sent to the national treasury via the sequestration commissioners and Goldsmith's Hall, though 1/5 part was supposed to be reserved for the maintenance of dependents, the local officials taking a small proportion for their expenses.[191]

Manchester, as the commander of the Eastern Association army, was also given responsibility for sequestrations in his area, and, with Capel's old friends, Lytton and Dacres, helped to mitigate the effects of the process on the Capel estates in Hertfordshire. Capel's mother, Theodosia, daughter of Sir Edward Montagu of Boughton, was closely related to Manchester and resided at Hadham Hall. Capel's wife, Elizabeth, was living at the Cassiobury mansion at Watford, inherited from her father, Sir Charles Morrison. However the estate was burdened with part of the £10,000 annuity granted to Lord General Essex, and her position was threatened when Essex was camped

---

[189] *CJ* II, pp756, 760-1, 785, 871; Skeet F J A, 'Arthur Lord Capell, Baron Hadham 1604-49, *East Herts Archaeological Transactions*, III, Pt III (1907) pp315-7; Ronald Hutton, 'Capel, Arthur, first Baron Capel of Hadham (1604-1649)' *NewDNB*; Kingston, *Herts*, pp24-6

[190] For Richard Fanshawe see Peter Davidson 'Fanshawe, Sir Richard, first baronet (1608-1666)' *NewDNB* & for Ann Fanshawe (nee Harrison ) see Peter Davidson, 'Fanshawe, Ann, Lady Fanshawe (1625-1680)', *NewDNB*

[191] *CJ* II, pp356, 683, 928, 949, 951; *CJ* III, pp217; F&R I, pp106-17, 254-60

at St Albans in October 1643. Furniture was seized from the mansion, and soldiers began to raid the estate, so Lady Capel fled to Oxford.

## Part 6: The organization of the sequestration process

A local Sequestration Committee was set up under the March 1643 Ordinance and Manchester's power to sequester strengthened under the 11 October Ordinance.[192] As he had friends in the county, Lord Capel's brother, William, was able to negotiate with the Hertford sequestration committee to become the main tenant, and therefore rent collector of the bulk of the Capel estates within the Eastern Association[193] **[149]**. He was then able to negotiate with interested parties and sub-let some of the properties. However it appears that not only did he have to spend a large proportion of his time touring the estates, collecting rents, maintaining property and making improvements, but that his brother was suspicious of his motives, and felt Lady Capel at Hadham was not being properly served by his position **[150-1]**. Some of Capel's woods were felled to pay soldiers and Sir William Brereton sought to lease part of the Langley estate.[194] Sir Thomas Coningsby's property was particularly badly hit, both his mansion house and woods suffering, and where there was no strong, local, permanent tenant to look after it, local people took advantage and invaded the property **[163]**. The general effects of this in other parts of the country have been analysed by O'Riordan, who saw many of the popular attacks on royalist property as opportunist, sometimes being justified in terms of customary rights. He also showed that rent strikes, the cutting of timber and estate takeovers all had dramatic effects on the estates and their former owners. His conclusions are supported by the evidence from Hertfordshire.[195]

The actual process of sequestration is vividly illustrated by the accounts of the two agents or bailiffs of the chief sequestrator for East Hertfordshire, Gabriel Odingsells. He sent his agents out to survey and value the goods and property

---

192 F&R I, pp113, 309

193 William Capel, as the brother of Lord Capel, had to pay yearly rent of £422 to the St Albans Sequestration Committee for various lands in West Hertfordshire including Bushey Mead, Cashiobury, Watford tithes etc. leased to him by the committee [*HMC Various Collections VII*, p346]

194 BL: Add Mss 40630 Capel Estate Papers *ff* 131, 134-41; TNA: SP20/1 *ff* 153, 232-5; HALS: Cassiobury Mss 8745 *ff* 68-75, 85, 139-41; HALS: Capel Mss 10602

195 O'Riordan, 'Popular exploitation of enemy estates in the English Revolution, *History*, 78, 253, (June, 1993) pp183, 187, 188, 190-4]

of so-called 'delinquents', a term used to describe those identified as royalist, or royalist sympathizers. The two key agents in East Hertfordshire were Edward Chandler[196] and Edward Heath[197]. In their claim for expenses **[145]** it is clear that, having assessed the value of the goods, some were immediately sold off and the property taken over to be leased out to tenants, who were sometimes intruded into the property. They had to pay rent to the committee and account for any losses and purchases, as was the case with Thomas Nicholls, who took on the Balls Park estates of Sir John Harrison **[153]**. In this case, because the newly built mansion was stuffed full of goods, furniture, kitchenware etc. that were only a few years old, it was decided to sell them at auction, much to the delight of local people **[161]**. However, Nicholls himself came under suspicion for not playing fair with the local committee and the Commons had to set up a committee to investigate the whole process. In the event, it appears that he might not have been deliberately lying, but was an inefficient farmer as well as an inefficient financial administrator, as he does not seem to have obtained as much as he could have done from the estate and allowed the sheep to pasture on land that gave them foot rot **[152-5]**.

## Part 7: The effects of Sequestration

The seizure of property and forced payment of rent was controversial, as it went against the key principles of many gentry, who had been opposed to Charles' arbitrary seizure of property and arbitrary taxation. The new Parliamentary system seemed no better that the previous royal one, and when the Sub-Committee of Accounts for the county was established, the role of the sequestrators became a major focus of attention for the more conservative members placed on that committee. William Capel had particular problems with trees being taken from his brother's estates without getting sufficient payment, but he was effective, in that the Committee at Hertford had to order

---

[196] Edward Chandler of Ware, draper had said in September 1642 that "John Watts was a malignant, contrary to our causes". He and his wife Elizabeth of Ware had at least 5 children: Susanna in 1630, John in 1634, Job in 1639, Roberta in 1642 and another son John in 1645. He had sold property in Bishops Stortford in 1636 and 1637 when he had been variously described as a linen-draper, silk-weaver and grocer. In March 1655 he was married again, to Bridget Stearne of Stapleford, and a son Edward was born in 1656, when he was still described as a draper. He was assessed for seven Hearths in 1663 [TNA: E179/248/23 f 113r; HALS: DP/116/1/1&2 Ware Parish Registers; QSMB2 no 443]

[197] Edward Heath was chosen surveyor of the Highways for Ware in 1652, in March 1656 he married Elizabeth Wickes of Ware and was assessed for five hearths there in 1663 [TNA: E179/248/23 *f*113v; HALS: DP/116/1/2 Ware Parish Register; Hunt, *Ware*, p122]

that no more should be cut down **[149]**. His task was very onerous as he had to collect the rents from a number of East Anglian counties as well as pay the local collectors their dues. He also had to provide for his brother's wife and family, as was required under the sequestration ordinances, as well as pay what was owing to the Earl of Essex out of Capel's Hertfordshire estates **[151]**.

The dramatic effect of having been put in The Tower is seen on the estates of Thomas Coningsby. Over £1,300 of goods were taken from his estate for compensating Sir William Brereton. Timber was cut down and sold, local people stole his fences and the bricks from his buildings and let their cattle graze on his property and when Cox and Carter investigated it in 1650 they found it in a ruinous state **[146, 163]**. Sir John Harrison's house was also denuded of its contents, the inventory of August 1643 listing their value as being nearly £500. Many animals were lost to the estate through seizure by soldiers or the poor management by Mr Nicholls. Ten months later further goods were found concealed in the barn, the partial list being valued at £72, though when they were sold, the total fetched over £350 **[148, 152-5, 156-7]**.

## Part 8: The sale of sequestered and concealed goods

Some of the royalists tried to get round what they feared might happen to their property and deliberately hid or concealed their goods, or gave them to friends to look after. However the sequestration agents became wise to this and found a considerable amount in different buildings and properties, including a large number of clothes and household linen, belonging both to the Harrisons and the Fanshawes, which was again sold off at an auction to local people **[156-61]**.

The clothes and artefacts revealed in these sources, give a glimpse of the lifestyle of the Fanshawes and the Harrisons, as rich bureaucrats, who had exploited the King's semi-privatized civil service and customs system to accumulate massive wealth. Sir John Harrison concealed vast quantities of linen in his barn as well as expensive bed furniture and fittings. Sir Simon Fanshawe concealed his clothes in the houses of neighbours or tenants, along with linen and expensive items belonging to his wife. When the contents came to be sold they also included curtains and curtain rods as well as a mass of kitchenware and bedroom furniture and the wood in the yard. One can imagine the glee when these were sold 'by the candle' to all the local people, who made offers for bed linen, pots and pans, and fancy finery, which would otherwise not normally have come their way.

The impact overall therefore of the war on the royalists could be devastating and Anne Fanshawe, the daughter of Sir John Harrison, described in her memoirs the estimated sums the former millionaire had lost as a result of leaving the Balls Park estate in the not so tender hands of Mr Nicholls and of Heath and Chandler, the 17th century equivalent of the broker's men. Her possibly exaggerated figure was more than £130,000, though this would have probably included not just losses to the estate in goods and kind, but dilapidations, loss of income from rents and from his other commercial interests centred on London. If a true figure and an appropriate multiplier were used, it would be the equivalent of £40-50 million today.[198]

## Part 9: The effect on sequestered clerics

Apart from the active secular royalists, it is clear from the lists that Catholics were also the target of the sequestrators, including Christopher Cressacre More, the descendant of Sir Thomas More, and even the ancient Lady Morley, a relative of the gunpowder plotters. As well as secular Catholics, those clergy who were considered to be Arminian, or to be inclining towards Catholicism, were also removed **[144, 146]**. From 22 January 1644 the Earl of Manchester was given authority to purge the clergy in the Eastern Association, and prosecute, sequester and remove 'scandalous ministers'.[199] However, in the case of Edward Jude of Hunsdon, **[164-9]** he was already being accused of scandalous behaviour in the autumn of 1642, and was ordered to appear before the local branch of the Parliamentary committee in November 1643, before Manchester obtained his extended powers. He was not only accused of papist activities, but also of immoral behaviour, a common tactic of anti-clericals ever since the reformation of the 16th century. Despite getting witnesses to speak in his favour, others seem to have provided sufficient evidence to condemn him and he was removed, having been hauled before the local sequestration committee to answer the charges levelled

---

198 Loftis J, (ed.) *The memoirs of Anne Lady Halkett & Ann Lady Fanshawe*, (Oxford, 1979) pp xv, 110. For the impact on the Verneys over the border in Buckinghamshire, where there was a similar radical committee see Broad, J P F, 'The Verneys and the sequestrators in the civil wars 1642-56', *Records of Buckinghamshire,* Vol 27 (Aylesbury, 1985) pp1-9

199 Holmes, *Eastern Association,* pp108, 122, 138

against him. The initial charges seem to have been later extended, as his answers seem to refer to a wider range than those initially put forward.

What the local committee were interested in was whether the cleric under suspicion had supported or hindered the war effort or the taking of The Covenant, and whether he had shown any signs of scandalous behaviour that would make him unfit to be a godly preaching minister. This could be both moral laxity as well as holding 'scandalous opinions'. They were also concerned about comments he had made on politics, the content of his sermons and his behaviour towards local officials. A royal proclamation of 18 June 1642 had specifically forbidden subjects to contribute to Parliamentary levies, and any refusal to do so would be seen as pro-royalist activity.[200]

However a compromise appears to have been reached with Viscount Rochford, whose father Lord Dover had instigated Jude's initial appointment through his control of the advowson.[201] With Dover absent in Oxford, and Rochford acting as a Parliamentary Colonel, Gabriel Barbor and the other local sequestration committeemen appear to have intruded a radical Independent, who was subsequently replaced by a more orthodox divine, whose views were more akin to those of Rochford's. Despite the radicals controlling the local committees, powerful members of the aristocracy who were on the Parliamentary sequestration committee, and who retained control of advowsons, were able to influence the final appointments. Copies of papers for this case survive locally, in contrast to many others that were handled centrally, the details of which are in the *Calendar for the Committee for Plundered Ministers*.

By the end of the conflict the religious structures locally had become fragmented and the political conflict between orthodox conservative Presbyterians and more radical Independents came out into the open. Gabriel Barbor and William Turner were by this time consorting with the radical millenarian, Christopher Feake, who was appointed to be Vicar of All Saints, Hertford. Joining up with their friends in the city of London, they tried to

---

[200] Larkin, *Proclamations*, pp770-5

[201] Rochford had been a colonel of a regiment in Essex's army, which had garrisoned Coventry before the battle of Edgehill, but had been disbanded by 28 June 1643 so had probably returned to Hunsdon by the autumn of 1643 [Davies, G, 'The Parliamentary army under the Earl of Essex, 1642-5', *EHR*, 49, No. 193 (Jan 1934) pp33, 48]

protect themselves against those attacking 'sectaries', the term used to condemn those that wanted local independent congregational forms of church government. Thomas Edwards, the ardent Presbyterian, was highly critical of 'the great sectarie' Feake and his activities in Hertford, where he claimed Feake had preached against the use of the Lords Prayer, had never sung psalms or baptized anyone and spoke against lawful forms of government. He also said there were four famous preachers in the shire including Field the bodice-maker of Hertford. Thus one significant aspect of the impact of the civil war was to further fragment the national church and to create a variety of religious groups and sects within the county. [202]

## Conclusion

The documents in this book show the reader particular features of the impact of the war on the county of Hertfordshire. In the first section they show how the county was initially organized through the lieutenancy to raise officers, men and horses to fight on behalf of Parliament. Secondly they identify the transition to the County Committee of effective control of men and supplies because of the inadequacies of the lieutenancy and the reluctance of the older established gentry to push forward rapidly with the war effort. The County Committee tended to be run by men from the main towns and the lesser gentry whose radicalism had supported the volunteers from St Albans, Hertford and Watford. The standing committees in the two main towns then not only raised horses, provided arms and ammunition, uniforms and saddles but also fortified the towns against possible royalist attack. They also provided men and supplies for three county regiments of volunteers and militia as well as men for the regional and national armies of the Earls of Manchester and Essex.

All of this had to be paid for and the County Committee came to take on the main burden of organizing and collecting the assessments, leaving it to individual taxation districts and parishes to spread the burden of assessment across their communities and appoint collectors for the different taxes as they arose. How they did this and how it was reported was left largely up to them. This gave the appearance of involving a measure of consent in the process, consent which had been lacking in the case of the Ship Money assessments by 1640. The enthusiasm of the radicals is shown in their willingness to lend

[202] Edwards, T, *Gangraena Part III,* (Exeter, 1977) pp81, 147-8

money, plate and horses under *The Propositions*, and in their determination, if they were on the committee, to ensure that the requirements of Parliament were effectively followed up.

Involved in this process was a delicate balancing act between central power and local consent, between the constant demands of war and the limitations imposed by the poverty of some men, the reluctance or opposition of others, and a concern that their own county should not be disadvantaged compared with others. There was also a difficult balance to be struck between the military and the civilian authorities. Initially some of the same men were the senior magistrates and the deputy lieutenants. As the lieutenancy became squeezed out, the senior magistrates continued to wield influence in the civilian sphere by sitting on the local bench and carrying out traditional duties. Thus some royalist sympathizers such as Sir John Boteler, and would -be neutrals such as Sir John Watts, senior and Sir John Caesar continued to run the bench until mid 1643. Gradually however with the appointment of the urban radicals, notably Gabriel Barbor, Joseph Dalton, and Dr John King, to not only the lieutenancy, but also the local bench, and with the replacement of the lieutenancy by the Militia Committee, the established county gentry found that they had largely lost control of both civilian and military affairs.

The piecemeal appropriation of power by the committees meant that on occasions, older county-wide committees, such as that for the Eastern Association, on which the established gentry were still entitled to sit, came to be used to try and restrain what were seen as the excesses of the radicals, and the grand jury was used to seek popular support for opposition to some of the worst effects of the war, notably those involved in free quarter, taken by successions of Parliamentary soldiers that wintered, were assembled within, or passed through the shire, on campaigns elsewhere. Not only were whole communities, particularly those around St Albans, dramatically affected, notably in winter, but many individuals felt particular grievances about the depredations and thefts of property and animals by soldiers from outside the shire. For a county that provided finance for local, regional and national forces, many felt particularly hard done by when they had those same forces imposed on them and living in their very own houses.

The effects on individuals, particularly those identified as, or accused of being, royalists, were dramatic as can be seen in the sales of goods belonging to Sir John Harrison, Simon Fanshawe and others, as well as the burdens imposed on William Capel to try and keep his family's property together. Others such as Boteler and Coningsby spent a number of years in prison for their actions which were deemed too pro-Royalist to be acceptable, despite not actually taking up arms against Parliament, and in the case of Boteler being forced to contribute considerable amounts to the Parliamentary war effort. A host of others had their property sequestered and taken over by the bailiffs and dealt with in an arbitrary manner, which the more conservative Sub-Committee of Accounts for the county was at pains to later investigate.

If there were losers, there may also have been those who gained from the war. Those, like the sequestration bailiffs, Heath and Chandler, who charged fixed fees for their work, the committee men such as William Gardiner who provided the uniforms for the local troops, or the saddlers in St Albans who provided equipment for the county cavalry units. Numerous committee men, collectors, agents and others were able to claim expenses for travel time, horse hire, meals taken at inns etc. all of which had to come out of the local taxation. Whether these men can be called 'war profiteers', is doubtful, as there is no clear evidence that they made excessive profits. However a number clearly prospered during the 1640s, when others were suffering, and some later became prominent members of their local communities paying considerable sums in the Hearth Tax returns of the 1660s. We know more about some of the prominent 'losers' such as Capel, Fanshawe, Coningsby, Harrison and Boteler than we do about the middle ranking 'winners', some of whom themselves were to become 'losers' at The Restoration. What the documents also reveal are the nitty-gritty details of everyday wartime administration and the often hand-to-mouth existence of the financial arrangements set up under numerous separate ordinances. Given the burdens imposed, it is remarkable that there was not more opposition within the county both to the war, the bureaucracy and to the Parliamentary activists.

# THE IMPACT OF THE FIRST CIVIL WAR

# ON HERTFORDSHIRE,

# 1642-1647

# IMPACT OF THE CIVIL WAR

## Section A Fighting the War

### Part 1 Officers, volunteers, the militia, impressment and uniforms

#### [1] HALS: DE/Lw/O3 Appointment of Sir John Wittewronge as Captain of a foot company of the trained bands, 25/8/1642

By vertue of an ordinance of Parliament authorising me, Charles Viscount Cranborne to be Lord-Leieuetenant of the countie of Hertford[1], I doe hereby nomynate and appoint you Sir John Witterong to be Captaine of the trained band for parte of Caishio and Decorum hundreds[2] to be mustered within the severall parrishes of the countie aforesaid. And further doe give warrant to you to lead, trayne and muster the said foote companie at such dayes and such places as by warrant from me or in my absence from my deputie Leieuetenants or anie one of them, you shalbe from time to time in that behalfe directed. Willing and commanding all inferior officers and soldiers of the said foote companie to be attending aydinge and assisting unto you for the better furtherance of this service by the said ordinance required. Given under my hand this five and twentith day of August 1642.

(***On reverse***) Lord Cranbornes grant to Sir John for Lieutenancy County of Hertford 1642

#### [2] HALS: DE/Lw/F18 Diary of Sir John Wittewronge[3] *f*17, 26/3/1643

March 26th 1642
Memorandum: I payde for a greate red velvett saddle with a case of red leather <to cover it> and a payre of pistoll cases, turned downe with the same of the saddle and a greate peece of leather to cover itt, when I should have the horse led in any wett weather, the stirrups, bitts, bridle, knobs[4] gilte, sutable to the saddle 09 00 00

---

[1] For Charles Cecil, Lord Cranborne and Sir John Wittewronge see Appendix
[2] The two hundreds largely in the western half of the county
[3] By 20 April the county had raised a regiment of volunteers, which was ready to march out of the shire. Wittewrong was appointed colonel of the regiment, which was to be paid out of the local money collected under *The Propositions*. The regiment could be sent out on orders either from Lord Grey of Warke the first commander of the Eastern Association, or by the Earl of Essex, the overall commander of the parliamentary forces. Warke had been appointed under an ordinance of 20 December 1642 [*LJ* VI, pp12-3; F&R I, pp151-2]

| | |
|---|---|
| Payde for a-nother of neats[5] leather for my man with all the furniture | 02 03 00 |
| Payde for a case of pistils for myselfe | 05 00 00 |
| Payde for ~~a payre~~ a case for my man | 02 15 00 |
| Payd for ~~my~~ the halfe-hide of which I made my buffe coate[6] | 08 00 00 |
| Payde for halfe a younge hide of buffe to make sleeves | 01 10 00 |
| Payde for a backe, brest and heade peeice[7] for my trooper | 01 05 00 |
| For a sworde | 00 06 00 |
| And for a flaske[8] | 00 03 00 |

### [3] HALS: DE/Lw/Z21 *f*30 Gabriel Barbor[9] from Hertford to Sir John Wittewrong at Aylesbury Garrison, 26/5/1643

Honored Collonell,
You shall by George Peach[10] or his captain receive <ther lacks *xxs*> £200 for your soldiers. I pray make a receipt and send itt. Also ther being your 6 horsses for waggon or scowts,[11] one bay gelding is reserved for my sonn John,[12] so that, he be willing his owne gelding may instedd thereof be imployed as you shall appoint. I am in great hast. The Lord preserve you, your officers and regiments with the towne you inhabite. I will be carefull to procure what may be gotten for you and yours before all others. The Lord give you stoute harts and faces like lyons.
I am your humble servant *Gabriel Barbor*
Hartford 26 May 1643
**(*On reverse*)** To our Honored Collonell, Sir John Wittwrong Knight

---

[4] A metal boss or stud holding different parts of the bridle together
[5] Neat = cattle
[6] A military coat made of very stout ox-hide, dressed with oil, having a fuzzy surface with a dull whitish-yellow colour.
[7] Armour consisting of back-plate, breastplate and helmet
[8] A flask or horn in which to keep gunpowder
[9] For Gabriel Barbor see Appendix. As chairman of the Hertford Committee he was responsible for supplying the volunteer regiment with pay now that it was stationed in Aylesbury garrison
[10] George Peach was a tailor and freeman of Hertford [HALS: HBR25 *f*6]
[11] Scouts were soldiers used for scouting out the land to see signs of the enemy
[12] Captain John Barbor was the second son of Gabriel Barbor and appointed to the Militia Committee in December 1643, rising to the rank of major and appointed to a number of other committees. He and his wife Elizabeth were living in Ware in 1648, when they had a daughter Elizabeth baptized, but buried 4 years later [HALS: DP/116/1/1 Ware Parish Register; *LJ* VI, pp342-3; Foster, *Gray's Inn Admissions*, p237; *Herts Vis*, p25]

(***In another hand***) Sir John Wittewronges account of his regiment

### [4] HALS: DE/Lw/Z22/11 Letter from the Earl of Essex[13] to Sir John Wittewrong in Aylesbury Garrison, 8/8/1643

Sir,
Considering the keeping safe of the garrison at Ailesbury to be of great importance, and understanding the House of Commons have taken speciall care for the raysing of six hundred pounds weekely[14] for maintenance thereof ~~wherefoure~~, I would have you use all the indevers you can to keepe the officers and souldiers of your regiment together and likewise of Collonel Tyrrills Regiment now at Ailesbury, notwithstanding any other forces sent by me to that place about which I expect your especiall care.
Your assured frend, Essex
August 8th 1643
If ~~sh~~ you shall desire any commissions from mee I shall upon notice thereof send them to you. And also that all care be taken that may be for strengthening both the regiments.
(***On reverse***) For Sir John Whittewrong and in his absence to the chiefe commander of the force now at Ailesbury these

### [5] TNA: SP28/154 Redbourn[15] parish accounts, 1643

Charges payd to volunteers of Captain Aylewards[16] Company one of the Captains of the militia of the county 1643
In primis John Dell payd to a soldier that served under Captain

---

[13] Robert Devereux, Earl of Essex, commander of the main parliamentary army until 1645. He wintered in St Albans in 1643-4, where he supervised the fortifications, and his troops spread out and took free quarter in the surrounding area, commandeering supplies from other towns and villages. He is often referred to as 'His Excellency' or 'The Lord General' in documents. [John Morrill, 'Devereux, Robert, third Earl of Essex (1591-1646)' *NewDNB*]
[14] In this ordinance Hertfordshire had to pay £200 a week [*CJ* III, p197]
[15] In 1642, 240 men over 18 had taken the Protestation Oath in Redbourn. 74 houses were assessed for Hearth Tax in 1663 [Munby, Lionel M, (ed) *The Story of Redbourn,* (Letchworth, 1962)]
[16] William Ayleward was on the Volunteers' Committee in September 1643 and on the militia committee in December, becoming the High Constable of the Hundred of Cashio in 1644. He was a yeoman farmer at New House St Albans, which was used for conventicles in 1669, and a member of a family with extensive lands in the area. He and his wife, Martha Nicholls, had at least 3 sons, James, William and Thomas [HALS: QSB2B *f*48d; *LJ* VI, pp244, 342-3; F&R, pp356-8; Smith and North, *St Albans,* pp12, 103, 106, 211-13]

Ayleward for one moneths pay 01 08 06
Item Jeremy Fynch[17] payd to a souldier that served under Captain Ayleward one moneth 01 08 06
Thomas Sylls[18] and Robert Beech payd to a Souldier that served under Captain Ayleward for one moneth 01 12 00
William Dollinge payd to a souldier that served under Captain Ayleward one moneth 01 08 00
William Beaumont gent[19] 26 October 1643 listed under Captain Ayleward one Corsleett and one musket compleat and delivered to the Captain lvis for one moneth pay for 2 Souldeirs Captain Ayleward delivered back all the Armes except one sword and belt one head peece and gorgett ~~back~~ 02 16 00
*William Beaumont, William Dollinge*

**[6] TNA: SP28/155 Sarratt parish accounts 1646 *f*1r - Mr Lane's[20] charges etc. 1642-3**

~~viii November~~ 1646 Hertford- Sarrat[21]
A List of charges, losses, payments and taxes to and by the parliament and their ordinances and by the parliaments soldiers since and by reason of the warres, susteyned and disbursed by Mr John Lane for his estate in Sarrat and by free quarter and plunder by parliament soldiers upon his tenants whereby hee was compelled to suffer greate loss.
About November 1642 about Edghill battell [22]Benjamin Randall tenant
Mr Lane fyndinge a musket and a halfe for his lands in Sarrat[23]

[17] Possibly a descendant of either John Finch of the George Inn (*d.* 1617) or Nicholas Finch of the Hill, (*d.* 1617) [Munby, *Redbourn*, pp40, 42]
[18] Thomas Sylls, (Sells) Yeoman, in 1645 granted a tenement called St Affables, alias St James' Chapel to his heir Francis [Munby, *Redbourn*, p25]
[19] For Beaumont see Appendix
[20] A John Lane married Elizabeth the widow of Thomas Kingsley, the former owner of both the Roos Hall and Goldington's estates in Sarratt. However it appears to have reverted to the Kingsley family, so it is unclear what lands this John Lane actually held in the 1640s [*VCH Herts* Vol II, pp438-43]
[21] This and subsequent underlined headings were in the left hand margin of the original. Some of this document is obscure or damaged. Only the first side has been extracted here.
[22] The Battle of Edgehill took place in Northamptonshire on 23 October 1642. These underlined headings were in the left hand margin in the original.
[23] Lane had to supply the finance for the equivalent of one and a half musketeers

and Benjamin Randall one of his tenants undertakeinge the discharge of the service for the halfe musket[24] gives Mr Lane an account that by order of Parliament everie musket was to attend the Lord Generall when hee came from Edge hill and the fynder of the musket to pay for his musketeere dureinge his attendance, which was a weeke and soe reckoned to Mr Lane and abated out of his rent for his halfe musket in this service. 00 10 00

22 August 1643

Deducted more by Benjamin Randall out of his rent[25] upon twoe severall ordinances of Parliament three monthes taxe <at 6s *per mensem*> for mayntenance of soldiers for whose (*obscured*) is for the Lord Generall (*blank*) and other 6s *per mensem*[26] for other 3 monethes for the associacon under the Earle of Manchester. 01 16 00

About the beginning <of> August 1643

The parliament soldiers (not settinge downe whose) passinge through Sarrat, quartered with Benjamin Randall at full quarter and toke away divers goods from him to his losse of 10s which hee reckons to Mr Lane and abated out of his rent. 00 10 00

Aron Lovet Tenant aboute Edghill ~~22 August 1643~~

Aron Lovet undertakeinge the service of the other muskett reckons of Mr Lanes rent for the lyke tyme and service as Benjamin Randall above. 01 00 00

---

[24] Randall agreed to supply half the cost of a musketeer

[25] Randall had his rent reduced as Lane, the landowner, was responsible for the tax

[26] Per month

**[7] TNA: SP28/230 Committee order to Turner re repayment to Colonel Hawes,[27] 8/11/1643**

To William Turner one of the treasurers for the committee of the volunteers companye

Wheras Collonell Hawes hath disbursed divers and severall sommes of money for the buyeinge of coullers, pattisions, drummes and holboards[28] etc. for advanceinge the three regiments,[29] wee desire you to paye into his hands the somme of threescore[30] pounds out of what you have received for our use, and this shalbe sufficient dischardge for the same. November 8th 1643

*John Garrard, Adam Washington, Thomas Michell,[31] Isaac Puller, William Carter, Edward Michell, John Gale,[32] Randall Nicoll[33]*

**[8] TNA: SP28/231 Captain Humphreys[34] bill for exercising the militia and conducting impressed soldiers, 10/5/1644**

| A true account of what is owing to mee and my officers for exercising 10 dayes and for poulder and mach May 7th 1644 | £ s d |
|---|---|
| Imprimis for my selfe for tenn days exercise | 03 15 00 |
| To my Leuetennant for tenn days | 02 00 00 |
| To my Ensigne for tenn days | 01 10 00 |

[27] Colonel Nathaniel Hawes (1621-1701) was put on the volunteer committee in September 1643. He may have been the son of Andrew Hawes, a London fishmonger. He went to St Catherine's Cambridge in 1633 and became treasurer of Christ's Hospital in the 1680s and '90s [*Al Cant* Pt I Vol. 2, p334; *LJ* VI, p244]

[28] Colours were regimental flags, pattisons possibly patterns or overshoes, and a halberd a weapon which was a combination of a spear and a battle-axe, consisting of a sharp edged blade ending in a point and a spearhead mounted on a handle five to seven feet long.

[29] The three county regiments, the Orange, Black and Green

[30] Three score= £60

[31] Thomas Michell of Michells Fee, Codicote, brother of Edward Michell, was a Captain, later Lieutenant-Colonel, who was added to the Hertfordshire Committee in October 1643 and in charge of the Black Regiment at Bedford in 1644 [TNA: SP28/231; *LJ* VI, p 257; *VCH Herts* II, p347]

[32] John Gale, gent (1585-1655) from Bushey, had given a silver chalice to his local church in 1633 and in his will left loaves and fishes to the poor of the parish. He was on the Volunteers' Committee in September 1643 [*LJ* VI, p244; *VCH Herts* II, pp185-6; Chauncy II, p464]

[33] Randall (Randolph) Nichol(ls) (c1605-1648), son of Randall Nicholl of London, gent, entered Grays Inn in 1623 and was put on the Volunteer Committee in September 1643. In 1650 he was living in Hendon, Middx when his son Randolph was born [*Al Cant.* pp3, 255; Will TNA Probate (95 Essex); *LJ* VI, p244]

[34] Captain Newman Humphreys was in the local militia regiment

| | |
|---|---|
| To my twoe Seargeants | 01 10 00 |
| To my twoe drummers | 01 00 00 |
| Layd out for drumsticks snares and a drum head[35] | 00 09 06 |
| The Summ | 10 04 06 |
| | |
| Thorley for pouder and mach[36] for twelve souldirs | 01 00 00 |
| Sabridgworth for fifty soulders[37] | 02 15 ? |
| Gilston for six soulders | 00 10 ? |
| Eastwick for foure soulders | 00 06 ? |
| The Summ | 04 11 10 |
| The Totall Summ | 14 16 04 |

To Mr Turner Treasurer
You are to pay unto Captain Humphryes the sum of fowerteene poundes sixteene shillings and fower pence and this shall bee your discharge given under our handes this 10th of May 1644
*Gabriel Barbor, Chairman; William Barbor,*[38] *William Love,*[39] *William Carter, Francis Clerke,*[40] *John Fowler*[41]
May 14th 1644
Received of William Turner Treasurer, acordinge to this order, the sume off fowerteene pound sixtenne shillings fower pence. I say *per me* £14-16s-4d
*Per me Numan Humphryes*

---

[35] The skin or membrane stretched across a drum

[36] Match was treated cord for lighting matchlock muskets and was sold by the yard length or by weight

[37] Part of the militia's role was to collect and conduct pressed men from their villages and towns to the point where they were enrolled in a regiment

[38] William Barbor of Redbourn was on the Militia Committee on 18/12/1643 and bought the St Paul's Cathedral lands at Kensworth in 1649, including the manor, but was forced to return them in 1669, by which time he was a Quaker holding meetings in his own house. His son William was imprisoned in the Liberty Gaol in 1660 for Quaker activities [*LJ* VI, pp342-3; *VCH Herts* II, p370; IV, p231; Crellin, C, *Where God had a people: Quakers in St Albans over three hundred years,* (St Albans, 1999)]

[39] For William Love see Appendix

[40] Clerke, from Berkhamsted St Peter and Hemel Hempstead, was on the Volunteers' Committee on 19/9/1643. As an attorney, he was appointed as steward of the manors of Great Gaddesden and Southall by John Earl of Bridgewater [HALS: Halsey Papers 12877; *LJ* VI, p244]

[41] Fowler was on the Militia Committee on 18/12/1643 [*LJ* VI, pp342-3]

**[9] TNA: SP28/231 Thomas Marsh's Account for Scouts, 15/11/1644**

November 15 1644

Captain Thomas Marsh his accounte for 7 wekes pay for him selfe and 6 men under his command as scowtes.

| | £ s d |
|---|---|
| *Imprimis* for him selfe 7 weekes | 19 12 00 |
| *Item* for 1 man 7 wekes paye | 07 07 00 |
| *Item* for 5 men 7 wekes paye | 30 12 06 |
| | 57 11 06 |

*Thomas Marsh*

To Mr Turner Treasurer

It is this day ordered that you paye unto Captain Thomas Marsh the som of twenty eaght pound fifteener shillings and ninepence in part of this acownte and this shalbe youer suffitient warrant

*Joseph Dalton Maior, Randall Nicoll, John Fowler, William Coxe,*[42] *John Finch,*[43] *Daniell Nicoll, Alban Coxe*

**[10] TNA: SP28/231 Payment to the county Militia (undated 1644-5)**

A particular of the dayes exarsis that was performed by Thomas Bowles Captain and his offisars

| | £ s d |
|---|---|
| Inprimis my selfe at Odsey 5 dayes | 01 17 06 |
| Item my lieutenant 4 dayes | 00 16 00 |
| Item my ensign 3 dayes | 00 09 00 |
| Item my sarjant thar 3 dayes | 00 04 06 |
| Item my drum thar 4 dayes | 00 04 00 |
| Item one other drum thar 4 dayes | 00 04 00 |
| Item my selfe at Stevenadge 1 day | 00 07 06 |
| Item my lieutenant there on day | 00 04 00 |
| Item my ensigne one day there | 00 03 00 |
| Item my sarjant one day there | 00 02 06 |

[42] William was the brother of Alban Coxe and lived at Shenley. He was put on various local committees between December 1643 and 1660 [F&R I&II, *passim*]

[43] John Finch, a tanner from Watford, was an active supporter of the Watford Volunteers and on the Militia Committee from 18/12/1643 and the Assessment Committee in November 1650. The Finch family owned land in Harrow and other parts of Middlesex [*LJ* V, p 441; F&R I, pp356-8; II, p468; *LJ* VI, pp342-3; Anon, *A History of the County of Middlesex,* Vol 4 (1971) pp211-18]

| | |
|---|---|
| Item my drum one day thar | 00 02 00 |
| Item my selfe at Hitching 4 dayes | 01 10 00 |
| Item my lieutenant there 4 dayes | 00 16 00 |
| Item my ensigne there 3 dayes | 00 09 00 |
| Item my sarjant there 2 dayes | 00 03 00 |
| Item my drum there 4 dayes | 00 04 00 |
| Summa Totalis | 07 14 08 |

*Thomas Bowles Captain*

The treasurer Mr Turner is required to pay this bill of $vii^{li}$ $xiiij^{s}$ $viii^{d}$ we say $7^{li,}14^{s}.8^{d}$[44]

*William Carter, Gabriel Barbor, William Plumer,*[45] *William Love, William Barbor, Edward Michell, Nathanial Manestie*[46]

**[11] TNA: SP28/230 St Albans Committee certificate re impressments for the New Model Army, 3/12/1645**

St Albans in *Comitatu*[47] Hertford

Wee the committee for the countey of Hertford sitting at St Albans do certify to the treasurers of warres in Guild-Hall London,[48] appointed by ordinance of parliament for receiveing of monies for the payment of the army under the command of the Right Honourable Sir Thomas Fairfax[49] that there was eighty

---

[44] The repetition of the sum in Arabic and Roman and the inclusion of the phrase 'we say' is for emphasis and for confirming that the money has been paid or received. It is similar to writing a sum on a cheque in words and numbers. My thanks are due to Professor John Miller for this point.

[45] For Plumer see Appendix

[46] Nathaniel Manestie(y), gent, with property at Welwyn and Brickendon, had refused to pay the Ship Money levied on him, and the sheriff's bailiff dared not distrain any of his goods, as Manestie had threatened to sue him. He was one of the original Watford volunteers in July 1642 *(see* below) and appointed to the Volunteers' Committee in September and the militia committee in December 1643. He was living in Watford in 1663, when he sent his son Samuel to Gray's's Inn [TNA: SP 16/376 *f*106; *LJ* VI, pp244, 342-3; Foster, *Gray's Inn Admissions*, p296]

[47] Latin for 'county'

[48] The London Guildhall was used as the parliamentary treasury

[49] Fairfax was the commander of the New Model Army from 1645, which quartered in the county in 1645 and subsequently in 1647, when troops under his command mutinied at St Albans, Luton and Ware. Taxes paid to the New Model were often listed by local people as payments to Sir Thomas Fairfax's army [Ian J Gentles, 'Fairfax, Thomas, third Lord Fairfax of Cameron, (1612-1671)' *NewDNB*]

men imprest within the two hundreds of Caisho and Dacorum in the countey aforesaid and inroled on the 20th of September last for the 4th recruit of Sir Thomas Fairfax army. For which the charges disbursed for imprest money, paying of the said souldiers, their guards and conductors amounts to the sum of seaventy five pounds and ten pence. Which said sum we desire may be allowed to William Hickman our High Collector[50] as so much money paid by him into the aforesaid treasury, and accordingly an acquittance given by him for the same.
Given under our hands and seales this third of December 1645
***(Signatures and seals down the side)***
*John Robotham, Johes King, William Foxwist*[51]

(***On reverse***) December 5th 1645
Received in full of this, by an acquittance from the treasurers at warre seaventy five pounds tenn pence. I say £75-0-10d
*Per me William Hickman High Collector*

***(On wrapper)*** 24 Mr Hickman High Collector for Cashio and Dacorum *Comitatu* Hertford, his certificate 5 December 1645 £75:0:10d

**[12] TNA: SP28/17 *ff*262-3 Mr Vaughan's account for Buff coats for Watford volunteers, 20/7/1642**

*f1r* Sould to Watford men the 20th of July 1642
Item 1 coate 1 pair of sleves for Mr Leonard[52] att
Item 1 Buffe coate and 1 pair of sleves for his man att
Item 1 Buffe coate and 1 pair of sleves for John Yewer att
Item 1 Buffe coate and 1 pair of sleves for Nathaniel Manistie att
Item 1 Buffe coate and 1 pair of sleves for William Sewell att
Item 1 Buffe coate and 1 pair of sleves for Jerima King att
Item 1 Buffe coate and 1 pair of sleves for John Nash att
Item 1 Buffe coate and 1 pair of sleves for John David att
Item 1 Buffe coate and 1 pair of sleves for Zakery King[53] att
Item 1 Buffe coate and 1 pair of sleves for William Yewer att

---

[50] William Hickman see Appendix
[51] For Robotham, Dr John King, and William Foxw(h)ist see Appendix
[52] Leonard was named as the commander of the troop in the ordinance of parliament
[53] King was the Treasurer. He and Manesty were given additional responsibility by Parliament in November 1642 to organize the defence of the Watford area [*LJ* V, pp440-2]

Item 1 Buffe coate and 1 pair of sleves for William Hunt att
Item 1 Buffe coate and 1 pair of sleves for William Hawkins att
Item 1 Buffe coate and 1 pair of sleves for John King att
Item 1 Buffe coate and 1 pair of sleves for Thomas Bedford att
Item 1 Buffe coate and 1 pair of sleves for John Hickman att
Item 1 Buffe coate and 1 pair of sleves for Thomas Aldin att
Item 1 Buffe coate and 1 pair of sleves for John Edlin, malter att
Item 1 Buffe coate and 1 pair of sleves for William Knight att
Item 1 Buffe coate and 1 pair of sleves for Daniell Mariall att
Item 1 Buffe coate and 1 pair of sleves for Richard Shepard att
Item 1 Buffe coate and 1 pair of sleves for John Lea att
Item 1 Buffe coate and 1 pair of sleves for Jonathan Finch att
Item 1 Buffe coate and 1 pair of sleves for Thomas Scott att
Item 1 Buffe coate and 1 pair of sleves for Simond Jold att
Item 1 Buffe coate and 1 pair of sleves for William Kelsey att
Item 1 Buffe coate and 1 pair of sleves for Francis Sherared att
Item 1 Buffe coate and 1 pair of sleves for Nicholas King att
Item 1 Buffe coate and 1 pair of sleves for Thomas Taylor att
Item 1 Buffe coate and 1 pair of sleves for John Reckett att
Item 1 Buffe coate and 1 pair of sleves for Charles Day att
Item 1 Buffe coate and 1 pair of sleves for John Tanner att
Item 1 Buffe coate and 1 pair of sleves for Ambrose Poke att
Item 1 Buffe coate and 1 pair of sleves for Ralph Twitcher att
Item 1 Buffe coate and 1 pair of sleves for Edward Allin att
Item 1 Buffe coate and 1 pair of sleves for John Gray att
Item 1 Buffe coate and 1 pair of sleves for John Twitcher att
Item 1 Buffe coate and 1 pair of sleves for Danyell Daye att
Item 1 Buffe coate and 1 pair of sleves for John Edlin, Yeoman att
Item 1 Buffe coate and 1 pair of sleves for John Edlin, Waginer att
Item 1 Buffe coate and 1 pair of sleves for Richard Eure att
Item 1 Buffe coate and 1 pair of sleves for Henry Baldin att
Item 1 Buffe coate and 1 pair of sleves for William Knaltor att

*f1v* Item 1 Buffe coate and 1 pair of sleves for Thomas Deakan att
Item 1 Buffe coate and 1 pair of sleves for Jeremy Ansell att
Item 1 Buffe coate and 1 pair of sleves for Samuel Harding att
Item 1 Buffe coate and 1 pair of sleves for Francis Andrew att
Item 1 Buffe coate and 1 pair of sleves for Ralph Hegbey att
Item 1 Buffe coate and 1 pair of sleves for the corporals brother att

Item 1 Buffe coate and 1 pair of sleves for John Nelson att
Item 1 Buffe coate and 1 pair of sleves for Edward Trapp att
Item 1 Buffe coate and 1 pair of sleves for Richard Dover att
Item 1 Buffe coate and 1 pair of sleves for Robert Manson att
Item 1 Buffe coate and 1 pair of sleves for Samuel Panton att

| | | |
|---|---|---|
| 11 | | |
| 42 one the other side[54] | | |
| 53 | 53 in all att 38s per coate | 100 14 00 |
| 39 | Simon Gould had noe sleeves | 000 05 00 |
| 424 | | £100 09 00 |

**(*Down the side*)** Mr Vaughans account for buff coats for Watford Troop
Dr Burges: Matsch; about: Pistols, carbines and saddles

**[13] TNA: SP28/231 William Gardiner's bill for coats and uniforms, 3/10/1644**

October 3rd 1644 William Gardiner of Hertford Draper[55] his bill

| | £ s d |
|---|---|
| Item: for 53 coates at 10s per coate | 26 10 00 |
| Item: for 25 pair of grey hoes[56] at 2s 6d a pair | 03 02 06 |
| Item: for 105 shirts at 3s 4d per shirte | 17 10 00 |
| Item: for 60 pairs of shooes at 3s 4d a pair | 10 00 00 |
| Item: for 40 pair of shooes at 2s 8d a pair | 05 06 08 |
| Item: for carrying the hoes shooes and shirts and coates to Alisbury[57] | 01 00 00 |
| Item: for 4 money bags[58] May 2nd which I gott made by order of the Committee | 00 02 00 |
| Item for Thomas Barnes his horse and himselfe carrying 120 snapsacks[59] to Alisbury | 00 07 00 |
| | 63 18 02 |

[54] i.e. on the first side of the document
[55] For Gardiner see Appendix
[56] Hose or breeches worn with a doublet
[57] To the Hertfordshire troops in the garrison at Aylesbury
[58] 17th century money bags found by the editor caught up with papers in SP 28 series for Hertfordshire were made of leather or sacking
[59] Snapsacks were haversacks for holding a snap or snack, a hasty meal, usually of bread, cheese and beer

Mr Turnor treasurer is required to pay to William Gardiner of Hartford, Draper, in full of this bill the somme of sixty three pounds eighteene shillings two pence wee say £63-18s-02d
*Gabriel Barbor, William Carter, William Love*

October 4th 1644
Received of Mr Turnor in part of this bill the somme of twenty three pounds eighteene shillings two pence. I say received *per me William Gardiner*

Memorandum when the rest is paid you call in quittance off mine for the remainder

October 18th 1644
Received more in part of this bill: the somme of twenty foure pounds tenne shillings I say received *per me* £24 10s 00d *William Gardiner*
October 23rd 1644
Received of Mr Turner in full of this bill the somme of fifteene pounds tenne shillings. I say received per me *William Gardiner £xv xs*[60]

**[14] TNA: SP28/231 Thomas Barnes'[61] bill re carrying coats etc. (undated 1644?)**

| Thomas Barnes his bill | £ s d |
|---|---|
| Item: for my selfe and 2 men more carrying 180 blew coates[62] and 180 snapsacks and for conducting 5 souldyers to the Committee at St Allbones | 00 05 00 |
| Item: I spent on the souldyers as they went | 00 00 04 |
| Item: for fetching the snapsacks from the castle and sacking upp The coates and loading them | 00 02 08 |
| | 00 08 00 |

Mr Turner Treasurer is required to pay to Thomas Barnes in full of this bill the some of eight shillings. Wee say £0.8.0d
*Gabriel Barbor, Thomas Nicholl, Joseph Dalton, Maior, William Carter*

---

[60] The payment in three instalments would indicate that there was probably a perennial problem with cash flow from local taxation
[61] A Thomas Barnes had been taken on as an apprentice by John Almond, the cutler, on 27 March 1638. However there was also a Thomas Barnes who was a Hertford maltster [HALS: HBR25 *f*6; 26 *f*49]
[62] This is the only reference found to the colour of the coats worn by Hertfordshire troops

Received of Mr Turner in full of this bill £0.8s.0d *per me Thomas Barnes*

### [15] TNA: SP28/232 Order re surgeon for county forces, 24/10/1645

Mr Turner,
You are desired to pay Mr Ayres entertained as Chirurgeon to this County the summe of ~~£iiiviiis~~ three pounds and eighteen shillings, being our proporcon for thirteene weeks due to him after the rate of tenn shillings per weeke according to order (upon record) from this Committee, dated att Hartford this 24th of October 1645 Wee say £3-18s-0d *Gabriel Barbor, John Barbor, William Carter, Thomas Meade, Joseph Dalton, George Banastre,*[63] *William Plomer*[64]
Receaved according to this order the some of: £3-18s-0d by mee
*Thomas Ayre*

## Part 2 Weapons, ammunition and supplies

### [16] TNA: SP28/17 ff 269-70 Receipts for arms for Watford Volunteers, 6-9/8/1642

*f269* Received of Mr Stephen Estwick the 9th of August 1642 the summe of seventy and five pounds of current mony, which was part of the five hundred pounds appointed by the Parliament to buy armes for Watford troope. I say received by me *C.Burges*[65] £75 00 00
I have laid out a good part herof for defective armes and the remainder will not satisfy for the rest that are defective

---

[63] George Banister(re) from Stevenage was on the Militia Committee from 18/12/1643. He later styled himself gent and was a trustee for the almshouse trust in Stevenage in 1649, with his son of the same name [*LJ* VI 342-3; Ashby, M, (ed.) *The Hellard Almshouses and other Stevenage charities 1482-2005* (Hertfordshire Record Society (Hertford, 2005) pp xv, 12-16, 25-6]

[64] Plumer (Plomer), William, gent, (c1613-60) son of Sir William Plomer of Radwell, had been to Richard Hale School, Hertford, and then to Christ's College Cambridge in 1629 and Gray's Inn in 1630, before becoming high sheriff in 1634. He served on various county committees from December 1643 to January 1660. He had married Anne, the daughter and co-heir of John Stamp of Malmesbury, Wiltshire. He had at least three sons, William, Thomas and John, Thomas being a trooper in Sir John Norwich's brigade. [*Herts Vis,* p83; *Al Cant* Pt I Vol 3, p373; Foster, *Gray's Inn Admissions*, p190; F&R I & II, *passim*]

[65] For Burges see Appendix

(***On reverse***) 9 August 1642 Dr Burges £75

| | | |
|---|---|---|
| *f270* 6 pair off furylock[66] pistols at 59s a pair | | 23 12 00 |
| 3 fuyrlock carbines an fornitur at 35s a pece | | 05 05 00 |
| 2 carbines scnaphances[67] an fornitur at 24s a pece | | 02 08 00 |
| | Som is | 31 05 00 |

Received off Mr Aystrias Tha som off tartyi pound fowertenn
schillins in fuall for this pistols an carbins Y sayr received 30 14 00
By mii *Werner Pin*[68]
Isu 6 off August 1642

(***On reverse***) 6 August 1642 Paid Pin for Watford troope 30 14 00

**[17] TNA: SP28/231 John Prichard's bill re carriage of new weapons, September 1644**

Brought from London by John Prichard[69] of Hertford carryer to Hertford by the appointment of Mr Love. Thes armes (videlt)
1644

| | |
|---|---|
| brought August 23rd once before 40ti musquettes and bandoliers at | 6s 8d |
| September 13th and after 3 basketts of armour at | 7s 6d |
| 17th bought downe 22 cases of pistols at | 4s 0d |
| Summa | 18s 2d |

Mr Turner treasurer you are appointed to pay this bill
*Gabriel Barbor, William Love*

(***On reverse***) Received in full payment of this bill *By me John Prichard*

---

66 Firelock was probably a wheel-lock mechanism for ignting powder in the firing pan
67 Snapha(u)nce was an early form of flint-lock mechanism for iginiting powder in the firing pan
68 Pin was probably a London arms dealer of Dutch or German origin
69 John Pri(t)chard was a freeman waggoner of Hertford Borough, who became a chief burgess of the borough in 1658, Mayor in 1671, and town clerk in 1674, by which time he styled himself gentleman. He was assessed for 20 hearths in All Saints, Hertford in 1663, as by then he was landlord of the Rose Inn. This may have been him or his father of the same name [TNA: E179/248/23 *f*121; HALS: HBR25 *f*6; Chauncy, I, p492]

### [18] TNA: SP28/231 Crowch's[70] bill for dressing[71] and repairing arms (undated 1644?)

| Thomas Crowch his bill | £ s d |
|---|---|
| Item for dressing 30 horse armes at 5d a piece | 00 12 06 |
| Item for dressing and mending 20 muskets at 4d a piece | 00 06 08 |
| Item for dressing and mending 20 pair of pistols at 7d a pair | 00 11 08 |
| In all | ~~02 15 00~~ |
| | 01 10 10 |

Mr Turner is required to pay this bill being xxxs- xd
*Gabriel Barbor, Thomas Meade, William Carter, Thomas Michell, Colonel, William Plomer, William Love, John Finch*

Received of Mr Turnor in full of this bill £1 10s 10d
*Per me Thomas Crowch*

### [19] TNA: SP28/231 John Almond's[72] bill for mending weapons, (undated 1644?)

John Almonds bill for worke don in mendinge of Armes for the Committies

| | £ s d |
|---|---|
| *Inprimis*: for mendinge and scowring twelve collivers and fower musquetts | 00 11 00 |
| for mendinge and scowringe eighteene musquetts more | 00 18 00 |
| The sum is | 01 09 00 |

Mr Turner is required to pay this bill of *xxix*$^{s}$ and this shall be your warrant $1^{li}$-$9^{s}$-$0^{d}$
*Gabriel Barbor, Joseph Dalton, Maior, Edward Michell, William Carter, William Plomer, Randall Nicoll, Dannill Nicoll*

---

70 Thomas Crowch was a master locksmith in Hertford, whose son of the same name became a borough assistant in 1670, having been taken on by his father as an apprentice in 1640. The father had however been poor in the early 1630s when he had been lent £3 for stock to maintain his trade as a 'poore freeman', and still appeared poor in 1663 [HALS: HBR26 *f*52; 75 *f*207d; Information from Alan Greening]

71 'Dressing' arms meant to trim, clean or make smooth

72 John Almond was a master cutler, who became a Hertford borough assistant in 1658 and was assessed for two hearths in All Saints, Hertford in 1663 [TNA: E179/248/23 *f*121; HALS: HBR25 *f*6; *VCH Herts* III, p257; Chauncy I, p493]

***(On Reverse)*** Paid full of his bill one pound nine shilling. I say $1^{li}$- $9^{s}$- $0^{d}$
Paid per me *John Alman*

**[20] TNA: SP28/232 Captain Pegg's bill for repairing weapons, casting bullets etc., 16/5/1645**

Monies paid and laid out for the committee for the Milicia 1644 and 1645

| | £ s d |
|---|---|
| *Imprimis* the dressinge of 300 swords and mendinge and dressing 200 muskets in the castle | 01 00 00 |
| *Item* paid Bird for castinge 4*C* weight[73] of bullets | 00 08 00 |
| The lead was Captain Roydens[74] | |
| *Item* for mendinge of 6 musketts | 00 02 00 |
| *Item* for my self, James Goodman[75], Richard Bettannie, and Hezekyas Downes[76] in executing a warrant at Stansted Abbott | 01 04 00 |
| *Item* for layinge in and takinge off of the drakes[77] 3 times | 00 03 00 |
| *Item* for grease for the drakes | 00 01 00 |
| *Item* for mending <and makeinge two> greate pinns of the drakes | 00 03 08 |
| *Item* for one day to Hitchin to finde the drake | 00 05 00 |
| *Item* 2 journies to St Albanes | 00 10 00 |
| *Item* for 4 drum heads when I was abroad | 00 08 00 |
| *Item* for dresinge 66 swords and 100 head peeces | 00 06 08 |
| ~~John Jones imprest for service~~ | 04 12 04 |

[73] Making 4cwt i.e. 1/5 ton of bullets i.e 203.2 kg

[74] Captain Marmaduke Roydon (Rawdon) (1583-1646), a succesfull London merchant and ship owner had married Elizabeth, heir of Thomas Thorowgood of Hoddesdon, having 13 of his 16 children survive infancy. He had built a house at Hoddesdon in 1622 and had a house and warehouses in Barking, Essex. He was referred to as Captain, as he was Captain-General of the Honourable Artillery Company. A former MP for Aldeburgh, Suffolk, he became a leading Royalist in London, and was involved in Waller's Plot to seize it for the King in 1643. He raised a regiment for the King and was knighted for defending Basing House. As a result he had his property sequestered and sold by July 1651 [Dale, T C, (ed) *Inhabitants of London 1638*, (2 Vols) (1931) pp3-8; *CJ* II, pp101-4, 131; *VCH Herts* III, pp330-40; Newman, *The Old Service*, pp127-8; John C Appleby, 'Roydon, Sir Marmaduke (1583-1646)', *NewDNB*]

[75] Goodman may have been the maltster who later was a copyhold tenant of the manor of Brickendonbury, holding the properties of "Cockabanhams" and Gilliaportis" in Castle Street. [HALS: DE/L/M36; Information from Alan Greening]

[76] Hezekia Downes was either the blacksmith father, who was the sergeant at mace for the borough of Hertford, or his son, the freeman ironmonger of the same name [HALS: HBR25 *f*6]

[77] Presumably putting on and taking off the drakes from their gun carriages

Maii the 16th 1645
Mr Turner is required to pay Captain Pegg out of the money raysed to provide horse and armes *£iiii xiis iiiid* wee say £4-12-4
*Gabriel Barbor, Joseph Dalton Maior, William Carter, Thomas Meade, John Barbor, William Plomer, John Fowler*

Received May *xvi*th 1645 of Mr Turner *£iiii.xiis.iiiid* by me *John Pegge*

**[21] TNA: SP28/17 *ff*266-8 Receipts for saddles for the Watford Volunteers, 15/7/1642**

*f266* London 15 July 1642
Received of Mr Stephen Estwicke by the hand of Doctor Burges the summe of thirty sixe pounds nineteene shillings <for 16 saddles> for great saddles for light horse delivered out to Mr John Leonard and Zachary Kinge of Watford for the troope of horse raised by the inhabitabts of Watford aforesaid. I say received for the use of Mr Thomas Harrison £36-19s
*William Geldy* for Thomas Harrison
So it is *Cornelius Burges*

| | |
|---|---|
| 425 | 36 19 00 |
| 75 | 23 01 00 |
| 500 | 69 00 00 |
| | ~~23~~ |
| | 129 00 00 |
| | 75 00 00 |
| | 204 00 00 |

**(*On reverse*)** 15 July 1642 paid £36 19 00 Watford troope

*f*267 London July 11 1642
Received of Mr Stephen Estwick by the hands of Doctor Burges the summe of Sixty and nine pounds lawfull mony for thirty great sadles for light horses delivered out to Mr John Leonard and Zachary King of Watford for the troop of horse raysed by the inhabitants of Watford aforesaid. I say received £69
By me *Thomas Harrison*
So it is *Cornelius Burges*
(*On reverse*) 11 July 1642 £69 00 00 for Watford Troope

*f*268 Receved this 29th day of July 1642 of Mr Stephen Estwick for ten sadles and furniture delivered to John Leonard and Zachary King of Watford in the county of Hertford Gents for the troope of horse there raysed, the summe of three and twenty pounds of lawfull mony. I say receaved £23 00 00
For the yoose of my father[78] Thomas Harrason by mee *William Geldy*
So it is *Cornelius Burges* and one shillinge more for carriage
23 0 0
00 1 0
23 01 -0

***(On reverse)*** 29 July 1642 - £23 01 00 Watford troope

**[22] TNA: SP28/231 Hertford Committee order to Turner to pay Redman and Jones for saddles 18/9/1644**

Hartford
Mr Turner treasurer is required to pay unto Thomas Reddman and William Jones of St Albones the sum of £20 for 20 great sadles and £3 5s for 10 little sadles att 6s 6d a peece towards the furnishing of 50 light horse and 50 dragoones[79] for the service of the Countie and this shall be your sufficient warrant given under our hands this 18 September 1644
*Gabriel Barbor, Thomas Meade, Captain William Carter, Thomas Lewins*

***(On reverse)*** September 18th 1644
Received off Mr Turner Treasurer in full £23-5s-0d
off his bill £23-5s-0d by us *William Jones. Thomas Redman*

**[23] TNA: SP28/231 Hertford Committee note re saddles and horse furniture 30/9/1644**

A note for saddles and other horse furniture for dragoones September 30 1644
*Imprimis* three saddles and bridles bought of John Pennyfather at
5s a peece 00 15 00

[78] Father-in-law
[79] The order for these relates to the ordinance of 12 July for raising forces in the Eastern Association, Hertford's share being 500 infantry, 50 horse and 50 dragoons. They were supposed to have been raised by 20 July [F&R I, pp462-6]

| | |
|---|---|
| Item one saddle bought of Thomas Finch[80] with one bridle | 00 06 00 |
| *Summa Totalis* | 01 01 00 |

Mr Treasurer is to pay unto John Pennyfather this bill of £1-1s 0d and this shalbe your warrant *Edward Michell, William Love, William Plumer*

(***On reverse***) October 5 1644
Received accordinge to this order of William Turner £1 -1s 0d
*Per me John Pennifather*

**[24] TNA: SP28/231 Payment for powder etc., 10/6/1644**

June 10th 1644
These are to desire you William Hickman Treasurer to pay unto Mr Thomas Brightwell for ten barrels of powder and five hundred of match fifty pounds and repay the other forty one shillings eight pence which you disbursed for the particulars above said in all fifty two pounds one shilling eight pence £52-1-8
*John King, John Heydon, John Marsh, Edmund Smyth[81], Ralph Pemberton Senior*

**[25] TNA: SP28/231 Hertford Militia Committee bills - Turner's powder and match account (undated 1644?)**

An account of what powder and match hath bin delivered to severall Captains by William Turner
January the 4th delivered to Captain Rutt[82] 12lb of powder 80

[80] Thomas Finch was a freeman collar-maker of Hertford Borough. That is he made the collar or leather covered roll round the neck of a draught animal [HALS: HBR25 *f*6]

[81] Edmund Smyth Esq, son of Nicholas Smyth of Westminster and Katherine Gardener of Southwark, had been one of the clerks of the Irish Privy Council, who had married Grace the daughter of John Percival of Kingsale. They had at five sons and five daughters. He was put on the assessment committee for the relief of the British Army in Ireland in October 1644 becoming a JP for the Liberty by February 1645 and for the county by 1652. In that year he was again put on the Hertfordshire Assessment Committee. He held the manor of Kingsboune Hall or Annables in Wheathampstead/Harpenden [TNA: C193/13/4/43d; HALS: DP/3/12/1; F&R I, pp531-9; II, p665; Chauncy, II p436; *VCH Herts* II, pp308, 436]

[82] Abraham Rutt was a Hertford ironmonger, who became a borough assistant in 1646, but was excluded when he refused to take the oath under the Corporations Act in 1662. He was assessed for five hearths in Saint Andrews, Hertford in 1663 [TNA: E179/248/23 *f*121; HALS: HBR20 *ff*422d-3; Chauncy I, p493]

| | |
|---|---|
| yardes of match | 00 18 06 |
| March the 21st delivered to Captain Pullers Leiftenant a pott to putt powder in and 8lbs of match | 00 03 02 |
| Aprill the 5th delivered to Captain Puller's Leitenant 3lbs ½ of match | 00 01 02 |
| Aprill 8th delivered to Captain Needham[83] 6lb of match | 00 02 00 |
| | 01 04 10 |
| Aprill 4th *et* 5th | |
| For buyinge the powder and the match for the militia beinge out 2 dayes | 00 08 00 |
| | 01 12 10 |

The treasurer is allowed to pay himselfe the said some of *xxxiis xd*. Wee say £1-12s-10d *Gabriel Barbor Chairman, William Barber, William Plomer, George Banastre, Isaac Puller, William Burre,*[84] *Anthony Stratford*[85]

**[26] TNA: SP28/231 Militia Committee order to pay Mr Barbor, 8/10/1644**

Att the Committee for the Millitia sitting att Hertford att the Kings Armes[86] this 18th of October 1644

It is further ordered by this Committee that Mr Turner Treasurer shall with all speed pay to Mr Barbor the summe of £67.10s.10d which hee hath paid to Mr

[83] Isaac Needham had held in 1629 a cottage on Baldock Street in Ware and two years before he and his wife Susanne had had a son Joseph [Trinity College Library Box 44 (VI) 7 No 99 Terrier of Ware Rectory; HALS: DP/116/1/1 Ware Parish Register]

[84] Captain William Burr was added to the Hertford Committee on 16 October 1643. By 1657 he was frequenting Quaker meetings in Baldock [*LJ* VI, p257; Rowe, V, *The first Hertford Quakers*, (Hertford, 1970) p13]

[85] Anthony Stratford of Meesden had married Abigail Dover of Gloucester where they both came from originally. He was put on the militia committee in December 1643. His brother George, had married Abigail's sister, Sibilla, and was a captain in the volunteers. He was also on the militia committee, having been added to the general committee two months before [*Herts Vis*, p95; *LJ* VI, p257; F&R I, pp356-8]

[86] The Kings Arms in Hertford was used by the Hertford Standing Committee for its meetings, being a corporation property. The landlady at the time was Mrs King. It was a significant inn, off the main hall of which were two little drinking rooms, the parlour, named the "Court of Gardy", and two other rooms one, called "The Greyhound" the other "the Brick Room". Upstairs there were six major bedrooms and another in the room next to Edward Chandler's shop next door. He was the draper and sequestration agent [Alan Greening, 'Innside Information', *Hertford and Ware Local History Society Journal*, (Hertford, 2005) pp21-2]

Deputy Peck for powder, match and ammunicon sent from London to Hertford Committee for the use of the County
*Thomas Michell, Joseph Dalton Maior, Edward Michell, Thomas Meade, William Carter, William Plomer, Randolph Niccolls*

28th November 1644
Received the day and yeare abovesaid the summe of £67.10s.10d according to this to the use of Mr Barbor my master. I saie againe received by mee
*Thomas Bevis*[87]

**[27] TNA: SP28/231 Account of militia charges for Colonel Washington[88] (undated 1644?)**

An account of what money my collonel have paid to Officers Extraordinary

| | |
|---|---|
| *Inprimis* paid to Benjamin Plummer for orderinge the drakes when there had an alarum at Hitchin | 00 05 00 |
| *Item* paid to the gunners of our regiment 3 weekes and one dayes pay at 1s 4d per day per weeke | 04 14 00 |
| *Item* paid to William Mullins for two teemes[89] to carry ammunicon from London to Hertford | 01 03 06 |
| For 2 drum heads | 00 06 00 |
| Total sum laid out | 06 08 06 |

An account for extraordinary charges

| | |
|---|---|
| *Item* for 5 weekes pay for the quartermaster of my regiment | 05 16 08 |
| For the clarke of my regiment | 02 10 00 |
| | 14 15 02 |

Mr Turner is required to pay this bill of *xiiij*$^{li}$ *xv*$^{s}$ *ii*$^{d}$ to Collonel Washingtons clerke   Wee say £14-15s-2d
*Gabriel Barbor, William Love, George Banastre, Thomas Michell, John Forester,*[90] *William Plomer, Thomas Meade*

---

87 Bevis was Barbor's personal clerk
88 For Washington see Appendix
89 Teams of horses
90 John Forester, citizen of London, married the daughter of Arthur Pulter (1604-1689) of Broadfield Hall, a former sheriff, who in 1642 resigned his offices as JP and militia captain and went into retirement [*VCH Herts* III, p211]

### [28] TNA: SP28/232 Hertford Committee order re payment for ammunition, 10/3/1644(5)

*Martii* 10th 1644 Att the Committee sittinge att the Kings Armes in Hartford It is this day ordered that Mr William Turner Treasurer shall pay out of the militia <money> to Mr Richard Willett of London marchant the summe of 74-00-00 being so much money bin appointed by this Committee to be paid unto him for powder and match. £74-00-00
*Gabriel Barbor, Joseph Dalton, Maior, William Carter, George Banaster, John Fowler, Thomas Meade, William Plomer*

Received of Mr Turner £74 for the use of Mr Willett according to the said order, I say £74. *Gabriel Barbor*

### [29] TNA: SP28/232 Order to Turner to pay Chandler and Heath[91] for lead for bullets, 21/3/1644(5)

Hertfordshire *Veneris 21st Martii*[92] 1644
Mr Turner, treasurer, is required to pay to Edward Heath and Edward Chandler the summe of five pounds six shillings for certain lead which they bought to make bullets <and most therof still remaining in the magazine> [93]And this shall bee your warrant. Geven under our handes the day and yeare abovesaid.
*Gabriel Barbor, Joseph Dalton Maior, Thomas Meade, George Banaster, William Plomer, Randall Nicoll, John Barbor.*

### [30] HALS: 70540 Silus Titus[94] to Alban Coxe, 29/8/1644

Sir,
I thinke my self fortunate that you are to be present at the Committee[95] at our sending forth, and ~~are are~~ am confident wee shall be the better supplyed when

[91] Edward Chandler and Edward Heath were normally employed as agents, collectors or bailiffs of the Hertford Sequestration Committee
[92] Latin for Friday 21 March
[93] The magazine was in Hertford Castle
[94] Titus had been born at Bushey, went to Oxford and the Middle Temple, and had been given a commission in the Hertfordshire Militia. He was at the siege of Donnington Castle, Berks, two months after this letter in October 1644 [See Appendix and Alan Marshall, 'Titus, Silius (1622/3-1704)' *NewDNB*]
[95] Committee for the Militia at St Albans

wee are to depend upon one that is acquainted with soldiers necessities. I heare sir some have beene over-carefull of our safeties and are as tender of us as they <would> be of theire monie, and have us march with a Convoy;[96] truly Sir my colours were never yet guarded by anie but those that marcht under them, and I suppose the charge of necessarie ammunnition will not be valued (by those that aswell respect the credit as the profit of the county) in comparison of the incongruitie of marching without. I speake this only cursorilie uppon a report which as careleslie I hearde, and as little credited. But, sir, it is reason to me that wee draw something farther from our soldiers homes, and leave them lesse incitation to returne by a longer journie. Wee are studious to keepe them together, wee are in hopes Sir wee shall not <want> conveniences to doe it. We are confident nothing shall be determined which relies uppon your care, and that wee shall have a universall ingagement as I have in particular to be

Your humble Servant

August 29th 1644 *S. Titus*

(***At right angles***) To his much honoured freinde Alban Cox Esq. these present

**[31] TNA: SP28/232 Order of Hertford militia committee re appointment of William Parr as gunner, 30/5/1645**

Hertford *Veneris* 30th Maii 1645

It is ordered that William Parr shall bee entertained as gunner for this County of Hertford and to have the allowance of fourteene shillings by the weeke out of which the Committee at St Albans is to pay 2 fifth parts, and wee 3,[97] and that hee immediately bee provide them <the guns> reddy mounted on there carriages with ball and match fitting for service, that soe they bee in a readiness at all times for action.

***(Names of committee listed down the left hand side)*** Gabriel Barbor Esq. Chairman, Mr Maior, Mr Meade, Mr Carter, Colonel Cox, Major Barber, Major Marsh, Colonel Michell, Mr Banastre, Mr Daniel Niccoll, Mr Randall Niccoll, Mr Plomer, Mr Fowler, Mr Marsh,[98] Mr Aylewood

---

96 Convoy used in the sense of a company under armed escort for protection

97 Traditionally the eastern and north-eastern hundreds paid 3/5 of all taxes and the two western and southwestern hundreds 2/5

98 Probably Henry Marsh, who was nominated to the Volunteer Committee in September 1643 and again in December [*LJ* VI, pp244, 342-3]

**[32] TNA: SP28/232 William Parr's bill, 5/6/1645**

| | s d |
|---|---|
| *Imprimis* | s d |
| *Item* for fixing the cheanes and staples, spikes and for locks[99] | 03 08 |
| For a lamb skin | 01 00 |
| For nayles | 00 02 |
| For helpe to mount the gunnes | 01 06 |
| For 3lb of grease | 00 10 *ob*[100] |
| | 07 02 *ob* |

Mr Turner treasurer you are to paie this abovesaid some unto William Parr Gent of the Ordnance for Hartfordshire and this shalbe your warrant, signed the 5th of June 1645. *Gabriel Barbor, Thomas Meade, William Carter*
Pd

**[33] TNA: SP28/232 Robert Draper's bill to the Militia Committee, 12/9/1645**

Hitchin in *Comitatu* Hertford
To the worshipfull the committee of the militia September 12th 1645 ys hereby presented:
A note of monyes disburst by the order and appoyntment of the <said> Committee of the militia of this County as followeth: £ s d
*Imprimis* for the new makeinge of a wheele for the drake and other apertinant charges in fixinge ytt and for baggs and carthages[101] of canvas for ytt as by perticulars maye apeare 00 14 02
*Item* disburst in findinge out of Scouts upon the alarme which was in Summer laste by the direction of the Committee 00 13 00
*Item* disburst in findinge out of Scouts, accordinge the order and warrant of the Committee, upon the last aproach of the enemye as by particulars maye apeare the soomme of 03 03 00
*Item* disburst in sendinge a prisoner (then one belongeinge to enemies army,) from Hitchin to Hertford by the direction of Collonell Coxe 00 09 00
*Item* disbursed in sendinge and receaveinge 2 severall messuages between Hitchin and Buntingforde in the tyme of our danger 00 01 06

---

[99] Chains and various pieces of metal for fixing the gun to the gun-carriage
[100] Shortened Latin form of *obolus* or a halfpenny
[101] Cartridges – i.e. canvas bags to hold the gunpowder for the drake

Soomme £5 -0s-8d *Robert Draper*

Mr Turner Treasurer you are required to paye unto Robert Draper the <aforesaid> soomme of five pounds and eight pence for the payment wherof this shalbee your warrant. Given by us of the Committee whose names are hereunto subscribed the daye and yeare abovesayd.
*George Banastre, Thomas Meade, William Plomer, John Barbor, John Fowler, Randall Nicoll, Danyell Nicoll*

**(*Endorsed down the left hand side*)** September 18th 1645
Received off Mr Turner five pound eight pence *per me Robert Draper*

## Part 3 Purchase, commandeering and use of horses

### [34] TNA: SP28/154 Standon parish accounts *f*16 re horses 18/2/1642-27/5/1643

Standon

| | |
|---|---|
| Maye 27th 1643 William Smeth had one black stone[102] horse taken from him by Captaine Robotham praised by Humphrey Packer and Edward Wood at Hertford at fower pounds | 04 00 00 |
| October 8th1642 David Chapman listed one black horse valued by the Comesaries John Smeth and Thomas Richardson[103] Comesaries at Tenn Pounds | 10 00 00 |
| August 18th 1642 George Hoye Inrowled at London a Black horse valued at eight pounds by the Comesaries John Smeth | 08 00 00 |
| August the first 1642 John Brooks Inrowled one Black horse Compleate[104] valued by John Smeth and Thomas Richardson Comesaries at two and twentie pounds | 22 00 00 |
| Maye 24th 1642 Edward Shipham Inrowled one Geldinge[105] at Hartforde valued by Joseph Dalton and Humphrey Packer Commisaries at five pounds | 05 00 00 |
| Maye 25th 1643 John Jones had a baye[106] Browne Geldinge taken | |

[102] Stoned or non-castrated
[103] Possibly the Thomas Richardson who was Salisbury's bailiff at Hatfield in the 1630s [Munby, *Stuart Household Accounts*, pp65, 188]
[104] Complete with all equipment or horse furniture.
[105] Gelding or castrated horse

from him by Captaine Robotham valued by Joseph Dalton and
Humphrey Packer Comesaries at seaven pounds 07 00 00
November 12th 1642 John Miller Inrowled one Browne Baye
horse valued by the Comesaries Mr John Smeth and Mr John
Richardson at nine pounds 09 00 00

**[35] TNA SP28/231 Hertford Committee note re money for horses kept by Commissary Fitch, 30/4/1643[107]**

A noate of moneis disbursed by Jeremiah Fitch, Commissary for horses for the Committee

| | |
|---|---|
| for foure post horses for goinge to Dunstable | 00 08 00 |
| for 2 horses 3 daies at hay and each a peck[108] of oates a day 6s and one horse two daies at hay and each a pecke of oates a day 2s? and one horse one day at hay and a peck of oates 1s, which horse went to Hertford for Sir John Norwich[109] in all | 00 09 00 |
| For 6 horses for the recrute of Collonel Crumwell.[110] 1 horse 3 daies at hay and one pecke oates 2s; five horses as at hay and half a pecke of oates a peece 3s 9d; and one horse was Edlins of Watford came from the Christopher[111] on Satterday and kept till Munday at hay 1s | 00 06 09 |
| Paid Samuell Wharton for listing of horses at the first under severall captaines | 00 10 00 |
| | 01 13 09 |

(***Along the side***) April 30th Jeremy Fitch £1-13-9 (6)

[106] Bay or chestnut-coloured

[107] Given that this refers to Colonel Cromwell the date will be 1643

[108] A peck was a measure of capacity for dry goods. It was ¼ of a bushel or two gallons

[109] For Sir John Norwich see Appendix

[110] The county had been specifically requested to provide horses for the Eastern Association cavalry

[111] The Christopher Inn was a medieval inn, rebuilt before the Civil War and later extended after the Restoration. One of the principal inns in St Albans it was run by Mrs Pollard, wife of Ralph Pollard the former Mayor [Smith and North, *St Albans*, pp35, 41, 65, 169, 176, 178, 207]

## [36] TNA: SP28/11 Pt I f99 Barkway – Horses for Colonel Norwich, 1643

| | £ s d |
|---|---|
| Sir Peter Saltonstall[112] by composicion in money for one light Horse and furniture imposed upon him and by him privately found as appeareth under the hand of Humphrey Packer | 10 10 00 |
| *Item* Sir Edward Chester[113] one light horse imposed upon him and furniture- private as appeareth | 09 08 06 |
| *Item* John Rowley gent[114] – sent a light horse and complete furniture for the said horse being privately by him found charge under Packer's hand | 14 00 00 |
| *Item* for a monthes paie for the saide horse and his ryder being likewise paid by him the said John Rowley | 03 10 00 |
| *Item* sent in a light horse with complete furniture for the same by the township of Barkwaye the value then as appeareth under Mr Packer | 12 00 00 |
| For a moneths pay for horse and ryder | 03 10 00 |
| Total | 52 18 06 |

Signed *George Gage,* Cunstable.

## [37] TNA: SP28/231 St Albans Committee order for draught horses for the artillery train, 29/4/1644

Whereas we have recieved a letter, dated 13 Aprill 1644, from the Knights and Burgesses of our county,[115] manifestinge that they have received a command from the <Committee of> Lords and Commons for both

---

[112] Sir Peter Saltonstall *(fl.* 1597-1645) fourth son of Sir Richard Saltonstall, Lord Mayor of London, admitted to Gray's Inn in 1597, was put on the Commission of the Peace by the King on 15 July 1642, having already been a commissioner for taxation in May. Married firstly Anne, daughter of Edmund Waller of Coleshill by whom he had a son Richard and secondly Christian, daughter of Sir John Pettus. His son James compounded as a royalist [Cambridge University Library: Ec.3.30 27 Taxation of the Hundreds of Hertfordshire May 1642; Foster, *Gray's Inn Admissions,* p71; *Statutes of the Realm,* V, (1628-80) (1819) pp145-67; *Al Cant* Pt 1, IV, p10]

[113] For Chester see Appendix

[114] John Rowley, Esq, (*fl.* 1604-63) son of John Rowley gent, attorney at law, educated at Halstead School, Essex, Caius College, Cambridge, and Grays Inn, sheriff in 1650 was assessed for eleven hearths in 1663 [TNA: E 179/248/23 *f*89; *Al Cant* Pt I, 3, p494; Foster, *Gray's Inn Admissions*, p167; *CJ* VI, p492]

[115] The six MPs representing the county and the two boroughs of Hertford and St Albans

Kingdoms,[116] as also from the Honourable House of Commons, for the speedy provideinge of 45 horse within our county; to be draught horses for the trayne of artillary, to be brought to St Albans with all expedition, on the 17th of this instant Aprill, where they ought to be delivered to such commissaries ~~th~~ as shallbe appoynted by the Lord Generall[117] to recieve them. And that a ticket under the said Commissaries hands shallbe sufficient for the county to receive the mony that the said horses cost, which is by the order of the house to be paid to the treasury of this county within this 14 daies after the delivery of the said horses. And, whereas 18 of the aforesaid 45 horses is the proportion of theise two hundreds, theise are to require you, William Hickman, treasurer, to issue out £106 16s 2d to Jeremy Fitch[118] and Fromabove Dove[119] authorized with your selfe by us to buy the said horses, for the payement of them, to such persons ~~th~~ of whom they were bought accordinge to the severall lists given him by the aforesaid persons intrusted and for that so doing, this shallbe your warrant dated this 29th Aprill 1644
*John Wittewronge, Johes King, John Robotham, Raphe Pemberton Esq.*

***(On reverse)*** Issued out in our presence the 15th day of Aprill in full of this order within written the severall sums for the eighteen horses which appears by the particulars the sum one hundred and six pounds sixteene shillings and two pence I say £106 -16s-2d *Per* us *Jeremy Fitch, Fromabove Dove*

***(Along the side)*** Jeremy Fitch £106.16.2 *£Cvi.xvis.iid*
Horse Arms and More pay No 15(2)

**[38] TNA: SP28/155 Tewin parish accounts re horses, 28/9/1644**

*f2r* Horses taken £149-00s-00d
Horses taken by Newman Humphryes Liutenant to Captaine William Salkaell

---

[116] This Committee, which contained representatives from the Parliaments of England and Scotland, was in effect the central executive committee for running the war for parliament
[117] The Earl of Essex who commanded the troops who had wintered in a garrison in St Albans and needed draught animals to move out to start the new season's campaign
[118] Fitch, (*fl.* 1627-1675) a baker, had become a St Albans Borough Assistant in 1627 and had been used before as a Commissary for horses. He had considerable wealth after the Restoration in terms of a business in Holywell Hill next to the Dolphin Inn, rated at four hearths in 1663 and stores of wheat and corn, servants, horses and carts. He later acquired another property in the town which he sold in 1675 [Chauncy, II, p304; Smith and North, *St Albans,* pp9, 154, 183]
[119] For Dove see Appendix

| | |
|---|---|
| From Mr Edward North[120] Senior 2 horses by the appointment (as he said) of Mr Gabriell Barber and Humphrey Packer upon a | |
| present expedicon with promise they should be returned within | £ s d |
| two or three dayes, apprized by Mr Humphrey Packer at | 16 00 00 |
| Also taken then a bridle and a sadle | |
| Horses taken by Captaine John Andrewes[121] by a speciall warrant (as he pretended) from the Lord Generall | |
| From Mr Edward North Senior 2 horses worth at the least | 28 00 00 |
| *f2v* Horses taken by one Captaine Knight[122] | |
| From Mr Edward North senior one horse worth | 13 00 00 |
| From John Asser one horse worth | 12 00 00 |
| Horses taken by Leiutenant Colborne, Leiutenant to Colonell Middleton,[123] by his warrant as he pretended in February 1642 | |

[120] Edward North senior (died 1650/3) held land in Tewin and Munden and had been serjeant at arms to Charles I. His son Edward had been admitted to Sidney Sussex, Cambridge in 1623 and to the Inner Temple in 1626. His other son George also went to Cambridge [Chauncy I, p542; *Al Cant* Pt I, 3, p265) Anon, *Students admitted to the Inner Temple 1547-1660* (1877) p248]. Given the general tone of this document and the number of horses taken from him, he may have been seen as a royalist sympathizer, without actually being sequestered as a delinquent

[121] Captain John Andrewes had used strong-armed methods in Hertfordshire to seize horses to the extent that the local committee had arrested him, proposing to return the horses to their owners. In May 1643, the House of Commons released him following a letter from Lord General Essex and allowed him to take 120 horses. Given this, he is probably not the John Andrewes who was employed by the local committee in 1644. However a Captain Andrewes sallied forth from the Newport Pagnell Garrison in March 1645 and captured 17 Royalists (BL: E274 [26] *Mercurius Civicus* No. 96 20-27 March 1645); Tibbutt, *Luke's Letter Book*, pp1233, 1238; Holmes, *Eastern Association*, p83]

[122] This may be Ralph Knights from Berkshire, a captain in Manchester's own regiment [Holmes, *Eastern Association*, p175]

[123] This is likely to be the Scot, John Middleton, who after service with the French became a colonel in the parliamentarian army. He was later promoted to lieutenant-general, and commanded the cavalry at Copredy Bridge, Oxon, in June and on the left at the first battle of Newbury, Berks on 20 September 1643. In April 1644 he joined Waller, when he was described as "a very worthy sober man" and "a brave man and as well understood in the command of horse as any of our side". Waller sent him with 2,000 cavalry to relieve Essex in Cornwall in July 1644. He was at the surrender of Wareham in mid August and dispersed some of the King's cavalry near Bristol, but was repelled at Bridgewater. He led a significant charge at the second battle of Newbury. With the creation of the New Model Army he resigned and returned to Scotland, where he became an Engager in 1648 and a Royalist therafter. His 'sober' reputation was tarnished somewhat in 1660 when he formed a brief 'drunken administration' in Edinburgh [*CJ* III, pp493-4, 589-01, 605-6, 615-6; Kishlansky, M, *The rise*

*Sir John Wittewronge in later life*

An Etching of Oliver Cromwel, from an Original Painting
by Cowper in Sidney Coll: Camb: — To the Master & Fellows of that
Coll: this Plate is most humbly inscribed by their Obed.t Serv.t J. Bretherton.


*Oilver Cromwell*

*Thomas Fairfax, 1647*

*Arthur Lord Capel*

From Dr John Montfort[124] 7 horses worth at the least 70 00 00
*Suma* paid
Horses taken by troopers belonging to Sir Samuel Luke[125] as they pretended
From Mr John Mynne[126] one horse worth 04 00 00
Taken by Isaack Puller[127] and Henry Gouge by warrant (as they pretended) from his excellency.
From Edward North one horse worth 06 00 00
Item 2 horses sent for to the parish for dragoones and delivered to Captain Butterfeild which cost the parish 07 00 00
*Summa Totalis* 149 00 00
*Edward North, Thomas Gray,[128] Robert Battale*

***(Endorsed on side)*** The return of the parish of Tewin this 28th September 1644

## [39] HALS: 70542 – Henry Ewer[129] to Coxe, 2/4/1645

To his worthie and mutche esteemed friend Alban Coxe Esq. Collonel of the horses raised for the defence of the Countie of Hertford these present.

Sir, I sent my horse, ryder and armes to Sandrige upon the last warninge before: haveinge noe commande then geven me. I have likewyse sent nowe to St Albans agayne: my Ryders name is John Dent, a Watford man and one that hath ben tryed alreadye in the service for twoe yeares heretofore, a very able younge man, I hope to your contentment. I praye list him for my Ryder. Thus

---

*of the New Model Army,* (Cambridge 1983) pp48-9; Haythornthwaite, P, *The English Civil War 1642-1651: An illustrated military history*, (1994) p94; Seymour, W, *Battles in Britain and their political background*, Vol II, (1975) p57; Adair J, *Roundhead General* (Stroud, 1997) pp176-7, 190, 201, 207, 215, 226; Henning, *Commons*, II, p61]

[124] Probably, in fact, James Mountford, Rector of Tewin, brother to John

[125] Luke of Cople, Bedfordshire had married the daughter of Ralph Freeman of Aspenden and was the commander of the Bedfordshire forces [Sean Kelsey, 'Luke, Sir Samuel (*bap.*1603, *d.*1670)', *NewDNB*]

[126] Possibly one of the sons of George Mynne of Hertingfordbury (d, 1651) civil servant, Clerk of the Hanaper, who died in 1652 [Aylmer, *The King's Servants,* pp 117-121, 189-90, 301-2]

[127] The organizer of the Hertford Volunteers and a Committeeman *(see* Appendix)

[128] Thomas Grey, yeoman, later moved to Hertford, where he died in 1658 when his estate was valued at £12 9s 6d. He held Cromer's Farm in Bengeo and Sacombe, land in Great Munden Manor as well as a house in Tewin. [Adams, *Hertford Wills*, pp3-5]

[129] For Henry Eure (Ewer) see Appendix

makeinge bold to trowble you with these fewe lynes. I rest: Your humble servant
*Henry Eure Esq.*
From the Lea in Watford parishe the second daye of Aprill 1645

**[40] HALS: 70545 Brockett Spencer[130] to Coxe, 2/4/1645**

Good collonell
I must request you would excuse the not sendinge my horse to wayt upon you this day, my wife beinge with child and lookinge[131] every hour, I can very ill aspayre either horse or man, I my selfe allsoe (beinge intrusted in a businesse at this tyme betwixt my sister and my nephew Jenyns)[132] which must not be neglected the day beinge agreed upon before I received your warrant, wherefore I would intreat you <not> to looke upon any thinge as neglect in me and henceforth I shall not fayle you in this or what else concernes the respect of your lovinge friend and servant

*Brockett Spencer*

Offley this 2nd of April 1645

To my much respected friend Collonell Cox at St Albans these present

---

130 Brockett Spencer Bt. (c.1605-68) of Offley Place, 2nd son of Richard Spencer, educated by Mr Plumtre at Ridge, at Sidney Sussex, Cambridge 1622, admitted to Lincoln's Inn in 1625, succeeded to the family estate on the death of his brother in 1633, JP for the County and Liberty from 1640 and created baronet on 26 September 1642, but remained neutral. He inherited the manors of Almeshoe in St Ippollitts, Offley and the Rectory at Kimpton. In 1646 he married Susan daughter of Sir Nicholas Cary (Carew) of Beddington, Surrey, by whom he had five sons, including Richard and William and four daughters, assessed for 24 hearths in 1663 [TNA: C231/5 *ff*374, 406; E 179/248/23 *f*12; GEC, *Complete Baronetage,* II, p200; Cussans, *Herts, Hitchin Volume* pp98, 103-6; *Lincoln's Inn Admissions Register,* p196; Chauncy II, pp183, 192-4, 201; *VCH Herts* III, pp26-7, 33, 41; *Al Cant* Pt I, IV, p131]

131 Expected to be delivered of it

132 Spencer's sister, Alice, was married to James Altham of Markeshall, Essex and his nephew Richard Jennings, was the son of Sir John and his aunt Alice [TNA: C 231/4 *f* 220v; *VCH Herts* III, p41; For Jennings see Appendix]

### [41] HALS: 70543 John Reade [133] to Colonel Alban Coxe re horses (undated 1645?)

Sir,
Having receaved satisfaction touching the equity of the horse layd upon me, I have now sent him, yet not as I intended two, bec~~au~~-ause I had warning but last night of your muster and one was ~~being~~ (sent) forth, this I feare will suddainly be made unserviceable in ordinary hands being never used to the saddle nor any imployment[134] but to draw my wife and mother to church. The other I ment to <have> sent is a plain gelding but an especiall going one and very hardy and soe accustomed to be hageld[135] about that I thinke a man can hardly rong him and any man that knows him would choose him rather then this or any I have. If you please I will send him the next muster and if upon triall he proves <not> to your mind, I will change him ~~as ells~~ <because> I cannot have my <wife> to church if this horse be out any time, otherwise I could spare this better then the other, likewise then I will send a rider. This man I got to goe this time for me because I could not soe sodainly procure a nother. This with my kind respects to you. I rest your loving frend *John Reade*
Thursday morn

**(*On the side*)** To my honored frend Collonell Cox at St Albans present these

### [42] HA 70544 H Morgan to Colonel Alban Coxe (undated 1645?)

Sir,
Not only Spring, but all my neighbours can testifie that the best horse I then had at home was sent you. For aboute an houre before your warrant came, I was unfortunately gon to London with two horses that are something better, and I did not returne till last night. When coming home I found <no> lesse then 53 horse and men quarterd at my house, which tooke up my care soe much that I could not well mind anything else. But having since enquired after itt, I doe not find that any can justly accuse my wife's diligence in obeying your warrant. For the testimony of all credible men shall witnes, that when Spring cam out upon the service, Harding refuseing to come along with him (which you promised me he should not ~~doe~~ dare to doe in case I could not

[133] Sir John Reade See Appendix
[134] To being ridden with a saddle or any other use
[135] Hageld – probably a contraction of 'handled roughly' from haggard = wild or rough

provide myself better) she freely dismised all her mounths men and made them a lender of all or any of five horse that were left aboute the house to come and serve you. Which offerr they all refused except one man, who voluntaryly went with our foote armes to serve the state under Captain Payne. This and something else I would have tould you by word of mouth but that Mr Jones would not give me leave to ride my owne horse to waite [136] upon you, though I desire him to accept of two other horses for him, or with him, soe I might have the rideing of my owne to your quarters. Those other two are herewith sent you. If you shall think good to returne me him home because I am to goe to London to morow upon busines that much concerns me, I shall take it for a favour from you. If not, soe there be occation to use them, I am very willing they should all three goe upon the servise. It is not long since I last spoke with you, I promised you then sire more than I intended, though this last alarum came upon us before things were soe well provided as I could wish. Quarter Master Jones is very civill; misunderstandings hath bin the cause of much mischiefe.
Sir I am your frend to serve you *H Morgan*

**(*On reverse*)** to my much honoured frend Collonell Coxe, this with my service present

**[43] HALS: 70546 Roland Lytton[137] to Alban Coxe, 26/8/1645**

Noble Sir,

If our horses attend you not punctually according to the summons, be pleased to take notice that your warrant came to the Constable of Walden in between nine and ten this present day; the party that formerly served on my horse is unwillinge longer to serve unless I would increase the countreys pay, the which as yett I am unwilling to doe, fearinge some ill consequence may proceede therof; wherefore I have here sent my horse and arms by one of my owne servants; I desire you would please ~~the man~~ to dismisse the man; bycause of my want of him; and put some honest fellow on my horse that would be carefull and should be thankfull to him; besides the ingagement ever to professe my selfe;

Your most respectfull friend and servant

[136] From this point the letter is written down the side
[137] For Lytton see Appendix

*R Lytton*

From the Hoo[138] this 26 of August 1645

***(On side)*** To my much honored freinde Collonell Cox present this

## Part 4 The committees, and wartime organization

### [44] TNA SP28/231 Letter from Committeeman John Kensey[139] at Much Hadham to Mr Turner, treasurer, at Hertford, 29/1/1643(4)

Mr Turner,
I had bin with you today but that some occasions intervening have prevented me. Nevertheless I must needs send you a challenge of your premise, for my pay, forasmuch as Great Hadham hath paid in the fourtnights pay[140] according to my request and I suppose Standon hath done the like, ere this time, but you said one more of my townes[141] <with Little Hadham> would make up the summe of my pay which, now it is come in, I should have it. The sum of my bill, as I told you before, is £17 - 11s as appears by the warrant. The clerke that wrote it mistooke the form and set down 13s but I mended it before the committees hands were to it, and made it 11s which is true according to the particulars which I have likewise sent you according to your desire. I pray send me the said summe by the bearer hereof, James Hampton, who is my brother in law and an honest man, tho' I say it. Remember my best respects to my brother and sister Till and tell them my will was good to do what I could in the business you wott[142] of, but Captain Heath,[143] upon whom I suppose

---

138 The Hoo was an estate in St Paul's Walden, inherited by Susan Hoo, who married Jonathan Keate. Lytton must have been renting the property or staying there [Chauncy, II, p404]

139 Captain, later Lieutenant-Colonel, John Kensey was a committeeman from Much Hadham, with an estate that his great- grandfather had purchased. He had been at Emmanuel College, Cambridge in 1633, had been a captain in the militia and had been added to the Hertford Committee in October 1643. He sat on numerous local committees from 1643 to 1659. He was put on the local bench in 1650 and 1656, when he was of the quorum. He married twice having two children by his first wife Joanne, and eight by his second wife Sarah (married September 1644), daughter of John Gardner of Farnham, Essex. He presumably is seeking repayment of his expenses for attending the Committee in Hertford (TNA: C193/13/3 *ff*30-31; 6 *f*41; HALS: 37693; *Al Cant* Pt I Vol. 3, p8; F&R I&II *passim*)

140 This would seem to indicate that collectors had to send in taxes on a fortnightly basis

141 i.e. townships which included villages

142 Wot – archaic form of know

143 Captain Thomas Heath, not Edward Heath the sequestration agent

they cheifely depend, told me he had done as much as could be done in it before I came so farre into the Citye, for indeed I was hindered in my journey. Remember me likewise to your wife, and till oportunity serves for other expression, accept of thanks from the part of your obliged friend *John Kensey.*
Hadham Magna[144] January 29th 1643

**(*On reverse*)** To his much respected and approved good friend Mr Turner Treasurer for the new Militia in Hertford these
Captaine Kensey His order for £17-11s

### [45] TNA: SP28/231 St Albans Committee order to pay chairman's attendance allowance 15/8/1644

Whereas the Committee sitting at St Albans have received a Commission from the right Honourable Edward Earle of Manchaster dated the 19th of Aprill 1644 for a standinge Committee of foure Gent of the committee to sit dayly at St Albans and attend the service of Parliament in the two hundreds next adjacent and for the defrayinge of theire charges; every committee (man) is to have 5s a day, to be paid by the Treasurers of the said county, as they shall receive warrant under three of the standinge committees hands. These are to authorise you , William Hickman Trasurer, to pay unto John King Dr[145] for his attendance 20 daies (dayly) upon the service of the Parliament accordinge to the said Commission at St Albans from the 10th of July to the 2nd of August followinge the sum of five pounds, and for the so doing this shallbe your warrant. Given under our hands this 15August 1644.
*John Robotham, Tobie Combe Esq,[146] Raphe Pemberton Esq.*

**(*On reverse*)** Received this 17th August 1644 in full of the order within written five pounds £5-00-00 *Per me Johem King*

[144] Much Hadham
[145] King's attendance at the committee would have meant that he had less time for his medical practice and thus a loss of fees. The attendance allowance would have made up for some of this
[146] For Tobie Combe see Appendix

**[46] HALS: 70555 Draft petition to the Commons from the Hundreds of Cashio and Dacorum about committee expenses[147] (undated)**

To the honourable the Howse of commons in Parliament assembled: The humble peticon of divers Knights, Gentlemen, Freeholders and others of the two hundreds of Cashio and Decorum within the Countie of Hertford.

Sheweth
That not withstanding your petitioners (since the beginning of those great and nationall troubles) have undergone farr heavier burthens then any other partes of this countie or of the kingdome that hath bene totally under the command of the Parliament which by deare experience they well knowe and can easily manifest. Yett divers of the standing Committee sitting at St Albanes, and there acting the affaires of the aforesaid two hundreds, little weighing our low condition, have, contrarie to the opinion of ~~you~~ theire honourable worthies sitting in this honourable house and the practice of those of the standing committee acting at Hertford, sent forth their warrants for the raising of £973 under colour of an Ordinance of both howses granted to the 7 counties of the Easterne Associacion for the reimbursing the severall committees thereof such monies as they were out of purse or stood engaged in, for defraying of alarums, scouts <and> intelligence.

Now in regard the intent of the said Ordinance is already soe fully and cleerely satisfied within the said County and hundreds, by vertue of an other Ordinance longe since granted to a particular committee of Militia within the said Countie and hundreds, thereby enabling them to rayse both men and monies for that purpose. Whoe, accordingly, have soe fully and faithfuly acted therein and make payment of all such somes as have accrued or growne due thereby, that the said standing committees cannot soe much as pretend to be engaged or out of purse therein, as alsoe that your Petitioners have bene by the said committee and theire agents, for not making soe cheereful and speedy payment thereof as they have usually done upon other rates, menaced, threatned, fyned, imprisoned and otherwise abused to theire great griefe and hinderance contrary, as we verily believe, to theire trust and the intent of this honourable howse.

---

[147] The date of this draft is not given but is probably the summer or autumn of 1644 or 1645, following the intense activity in relation to a perceived royalist threat. The previous document in the series, 70554 appears to be an earlier draft.

Your petitioners therefore most humblly crave that by order from this most honourable howse they may bee commanded to forbeare theire further proceedes therein, speedily to repay such sommes as have bene by them collected or received and for the future enjoyned to carry them selfes with more moderacon and lesse aserbity etc. And they shall pray etc.

**(*On reverse*)** The humble peticon of divers Knights Gentlemen and Freeholders of the two hundreds of Cashio and Decorum in the County of Hertford

**[47] TNA: SP28/231 County Committee order re John King's London expenses, 18/5/1645**

May 18th 1645 Att the Committee at their generall meeting at Hatfield the day and year abovesaid
Ordered that William Priestley Esq[148] and John King Dr in phisicke shall attend the committee of the Honourable House of Commons for considering of the petition and propositions of the County of Hertford;[149] and that they shall repaire to London, and meete in Westminster Hall[150] the 28th of May 1645 by nine of the clock in the morning. And that each of them shall have 5s a day to beare their charges during their attendance of the aforesaid service, to be paid by order from the Committee out of the third parte of the sequestrations.
*Vera copia*[151]
According to which order, I John King did repaire to London and attended to the aforesaid service as followeth

| | |
|---|---|
| Attended from the 28th of May to the 4th of June | 2 00 00 |
| Attended from the 16th of June to the 20th June | 1 00 00 |
| Attended from the 30th of June to the 3rd of July | 1 00 00 |
| Attended from the 22nd if July to the 26 of July | 1 05 00 |
| Attended from the 4th August to the 9 of August | 1 10 00 |
| Summe | 7 00 00 |

August 22nd 1645

---

148 For William Priestley (Presley) see Appendix
149 This would have been the petition which was read in the Commons on 10th May and related to the 'grievous oppression' on the county by the forces in it, the people being unable to bear 'endure the burden of them' [*CJ* IV, pp138, 139]
150 Parliament met in Westminster Hall at this time
151 Latin for 'a true copy'

These are to desire you William Hickman Treasurer to pay unto Dr King the summe of seaven pounds abovesaid for the abovesaid service according to the abovesaid order; out of the third parte of the Sequestrations; and for your soe doing this shalbe your warrant
*Alban Coxe, William Foxwist,*[152] *Tobie Combe, John Wittewronge, Edmund Smythe*

Received this 25th of August 1645 in full of the abovesaid order of William Hickman, Treasurer the sum of seaven pounds £07:00s:00d
*Johes King*

**[48] TNA: SP28/232 Hertford Militia Committee order re payment for obtaining release of regiment, 23/5/1645**

23 Maii 1645 Mr Turner is required to pay unto Lieutenant Collonel Puller[153] and to Captain Dawges[154] for 5 dayes attendance on the Committee of both kingdoms in getting release of our regiment from marching out of the County the some of 5s per day, which is xxvs a peece the totall is £2-10s-0d Wee say *£ii xs Gabriel Barbor, Joseph Dalton Maior, William Carter, John Barbor, Thomas Meade, George Banastre, William Plomer*

Received accordinge to the above written order fifty shillings *per me William Dawges*

**[49] TNA SP28/231 Bill of charges of the Hertford Committee at the King's Arms (undated 1644?)**

| The bill of charges for the Committee at the Kings Arms | £ s d |
|---|---|
| *Item* 15 November for fire, committis dinners | 00 05 00 |
| *Item* for fyer, paper, beare and ayle | 00 03 06 |
| *Item* for Goodman Goliges dinner and supper | 00 01 00 |
| *Item* for fire, Commitis supers | 00 04 00 |
| *Item* for bear and fyer and paper | 00 03 06 |

[152] For Foxwist see Appendix
[153] Isaac Puller the committeeman as an officer in the militia See Appendix
[154] William Dawges Esq of Hatfield was a captain in the militia and the Hertfordshire solicitor for sequestrations, later parliamentary surveyor. He was on the Hertford Committee until 1649 then again in 1659 being a JP 1656-9. He was assessed for 23 Hearths in 1663 [TNA: C139/13/6 *f*41d; E170/248/23 *f*24; F&R I&II, *passim*]

| | |
|---|---|
| *Item* for a quart of sack[155] | 00 01 02 |
| *Item* for beare and sugger, bread and cheus[156] | 00 02 00 |
| | 01 00 02 |
| *Item* for twelve commitis dinneres the 17 not whear off Mr Barbar and Mr Carter payd | 00 10 00 |
| *Item* for 2 mens dinners and for fyer and beare | 00 02 00 |
| | 01 12 02 |

Mr Turner you are to pay Mrs King[157] this her bill which cometh to *i*$^{li}$ *xii*$^{s.}$ 4$^{d}$
*Gabriel Barbor, Joseph Dalton, Maior, William Love, Thomas Meade, George Bannister, William Plummer*
Received this bill by me £1-12s-4d *Elizabeth King*

**[50] TNA: SP28/232 Gabriel Barbor's bill for celebrating victory at Naseby,[158] June 1645**

| Hertford | s d |
|---|---|
| Paid the second soldier that brought newes of the victorie[159] | 3 00 |
| Paid the first man which was hardly believed | 1 00 |
| Paid the third man which confirmed it with letters | 2 00 |
| Paid All Saints[160] ringers | 2 06 |
| Paid the sexton | 1 06 |
| Paid Andrew parish ringers | 2 00 |
| Paid the sexton | 1 00 |
| Paid for diverse things being for the committee | 1 06 |
| | 14 06 |

Mr Treasurer is to pay this bearer this bill which is *xiiiis vid*
*Gabriel Barbor*

Paid this bill to Peter Gins wife for Mr Barbor

[155] Sack was white wine from Spain or the Canaries
[156] Cheese
[157] Mrs King was lucky to have her inn used by the Committee given her involvement in a case in 1638 [Alan Greening, 'Much ado about tippling', *Hertford and Ware Local History Society Journal* (Hertford, 2004) pp3-8]
[158] The battle of Naseby took place on 14 June 1645
[159] It was the custom in this period to reward those who brought good news
[160] Ringers of All Saints Church Hertford paid to communicate the victory to the inhabitants of Hertford by bell-ringing

### [51] HALS: 70538 Hertford Committee to Colonel Alban Coxe (undated 1645?)

Noble Sire
We received yours of the 6th of this instant wherin we perceive that you have called in the horsses listed for you out of thes divicions of Hartford and that you are recuire to <doe> service for the defence of this Countie and Kingdome. Wee desire you to send to the Committee and tresurer at St Albons for ther paie, for we conceive that a troupe, to be paid some from Hartford and some from St Albons, will make much trouble and differences, and yet boathe yours and the Majors[161] muste be soe, if wee should paie thes as you mention, because the Major have some in your divicions also. Beside our tressurie is verie thine at this time and the more for the wante of the £200 behinde, which was ordered to be paid from your tressurer to Hartford. And that other mony, which your standinge committee was ordered to paie to our treasurer out of the Earle of Manchesters, ~~and of th~~ money, due to him, to paie his souldiers free quarter on this side of the Countie, which maketh divers denie to paie any more money for want of that which is ther due which they have longe expected. Therfore we desire you to expedite the souldiers paie of these somes soe much as you cann; allthough you paid more souldiors then your parte cometh unto, yet <we> will assure you that we shall paie our parte, ~~and we~~ whatsoever it be and desire that the soone as may be, an accounte may be taken, and soe made even what is due to you, or to us, and soe continewe for after times.
Sir we desire you to houlde for us, as well as for your owne side of the countie, which we have hitherto found and we shall sticke as close to you, in any friendly waie and doe reste. Your friends assuredly
*Gabriell Barbor, William Carter, George Banestre, William Plomer*
***(One reverse)***To our honoured and assured freinde Collonell Coxe Esq. these present with speede

### [52] HALS: 70549 St Albans Militia Committee to Coxe, 27/8/1645

Sir,
Wee haveinge perused all intelligence doe conceive it best conduceinge to our service and safetye that you drawe your regiment towards Hitchin where you

[161] I assume this though written maior it is Major (probably Marsh) rather than Mayor. This is a common practice at the time

beinge somewhat in the Champion,[162] you maye better observe the mocon of the enymye, either the body or partyes. Wee shall soe dispose of the foot to quarter in the inclosures[163] neere you, that they maye be alwayes ready to assist you upon anye alaram. Wee conceive it necessary the Black Regiment might joyne with others conceivinge the kings intencon for Oxford. Sir you maye be readye to move upon the edge of the Champion accordinge to their motion. Wee heare by Major Marsh[164] the Kings armie (has gone) to Bedford <also Wobourne Abbye>house[165] last night att 10 a clock, with some 2000[166] horse the rest very neere behinde. Soe that since the wrightinge herof wee have ordered the foote to quarter this night att and about Hardinge[167] and thinke it fitt you drawe towards Luton with your whole regiment and the Black Regiment neere our other foote. Thus desireinge you to hould your intelligence with us, wee rest your assured loving freinds
*John Gale, Zacharie King, John Marsh Collonel, Francis Clarke Esq, William Barbor, William Smyth,[168] Christopher Loefts, William Shawarde,[169] William Finch[170]* St Albans August 27th

**[53] HALS: 70547 John Barbor to Coxe, 26/8/1645**

Sir,
The alarme continewes warme, a trooper come from Cambridg tells us that the enemy faced it about 10 of the clock with 3 troopes of horse. Either they intend to attempt the Isle[171]or otherwise to plunder the countrey, and away, it may bee, to Oxford. I send you the copy of the Lords letter to us. To morrow morning I intend to march to Buntingford, where I hope wee may meet. Till when I remaine (Sir)

---

[162] Open ground
[163] The enclosed, as opposed to the open, fields
[164] Parliament ordered Coxe and John Marsh of St Albans to train their volunteers on 10 August 1642. Marsh (1603-81) was a local inn holder in St Albans who bought the manor of Garston from William Carter having been an officer in the local militia [*CJ II*, p 712; Smith and North, *St Albans*, p98]. Marsh was in charge of the Scouts
[165] Home of the Earls of Bedford
[166] Probably an exaggeration
[167] Harpenden
[168] William Smyth of Sandridge, added to the county committee in December 1643 [F&R I, pp356-8]
[169] Shawarden family had been resident in Datchworth [*VCH Herts* III, p79]
[170] Finch was the son of Thomas Finch of St Michaels and Dorothy the daughter of a brewer from Markyate and held land in St Michaels Street, St Albans [HALS: 78660]
[171] The Isle of Ely, i.e. in North Cambridgeshire

Yours to serve you *John Barbor*
Hartford August 26, 1645

**(*On reverse*)** For Colonel Alban Coxe these present

**[54] HALS: 70548 Committee of Hertford to Alban, Coxe 27/8/1645**

Collonel Coxe
Wee having received certaine informacon this morninge from Collonel Michell given notice of the enemies marchinge to Bedford the last night, and that ~~you~~ wee are desired by some of the inhabitants of Hitchin to send some forces thither for there asistance, which towne with the partes adjacent, wee apprehend are now most in danger. Wee therefore (uppon debate of the bussiness) conceive itt most conduceinge to the Counties safety that you remove your regiment to ~~Stevenage~~ Hitchin and the townes next adjoyninge or to such places (as by the intelligence of the enemies mocon) may bee more advantagious for our Countries defence, provided that you doe not expose them too much upon the Champion[172] for feare of sudden supprisall. Wee desire your care and vigilancie to take all opportunities and advantages and to acquaint us with what intelligence comes to you. What comes to ~~you~~ us wee shall impart to you both intelligence and advice, and shall remaine: Your loveinge freinds
*Joseph Dalton Mayor, Isaac Puller, George Banestre, Gabriell Barbor, William Carter, Thomas Meade, William Plumer*

Hartford 27th August 1645
**(*On reverse*)** For our loveinge freind Collonel Alban Coxe these att his quarters

**[55] HALS: 70550 Silius Titus to Alban Coxe, 27/8/1645**

Sir,
I am at Curricot,[173] and desire to heare from you with as much speed as may be. My horses have had pretty large marches this weeke and to day we were called to Luton by a verie strong alarum,[174] which will make this dayes march

[172] The champion or open country, which was unfenced or without hedges
[173] Probably Codicote between Luton and Welwyn
[174] This was probably as a result of royalist cavalry infiltration from Buckinghamshire into South Bedfordshire

longest ere we joyne. I desire that you would sende me orders where I shall quarter, and where I shall have the good fortune to meet with your self. I beseech you, to hasten and despatch this far.

Your Obliged Servant

August 27th 1645 *S Titus*

For his much honoured friend Collonel Cox

**[56] HALS: 70553 Hertford Committee to Coxe, 31/10/1646**

Noble Colonell,
It is still our desires that you would bee att Bury[175] on Tuesday next. But for Instruccions, wee knowe not what your busines will bee and therefore desire you to use your owne discrecon in what shall bee propounded either for matter of government or any thinge els for our Countyes good. There is none on this side to bee there, therefore wee desire your greater care in the busines that shall bee there acted. And rest your very loveinge freinds
*Gabriel Barbor, William Prestley, Thomas Tooke,[176] Thomas Meade, Isaac Puller, Joseph Dalton*
Hertford 31st October 1646

**[57] HALS: 70557 Silius Titus to Alban Coxe from Durham[177] 3/2/1646(7)**

Sir,
The usuall post not coming through St Albans it discouraged me to write to you because my newes upon necessitie must grow old in the conveyance. Nor

[175] Bury St Edmunds Suffolk, where the Committee of the Eastern Association was to meet
[176] Thomas Took(e) and his brother John of Wormley were both put on the county assessment committee in October 1644. Their father, also Thomas, was auditor of the Court of Wards and had been the muster master for the county in the 1630s, and became a Royalist, disinheriting two sons, the elder brother John having married the daughter of Sir Thomas Dacres in 1638. However their brother George married a daughter of Thomas Coningsby the Royalist. Thomas inherited through his brothers the manors of Wormley, Popes Park, Essendon and Holbeaches Hatfield, was put on the Eastern Association Committee and became a county JP [HALS: Pegram, A W, 'Descriptive list on Title Deeds of Wormley Manor', Typed MS 1962; *VCH Herts* III, pp91-111, 458-62, 487-90; Daniell, H C N, 'Popes Manor Essendon with a note on Edlins', *East Herts Archeological Society Transactions*, VII, pp148-60 (1924); Bushby D, *Wormley in Herts* (London, 1954) pp47, 52]
[177] Titus was part of the English force at Durham which had collected the King from the Scots Commissioners who handed him over at the end of the First Civil War

can any letter yet come to you till it hath visited many shires, and past at the least 20 stages[178]. However (Sir) I must be as good as my worde and tell you that wee are now attending the king to Holmeby[179] and expect to be there (*Jus Fortunantibus*)[180] on Munday the I5 of this instant. God grant the journie may defeat bad mens hopes and good mens feares; but sincerely as yet (for anything we can collect from the kinges comportment and expressions) there is as little hope of compliance nowe as ever, and his language I thinke is no much altered from what it was before Naseby.[181] Pray take the paines to come with Captain Cocke to Holmeby and then I shall (besides the accompaning you backe) tell you something will not be altogether fit to write though I care not how publique I make the professions of being[182]
Sir, Your most affectionate humble servant *S Titus*
Durham February 3rd 1646

**(*On folded section at right angles*)** To his honoured freinde Collonel Cox
Deliver this at the Bull in St Albans to be sent as above

## Part 5 The secretariat and communications

### [58] TNA: SP28/231 Anthony Mowry's account as secretary to the Militia Committee, 30/3/1643(4)[183]

March 30th 1643 An Account for writinge for the Committee

| | |
|---|---|
| In primis for writinge 50 warrants for horse | 01 00 00 |
| For writinge out warrants for the £900 | 00 05 00 |
| For attending upon the Committee at Hitchin | 00 04 00 |
| For attending upon the Committee at Stephenage being to | |

[178] This is a comment on the slowness of the post stages established up and down the Old North Road from Newcastle to London
[179] Holmby or Holdenby House in Northamptonshire was decided upon as the place where the King would be lodged while post war negotiations continued
[180] According to fortune's law
[181] Before the battle of Naseby in June 1645- i.e. the King, despite being defeated, had not changed his attitude
[182] This could be interpreted as meaning that he was more sympathetic to the King, something he could not write. Later the same year he was to defect to the Royalist cause
[183] This is probably March 1644 as the committee was not called the militia committee until December 1643

| | |
|---|---|
| compleate the Black Regiment[184] | 00 04 00 |
| For attending uppon the Committee at Ware | 00 04 00 |
| For attending uppon the Committee at Buntingford | 00 04 00 |
| For att<end>ing uppon the Committee divers severalle times at Hertford | 00 10 00 |
| Summ is | 02 11 00 |

To Mr Turner Treasurer
You are required to pay unto Anthony Mowry, clerke to Collonel Washington, fifty one shillings, and this shall bee your discharge ~~date~~ given under our hands this $30^{th}$ of March
*Gabriel Barbor, John Fowler, William Carter, Thomas Niccolls, Adam Washington, William Burre, John Kensey Esq.*

**[59] TNA: SP28/231 Adlord Bowd's bill to Hertford Committee, 22/8/1644**

| | |
|---|---|
| Adlord Bowd his bill | |
| July $2^{nd}$ 1644 Item 3 dayes writeing letters to the gentlemen of the country to borrow money | 4s-0 |
| July $19^{th}$ 1644 Item for writeing 3 long warrants to raise money to pay the regiments | 1s |
| August 1st Item for writeing 3 long warrants for money to rayse 500 foote and 100 light horse and dragoons | 1s |

The treasurer, Mr Turner, is required to pay Adlord Bowd the somme of six shillings - I say *vis* *Gabriel Barbor* Chairman

August $22^{nd}$ 1644
Received of Mr Turnor in full of this bill the somme of six shillings. I say received $o^{li}$: $6^{s}$. $0^{d}$ *Adlord Bowde*

[184] This would indicate that the formation of the Black Regiment of militia volunteers was completed sometime in March 1643, and this and subsequent items suggest that the Committee had been active in different towns, not just meeting in Hertford

**[60] TNA: SP28/231 Adlord Bowd's second bill, 16/9/1644**

Adlord Bowde his bill
September 16th 1644 Item for writeing 4 longe warrants to warne the country to bringe in horses 00 00 08
October 2nd Item for writeing 3 warrants upon assessment 00 00 03
October 4th Item for writyeing 6 long warrants for the apprehending of the imprest souldyers that run away from theyr colours 00 01 00
November 15th Item for writeing 26 warrants to send out to warne in horses for the safety of the County 00 02 02
November 22nd Item for for writeing 20 warrants for Captain Carter to send to severall townes to rayse his foote companys 00 01 08
November 2nd Item for writeing 12 warrants for Captain Dagurs[185] to send to several townes for him to pay his foote company 00 01 00
00 06 09
Mr Turnor treasurer is required to pay Adlord Bowd in full of this bill the some of *vis ixd* I say *vis ixd Gabriel Barbor* Received per me *Adlord Bowde*

3
26
20
12
61 at 1d =5s 1d
10 at 2d+ 1s 8d
6s 9d[186]

**[61] TNA: SP28/232 Bevis'[187] bills for stationary supplies, 5/8/1645**

| Thomas Bevis his Bill | s d |
|---|---|
| For quills | 01 04 |
| For a pynte of inke | 01 04 |

[185] Probably Captain William Dawges
[186] This sum, jotted at the bottom of the paper, indicates that Bowde was paid 1d for writing an ordinary warrant and 2d for a long warrant
[187] Thomas Bevis personal clerk to Barbor was in 1652 to be the treasurer for the eastern part of the county for the repayment of loans and in 1656 was clerk to the Decimation Tax Committee, also acting as a witness to a will in Hertford in 1658 and as overseer of another in 1661 when he was styled 'gent'. He was assessed for six hearths in St Andrews, Hertford in 1663 [TNA: E179/248/23 *f*121; SP28/197 Pt II *ff*6-18, 22-3; Adams, *Hertford Wills,* pp3, 4, 5, 10]

| | |
|---|---|
| For wax[188] | 00 05 |
| For quills | 00 10 |
| For hay at Hatfield for my horse | 00 02 |
| For a letter from Ware which came from Cambridge | 00 03 |
| To a porter that brought letters from the Committee of Both Kingdoms sent by Mr Leman about the raysing out of one of our regiments | 06 00 |
| For a pynte of inke | 00 03 *ob* |
| Paid for a letter to the committee from Ware | 00 04 |
| Paid for wax 6d | 00 06 |
| Paid for quills | 00 04 *ob* |
| Paid for quills | 00 06 |
| For a pynt of inke | 00 03 *ob* |
| Paid for bringing a letter from St Albans | 00 06 |
| For laces[189] | 00 05 *ob* |
| | 11 02 |

5 August 1645
Mr Turner is to pay this summe of eleaven shillings twoe pence to Thomas Bevis *Gabriel Barbor*

Received the said summe of *xis iid* by mee *Thomas Bevis*

**[62] TNA: SP28/232 Petition of Thomas Bevis, clerk to the Hertford Militia Committee, 1/1/1646(7)**

*f1r* Gentleman,
You may please to bee informed that about 2 years and 8 monethes since,[190] when I came first to Hertford, tymes were exceeding troublesome and daingerous and ther were many alarums, which made mee very full of imployment. In soe much that I have sitten upp 2 or 3 sometymes 4 nights in a week till 2 and sometimes till 4 of the clock in the morning and other tymes I have risen att 4 in the morning to wright warrants for the militia committee and other things, the particulars I cannot well remember it being soe longe since, And this was done by me att my master's house for the space of one

[188] Wax for sealing letters
[189] Laces to tie papers together. Examples of this exist in the SP28 series boxes for Hertfordshire
[190] In about May 1644

whole yeare and a halfe, by my master's[191] command, (hee being chaireman), and all had recourse to him in the night and at all other tymes in the committee's absence, for which I received not any satisfaccion, thinking indeed that there had not bin any allowance for the same.

But att your last full meeteing heare, I understood that there was an ~~salareye~~ allowance of £13 per quarter to the clerke, of which I received not one penny, in regard I was not taken notice of by you, because the third parte and more of what I did <for you> was done att my master's house by his command as aforesaid I being then, only clarke to the other Committee visibly. But if I had not done the business, it must have bin lefte undone, unles hee that was in pay had bin sent for,[192] which you knowe could not bee with convenience or that hee had hyred one to doe it for ~~hence~~ which was never done.

And further when Alarums were frequent  I have hardly gone into my naked bed, for a whole weeke together because I have bin forced to rise divers tymes in a night to wright warrants and letters, and to answere other letters, which to my master as chaireman and the clerke that received the pay felt none of this.

And when the Country hath bin raised <suddenly> I, not another, have sometymes written above 100 particular warrants to all the petty constables in these 3 divisions[193] and handed[194] them and sent them away.

Likewise then I writt above halfe the warrants upon the militia rates before the printed blanck warrants were invented,[195] for they would come dropping in almost every day, some to my master's house as they doe now with other rates, which was farr greater labour then it is because nowe I have blanckes, and then I writt them wholly and handed them in your absence.

The Clarke which was then paid did most of the business on Fridays when hee was here, but I did it on all the dayes in the weeke besides and yet hee was not

---

[191] Gabriel Barbor see Appendix
[192] This was probably either Anthony Mowry or Adlord Bowd
[193] These were the three taxation divisions of the hundreds of Hertford and Braughing, Edwinstree and Odsey and Broadwater and Hitchin
[194] 'Handed' meant put my hand to them, i.e. signed them
[195] Printed warrants were later produced into which clerks only had to insert a few details by hand instead of writing them all out individually longhand

here every Friday neither, and then likewise I did it in his absence for all which I received nothinge.

If hee had done his service for nothinge, I should not have desired any thing for myne, which was farr exceeding his, both in wrighting and being deprived of my rest and sleepe many tymes and often. But since hee had such a competent allowance as is afore menconed, I hope you will please to thinck mee worthy of some reward. And I shall thanckfully accept of what you shall please soe to bestowe upon mee and rest your faithfull and ready servant
*Thomas Bevis*
$1^{st}$ January 1646

Likewise I have then coppyed out most of the letters that came in the tymes of Alarums (to informe this Committee of the enemyes mocons) and have sent them (by my Masters command) to St Albans, and to the Colonells sometimes and at other tymes to the Committee of both Kingdoms etc. and Cambridge and many other services which I doe not perfectly remember.

### [63] TNA: SP28/231 The Widdow Faireman's[196] bill re stabling horses, 27/9/1644

<u>From March 22 1643(4) to May 14 1644 The widdowe Fairemans Bill</u>

| | £ s d |
|---|---|
| For the blacke mares standinge at hay in her stable seaven weekes and foure dayes at three shillings ye weeke comes just to | 01 03 00 |
| And for oates the which shee had in that time they beinge three bushels three peckes and an haufe at five groates the bushelle[197] comes to | 00 06 $05^{1/2}$ |
| The mare being absent a weeke and foure dayes within that time above mentioned theire is to be abated | 00 05 00 |
| And then the bill comes just to $1^{li}$-$4^{s}$-$5^{d-}$*ob*$^{ob}$ | |
| Likewise for her own nagg goeinge out to Starfurd and to | |

[196] Lucy Fair(e)man, despite her sex, was listed in the Hertford Freemen's List of 1648 as a brewer [Greening, A, 'Needful and necessary men'?: Hertford Borough Freemen 1640-1715', in Jones-Baker, D, (ed) *Hertfordshire in History: papers presented to Lionel Munby*, (Hertford, 1991) p186]

[197] A groat was a silver coin worth 4d and there were 4 pecks to a bushel, hence the sum.

| | |
|---|---|
| Watfourd with Goodman Kinge[198] upon the Committes businesse | 00 03 00 |
| Summa Toto | 01 07 05$^{1/2}$ |

Mr Turner is to pay this bill of *xxvii$^{s}$, v$^{d}$ ob,* being due for a bussynes belonging to the Millicia; wee say 1$^{li}$- 7$^{s}$ 5$^{d}$
*Gabriel Barbor, Joseph Dalton, Maior, Thomas Niccolls, Daniel Nicoll, George Banastre, Henry Marsh , John Finch*

Received in full for this bill September 27 1$^{li}$- 7$^{s}$- 5$^{d}$ *William Faireman*

**[64] TNA SP28/231 John Andrews[199] bill, 3/10/1644**

<u>8 of August to the third of October 1644</u>

| | |
|---|---|
| *Inprimis*: 9 days to Lincolne[200] with letters to the Earle of Manchester with letters at 3s *per diem* | 01 07 00 |
| 2 days to London with letters to the Lords at 3s per day | 00 06 00 |
| 1 day with warrants to impresse at 3s *per diem* | 00 03 00 |
| 2 days to London with letters to Mr Love[201] | 00 06 00 |
| 1 day with warrant to the high constables for bringeinge in runaway soldiers[202] | 00 03 00 |
| 1 day to the high constables and other plases for the militia meetings | 00 03 00 |
| 1 day for goeinge to Waterford and Hatfeild | 00 03 00 |
| 2 days to Alsbury with two soldiers[203] | 00 06 00 |
| Layd out for diet for the soldiers | 00 01 06 |

[198] This is probably John King(e), grocer of Hertford, nephew of William Turner, later a prominent Quaker who was assessed for three hearths in All Saints Hertford in 1663 [TNA E179/248/23 *f*121; Rowe, *Hertford Quakers*, pp55-6]

[199] This may be Captain Andrewes, later in Newport Pagnell Garrison [Tibbutt, *Luke's letter Book*, pp1233, 1238]

[200] Eastern Association forces under Manchester were travelling through Lincolnshire following the fall of York on 16$^{th}$ July [Ian J. Gentles, 'Montague, Edward, second Earl of Manchester (1602-1671)', *NewDNB*]

[201] William Love, a committeeman, was putting pressure on the Commons on behalf of the Militia Committee

[202] Runaway soldiers were a particular problem when men left their posts to get in the harvest in late summer

[203] Aylesbury garrison needed a steady number of new recruits to replace those dying or deserting

| | |
|---|---|
| ~~6 days to Cambridge and Lincolne with letters~~ | ~~00 18 00~~ |
| 1 day to St Albans with letters to the Committee | 00 03 00 |
| 1 day with warrants for the horses to come in | 00 03 00 |
| Layd out at Hattfeild for horsemeate[204] and 3 mens dinners | 00 02 06 |
| 2 days to London with letters to the Earle of Manchester | 00 06 00 |
| 3 days to Huntington with the horses | 00 09 00 |
| 1 day to Hatfeild to Hatfeild (*sic)* to wayt on the Committee | 00 03 00 |
| Paid for the horses there | 00 01 02 |
| 2 days to the Earle of Manchester to Maydenhead | 00 06 00 |
| Layd out for sendinge warrants for the months tax | 00 00 06 |
| 3 days to Readinge[205] with the dragoone horses | 00 09 00 |
| Totall $5^{li}$:$01^{s}$:$08^{d}$ | 05 01 08 |

Mr Turner you are required to pay John Andrews the summe of five pounds on shillings eight pence and this shall be your warrant.
We say the sum e of £$5^{li}$: $01^{s}$: $8^{d}$
*Gabriel Barbor, Joseph Dalton, Maior, William Love, Thomas Meade. Thomas Michell, William Carter, William Plomer*

Received of Mr Turner the sum of $5^{li}$-$1^{s}$-$8^{d}$ the 16 of October 1644 by me
*John Andrews*

**[65] TNA: SP28/232 Bill for Clarke[206], Daltons and King re work for Hertford committee, 1/8/1645**

John Clarke, Morrice Dalton, Daniell Dalton,[207] and John Kinge theire bill the $1^{st}$ of August as followeth viz:
John Clarke and Maurice Dalton
For fetching of souldiers to Hartford that ran from there colours as they marched from Northamton towards Lester ~~for Daniell Dalton for the like~~ for foure daies £1-4s

[204] Horsemeat meant fodder or food for horses, not the meat of horses

[205] Hertfordshire troops were sent to reinforce the garrison at Reading to protect traffic along the Thames from royalist attack as Manchester did not reach there until the end of September [Ian J Gentles, 'Montague, Edward, second Earl of Manchester (1602-1671)', *NewDNB*]

[206] John Clarke had been made free of Hertford Borough and an assistant in 1639, was a chief burgess 1645-80, Mayor 1649, 1659 and 1670 as well as an Alderman 1680-4. He therefore managed to survive the Restoration, being assessed for eight hearths in 1663 and dying in 1684 [Information from Alan Greening]

[207] Possibly sons of Joseph Dalton, Mayor of Hertford

For one day for Morris Dalton and his brother for carringe out of warrants for our horses <which> went to Bedford the first day ~~one day~~ 6s
For Morris Dalton and John Kinge for caringe out of warrants for our horses when wee went to Bedford the last time 2 daies 12s

For Morris Dalton for one day for carriage out of Prockelamations for souldiers to ride the horses that Leuetenant Randall conducted to the army 3s
Some is 45s

Mr Turner Treasurer you are to pay this above bill of £2-5s to John Clarke that he may paie him selfe and the others and this shalbe your warrant given under our hands this firste of Auguste 1645 *Gabriel Barbor, Joseph Dalton, Maior, George Banstre, Thomas Meade, William Plumer, William Carter, John Fowler*

**(*On reverse*)** Reseaved by mee John Clarke the some of two pounds five shillings of Mr Turner Treasurer. I say reseaved the some of £12-05s-00d

## Part 6 Fortification of Newport Pagnell, St Albans and Hertford

### [66] TNA: SP28/230 St Albans Committee order re money for Newport Fortification,[208] 3/11/1643

St Albans *in Comitatu* Hertford November 3 1643
Theise are to desire you to pay out of the <treasury for the> 5 and 20 part and out of the treasury for association money <in St Albans> in the sum of two hundred pounds which if you shall want in those said treasuries, the said sum that you borrow out of the treasury for the Earle of Manchesters foot to make

[208] Newport Pagnell was taken from the royalists in late 1643 and on 8 November it was decided to send the Hertfordshire Regiment, then at Luton, to join those in Middleton's and other regiments to garrison it. The sums allocated for fortification anticipated the December Ordinance which fixed Hertfordshire contribution at £150 and £500 a month for maintenance. A further 125 troops were to be sent from the County and later Sir John Norwich joined the garrison [Roundell, H, 'The garrison of Newport Pagnell during the civil wars, (Pt 1) *Records of Buckinghamshire,* Vol. II, 5, (Aylesbury, 1861) pp206-216]

it up to be repaid upon account out of the 5 and 20 part.[209] Any sum you are to pay over to John Pollard Esq. dwellinge at Leckhamsteed in Buckinghamsheire, or in his absence, to Collonel Terrell now at Newport,[210] and to take accompt under theire hands, being that part <of Hertfordshieres> apportioned by the Committees of the Countyes of Northampton, Bucks, Bedford and Herts agreed one at theire meting at St Albons, the first November, according to the order of the houses[211] for the makeing up of the fortifications at Newport and for that so doing this shall be your warrant. Given under our hands the date abovesaid
*John Robotham, John Pemberton, Johes King, Raphe Pemberton Esq.*

To William Hickman Treasurer for the hundreds of Caishoe and Decorum

**(*On reverse*)** November 4 1643
Receaved the same day of William Hickman the some of two hundred pounds accordinge to the within menconed order towards the fortifications att Newport Pagnell.
I say received £200 *Thomas Tyrrill.*

**[67] TNA: SP28/230 St Albans Committee order to pay Adjutant English for fortifications in St Albans,[212] 10/11/1643**

St Albans in *Comitatu* Hertford 10th November 1643
These are to desire you to pay unto Adjutant <General> English[213] twenty five pounds six shillings and eight pence out of the 5th and 20th part treasury for the payment of the workemen for the works about St Albans according to his Excellencys warrant. And that you reimburse yourself againe out of the moneys raysed in the County for the fortifications of the said towne and for your soe doing this shalbe your warrant. Given under our hands the day and yeare abovesaid.

---

[209] This piece of creative accounting suggests a dire shortage of hard cash
[210] The new garrison at Newport Pagnell, Bucks, which was jointly financed by four counties
[211] The House of Commons had ordered on 30 October that the standing committee at St Albans should attend the Lord General at St Albans to consult with others and receive directions concerning 'placing and settling a garrison at Newport' [*CJ* III, p295]
[212] According to Toms the defences were made strong near St Peter's Church and near St Stephens and Essex made the pillory movable so that it could be set up in the parts of the town where the army was billeted [Toms, *St Albans*, pp101-2]
[213] An adjutant-general was an officer who assisted superior officers in the details of a duty, in this case, organizing the details of fortification

*John Robotham, Johes King, Tobie Combe, Raphe Pemberton Esq.*
To William Hickman Treasurer

**(*On reverse*)** Received this 10th November 1643 in full of this order within written the summe of twenty five pounds six shillings eight pence £25-6s-8d
Per me *Jacob Culenburgh* Cijf Ingenieur 1643[214]

**[68] TNA: SP28/230 St Albans Committee order re payment of workmen's bill for making St Albans defences, 16/12/1643**

Theise are to authorize you William Hickman Treasurer to pay unto Robert Michell and Richard Chamberlayne etc. for the making of ~~fower~~ five pole[215] and a quarter of breast works[216] towards the fortifications of St Albans the some of thirty six shillings nine pence and for that so doing ~~you~~ this shall be your warrant dated this 16 December 1643
*Johes King, John Robotham, Raphe Pemberton*

**(*On reverse*)** Received this 16 December 1643 in full of this order within written thirty six shillings nine pence £1-16s-9d
Robert ***X*** Michells marke Richard ***R*** Chamberlayne marke
Orders for the fortification of St Albans

**[69] TNA: SP28/230 St Albans committee order to pay Colonel English re fortifications at St Albans, 19/12/1643**

Theise are to will and require you William Hickman Treasurer to pay unto Collonell Anglis[217] out of the monies for the fortifications towards the works the some of foure pounds five shillings and for you so doing this shall be your warrant dated 19 December 1643 also pay unto the said Collonell more five pounds, in all the some of nine pound five shillings and this shall be your warrant *Johes King, John Robotham, Raphe Pemberton Esq.*

**(*On reverse*)** Receaved upon the full of this order nyne pounds fyf shillings the 19th of this instant December 1643 *David Inglis*

---

214 English had employed as his chief engineer for the works a Dutch military expert.
215 A pole was 5 ½ yards or just over 5 metres in length
216 Breast works were breast high fortifications for defence
217 I am assuming that Inglis, Anglis and English are the same person and, as he may have been a Scot, there was some confusion over his name and rank

Theise are to authorize you to pay to Jacob Cullumburgh Chife Ingineer the somme of twenty five pounds six shillings eight pence out of the money that is come in for the fortifications of St Albans, which sum is the second payment towards the works and for the so doing this shall be your warrant dated this 17 November 1643
*John Robotham, Tobie Combe, Raphe Pemberton Esq.*

To William Hickman Treasurer

**(*On Reverse*)**Received this 17 November 1643 in full of his noate the sum within specified being the summe of twenty five pounds six shillings eight pence being the second payment of the 2/3 towards the fortifications of St Albans *Per me Jacob Culenburgh* Chijf Ingenyeur 1643
Dit is op yet threed derds vart outfang [218]

**[70] TNA: SP28/230 St Albans Committee order to pay Jacob Culumber for fortifications of St Albans, 22/12/1643**

St Albans December 22nd 1643
These are to desire you William Hickman to pay unto Captain Jacob Culumber Engineer for the finishing of two redoubts[219] consisting of 39 poles together called No 1 and No 5 the remainder of the summe which comes to £14.7s.8d and this shalbe your warrant.
*Johes King, John Rowbotham, Raphe Pemberton*

**(*On reverse*)** Received this 22nd December 1643 in full of this order within written foureteene pounds seaven shillings ~~foure~~ eight pence £14-7s 8d
*Per me Jacob Culenbourgh* Chijf Ingenieur 1643

**[71] TNA: SP28/230 St Albans Committee order to pay John Branch for fortifications of St Albans, 23/12/1643**

Theise are to require you William Hickman Treasurer for the hundreds of Caishoe and Dacorum upon the sight hereof to paye unto John Branch for 8 dayes worke and a halfe twelve shillings and seven pence for rayles, planck

[218] This note in Dutch implies it is the second of three instalments to be paid him for the fortifications work
[219] A redoubt was a square or multisided extension of a fortification. 39 poles would be about 200 metres of fortification

nayles and for a lock ymployed about the turnpikes[220] at Hollowell and New Lane alias Cock Lane and for setting up a litle howse there for the Court of Guard[221] eighteene shillings and tenn pence in the whole the some of *xxxis* 8d. And for your soe doeing this shalbe your warrant *John Pemberton,*[222] *John Robotham*

**(*On reverse*)** Received this 23 December 1643 in full of this order within written thirty one shillings eight pence *xxxis viijd Per John Branch*

### [72] TNA: SP28/231 St Albans Committee order to pay English's bill for fortifications at St Albans, 3/1/1643(4)

These are to authorize you William Hickman treasurer to pay to Lieutenant Colonell English the summe of £9 12s 6d to be paid (out of the money for the works) for the two redoutes in Mrs Powells and John Cullets grounds, And for your soe doing this shalbe your warrant. Given under our hands the 3rd of January 1643

To William Hickman Treasurer
*Johes King, John Robotham, Raphe Pemberton Esq.*

Receaved in full of this order nyne pound twelff shillings 6 pence
*David Inglish*

**(*On Reverse*)** Adjutant Anglis 9-12-6
Fortifications of St Albans 12 of them *£ix xiis vid*

---

[220] A Turnpike was a spiked barrier fixed across a road as a defence against sudden attack by horsemen. Holywell Hill goes south to St Stephens, and Cock Lane ran east from the southern end of St Peter's Street

[221] A Court of Guard was a guard house or sentry box

[222] John Pemberton was the eldest son of Roger Pemberton of St Albans. He had been the county treasurer for the western side of the county in 1637. He served on the Assessment Committee from March 1643 and the Sequestration Committee from June. He married Elizabeth Audley, widow, but died by April 1645 leaving an elder son of the same name and a second son Robert. The younger John then sat on the Assessment Committees for the county and Liberty from 1647-9 [HALS: QSB2A *f*210d; *Herts Vis*, p81; *LJ* VI, p76; F&R I, pp119, 967, 1084; II, pp36, 300]

**[73] TNA: SP28/230 William Gardiner's bill for fortifications etc. in Hertford, 28/1/1644(5)**

William Gardiner his bill January 28th 1644

| | £ s d |
|---|---|
| Item for taffitye ribbin for the Militia booke | 00 01 00 |
| Item for mending the drum to set the guard at night | 00 04 00 |
| Layd out for 92 souldyers a day for 2 dayes of exercises | 00 08 00 |
| Layd out on the workmen that fild the workes about the towne at severall times | 00 05 00 |
| For my paines in overseeing the workmen in filling and making upp the workes about the towne | 00 12 00 |
| | 01 10 00 |

Mr Turner you are required to pay this bill being *xxxs* out of the monies for raysing horse and foote and this shalbe your warrant *xxxxs*

*Gabriel Barbor, Joseph Dalton Maior, Thomas Meade*

Received in full of this bill the somme of one pound ten shillings. I say received *per me William Gardiner* £1-10s

**[74] TNA: SP28/230 John Holland's[223] bill re fortifications at Hertford, 6/2/1644(5)**

John Holland, his bill for worke and stuffe about the turnpikes and the sentinel howses and the bullwarkes[224]

| The 6 February 1644 | £ s d |
|---|---|
| Item: for 400 of board to board in the Old Crosse[225] | 01 13 04 |
| Item: for 7 studs[226] for it | 00 04 06 |
| Item: for a doore stud and a grunsell and a foyle[227] | 00 02 06 |
| Item: for 3 posts and other pieces of timber for the turnstile[228] and turnpike by the old crosse | 00 08 00 |

[223] John Holland a carpenter lived in All Saints parish and had taken on an apprentice in 1639 He became a borough assistant in 1650. [HALS: HBR26 *f*51]

[224] Sentinel houses were guard houses or sentry boxes, and bulwarks were defensive fortifications, in this case of wood, normally with earth behind

[225] The remains of Old Cross in Hertford

[226] A stud is an upright timber or support

[227] A grunsell, was a groundsel or ground-sill, a timber serving as a foundation to carry a wooden superstructure and a foyle was a flat thin piece of wood or metal

[228] A turnstile made of wood to allow in only foot passengers

| | |
|---|---|
| Item: for 2 posts for the turnstile against the tower[229] and 2 pieces for the stile | 00 05 00 |
| Item: for 4 posts for the pailing[230] against the tower | 00 02 00 |
| Item: for 25 pailes for the pailing of the Bullwarkes | 00 12 06 |
| Item for 120 pailes for the Bullwarkes | 00 10 00 |
| Item: for spares and other pieces to fasten in the railes and posts for the Bullwarkes | 00 07 06 |
| Item: for a post for the passage by old Northes[231] howse | 00 01 08 |
| Item: for 3 grunselles and 2 casserns[232] and 2 beames and 20 studs and 3 posts for the sentinel howse Mr Keilings Barne | 00 12 00 |
| Item: for 14 sparres for it | 00 05 00 |
| Item: for 30 of board for the top and sides of the howse | 01 15 00 |
| Item: for 3 studs and 330 foote of ½ inch board for the sentinel against Mr Barbors[233] howse | 00 02 10 |
| Item: 2 Mantell trees[234] for the chimneys in the old Crosse and the house of Mr Keilings | 00 02 08 |
| Item: for stuffe for 2 forms for the howses | 00 01 06 |
| Item: for worke of John Holland about this business | 01 00 00 |
| Item: for 6 days work of John Field | 00 09 00 |
| Item: for 13 dayes worke of John Pratt | 00 19 06 |
| Item: for 6 dayes worke of Edward Clarke[235] | 00 09 00 |
| Item: for 4 dayes worke and a halfe of Edward Gamblin | 00 06 00 |
| Item: for 6 dayes worke of John Younger | 00 07 00 |
| Item: for nails from Mr Turnors for this worke | 00 03 10 |
| Item: for 2 pair of hookes and hangers and nails from Abraham Rutts[236] | 00 06 04 |
| Item: for 2 pair of hookes and hangers and 2 lathes and 2 locks and nails from Goodman Downes[237] for this worke | 00 13 05 |

---

[229] This was the old tower of the castle

[230] Pailing or paling was fencing

[231] Mr Hugh North, the attorney, who was assessed at 10s for Ship Money in 1637 and reckoned to be able to spend £20 p.a. in the Poll Tax of 1641 [HALS: HBR46 *ff*908, 933]

[232] A casern was a small temporary building between the houses of a fortified town

[233] Gabriel Barbor's house

[234] A mantel-tree was a beam across the opening of a fire place supporting the masonry

[235] Field, Pratt and Clarke were all freemen carpenters of Hertford. Pratt became a borough assistant in 1642, Field in 1657, but had taken apprentices as early as 1640 [HALS: HBR25 *f*6; 26 *f*174 Chauncy, *Herts* I, p493]

[236] The ironmonger

[237] The blacksmith

| | |
|---|---|
| Item: for ironworke for 2 turnpikes and for greate nailes | 00 09 07 |
| Item: for 400 of bricks for the Chimneys from Goodman Yardleys[238] and for 50 tiles to mend the old cross | 01 06 10 |
| Item: for a quarter of lime and a load of clay and for sand to make chimineys and to mend the tileing on the old crosse | 00 07 00 |
| Item: for 4 dayes a piece of a bricklayer and a labourer about Making the chimineyes and mending the tileing | 00 10 00 |
| The somme is | 14 03 06 |

Mr Turner is required to pay John Holland this bill of *£xiiij iijs vid* out of the monies upon the ordinance of 500 foote and 100 horse. Wee say £14-3s-6d
*Gabriel Barbor, Joseph Dalton Maior, Thomas Meade*

Received of Mr Turnor in full of this bill the somme of fourteene pounds three shillings sixpence. I say received per me *£xiiij: iiis: vid* *John Holland*

**[75] TNA: SP28/231 Holland's bill re turnpikes in Hertford (undated 1645?)**

| John Holland his bill for mending the turnepickes | s d |
|---|---|
| Item for a part to mend the top of the turnepick near Master Bulles | -00-04 |
| For a post to stand in Master Bulles[239] garden and a raill over the top of it to stay horsemen | -02-00 |
| for a post for the turnpick near Thomas Fulches | -01-00 |
| for 2 railles and paillers[240] for the turnepicke near Master Kelling[241] garden | -01-00 |
| for nailles about them | -00-09 |
| for work about meanding of them | -03-06 |
| | 08-07 |

[238] The Yardley family were brickmakers from Brickendon Liberty. John Yardley senior was dead by 1678 and this may be his son, John Yardley junior, who was a witness to another carpenter's will in 1680 and an appraiser for an inventory in 1698 [Adams, *Hertford Wills*, pp83, 97; Information from Alan Greening]

[239] Either Richard Bull Senior gent, or his son, of the same name, who paid Ship Money in St Andrews parish in 1637-8 [HALS: HBR46 *ff* 907-8]

[240] Rails and pales i.e. the horizontal and vertical parts of a fence or barrier

[241] Either John Keeling Esq or the son of the same name who paid Ship Money in All Saints parish in 1637-8 [HALS: HBR46 *f*907] For the younger Keeling see Appendix

Mr Turner is desired to pay this bill being *viiis viid*
*Gabriel Barbor*

**[76] HALS: HBR9 *f*183 Information from the guard at Hertford, 22/7/1645**

John Harvey and John Cross came yester night about 9 of the clock quarrelling to the guard at the turnpike, being on foot, and would have them to unlock the turnpike and the guard bidd them stopp if they would in regard they had noe horses, whereupon the said Cross and Harvey did vapour[242] and quarrel with the guard, railing and vapouring in such a manner that John Daniells tapster[243] desired the watchmen to stoop to their humour by unlocking the turnpike which they did.

And then the said Cross thrust it too and shutt it againe And Cross and Harvey would not goe out of the towne, but returned back to the alehouse againe, and about 11 of the clock the same night they both came up the towne againe making a great noyse and singing base cavileeres songs. Whereupon Phillip Hoeye, standing sentinel[244] with his musket charged, bad them stand and demanded their names and their business at that tyme of the night and they obstinately denied to tell him or to stand, but came up desperately upon the said sentinelle and Crosse said I am a faire marke why doe you not shoote and came up and strived with the sentinel to take away his armes and if help had not bin, they had disarmed him. And hereupon the watch seized upon them, fearing they came to doe some mischiefe in the towne because they had been taken twice or thrice in a weeke formerlie in such a disorderly manner.

They the said Cross and Harvey strugled and swore and called them all manner of rogues, damned rogues, sonns of whores, And so wee forst they to come to Mr Barbor House, who rising from his sleepe, commanded them to the counter and by the way they rayled and called cropeared[245] rogues and said they had eares as long as asses, wearing the corporals band and Harvey swore many but wee (tried to) put them in prison, but they stirred and would have gone to the gaole contrary to the justices command, and said they could

[242] To vapour = to swagger or bluster

[243] A tapster= the man who drew or tapped the ale or beer in an alehouse or inn

[244] Sentinel= sentry

[245] Cropeared refers to the custom of cropping, or having the hair cut short, so that the ears are conspicuous, as the Roundheads were supposed to cut their hair

have noe justice but wished the pox of God[246] might confound Mr Barbor and which words were spoken by Crosse and they swore divers bitter oaths, 6 a peece as Ben Bradly and George Bringford depose.

Henry Yates, Phillip Hodges, Thomas Crouch, Benjamin Bradly, Hezekiah Downes, John Pratt

*Gabriel Barbor*

# Section B Raising the money and paying the troops

## Part 1 The Propositions, loans and contributions

### [77] TNA: SP28/155 North Mymms parish account for The Propositions, 22/3/1644(5)

*f1* The Informations from North Mimmes brought in by us hereunder named The 22nd day of March *Anno domini* 1644 Thomas Fish, Arthur Hollingsworth, Thomas Pursey Insubscribed £126-5s-11d

*f 2* North Mymmes -An account of the charges of the abovesayd parish of Northmymmes raysed by Ordinance of Parliament upon the Propositions, weekly assessment, subsidies, 5th and20th part etc.

Propositions

| | |
|---|---|
| Mr John Grubbe[247] lent at London | £ s d |
| August. 6.1642 One Browne horse valued at | 10 10 00 |
| August.9.1642 Silver plate.96.oz at 5s-4d per oz | 25 14 04 |

[246] Probably either smallpox or syphilis

[247] John Grubbe gent, (c.1590-1647) son of Eustace (died 1642) and Constance Sheppard of Hockly, Bedfordshire, was admitted to Lincoln's Inn in February 1606-7. He had married Mary, daughter of William Preston of Childrick and had a son John Grubbe. The Grubbe family held the advowson of North Mymms Church. He was added to the County Committee in December 1643 and the Hertford and St Albans Assessment Committees in 1649. In 1643 he had been nominated by the Royalist sheriff, Coningsby, to be the constable at North Mymms but claimed he could not serve as constable, as he was serving on a committee for parliament and had moved out of the parish, probably to Shenley, where he was living when he left bequests to his grandson John [TNA: Probate (230 Fines); HALS: QSB2B *f*43d; Anon, *Lincoln's Inn Admissions*, p142; F&R I, pp356-8; II, pp36, 300; *Herts Vis*, pp59-60; *VCH Herts* II, pp251-61]

| | |
|---|---|
| John Roberts. Service | |
| October.27 1642 A gold ringe valued at | 05 10 10 |
| John Dell. Lent at London | |
| June.13.1643 I browne stoned horse valued | 14 10 00 |
| November 23. 1642 Paid to Dr. Kinge Mr Robottam and others by | |
| Mr Younger vicar a silver bowle | 02 12 00 |
| Mr Fish | 02 10 10 |
| Mr Brooke | 03 10 10 |
| | |
| Mr Pursey[248] | |
| John Rushley | 03 00 00 |
| John Nichols | 01 00 00 |
| John Redwell | 00 08 00 |
| Thomas Norris | 00 02 06 |
| Joseph Anderson | 00 03 00 |
| Richard Chappell | 00 08 00 |
| William Francis | 00 10 00 |
| Thomas Griggs | 00 50 00 |
| Robert Salter | 00 50 00 |
| Thomas Beech | 00 10 00 |
| Thomas Hill | 00 01 00 |
| John Jeames | 00 10 00 |
| Hugh Todde | 00 05 00 |
| John Dell | 01 10 00 |
| May.16.1643 | |
| John Howard | 01 00 00 |
| Richard May | 00 03 00 |
| Robert Timerton the elder | 00 02 06 |
| Which amounts to: | 17 15 00 |

[248] No sum is listed against Mr Pursey. He may have been allowed not to contribute in lieu of a fee as either an assessor or collector

**[78] TNA: SP28/154 Hemel Hempstead parish account for The Propositions etc., July 1641-14 February 1643(4)**

*f*1r Hemelhemsted
Moneys <and plate> lent upon the proposicons by the Inhabitants of Hemel Hemsted aforesaid and for the 5th and 20th parte and the review therof and paid as followeth-
Tobie Combs Esq 19 Aug 1642 to John Wollaston[249] and John Warner[250] in money and plate 50 00 00
Paid more then 29 November 1642 05 00 00
John Besowth[251] 5 August 1642 to Thomas Andrewes[252] and Towse[253] Treasurers 50 00 00
Mary Kinge widdowe 17th August to John Wollaston and Thomas Andrews 20 00 00
Also paid to William Turpin one of the commissioners for review of the 5 and 20th parte which shee gave freely towards the

---

[249] Sir John Wollaston, Thomas Andrewes, John Towse, and John Warner were all aldermen of London, who were treasurers at Guildhall appointed in June 1642 for the collection of money, plate and horses for the impending war. Wollaston was a political survivor, who though rather conservative, supported the more radical aldermen in setting up the London Militia Committee. He was a colonel of one of the six London militia regiments [Lindley, *Popular politics* pp176, 183-4, 199, 200 n7, 208 n46, 218]

[250] John Warner was the fourth Guildhall treasurer who was a wealthy colonial merchant, member of the Grocer's company, a puritan activist and one of the most radical aldermen on the London Militia Committee. He also was a third colonel of a city militia regiment, who fought at the first battle of Newbury and became a leading London Independent. An alderman in 1640 he served on the City Lands Committee 1642-6 and was Lord Mayor 1647-8. He became a lay trier, an elder and a representative on the London Provincial Assembly of the new Presbyterian Church. His sister Elizabeth married William Thompson, brother of Maurice, George and Robert *(see* Appendix) [Lindley, *Popular Politics,* pp46, 166, 176, 199, 200 n7, 201, 208 n46, 218, 224, 308 n13, 388, nn165-6 and 168, 389 nn171-2 and 174, 390]

[251] John Besouth had a shop in Hemel Hempstead in 1632 [Dacorum Borough Council: Hemel Hempstead Bailiwick Minute Book, I, *f*29]

[252] Andrewes, like Towse and Warner, was a radical puritan, active in promoting the London Militia Committee, on which the Hertfordshire version was later modelled. Andrewes had been a common councillor, sheriff of London, and a member of Simpson's Independent church. An active trader with the colonies, he invested heavily in the Irish Adventure, became an Alderman in 1642 and Lord Mayor in 1649 and in 1650-1. He also provided the army with arms and provisions [Lindley, *Popular Politics*, pp199 n2, 284, 388 nn165, 168, 389 nn169, 170-2, 174, 390 n181, 391 nn187-8]

[253] Alderman John Towse was a leading puritan activist in the Grocer's company who managed the new Common Council elections in 1641 and was colonel of a city militia regiment [Lindley, *Popular Politics*, pp166, 176, 182, 199, 200 n7, 208 n46, 218, 308 n13]

buyeinge of horses for Colonell Cromwell[254] 01 00 00
Nathaniel Axtell paid to Thomas Oxton[255] and Raphe Gladman[256]
10 December 1642 03 00 00
Nicholas Stratford in money and plate att Guildhall 09 00 00
paid more to William Turpin toward horses for Colonel
Cromwell 00 10 00
Henry Turner 24th November for his 5 and 20th parte to William
Hickman Tresurer 01 00 00
Paid more to William Turpin upon reveiw 01 10 00
John Binn[257] of Eastbrookehaye 14th February 1643 for his 5 and
20th parte to William Hickman 05 10 00
John Nashe 15th August 1642 to John Towse and Thomas
Andrewes 10 00 00
John Gate 15 August <1642> to John Wollaston and John Towse 10 00 00
Francys Clarke July 1641 paid poll money[258] beinge an Attorney
to Roberte Pye and William Bell 03 00 00
paid more to William Turpin as a free guifte to Colonel
Cromwell 00 05 00
Richard Salter in money and plate to John Wollaston and
Thomas Andrewes 10 00 00
Henry Kinge[259] in money and plate to the same 10 00 00

---

[254] Cromwell was recruiting cavalry in West Hertfordshire when he arrested Coningsby in January 1643

[255] Thomas Oxton, (*d.* 1677) tanner, Chief Burgess in 1632, and Mayor of St Albans in 1636, 1644, 1656 and 1667, held office in the town for more than 40 years. He lived in a large house in Fishpool Street assessed for six hearths in 1663 [Chauncy, II, pp301, 303; Smith and North, *St Albans*, pp14, 46-7, 163, 169-70]

[256] Ralph Gladman, (*fl.* 1622-1670) baker, became a St Albans Borough Assistant in 1622 and a treasurer for the Propositions in 1642. A Chief Burgess in 1649 he became Mayor in 1652, and was responsible for securing the Borough Charter under the Commonwealth. He lost his place under the new Borough Charter after the Restoration. He had considerable wealth and at his death styled himself 'gent' He was then living in a large house in Holywell ward, with a parlour, containing a curtained bedstead, a table, 3 stools and 2 chairs, a pair of virginals in the hall and pictures in the chamber over it. In his inventory he listed six silver drinking vessels [Chauncy, II, pp301, 303, 304; Smith and North, *St Albans*, pp64, 183, 220, 241, 229-30]

[257] John Binn had been on the Bailiwick Jury in 1630 [Dacorum Borough Council: Hemel Hempstead Bailiwick Minute Book, I]

[258] The Poll tax levied in 1641 to pay for the Scots War

[259] Henry King, mercer in Hemel Hempstead since at least 1630, when he was on the Bailiwick jury, was put on the Hertfordshire Volunteer Committee in September and Militia Committee

| | |
|---|---|
| paid moiety to Mr Turpin- given to Colonel Cromwell | 00 10 00 |
| Samuell Sowthen in money and plate 18 August 1642 to John Towse and Thomas Andrewes | 20 00 00 |
| John Hull[260] in money and plate 1st November 1642 to John Warner and John Towse | 12 00 00 |
| Paid more to Mr Turpin given to Colonel Cromwell | 00 10 00 |
| | 243 15 00 |

| | |
|---|---|
| *f1v* Francys Hodges 7th October 1642 to John Warner and John Towse | 10 00 00 |
| paid more upon reveiew 3rd Junii 1644 to William Turpin | 01 00 00 |
| John Gaze 18 August 1642 in money and plate | 10 00 00 |
| Edward Wheeler for his 5 and 20th parte 11th November 1643 to William Hickman | 02 00 00 |
| paid more to William Turpin upon the reveiw | 00 10 00 |
| John Brandley 10 September 1642 to John Wollaston and John Warner | 03 00 00 |
| John Knight 7th October 1642 to John Warner and John Towse | 02 00 00 |
| John Field of Lovettsend 21 December <1642> to Thomas Oxton and Raphe Gladman | 05 00 00 |
| Mrs Marston Widdowe 24 August <1642> to the same | 10 00 00 |
| more lent 23 August and paid to the same | 05 00 00 |
| Nathaniell Wilkinson 24 January 1643 to William Hickman | 05 00 00 |
| Paid more <to> William Turpin upon review | 00 10 00 |
| William Marshall 11th November 1643 to William Hickman for his 5 and 20th parte | 03 15 00 |
| Nathaniell Field of the Hill, Clerke, 3rd February 1643 paid by John Binn to the same for his 5 and 20th parte | 08 00 00 |
| John Binn of the Wood 3rd Junii 1644 to William Turpin upon reveiwe for his 5 and 20th parte | 00 10 00 |
| John Mourton 7 October 1642 to John Warner and <John Towse> ~~Thomas Andr~~ | 05 00 00 |
| Abraham Crawley 11th October 1643 to John Wollaston and Thomas Andrewes | 03 02 08 |

in December 1643 [HALS: 20117; Dacorum Borough Council: Hemel Hempstead Bailiwick Minute Book, I; F&R I, pp289-91, 356-8]

260 John Hull had been paid by the burgesses of Hemel Hempstead for powder and match in 1641 [Dacorum Borough Council: Hemel Hempstead Bailiwick Minute Book, I, *f*59]

Paid more for his 5 and 20th parte to William Hickman 02 17 01
11th November 1643 paid more to William Turpin upon review 00 05 00
Jane Longe of Coppend widdowe 10 December 1642 to Thomas Oxton and Raphe Gladman 05 00 00
William Longe to the same then 10 00 00
Elizabeth Hill, widdowe to the same then £5
~~John Guston 24 Januarii 1643 to William Hickman 06 13 04~~[261]
~~Paid more upon review to William Turpin 30 May 1644 01 05 00~~
Total *(damaged)* 9

*f*2r Henry Sawcer, Attorney for Poll money 14 July 1641 to Robert Pye and William Bell 03 00 00
For Robert Sawcer his sonne the like 03 00 00
Lent more by the same Henry Sawcer and paid 8 April 1643 to Thomas Oxton and Raphe Gladman 05 00 00
Paid more 4th November for his 5 and 20th parte to William Hickman £2-10/-
Joseph Turner 3 August 1643 paid to John Warner and Thomas Andrewes £5
Grace Mitchell, widow, 24 January 1643 to William Hickman £2
Henry Rutland then to the same £5
Henry Keles 10 December 1642 to Thomas Oxton and Raphe Gladman £4
William Younge 17 November 1643 to William Hickman for his 5 and 20th parte £2
Henry Goodwyn 4 November 1643 to the same for his 5 and 20th parte £9
William Gould 17 November 1643 to William Hickman for his 5 and 20th parte £4
Paid more upon reveiew to William Turpin 3rd Junii 1644 £5
Christofer Besowth 11th November 1643 to William Hickman for his 5 and 20th parte £9
paid more upon reveiew to William Turpin £1
Jonathan Kinge 23 August 1642 in money and plate to John Wollaston and John Towse £10
Paid more to Mr Turpin which he gave to Colonell Cromwell toward raisinge of horses 10/-

[261] This was obviously inserted in the wrong place see below

| | |
|---|---|
| Jeames Rolfe 17th February 1643 to William Hickman for his 5 and 20th parte | £1-10/- |
| Paid more to William Turpin upon reveiew | 5/- |
| Henry Sallow 4 November 1643 to the same for his 5 and 20th Parte | £3 |
| Paid more into the hands of Francys Hodges Constable of the parish towards the raisinge of dragoones for the defence of the countye | £1-10/- |
| John Gunston 24 January 1643 to William Hickman | £6-13s-4d |
| paid more upon reveiew to William Turpin 30 Maii 1644` | £1-5/-[262] |
| £83-13s-4d | ~~£97-11s-4d~~ |

| | |
|---|---|
| *f2v* John Gladman[263] 17th February 1643 paid to William Hickman for his 5 and 20th parte | 07 00 00 |
| paid more to William Turpin upon review | 00 10 00 |
| Jeames Payne 4th November 1643 paid for his 5 and 20th parte | 04 00 00 |
| Paid more upon review to William Turpin | 00 10 00 |
| Nathaniell Field of Lovettsend Paid to William Hickman 10 November 1643 for his 5 and 20th parte | 06 00 00 |
| Widdowe Longe of Corner Hall paid to the same 3 February 1643 for her 5 and 20th parte | 02 10 00 |
| Thomas Hackett 10 April 1643 lent and paid to Thomas Oxton and Raphe Gladman | 02 00 00 |
| Paid more to William Hickman for his 5 and 20th parte | 04 10 00 |
| Paid more to the same for his 5 and 20th parte 13 February 1643 | 03 10 00 |
| Thomas Axtell 17th February 1643 paid to William Hickman for his 5 and 20th parte | 02 00 00 |
| Total | 456 18 01 |

*Henry Sallow, Christopher Besouth*

[262] See above for deleted item which is the same as this

[263] This is possibly the John Gladman who became a Captain in Cromwell's, then later Fairfax's regiment. In 1657 he was put on the Assessment Committee for Hertfordshire and in 1659 on the local Militia Committee [F&R, II, pp1058-97, 1320-42; Robert Zaller, 'Gladman, John (*fl.*1644-1685)', *NewDNB*]

**[79] TNA: SP28/155 Tewin parish account for the Propositions (undated 1642-3?)**

Tewine
The returne of the Inhabitants to the warrant sent by the Committee appointed to take the accompts to the said parish of Tewin

| Money advanced upon the Propositions and paid to Mr Humphrey Packer and Joseph Daulton | £ s d |
|---|---|
| *Imprimis* John Mynne Esq[264] | 05 00 00 |
| Edward North Senior gent | 20 00 00 |
| Thomas Gray | 04 00 00 |
| John Asser | 01 10 00 |
| Ellen Adams widow | 01 00 00 |
| William Bayford | 02 00 00 |
| Edward North | 02 00 00 |
| John Kimpton | 01 00 00 |
| Ralph Battell | 02 00 00 |
| William Mayes | 00 10 00 |
| Upon the Propositions | 39 00 00 |

**(*In the left hand margin*)** On the Propositions £114 00 00

| Money paid to Mr Gabriell Barber | | £ s d |
|---|---|---|
| John Mynne Esq for Gabriell Armstrong gent | | 50 00 00 |
| Money paid to Mr John Warner and John Towse | | |
| John Welsh | *Summa per* | 05 00 00 |
| | | |
| Money paid to Mr John Wolleston and Mr John Towse | | |
| Thomas Gray | *Summa per* | 10 00 00 |
| Listed by Thomas Gray one horse price | | 10 00 00 |
| *Summa totalis* | | 114 00 00 |

[264] John Mynne Esq of Tewin and King's Walden sent his son to three successive local schools, Richard Hale, Hertford, under Mr Minors, and schools at Rushden and Walden before gaining a place at Caius, Cambridge in 1646 [*Al Cant* 3, p231]

**[80] TNA: SP28/154 Redbourn parish accounts *f*1 for the Advance of the Scots and the Irish money, 1642-3**

<u>Moneys lent towards the advance of our brethren the Scotts 1643</u>

| | £ s d |
|---|---|
| *In Primis* lent by William Beaumont gent <and payd> into the hands of Thomas Cowley[265] and Thomas Oxton Treasurers *viii*$^{li}$ | 08 00 00 |
| *Item* lent by John Thewer[266] gent *xl*$^{s}$ | 02 00 00 |
| *Item* lent by William Dollinge *xl*$^{s}$ | 02 00 00 |
| *Item* lent by John Hayward of Beasmead[267] *xl*$^{s}$ | 02 00 00 |
| *Item* lent by John Dell x$^{s}$ | 00 10 00 |
| *Item* lent by Tymothie Axtill[268] *l*$^{s}$ | 02 10 00 |
| *Item* lent by John Hayward Woodend *l*$^{s}$ | 02 10 00 |
| *Item* lent by Daniel Kelsey[269] *x*$^{s}$ | 00 10 00 |
| *Item* lent by Jeremy Fynch *x*$^{s}$ | 00 10 00 |
| *Item* lent by George Carpenter[270] | 02 10 00 |
| *Item* lent by John Martin *v*$^{s}$ | 00 05 00 |
| *Item* lent by John Field *ii*$^{s}$*vid* | 00 02 06 |
| *Item* lent by Richard Kimpton *v*$^{s}$ | 00 05 00 |
| *Item* lent by Francis Wethered *ii*$^{s}$ | 00 02 00 |
| *Item* lent by Anthony Gotheram *ii*$^{s}$ *vid* | 00 02 06 |
| *Item* lent by Robert Beech *x*$^{s}$ | 00 10 00 |
| *Item* lent by Robert Whitely[271] *xv*$^{s}$ | 00 15 00 |
| *Item* lent by Bartholomew Band *iii*$^{li}$ *xv*$^{s}$ | 03 15 00 |
| *Item* lent by Saloman Trott[272] *v*$^{s}$ | 00 05 00 |

---

[265] For Thomas Cowley See Appendix

[266] John Thewer assessed at Digswell in 1636, said he had been unequally rated for Ship Money and refused to pay it. He was nominated to the Assessment Committee for the county in March 1643 [TNA SP16/376 *f*106; F&R, I, pp117-23]

[267] Beason End

[268] Axtill was the tenant of a 158 acre farm called Butlers [Munby, *Redbourn,* p22]

[269] A Daniel Kelsey took a 21 year lease of Fish Street Farm in 1692 [Munby, *Redbourn*, p26]

[270] There were a number of members of the Carpenter family, Anthony having just died in 1641. In 1634 William Carpenter, yeoman and his son Thomas had forcibly ousted Thomas Carpenter of Wheathampstaed, gent, from seven acres of land (Munby, *Redbourn*, pp39, 40, 72]

[271] Members of the Whitely family leased the Redbournbury Manor house plus 190 acres for £90 p.a. in 1654, and later bought 10 acres of former parkland for £450, the house having five hearths in 1663 and 10 identifiable rooms six years later [Munby, *Redbourn,* pp26, 38]

[272] A Thomas Trott had held 7 ½ acres of the Priory Manor in 1632 and Richard Trott was a collar-maker in the village [Munby, *Redbourn,* p23]

All the severall sommes above written were payd into the hands of Thomas Cowley and Thomas Oxton the receyvers above named

| For the Affayres in Ireland 1642 | £ s d |
|---|---|
| *In primis* payd by John Thewer gent to the propositions for the reducinge of the Rebells ther *£xxv* into the Chamber of London to the hands of John Towse, Thomas Andrewes and John Warner Treasurers[273] | 25 00 00 |
| Item payd by Robert Beech Churchwarden for the yeere of our lord 1643 for the poore Clergie in Ireland being the first gifte of the parish $i^{li}$ $vi^{s}$ into the hands of Zachary Kinge Treasurer | 01 06 00 |
| Item paid by Thomas Salter Churchwarden for the yeere of our Lord 1643 for a contribution for the whole of the poore people of Ireland $ii^{li}$ $x^{s}$ $x^{d}$ payd into the hands of John Kendrick and Benjamin Goodwin | 02 10 10 |

**[81] TNA: SP28/155 Tewin parish account for the advance of the Scots (1643?)**

Money payd for the advance of the Scotts to Isaack Puller and William Turner

| | | £ s d |
|---|---|---|
| For the Advance of the Scotts | Edward North Senior | 06 00 00 |
| 20li-11s 00d | Young Dixie[274] Clarke | 05 00 00 |
| | Thomas Gray | 05 00 00 |
| | John Asser | 00 05 00 |
| | William Blindell | 00 10 00 |
| | Ellen Adams and Thomas Shepheard | 00 16 00 |
| | Willam Bayford | 00 10 00 |
| | John Asser and Edward Welsh | 00 15 00 |
| | John Kimpton | 00 10 00 |
| | Ralph Battell | 00 05 00 |
| | Samuell Smart | 00 10 00 |

[273] Treasurers at Guildhall

[274] Young Dixie, (*b.* *c*1601-1664) the son of Wolstan Dixie, vicar of Brampton St Mary, Northamptonshire, having been to Emmanuel, Cambridge, became Rector of Cadeby Leicester and was then sequestered to Tewin on 27 July 1643, later returning to Leicester as minister at St Margaret's in 1659 [*Al Cant* Pt 1, III, p46]

| | | |
|---|---|---|
| | William Mayes | 00 10 00 |
| | Summa | 20 11 00 |

Money imposed and payd for the advance of the Scotts to Isaack Puller and William Turner

| | | £ s d |
|---|---|---|
| Imposed for the | {Mr Edward North Senior | 14 00 00 |
| advance of the Scotts | {Dr John Montfort | 15 00 00 |
| 39li 00s-00d | {Mr Edward North Junior | 10 00 00 |
| | Summa | 39 00 00 |

**[82] TNA: SP28/155 Bushey parish accounts –*f*1 various contributions and rates, 1643-4**

| | |
|---|---|
| Sammuell Hickman and Edward Broadgate in February 1643 collected for Sir Sammuell Luke[275] which was for two great nags | 11 18 04 |
| Roger Nuttkin collected £15 which was for carreinge for my Lord Generall, for workes about St Albones for salt peter[276] and for diverse things for his power | 15 00 00 |
| Another rate for 50 light horse and 50 dragoons in September 1644 | 11 16 00 |
| The parishioners of Bushey contributed towards the poore Protestants in Ireland the 19th of May 1643 was paid to Mauris Thompson[277] and John Kendricke the summe of | 09 00 00 |
| The 16th of May 1643 to Jeremy Sibley[278] our High Constable for the relieffe of the poore Protestants in Ireland | 21 10 08 |
| Subscribed for the reducinge of Wales | 09 00 00 |
| John Fyndall collected for the (levy) of horse and armes for the earle of Manchester about July 1643 | 46 11 10 |
| More about the same time for raysing of souldiers and armes for the parliament service | 44 09 06 |
| | 169 06 04 |

[275] For the garrison at Newport Pagnell

[276] Saltpetre- a key constituent of Gunpowder

[277] For Maurice Thomson, originally from Watton at Stone, see Valerie Pearl, 'Thomson, Maurice (1604-1676)', *NewDNB*

[278] Jeremy Sibley of Wheathampstead was High Constable of the Hundred of Dacorum from 1641-4 and later treasurer of the western half of the county from 1656. The Sibley family also held lands in Great Gaddesden and Studham [HALS: QSB2B *ff*29, 46; QSB3 *f*448d; *VCH Herts* II, pp274-80]

**[83] TNA: SP28/154 Charges of the Inhabitants of Redbourn for the Excise, 1643**

| | £ s d |
|---|---|
| *In primis* payd to William Beaumont gent for 1 yeeres | |
| excise for beere | 01 00 00 |
| and for flesh as he thinketh | 00 00 09 |
| *Item* payd by Tymothie Axtill | 00 10 00 |
| *Item* pad by Thomas Saunders[279] | 00 05 00 |
| *Item* payd by Robert Beech | 00 08 00 |
| *Item* payd by William Dolling | 00 10 00 |
| *Item* payd by Bartholomew Bond | 02 14 06 |

**[84] HALS: DP/71/5/2 Little Munden Account Book - Subscriptions for supporting a regiment, 27/10/1644**

Munden Parva The names of those who have subscribed for the inabling of Sir Thomas Middleton[280] October 27th 1644 these have not tickitts

| | £ s d |
|---|---|
| Mr Ayres | 00 05 00 |
| Thomas Kitchen | 00 05 00 |
| Thomas Rowley | 00 05 00 |
| John Lanckthorne | 00 05 00 |
| Thomas Colt Junior | 00 05 00 |
| Michael Ireland | 00 05 00 |
| John Chandler | 00 01 06 |
| | 01 11 06 |

[279] Thomas Saunders Esq and others had acquired the Priory Manor of St Amphibals, which they had then sold to William Beaumont in 1637 [Munby, *Redbourn,* p23]

[280] In 1643 Sir Thomas Middleton (1586-1666) of Chirk Castle (Denbigh) (later taken by royalists under John Watts of Mardocks), was the greatest landowner in the county and one of the few influential men in the area to support Parliament. He was put in charges of Parliamentary forces in North Wales and the northwest. Those providing horses for him were to have the value repaid on the public faith. It was suggested that, to fund his forces, timber from Capel's woods be sold. In September 1644 he and forces under Sir John Meldrum, another Scot, defeated the Royalists near Montgomery Castle. The continual under-funding of his troops presumably led to this request for subscriptions. By 1651 he was seen as a Presbyterian moderate, who later supported Booth's rising [*CJ* III, pp142-4, 320-2, 636-7; Henning, *Commons* II, pp124-5]

## Part 2. Assessment and local rating

### [85] TNA: SP28/154 Kings Langley parish assessors and collectors, 22/6/1642-19/4/1643

Langley Regis A Seasment made <for> the first part of the great taxe,[281] the 22nd June Anno Domini 1642 the sessers were:

Thomas Masssingale gent          John Baldwyn }
William Knight Junior[282]          Robert Gates }Collectors
Nicholas King Junior[283]
Edward Puddefat          The sum being £27-17s-7d
Payd to Thomas Goddard high collector the some of £27-17s-7d

A seasment made the 22nd of March Anno Domini 1642 for the Lord Generalls army for the three months, being £3-4s-6d the weeke[284] for Kings Langley paid
The sessers beinge:
John King Gent
Nicholas King Junior          George Weedon}
Robert Cartwright          James Alden } Collectors
William Knight Senior

A sessment made the 19th of Aprill Anno Domini 1643 for the assotiation of the Countie being £3-4s-6d the week for Kings Langley 8 months paid
The sessers beinge:
John King Junior
Nicholas King Junior
William Kelsey          Thomas Bigge[285]}
Robert Cartwright          James Puddifate } Collectors
Nathanill Humphrey

---

[281] The tax for £400,000 of March 1642

[282] William Knight senior (died 1644) held the manor of Bulstrodes [*VCH Herts* II, p241]

[283] Nicholas King was added to the Hertfordshire Committee in October 1643 and the Militia Committee in December. He does not seem to have served on a committee again but was High Constable of Dacorum Hundred between October 1659 and January 1663 [HALS QSB3 *ff*75, 101; *LJ* VI, p257; F&R I, pp356-8]

[284] This would have been for the Weekly Assessment ordinance passed on 24 February 1642/3

[285] Thomas Bigg of Porters End had been the High Constable for Hitchin 1639-41 and was added to Hertfordshire Committees from October 1643. He became a JP in 1650 [TNA C193/13/3 *ff*30-1; HALS: QSR5 *f*65; *LJ* VI, p257]

**[86] TNA: SP28/154 Northchurch parish assessors and collectors (undated 1643?)**

A returne of all those names which have been assessors and collectors within the parish of Northchurch

Assessors for the Pole-money per acquittance paid £29- 2s

| | | | |
|---|---|---|---|
| Jeames Daveney | } | | |
| William Edlin[286] | } | Collectors: | Daniell Ewer |
| Jeames Fenne | } | | Richard Ivory |
| Ephraim Howe | } | | |

The first part of the fower hundred thousand pounds
Assessors

| | | | |
|---|---|---|---|
| James Daveney | } | | |
| William Edlin | } | | |
| Jeames Fenne | } | Sub collector | Robert White |
| Daniell Ewer | } | £41-16s-5d | unpaide |
| Ephraim Howe | } | | |
| William Willett | } | | |

Assessors for the weekly assessment for my Lord Generalls army

| | | | |
|---|---|---|---|
| William Edlin | } | | |
| Robert White | } | | |
| Henry Putnam | } | Collectors: | Richard Ivory |
| Jeames Fenne | } | | James Fenne |
| Thomas Whitnay | } | | £4.12s.3d |

Assessors for the Assosiation taxe

| | | | |
|---|---|---|---|
| Richard Ivory | } | | |
| Roger Deacon | } | | |
| William Willett | } | Collectors: | Richard Story |
| Henry Norris | } | | Daniell Ewer |
| Henry Climson | } | | £4.12s.3d |

[286] William Edlin (died 1649) held the manor of Norcott Hill [*VCH Herts* II, p246]

**[87] TNA: SP28/154 Coleshill hamlet[287] assessors and collectors (1643?)**

Coleshill
The names of such persons as have bene assessors and collectors for the Subsidies, Polle mony and other money to the severall sommes for the hamlett of Coleshill

William Tredway }Assessors for all these somes
Edmund Ball }
For the polle mony paide in Guild Hall

| | £ s d |
|---|---|
| For the £400000 pounds the charge | 12 19 11 paid |
| For my Lord Generalls Armie charge | 18 00 00 <paid> |
| For the Assosiation mony the charge | 18 00 00 2 moneths paid |

Joseph Bonindon }
Giles Aldridge } Collectors for Polle Mony
For the 1st part

Joseph Bonindon collector for the £400000 the charge 12 pound 10 shilling 11 pence wherof 5 pound remanes in his hands

Walter Tredway }Collectors for my Lord Generall Armie
Edmund Ball } the charge £18 paid at Guild Hall

Hugh Wingrave }Collectors for the Assosciation mony
John Dean }the charge £18 wherof £12 paid to Tobie Combe Esq. the rest to collect

Edward Clarke collector of the voluntary benevolenc towards the releife of Ireland ~~the charge 2~~ is his hand and unpaide the some £2-11s-1d
*James Child Constable*

---

[287] This was the detached part of Hertfordshire in East Buckinghamshire. For a detailed analysis of the inhabitants of Coleshill and their houses in the 17th century see Chenevix Trench, J, 'The houses of Coleshill: the social anatomy of a seventeenth century village', *Records of Buckinghamshire,* Vol. XXV (Aylesbury, 1983) pp61-109

**[88] HALS: DP/71/5/2 Little Munden parish accounts for the Earl of Manchester's rate, 14/5/1644**

| Goods att 12d the score[288] | £ | s | d |
|---|---|---|---|
| Daniell Nash | 1 | 0 | 0 |
| Mr Lake | 0 | 13 | 0 |
| Michaell Ireland | 0 | 13 | 6 |
| Mr Cordwell | 0 | 9 | 6 |
| Henrie Ayres | 0 | 7 | 6 |
| Thomas Rowley | 0 | 4 | 6 |
| John Kimpton | 0 | 5 | 0 |
| Jeremie Laundie | 0 | 3 | 0 |
| John Chandler | 0 | 2 | 6 |
| Martha Kirbie | 0 | 0 | 9 |
| William Andrew | 0 | 0 | 6 |
| Thomas Miridith | 0 | 0 | 8 |
| Richard Hutchin | 0 | 0 | 8 |
| Phillip Trundley | 0 | 0 | 6 |
| Simon Michell | 0 | 0 | 8 |
| Thomas Colt Senior | 0 | 2 | 3 |
| Thomas Edwards | 0 | 6 | 6 |
| John Cuffley | 0 | 0 | 6 |
| Thomas Colt Junior | 0 | 1 | 6 |
| John Toms Junior | 0 | 1 | 6 |
| Richard Goodwine | 0 | 0 | 9 |
| William Walker | 0 | 2 | 0 |
| Thomas Gable | 0 | 0 | 8 |
| James Bardell | 0 | 5 | 0 |
| John Granwell | 0 | 5 | 0 |
| William Woods | 0 | 2 | 6 |
| Robert Addams | 0 | 1 | 0 |
| John Snell | 0 | 0 | 8 |
| John Hill | 0 | 0 | 6 |
| Leonard Humberstone | 0 | 0 | 8 |

[288] I assume this is 12d or one shilling for every 20 pounds sterling in value, of goods owned. This would mean Daniel Nash had goods valued at £400 and Robert Adams, goods valued at £20

Hertfordshire
Wee the Committee at Hertford doe approve of this assessment within written and doe order and appoint the within named Henrie Ayres and Robert Addams to be collectors thereof. And if anie of these who are within assessed shall refuse to pay theire tax imposed upon them or anie of them, then wee doe authorize and appoint the aforesaid collectors to distraine for a treble vallew and make sale of the goodes for the valew of this tax imposed upon them, or anie of them. And the said collectors are to make the returne of theire monie by them collected to Thomas Niccolls Esq[289] one of the Committee at Hertford on Tewsday the 22nd of May next as they will answer the contrarie att theire perrills,

Given under our hands this 14th of May 1644
*Thomas Nicholls, William Prestley, Gabriel Barbor*

May 26th 1644 Received in parte of this rate the some of £29 -5s -0d
*Thomas Nicholls, Edward Haborley*

June 22nd 1644
Received then of Robert Addams collector for the township of Munden Parva in the hundred of Broadwater, in full for the 2 last monthes Association proportioned for this countie of Hartford for maintaining of forces raised under the command of the Right Honourable the Earle of Manchester for the associated counties the some of £29-1s *Thomas Niccolls, Edward Haborley*

**[89] HALS: Off Acc 1162 No. 983r-v Committee order and bill for taxes paid out of the church and poor's money in St Albans (1643-4)**

*f*983r By order of Committee such lands as are guiven <by feoffment> for reliefe of the poore and to be exempted and saved from all rates and taxes wheras Thomas Mason, Thomas Knowlton, John Scott, Nicholas Sparling and Thomas Richardson doe pay a third parte of theyr rents to the use of the poore the said <same> persons are to be exempted for the tyme to come from the date hereof from all taxes what soever ~~dated~~ <given under our hands> this 19th of October 1644. *John Robotham, John King*

[289] For Nicholls see Appendix

To the assessors for all rates within the towne of St Albans and others whom it may concearne.

Taxes payd out of the Church's and pores mony.

*f*983v Thomas Mason's Bill for rent paid
Item payed the 16 day of June the sum of 1 shilling for my house 1643 Rent
Item payde the 10 daye of Auguste the sum of 1 shilling of my house 1643
For my Lord of Manchester
Item payd the sum of 8d destres[290] and 6d which 1 shilling 2d according to ordere of parllement one for 20 daye February Rent
Jeremye Loattemurd?[291]
Item payd for my house for the voluntary sogers 4d the 27 daye Marche 1644 Rent
Item payed the som of 1s the 6 daye of Aprill for my house 1644 Rent
Item paid the sum of 1s iiiid for mye Lord generall for mye house the 8 daye of Aprill 1644 Rent
Item payd the 29 day of Aprill for mye house the som iiiid to my Lorde of Manchester for seting out of horse for the Countye of Harford 1644 Rent
Item payd the 3 daye of Maye for my house the some of 1s for the ssosiation[292] 1644 Rent
Item payd the fyrste daye of June the some iiid for the solgers for Countye of Harford for my house 1644 Rent
Item payde the 3 daye of Julye for mye house the some of 1s 1644 Rent
Item payd for my house the some of vid the 8 day of June 1644 Rent
Item payd for my house the some of vid the 10 day of August Rent
Item payd for my house the some of *xviiid* Rent
Item payd for my house the some of iiiid rent the 21 August
Thomas Masons Bill. The Hole[293] some come to xis 4d

[290] Distress
[291] This name is indecipherable and it is unclear why it is there
[292] Eastern Association
[293] Hole - i.e. the whole sum

**[90] HALS: Off Acc 1162 No. 978 Abatements on assessment on income from church lands and for the poor for the 20th part in St Albans, 1643-5**

| 1643 | £ | s | d | q[294] | |
|---|---|---|---|---|---|
| The 20th part of £14-17s-6d is | | 14 | 10 | 2 | |
| Halfe the remainder is | 7 | 1 | 3 | 3 | |
| To which add the 20th part | 0 | 14 | 10 | 2 | |
| | 7 | 16 | 2 | 1 | due to the church |
| | | | | | |
| The other halfe of the remainder is | 7 | 1 | 3 | 3 | |
| Out of which abate | 5 | 9 | 0 | 0 | |
| | 1 | 2 | 3 | 3 | due to the poore |

| 1644 | | | | | |
|---|---|---|---|---|---|
| The taxes and quitrent and charges being paid the remainder | 11 | 6 | 9 | | |
| out of which abate the 20th part which is | | 11 | 10 | | |
| and there remaineth | 11 | 4 | 11 | | |
| Halfe the remainder is | 5 | 12 | 5 | 2 | |
| To which add the 20th parte | 0 | 11 | 10 | 0 | |
| | 6 | 4 | 3 | 2 | due to the church |
| The other part of the remainder is | 5 | 12 | 5 | 2 | |
| Out of which abate | 5 | 4 | 0 | 0 | |
| | 0 | 8 | 5 | 2 | due to the poore |

*(On reverse)* 1645

The taxes quitrent and charges paid

there remaines 12 7 0

Out of which abate the 20th part which is 12 4d

and there remaines 11-14-8d

Halfe the remainder is £5 -17s-4d

To which add the 20th part 0-12-4d

6 – 9 -8 due to the church

To other part of the remainder is £5-17-4d

Out of which abate 5- 4- 0

0 13 -4 due to the poore

294 A column for quarters or farthings i.e. a halfpenny is 2 in the final column

**[91] HALS: Off Acc 1162 No 988 Thomas Knowlton's Bill (1644)**

1644 Thomas Knowlton's bill of taxis set upon the scowlground[295]
Item payed to Thomas Samson constable januari 13 for seting forth the prest solgars[296] vid
Item payd to Goodman Joyner Colector March 9 for relif of Ireland iiis 2d
Item the 15th of March paid to Mr Oxton for the 4 monthes tax for the earle of Manchester 18s
Item paid to Richard Woodward and John Brocke for the militia 3s
Item to John Smith for Newport[297] 3s 4d
Some is £1-4s-4d
*Thomas Knowlton*

**[92] HALS: DP/71/5/2 Little Munden account book- Rate for impressments etc., 20/10/1645**

Munden Parva A rate made for the prest souldiers charges and other necessarie charges for the parliament service October 20th 1645:- Henry Andrewes and Thomas Rowley Constables

| At 1s 8d the scoare[298] | Acres | £ | s | d |
|---|---|---|---|---|
| Doctor Goad[299] | 410 and quitt rents | 1 | 19 | 2 |
| Mr Bateman Minister[300] | | 1 | 0 | 0 |
| Mr Berisford[301] | 98 | 0 | 8 | 2 |
| Mr Spence | 164 | 0 | 13 | 8 |
| Mr Scroggs[302] | 95 | 0 | 7 | 11 |

295 i.e. Taxes on the school ground
296 Impressed soldiers
297 Maintenance of Newport Pagnell garrison
298 This meant every occupier paid 20d per score of acres or 1d per acre rate. However Goad paid an additional 5/- for quit rents and presumably Bateman shared this
299 This is Thomas Goad DD, (c1595-1666) the cousin of the more famous Thomas Goad (died 1638). This Thomas had been Archdeacon of St Albans and Regius Professor of Laws at Oxford in the late 1630s . [N. G. Jones, 'Goad, Thomas (*c*.1595-1666)', *NewDNB*]
300 Possibly a minister who had been intruded
301 Possibly John Berisford of Rickmansworth (*c*.1621-86), later sheriff and member of the Hertford Assessment Committee in 1657 [F&R II, p1070]
302 John Scroggs Esq. (1612-1692) of Patmer Hall, Albury, was the second cousin of Sir William Scroggs the Lord Chief Justice after the restoration. He married, as his second wife, Elizabeth the daughter of Sir William Lytton. He was appointed to the Hertfordshire Assessment Committee in March 1643, the Sequestrations in June and Eastern Association in September, when he was described as a captain. A JP in the early 1650s, he was treasurer for

| | | | | |
|---|---|---|---|---|
| Mr Churchman | 100 | 0 | 8 | 4 |
| Mr Birchinhead | 46 | 0 | 3 | 10 |
| John Kempton | 100 | 0 | 8 | 4 |
| Thomas Rowley | 88 | 0 | 7 | 4 |
| Docter Mountfort[303] | 60 | 0 | 5 | 0 |
| John Lanckthone | 05 | 0 | 0 | 5 |
| Henrie Ayres | 30 | 0 | 2 | 6 |
| Sir John Boteler[304] | 13 | 0 | 1 | 1 |
| John Bydes | 10 | 0 | 0 | 10 |
| William Chapman | 48 | 0 | 4 | 0 |
| Mr Newton | 15 | 0 | 1 | 3 |
| Martha Kirbie | 15 | 0 | 1 | 3 |
| George Addams | 47 | 0 | 3 | 11 |
| Thomas Kitching | 36 | 0 | 3 | 0 |
| Thomas Kitching for Mr Scrogs land | 25 | 0 | 2 | 1 |
| Henry Cater | 20 | 0 | 1 | 8 |
| Henry Cocke | 14 | 0 | 1 | 2 |
| Leon Humberstone | 08 | 0 | 0 | 8 |
| Mr North[305] | 22 | 0 | 1 | 10 |
| Mr Condell | 14 | 0 | 1 | 2 |
| Michaell Colt | 20 | 0 | 1 | 8 |
| William Morris | 10 | 0 | 0 | 10 |
| Thomas Colt | 30 | 0 | 2 | 6 |
| Widdow Perrie | 30 | 0 | 2 | 6 |
| Richard Goodwin | 14 | 0 | 1 | 2 |
| Katherine Walker | 10 | 0 | 0 | 10 |
| Thomas Gable | 8 | 0 | 0 | 8 |
| Robert Cocke | 10 | 0 | 0 | 10 |

maimed soldiers in 1659 and assessed for 14 hearths in 1663 [TNA: C193/13/3 *ff*30-31; 4 *f*43d; E179/248/23 *ff*77-8; BL: Lansdowne MSS 255 *f*5; HALS: QSB3 *ff*70, 79d; F&R 1, pp19, 117-23, 170; *LJ* VI, p76; Cussans, *Herts* Pt II, p162]

[303] This is probably James (Rector of Tewin died 1647) one of the sons of Thomas Mountford (Rector of Anstey and Tewin died 1632) and the brother of John Mountford, (Rector of Anstey died c. 1640). He held land in at least eight different parishes at his death [HALS: 28529-31; Urwick, W, *Nonconformity in Hertfordshire* (1884) p553; Hennessy, G, *Novum Repertorium Ecclesiasticum Parochiale Londinense* (1898) pp xxxx1v, 294, 305]

[304] For Boteler See Appendix

[305] Probably Roger North of Tewin

| | | | | |
|---|---|---|---|---|
| William Walker | 5 | 0 | 0 | 5 |
| John Chapman | 4 | 0 | 0 | 4 |
| George Rowley | 4 | 0 | 0 | 4 |
| Mr Walters | 40 | 0 | 3 | 4 |
| Jeremie Adkinson | 40 | 0 | 3 | 4 |
| Mrs Gardner | 15 | 0 | 1 | 3 |
| Mrs Baker | 15 | 0 | 1 | 3 |
| John Hyne | 07 | 0 | 0 | 7 |
| John Cuffley | 06 | 0 | 0 | 6 |
| Simon Michell | 04 | 0 | 0 | 4 |
| Lady Casar[306] | 15 | 0 | 1 | 3 |
| Francis Clarke | 05 | 0 | 0 | 5 |
| John Hill | 06 | 0 | 0 | 6 |
| Moses Rowley | 03 | 0 | 0 | 3 |
| Edward Chandler | 47 | 0 | 3 | 11 |

*Daniel Nash, John Kempton, John Lanckthone*: Sessors

## Part 3. The Collection of rates, loans, taxes and contributions

### [93] TNA: SP28/154 Redbourn parish accounts *ff*3-4 - Rates for the militia, Eastern Association and subsidies, August 1642 to June 1645

| *f*3 Seaven Rates for the Militia | £ s d |
|---|---|
| The first rate payd to Mr Zachary King our Treasurer in October 1643 | 10 13 08 |
| The 2nd to the saide Zachary in February 1643 | 10 13 08 |
| The 3rd to the Zachary in Aprill 1644 | 21 07 04 |
| The 4th to the said Zachary in June 1644 | 21 07 04 |
| The 5th to the said Zachary in July 1644 | 21 07 04 |
| The 6th to Captaine Tanner[307] in September 1644 | 21 07 04 |

[306] This is probably Jane the second wife and widow (died 1661) of the former Master of the Rolls, Sir Charles Caesar, (died December 1642), whose first wife, Anne's, dowry had included the Manor of Little Munden [L.M. Hill, 'Caesar, Sir Charles (1590-1642)', *NewDNB*; *VCH Herts* III, p131]

[307] This may be Thomas Tanner, a tanner, who was a Borough Assistant in St Albans for 22 years and was wealthy enough at his death to leave £100 each to five of his seven daughters. He had refused to pay Ship Money in 1638. He was put on the St Albans Assessment

| | |
|---|---|
| The 7th to Captaine Tanner in November 1644 | 21 07 04 |
| | £128 09 00 |

Collected for the Earle of Manchester

| | |
|---|---|
| Robert Field Collected 3 monthes for the associacion and payd it to Mr Combes of Hempstead treasurer in August 1642 | 59 01 04 |
| And to William Hickman treasurer | 04 07 08 |
| Samuell Hickman[308] collected and payd to William Hickman in February 1643 | 64 02 00 |
| William Field and Michaell Page collected 2 monthes and payd it to William Hickman in April 1644 | 64 02 00 |
| | |
| John Weedon[309] in July 1644 collected | 64 02 00 |
| Raph Haward[310] collected in August 1644 | 64 02 00 |
| Raph Haward collected for the monthly tax from the first of June 1642 for 3 monthes paid att London June 1645 | 64 02 00 |
| Raph Haward collected two monthes from the first of August 1643 and payd it to William Hickman of St Albans | 42 01 05 |
| Raph Haward collected the 29th of August 1644 and payd to William Hickman | 64 02 00 |
| Tho: Bigge[311] and Bryan Shepherd collectors two moneths payd to Mr Hickman in November 1644 | 64 02 00 |
| | £515 09 00 |

| *f*4 | £ s d |
|---|---|
| The first and second subsidies collected by William Bucley and payd to Richard Daggnall of Tringe which was | 19 06 08 |
| The 3rd and 4th to Mr Roberts of Myms | 19 06 08 |
| The 5th and 6th to Mr Daggtoll of Barkhamsted | 19 06 08 |

Committee in 1657 and 1660, when he styled himself Esq [TNA: SP16/399 *f*81; F&R II, pp1070, 1370; Smith and North, *St Albans,* p171]

308 The Hickmans were the millers at Redbournbury Mill. It was leased to the St Albans Treasurer, William Hickman, in 1651 for seven years at £100-5/- down and 5d a year rent. [Munby, *Redbourn,* p15]

309 The Weedon family were associated with a corn-grinding watermill near Watling Street, and held a number of acres of the Priory Manor in 1632 [Munby, *Redbourn*, pp15, 23]

310 A John Hayward had bought 35 acres from George Neale for £300 in 1617 and in 1656 a Thomas Hayward died, holding Beson End Farm, of 101 acres [Munby, *Redbourn*, p21]

311 Thomas Bigg, yeoman, was reported as entertaining Quakers in his house with William Barber, gent, in 1689 [Munby, *Redbourn*, p63]

£57 18 00

Sum Totalis £213 -19-4

*John Gale William Bankes*

**[94] TNA: SP28 /154 Return of names of Busshey parish assessors and collectors, 4/7/1643**

Busshey 1643 4 July

A Retorne made by us the constabels of Busshe conserning a warrant sent unto us for to Inquire the names of sutch as have bine sesers or collectors for these sumes heare under writen.

| | |
|---|---|
| Asesars for our part of the 400000li | Mr John Seale<br>Mr William Bayle<br>Mr Thomas Nickolls |
| our towne was laid at 44li-8s 0d | |
| Collectors | Roger Nuttine<br>Thomas Banck |
| Asesers for polemomies | Mr William Ewer<br>Mr William Bayle<br>Thomas Ludell<br>Thomas Scott<br>George Hickman<br>Kenys Hayward |
| the sume levied 57li- 10s-4d | |
| Collectors | George Hickman<br>Edward Adams |
| Abeated for | Mr Seale<br>Mr Thomas Nickols<br>Mr Simon Halborne |

The Sume of 19-13-4 paid in att London Guildhall

Contribution monies to the kinge and parliment first *viiii* horse and *£xxxx*

Conserninge the weekely taxe for my lord generall asesers

Mr John Seale
Mr William Bayle
William Field ledget?
Thomas Hundell
Roger Nutkine
Rowland Frend

| | |
|---|---|
| The Collecttors for the weekly taxe of five pound sixe shillings and ten pence | Ralph Hayward and Hendry Jeames |
| accounted for at Lundun | |

Conserning the ascotiation and weekly taxe for that the whitch is 5li-6-10d

| | |
|---|---|
| Collectors | Robert Feilld and |
| | Edward Cooke |
| Asesers | William Bayle |
| | Thomas Hundell |
| | Roger Nutkine |
| | Rowland Frend |
| Constables | Thomas Scott |
| | John Fendall |

**[95] TNA: SP28/154 Kensworth[312] return of collectors' names (undated 1645?)**

Hertford Kensworth A Note of the hi collectors and subcolecttors that have receaved and gathered these somes of mony here under written

Collectors

| | |
|---|---|
| Thomas Lodge and Thomas Halsey paid to William Tramshers at Guildhall for 2 monthes to my Lord Generall | 24 00 00 |
| Thomas Lodge and Thomas Halsey paid to John Haydon at Watford for my Lord Generall | 11 06 08 |
| The same man paid to Thomas Oxton at St Albans for my lord General | 12 00 00 |
| The same man paid to William Hickman for my Lord Generall | 11 15 06 |
| Thomas Lodge and William Turner paid to Zacari King of Watford for the valonters | 12 00 00 |
| Mordica Knite, Thomas Robines paid to Zacari King for the Militia | 12 00 00 |
| Henry Haward, Thomas Haward paid to Zacari King £5 for the militia and to Capten Marsh[313] £1 | 06 00 00 |
| Mordica Knite and Will Abut paid paid (sic) to Mr Hickman for the Earle of Manchester | 36 00 00 |

[312] Kensworth was then in Hertfordshire, but now is in Bedfordshire
[313] This is John Marsh who trained the St Albans Volunteers

George Barber and John Warner paid to Mr Combs of Hemsted
£27 4s and to Mr Hicman of St Albans £8 16s 36 00 00
Henry Howard and Thomas Howard paid to Mr Hickman for the
Earle of Manchester 36 00 00
Thomas Howard Churchwarden paid to Benjamin Goodwine and
John Kendrik at Guild Hale for the contribution of Ireland 02 16 10
The same Thomas Howard paid to William Beamont hi
constable for the clargi of Ireland 00 12 00
Robert Pepit, Henri Straite paid to Mr Hicman for the Earle of
Manchester 36 00 00
Simon Freeman, William Turner listed in 2 horses for the for the
(sic) parish of Kensworth valued by the Comisaries at 28 00 00
Paid for a months pay for the riders and for ther armes to William
Hicman 11 00 00
Robert Pepit paid 2 subsidies to Samual Dagnal his collectors
whereof £3 4s was paid in tickats 10 13 04
William Haward and Samuel Halsey paid in to William Hicman
treasurer for the earle of Manchester 36 00 00
William Haward, Thomas Grigori paid to William Hickman for
the raising of horse and dragoons 06 13 04
Mr Barber paid to Captain Tanner for the militia 12 00 00

(***On Reverse***) 7 December Dacorum Hundred return of the names of the collectors etc. of Dacorum Kensworth Parish folio 9

**[96] TNA: SP28/154 Return of collectors names for Northchurch parish (undated 1645?)**

Hertford Northchurch
For the poolemoney[314] Richard Ivory and Daniell Eawer Collectors
For the Subsidie Royall Robert White collector
The weekely taxes for my Lord Generalls armie for five monthes Richard Seare collector
Weekely taxes for the Assotiation for the three monthes Richard Ivory collector
for the Militia Henry Dagnall collector
for the Militia Russell Webb collector

[314] The Poll Tax authorized by Parliament in 1641

for the Earle of Manchester Richard Wood collector
for the Earle of Manchester Richard Wood collector (sic)
horse to recrute the Earle of Manchester William Allen collector
for the Militia Theophelus Joyce collector
for the Earle of Manchester William Edlyn collector
for the Blacke Regiment Roger Deacon collector
for the Earle of Manchester Timothy White collector
for meamed Soljours and Widdowes[315] Thomas Hill collector
for three horse bridles and sadles Thomas Hill collector
for the Earle of Manchester Robert White collector
for the Militia Henry Norris collector
for the Earle of Manchester Richard Seare collector
for horse to the Earle of Manchester William Willett collector
for the Militia Timothy Halliday collector

Sub collectors for the subsets Ephraim How and Thomas Witney and William Willett

**[97] TNA: SP28/154 Return of collectors names from Little Gaddesden parish (undated 1645?)**

Gadsden parva The names of all the subcollectors

Danniell Garrett }
Edward Wesscott } Lord Generall Tax

William Newman }
Joseph Goshill } for the Assotiation

John Wesscott }
Francis Mores } Assotiation

Thomas Figgs }
Samuel Barford } the fifft and twentieth part

Thomas Hill }

[315] The collection for maimed soldiers and their widows was a local Tudor tax, that was continued into the civil war period

Edward Keene }Earle Manchesters tax

William Keene }
Jaimes Haydon }Earle Manchesters

Daniel Hall }
William Keene } for the militia

John Eames }
John Feild } militia

Thomas Portris }
Edward Alea } militia

Francis Mores }
Daniel Nowell }Earle Manchesters

Edward Keene }
Joseph Goshill } for horse and foote
*John X Wesscott Constable*

**[98] TNA: SP28/154 Toby Combe's[316] high collector's accounts, 8/3/1644(5)**

*f1* A true copie of that book which I delivered to Mr Foxwist[317] and the rest of the comissitioners of the Accompts of the Kingdome sitting at St Albans 8th March 1644 in the words following:
Proposition money collected in *annos*[318] 1642 and 1643 etc. by me Tobie Combe of Hemsted in the countie of Hertford Gent and paid also by me into the Guildhall, London, by order from the Committee of Hertfordsheire collected in part of the Hundred of Dacorum in such townes and parishes as hereafter is shewed.
<u>Hemsted</u>
First the money which I, Toby Combe lent uppon the propositions for my self in plate and money fiftie pounds, I say £50

[316] For Combe see Appendix
[317] Foxwist was chairman of the local sub-committee of accounts based in St Albans to check up on all wartime expenditure *(see* Appendix)
[318] *Annos* = Latin for years

*Item* again, I lodging with my famelie in Pater Noster Roe, London in St Faiths paris under Pawles,[319] I lent again more upon the propositions five pounds, I say £5

*Item* Mrs Hester Martin,[320] widow <in plate and money> £10

*Item* Mrs Marie Marston,[321] widow £10

*Item* the same Mrs Mary Marston againe lent more five pounds, I say £5

*Item* Mr Joseph Marston[322] of Woodhall in Hemsted parish £5

*Item* John Gaze in plate and money £10

*Item* Mrs Mary King, widow <twentie pound> I say £20

John Gate of Boxted plate and money £10

Francis Hodgis £10

John Bramley Junior £3

Joseph Turner £5

Richard Salter Junior <plate and money> £10

Abram Crawley a silver boule at price at the Guildhall, London £3

Joseph Partridge £2

John Puddivat of Pigotsend in plate and money £10-0-6d

Thomas Lovejoy £3

Robart Putnam £2

John Knight £2

John Moorton of Candles £5

Samuell Sowthen plate <and money> £20

Samuell Baker plate and money £10

Thomas Mun

***(In margin)*** This Thomas Mun is set in the latter end of the book.

These sums above first received and afterward paid unto Guildhall by me Tobie Combe. Som £210-2-6d

*f*2 Paid these sums following into the Guildhall London

Little Gadsden

---

[319] In the old St Faiths parish near the old St Paul's Cathedral

[320] John Martin, the owner of Aignells manor in Hemel Hempstead, died in 1643, leaving as his heirs his daughters, Mrs Hester Martin and Mary King (below), who jointly held the manor until 1650 [*VCH Herts* II, pp215-30]

[321] Mrs Mary Marston, daughter of Thomas Porter of Ayot St Lawrence and widow of Joseph Porter, senior, died 1637 [*VCH Herts* II, pp215-30]

[322] Son of Mary and Joseph Marston, and held the manor of Woodhall in Hemel Hempstead [*VCH Herts* II, pp215-30]

| | |
|---|---|
| Daniell Hall | £5 |
| Samuell Hall | £5 |
| Daniell Garret | £1 |
| | |
| Bovingdon | |
| Thomas Gould of Newhall | £10 |
| Thomas Hay | £5 |
| Thomas Gould of Halfacre | £6 |
| John Partridge | £5 |
| Great Gadsden | |
| | |
| Mrs Lettice Halsey[323] | £50 |
| Thomas Halsey de Townsend | £10 |
| Timothy Weedon de Corner | £10 |
| Robart Smith de Taggsend | £10 |
| Mordecay Halsey | £10 |
| Fawstin Knight | £10 |
| William Halsey de Woodd | £10 |
| George Rose | £5 |
| Thomas Wells | £5 |
| John Beech | £5 |
| Josias Rutland | £2 |
| Thomas Dogget | £2 |
| James Long | £2 |
| Allin Batman | |
| Thomas Clerk | |

(Thomas Clerk and this Allin Batmnan are set at the end of this last hereafter)
These above received first and afterwards by me paid into the Guildhall London
Sum £178 *per me Tobias Combe*

*f*3 A noat or particular of such proposition money as was first collected by me Tobie Combe and afterwards alsoe paid the same money again by me the same Tobie Combe to Mr Ralph Gladman of St Albans the (then) treasurer. I

323 In 1611 Lettice Williams married William Halsey (died 1637) and members of the Halsey family held the Golden Parsonage estate in Gaddesdon Row throughout this period [*VCH Herts* II, pp201-7]

being appointed to pay the same return by warrant from the Committee of Hertford since as appeers by the same warrant

| Of Hemsted | £ |
|---|---|
| Joan Long of Coxpond Widdow | £5 |
| William Long of <the same> Coxpond | £10 |
| John Long | £5 |
| Michaell Heyward | £2 |
| Henry Eles | £4 |
| Henry Cock | £5 |
| Nathaniell Axtell | £3 |
| Jeremie Hobbs | £2 |
| Elizabeth Hollander | £5 |
| William Coleman | £2 |

Of Barkhamsted
Oliver Babb
**(*In margin*)** This charge Babb is set £10 at the end of this book

| | |
|---|---|
| Michaell Yong | £20 |
| Jeremie Rolfe | £5 |
| John Sell? | £5 |
| Francis Nickson | £10 |

| Of Tring | |
|---|---|
| Mrs Lake | £5 |
| Jane Sebrooks | £5 |
| John Switser | £10 |
| John Lake of Tring | £10 |
| John Foster | £5 |
| Robart Harding | £10 |

Sum £133
These sums all first received and afterwards paid to Mr Raphe Gladman by me
Tobie Combe Esq.

*f*4 The sums also under written first collected by me Toby Combe and afterwards paid by me to Mr Raph Gladman of St Albans (then) Treasurer by the appointment of the Committee of Hertfordsheire as by the warrant from the said committee appeers.

| | £ s d |
|---|---|
| Of Putnam William, Stowell <the younger> | 20 00 00 |
| Of Kensworth Mordecay Knight | 05 00 00 |
| Of Flamsted Walter Hickden <£10> who is set hearafter at the end of the book | 10 00 00 |
| Also of Flamsted William Halsey of the Hill | 10 00 00 |
| Also of Flamsted William Hickden | 05 00 00 |
| Martha Lea of Flamsted | 01 10 00 |

Great Gadsden

| | |
|---|---|
| William Cannum | 01 00 00 |
| Thomas Norton | 02 10 00 |

Thomas Sebrook hath paid £1 but casually hath bin and must be set in William How his ticket of Redburne his tickett of Redburne for each of them Vizt How and Sebrook lent uppon the propositions 20s a peece but the whole fortie shillings is set in William Hows tickett of Redburne for whom and in whose name I paid the same as heerafter if Redburn is shewed and I keep the tickett to both ther uses.

| | |
|---|---|
| Of Northchurch Sara Fen | 10 00 00 |
| Of Abbots Langley Timothy Birchmore | 01 10 00 |

Of Redburn these below

| | |
|---|---|
| Thomas Birchmore | 02 00 00 |
| Thomas Aberrie | (*torn*) |

William How of the woodd is set in his tickett to pay £2 but one of the pounds was Thomas Sebrooks money of Great Gadsden which was overseen that each of them had not had a severall ticket because they both lent each of them but 20s a peece. Wherfore now they are both to share together in How his tickett of 40s which I still keep to both their uses. Sum £61 10 00

*Per me Tobias Combe Esq*

*f*5 Here after <now> followeth a noat or remembrance of such proposition money as hath bin first collected by me Tobie Combe of Hemsted gent and afterward againe paid by me the ~~said~~ <same> Tobie Combe to William Hickman Treasurer, by warrant of the Committee of Hertfordsheire

| Of Hemsted | £ s d |
|---|---|
| John Gunston | 06 13 04 |

| | |
|---|---|
| Henry Rutland | 05 00 00 |
| Henry Turner of Waterside gave | 01 00 00 |
| Grace Mitchell | 02 00 00 |
| Nathaniell Wilkinsonn | 05 00 00 |
| Widdow <How> of Gadbridge | 00 10 00 |
| Of Kings Langley William Knight | 10 00 00 |
| Of Great Gadsden William Doggett | 02 00 00 |
| And Samuell Dayton | 00 10 00 |
| Sum | 32 13 04 |

These sums above I first collected and afterwards were paid to William Hickman by me *Tobie Combe Esq*
A noat or remembrance of such money furthermore which I Tobie Combe have received upon the propositions

| | |
|---|---|
| Tringe: Of John Geery of Tring | 20 00 00 |
| Barkhamsted: Of Oliver Babb of Barkhamsted | 10 00 00 |
| Flamsted: Of Walter Hickden of Flamsted | 10 00 00 |
| Flamsted: Of Jonathan Mun of Flamsted | 02 10 00 |
| Great Gadsden: Of Thomas Clerk of Great Gadsden | 05 00 00 |
| Also of Great Gadsden: Alin Batman | 02 00 00 |
| Of Hemsted: Thomas Mun | 02 00 00 |
| Sum | 51 10 00 |

Which money was then laid out by me Tobie Combe by warrant under written as ensueth; vizt
Wheras the Deputie Leiutenants of the Countie of Hertford have received severall orders for the raysing and bring the volunteers and trained bands wher they shalbe appointed by order of both houses of Parliament. And wheras by the said orders power is given to us to appoint wayes and meanes for the payment of such souldiers, as we shall by such orders rayse, these are therefore to require Tobie Combe Esq Treasurer apointed for the hundred of Dacorum, to pay unto Captaine Decon £20 for the paying of his souldiers and this by the authoritie of both houses shalbe his discharg and by the consent of the Committee for the Safty of the Kingdome shall require tickets out of the Treasurie of London for the same sum.
Subscribed hereunto *John Garrard, John Wittewronge, Thomas Dacres, John Read, W. Lytton*

*f*6 The said £20 last before resited, I paid to the said Captaine Deacon, as by his acquittanc therof (bearing date the 21st October 1642)

appeers – I say 20 00 00
And to Captaine Turner of Hemsted for the like (watching at
Pancras in those feilds)[324] for the Cittie of Londons saftye his
souldiers many gone from him and the rest ready to leave him for
want of pay, I disbursed to him ten pounds I say 10 00 00
And for one hundred and one horses and horse harness procured

by warrant (procured by Doctor Burgess)[325] from <some> Lords of
the house of Parliament, <the horses> to be imediatly sent to
his Excellency the Erle of Essex, to draw up the amunition
towards the Cittie of London, (as they were in their march from
Kenton Field (neer Banburie)[326] to the said Citie of London with
all possible expedition, at which tyme, viz about November
1642, from Hemsted and the towns adjacent, ~~by Doctor Burgess~~
~~of Watford meanes,~~ the said 101 horses and horseharness towards
listing of which ~~horses~~ I Toby Combe tooke paines and was
commanded to disburse towards their charges, which I paid to
the present commissaries, <Mr>Henry King (one of the members of
Committee for the militia) and Timothy Weedon, appointed ~~to~~
then to value those horses, and towards the said horses charges
and their riders, to Mr Henry King aforesaid who went with
the said horses to Dunstable and delivered them to the Wagon
Master Generall. I paid, I say, to the said Mr Henry King of
Hemsted <and Tomothie Weedon>, I paid, I say, five pounds as by
ther acquittance dated 10th day of November 1642 appeereth.
I say 05 00 00

Soe of £51 as is shewed before by me to be collected And
wherof £35 of is last <of all> above < in like manner> before
shewed how by me laid out. And then only £16 10s in my
hands remaining (of the said £51). Out of which (said £10 and 10s)
my fees by the Ordenance of the parliament allowed at three pence
in the pound for collecting and charges of paying of it (much of it
paid above 20 miles yea almost 30 miles from the place I

---

324 This presumably refers to when the Hertfordshire troops were sent to St Pancras when royalists threatened London after Edgehill

325 Dr Cornelius Burges(s), vicar of Watford *(see* Appendix)

326 i.e. Their march south after the Battle of Edgehill to Turnham Green

collected it) The sum which I collected being in the wholl
£667 5s 10d At 3d in pound the fees amounting to £8 6s
So ther remaynes £8 4s in my hands this 8th March 1644 by me
of the proposition money
*Toby Combe*

Plus *in dorsoe*[327]

*f7* And soe ther is a true accompt to my best knowledge and remembrance wherof I doe depose and take my Oath and heerunto subscribe with my <owne> hand *Tobie Combe Esq*

But of the Association money and accompt <therof> (which I brought in before (vizt about 3 months <since>) to the Committee of the Accounts of the Kingdome of that money and in that account, I laid out for the state ninety and ~~foure~~ <three pounds> and fifteen shillings <and 10d> of myne owne propper and peculiar money, more then that which I had received, as by the said Accompt delivered also in by me Toby Combe unto William Foxwist Esquire, and the rest of the Commissioners for the Accompts of the Kingdome sitting at St Albans, more plainly appeareth. Which I hope shalbe returned to me back againe *Tobye Combe Esq*
Soe in conclusion and in fine I Tobie Combe am (by this account) eight pounds and fower shillings in the states debt.
And the state is my debt (for money paid when I was Treasurer) by the Committees warrants, Ninety and three ~~fower~~ pounds and fifteene shillings and ten pence wherof I Tobie Combe am all ready sworne and will depose.
*Tobye Combe Esq*

(***Endorsed on edge***)– Mr Combes his Accounts examined upon oath 9th March 1644)

[327] Latin for in or on the back, hence endorsed

## Part 4 Allocation of, opposition to, and repayment of moneys raised

### [99] TNA: SP28/230 Order of Standing Committee of St Albans re Excise Money, 15/3/1646(7)

By the standing committee for the Countey of Hertford sitting at St Albans 15th March 1646
It is this day ordered that Mr William Hickman Treasurer to this Committee, doe, upon sight hereof, repaire unto Mr William Turner, Treasurer to the Committee at Hertford, and do demand and receive two full fift parts of six hundred and fower pounds ten shillings, being two hundred fortey one pounds sixteen shillings as soe much due to this committee and treasury upon the second payment<out> of the excise, which is for moneys by us disbursed formerly for our part of the pay of 70ty horse sent out of this countey as parte of the 800 horse to be raised within the Easterne Association, according to an ordinance of parliament dated the 28th February 1645. With which said summe of £241-16/- the said William Hickman is hereby appointed to repay the treasuries out of which he disbursed the same. And for his so doing, as also for the said Mr Turner, payment of the said summe too him, this shalbe to them sufficient warrant. Given under our hands the day and yeare first above written.

*John King, John Robotham*

Received of Mr William Turner this 19th March 1646 in full of the abovesaid order the summe of two hundred fortey one pounds and sixteen shillings £241-16/- *William Hickman*

### [100] HALS: 70552 William Lytton and Thomas Dacres to Zachary King, 6/10/45

Mr Zachary King,
Having bine desiared by the gentlemen of St Albanes that wee woold put an end to the differance ~~betwixt~~? touching them and your townes in the Hundred of Cashioe[328], their desiar being in ~~deleted~~ no wise to charge your fower townes[329] with the fourth parte, that is by the <order of the> Committee of this Countie sitting at <St Albans> taken of(f) from St Albans, but rather that

[328] The Hundred that was roughly co-terminus with the old Liberty of St Albans
[329] The four most prominent towns in Cashio apart from St Albans were probably, Watford, Rickmansworth, Bushey and Barnet

it shood take upp on the whole hundred. Wee thought it fit to acquaint you ther with, intreating you to recommend it unto the gentlemen of the fower townes further considerations and desareing your answer with what convenient speed you can, wee resolving to stay the request untill wee hear from you soe in hast wee rest your assured friends *William Lytton, Thomas Dacwers* Hertford October 6th 1645

**[101] HALS: QSR7 *f*151 Information re the opposition to the excise, 6/3/1646(7)**

*f*151 The informacon of me, George Thompson, one of the collectors for the excise within the Hundreds of Hertford and Braughin etc. as followeth: That upon 16th of February 1646 ~~or thereabouts~~ one William Wilkinson of Ware, in the street before divers hearers threatened me and said that he and others would beate me out of the country very shortly and that the excise howse was burnt downe at London and they would burne the house where I lived and me also and that they that set the excise first on foote were Roges and rascalles and Alice Creed of Ware, sister to Wilkinson spoke to the same effect and Thomas Houlton[330] of Hartford, butcher, about the same tyme came to Ware for no other end or purpose as I can learne or doe beleeve but to raile at me and the proceedings of the excise and tould me I had undone him and I must not thinke to goe free nor the committee themselves for they might as well have robbed him of his money as to take it for excise with many other railing expressions. *George Thompson*

[This informacon was prosseded before us this 6th of March 1646 upon oath before us the committees of the county of Hartford]

**[102] HALS: QSR7 *f*152 Depositions of William Hunt and Jonas Odison against Robert Humberstone, 29/1/1646(7)**

29 January 1646
*f*152 William Hunt deposeth that hee went by Robert Humberston on the last Day of Humiliacon,[331] as hee was makeing of fagotts[332] and asked him whie

---

[330] Thomas Ho(u)ton, from all Saints had been made free of the Borough in March 1641 [Information from Alan Greening]
[331] A day of humiliation was a day, set aside by Parliament, so that all should pray and confess their sins publicly (humiliate themselves) before God, so that he would look more favourably on the Godly people, i.e. parliamentarians

hee wrought on that day.[333] Whereupon the said Humberstone replyed and said what doe you thinck I will obey these rogues dayes and said further what did they pray for the money that went to the rogues the Scotts. And further saith not. *William Hunte*

Jonas Odison deposeth that hee lately asked the said Robert Humberstone why hee did not kill hoggs as hee used to doe, whereupon the said Robert Humberstone replyed that hee would never kill nowe to pay excise for the committees att Hertford to sitt and drinck it. And further said not.
*Jonas Addison* *Caput Coram* [334]*Gabriel Barbor*

**[103] TNA: SP28/231 Order of Militia Committee re repayment of loan, 18/10/1644**

Att a full Committee for the militia sitting att the King's Armes in Hertford this 18th of October 1644:
It is this day ordered that Mr Barbor shall have the fowre hundred pounds (which he hath lent towards the payment of the arrerages of the Oringe Regiment) paid him againe by Mr Turner Trasurer out of the first moneys which hee shall receave, And it is further ordered that Mr Love having received the said £400 to to pay the Captaines, Officers and Souldiers of the Oringe Regiment shall also take acquittances for the said money that hereby hee may give an account hereof to this committee and to Mr Turner Treasurer.

*Joseph Dalton, Maior, Edward Michell, Thomas Meade, Thomas Michell, William Carter, Randolph Niccoll, William Plomer*

***(On reverse)*** This is nott paid
(***Lower down on reverse***) December 18th 1644
Received accordinge to the within written order the sum off Fower hundred pounds *Gabriel Barbor*

---

[332] Firewood
[333] On Sundays godly sabbatarians were not supposed to work
[334] Latin for 'head of the court' or magistrate

**[104] TNA: SP28/231 Order from Hertford to St Albans Committees, 20/03/1643(4)**

20 March 1643
It is this day ordered by the Committee sitting at Hartford that foure hundred pounds be issued out of the treasury at St Albans for there proporcon of a thousand pounds <to be paid by our county by virtue the last ordinance> towards the Associacion.

To William Hickman Threasurer at St Albans
Given under our hands this xxth March 1643 *Gabriel Barbor, Thomas Niccolls, William Presley, Alexander Weld,*[335] *William Carter, Thomas Meade, William Dawges*
This money is to be sent immediately to Cambridge[336] and therefore pray lett the Threasurer ~~bring~~ send it to Hartford to morrow that soe wee may convey it with all speede.

**(*On reverse*)** Receaved according to this order of Mr William Hickman fowr hundred pounds this 22nd March 1643 £400
*Per me Fromabove Dove*

**[105] TNA: SP28/231 St Albans Committee receipt from the Eastern Association treasurers, 30/3/1644**

30th March 1644
Received by us Gregory Gawsell[337] and William Leman,[338] Treasurers, the sum of five hundred and thirty eight pounds thirteen shillings and foure pence, of William Hickman out of the Treasury att St Albanes, being arrears of the

---

[335] Weld (Wilde) held the manor of Widbury in Ware until 1665. He was probably the son of Sir Humphrey Weld, grocer, who had died in 1610. The family came from Chester and he had married Rose Butcher of London, having a son Alexander *c*1624. Weld became an active JP from 1654-60 [HALS: QSB3 *passim*; Beaven, *Aldermen*, pp147, 219; *VCH Herts* III, p390; *Herts Vis,* p103]

[336] To the main treasurer of the Eastern Association

[337] Gawsell, inherited estates from an old gentry family, had been educated at Cambridge, was related to a number of New England colonists, and had, like Gabriel Barbor and Maurice Thomson, been a member of the Providence Island Company. He had also been an agent for the Earl of Warwick's Norfolk lands and an efficient estate manager [Holmes, *Eastern Association*, p127]

[338] For Leman see Appendix

5th and 20th part of and weekly assessments before the first of January 1643. We also receive this 9th of Aprill 1644 of the said William Hickman the summe of sixe hundred pounds more beinge arrears of the 5th and 20th parte and weekely assessments before the said first of January. Wee say received in all the summe of £1138 : 13s : 4d

*Gregory Gawsell, William Leman*

## Part 5 Payments to troops

### [106] HALS: D/Z55/02 Payments to the Hertfordshire Regiment (April to July 1643)[339]

*f*1v A perticular of all such summes of money as were sent from the County of Hertforde to the Regiment ~~Aylesbury~~ under the command of Sir John Wittewronge Knt beginning from their advance out of the countrey which was on the 24th day of Aprill 1643 and ending the 10th of July following; when by Commission from the Deputy Leiutenants and Committees, for the sayd County; Commissary Sterne[340] was appoynted to muster and pay the <same> Regiment.

| | £ | s |
|---|---|---|
| There came to the Regiment from Hertforde about the 26th of Aprill | 50 | |
| And from St Albans the same day | 100 | |
| From ~~Hertford~~ St Albans May 10th | 200 | |
| From Hertford May 16th | 200 | |
| From thence May the 26th | 200 | |
| From Hertford and St Albans togeather, June 3rd | 400 | |
| From Hertford June 6th | 100 | |
| From St Albans June 12th | 280 | |
| From Hertford ~~July~~ June 14th | 999 | 18 |
| From Hertford July 5th | 300 | |
| Summe is - | 2829 | 18 |

[339] On folios 1r and 2v are various random additions which have not been included here as it is not clear as to what they refer

[340] Captain Edward Sterne was from Hoddesdon and was on the Militia Committee in 1643. He had married Mary Pedley widow, and had a son Robert. He died in 1645 [*Herts Vis*, p93; F&R I, pp356-8]

| | |
|---|---|
| Besides Receaived ~~for the~~ by the Collonell ~~Officers of the Staff~~ of moneys that came to the Regiment July 14th – 15th of Mr Dagnall and Robert Gregory of Tringe £20 ~~soe~~ in all | 35 |
| The totall of all is | 2864 18 |

*f*2r

A perticular how the moneyes sent to the Regiment (as on the other side) have binne ~~disbursed~~ receaived by the generall officers and captains thereof as followeth viz

| | £ | s |
|---|---|---|
| Receaived By the Collonell | 504 | 5 |
| By the Leuitenant Collonell[341] | 338 | |
| By the Sergeant Major | 335 | 13 |
| By Captain Earle | 247- | |
| By Captain Noake | 231 | |
| By Captain John Barbor[342] | 259 | |
| By Captain Fairclugh[343] | 178 | |
| By Captain William Barbor[344] | 256 | |
| By Captain Rocke | 248 | |
| By Captain Feild[345] | 278 | |
| Summe is - | 2874 | 18s |
| | | |
| £2864-18 sent from the <countrey > | 2874 | 18 |

341 Thomas Sadler Lieutenant Colonel in Wittewronge's regiment was the acting governor of Aylesbury garrison. He was probably the Thomas Sadler of Sopwell, St Albans, to whom pikes of those fleeing Edgehill, were given, who later became a JP for the Liberty, rather than Thomas of Preston near Hitchin, who was appointed to a number of local committees 1643-9 [*LJ* VI, pp76, 257; *CJ* II, p845; F&R I, *passim*]

342 Gabriel Barbor's son

343 Probably the son of Litton Fairclough, of Fairclough Hall in Weston, though he could be a nephew. He was added to the assessment committee in March 1643 and the Sequestration Committee in June. At the Restoration he was assessed for seven hearths [TNA: E179/248/23 *f*29; F&R, I, pp117-23, 168-71; *LJ* VI, p76; *Herts Vis,* pp52-3, 634]

344 Gabriel Barbor's other son

345 Probably Captain Field of Tring, who was one of the first volunteer captains to go into Aylesbury, and was put on the Volunteer committee in September 1643, rather than William Field of Watford, who was put on the Militia Committee in December and subsequently served on committees on and off until 1660. Field had petitioned the Privy Council in 1638 over his treatment, when Ship Money collector for Tring. His widow received his arrears after his death on active service *(see* below) [TNA: SP16/395 *f*111; *CJ* II, p935; F&R I&II *passim*]

| | | |
|---|---|---|
| £2874-18 | Payd to the <Regiment> | 2864 18 |
| £10-00 | Remaynes | 0010 00 |

This remaynder of £10, I conceaive was in my hands~~, for which I am of possessed of~~ whereof £9-9s-4d was accepted by me in part of my ~~pay~~ arrears to the 20th of July

**[107] TNA: SP 28/130 Part II *ff*24-8 Humphrey Packer Junior's account (October 1643)**

The accompt of Humphrey Packer Junior paymaster of the regiment or Sir John Norwich[346] of all such moneyes hee hath received and payd for accompt of the said regiment. *Humphrey Packer*

*f*26 Received of My Colonell Sir John Norwich

A list of the gentlemen and souldiers under the command of Sir John Norwich beinge payd after theire march from Hertford from the third of October to the tenth of the same month 1643.

| | | £ s d |
|---|---|---|
| Sir John Norwich as Major Generall Collonell and Captaine | | 24 03 00 |
| Nicholas Deane - Captain Leiuetennant | | 08 08 00 |
| John Ediwin - Coronett | | 04 14 06 |
| Humphrey Packer - Clarke | | 03 10 00 |
| John Gardiner - Scoute Master | | 03 10 00 |
| Daniel Ventris - Marshall | | 01 15 00 |
| Thomas Hunt - Master of the Armes | | 01 15 00 |
| John Maihewe - Quarter Master | | 03 03 00 |
| William Joyce | } | |
| John Smith | } Corporalls | 03 03 00 |
| Thomas Muncaster | } | |
| John Eales | } | |
| John Hawkins | } Trumpiters | 02 06 00 |
| Thomas West – Sadler | | 01 01 00 |
| Thomas Hubberd | | 00 17 06 |
| Henry Goodyeare | | 00 17 06 |
| William Braughton | | 00 17 06 |

346 For Sir John Norwich see Appendix

| | |
|---|---|
| Christopher Kimpton | 00 17 06 |
| Robert Dixon | 00 17 06 |
| John Scarborough | 00 17 06 |
| Martin Hall | 00 17 06 |
| Thomas Lashbrooke | 00 17 06 |
| John Gates[347] | 00 17 06 |
| Thomas Springe | 00 17 06 |
| Gabriell Baskervile | 00 17 06 |
| John Whithe | 00 17 06 |
| William Sherringham | 00 17 06 |
| William Stewarte | 00 17 06 |
| Richard Munday | 00 17 06 |
| Jonas Collop | 00 17 06 |
| Richard Gwine | 00 17 06 |
| Richard Hayle | 00 17 06 |
| Edward Shelton | 00 17 06 |
| Richard Steevens | 00 17 06 |
| Robert Longe | 00 17 06 |
| Edward Cowles | 00 17 06 |
| John Rawlins | 00 17 06 |
| Christopher Peirson | 00 17 06 |
| Henry Ingram | 00 17 06 |
| Edward Walker | 00 17 06 |
| Tobias Crispe | 00 17 06 |
| William Proctor | 00 17 06 |
| Nicholas Symonds | 00 17 06 |
| Edward Wilkinson | 00 17 06 |
| Mathewe Kinge | 00 17 06 |
| George Herryott | 00 17 06 |
| Edward Coxe | 00 17 06 |
| Launcelett Whiteinge | 00 17 06 |
| Robert Dunne | 00 17 06 |
| William Ayres | 00 17 06 |
| John Eteridge | 00 17 06 |
| Paule Browne | 00 17 06 |

[347] John Gates of Hemel Hempstead, High Constable of the Hundred of Dacorum 1639-41 and on the volunteer committee and militia committee in September and December 1643 respectively [HALS: QSB2B *ff*11d, 24; *LJ*, VI, pp244; 342-3]

| | |
|---|---|
| John Harlowe | 00 17 06 |
| Richard Bucke | 00 17 06 |
| William Allen[348] | 00 17 06 |
| Daniell Howe | 00 17 06 |
| William Heath | 00 17 06 |
| Henry Gates | 00 17 06 |
| William Hatton | 00 17 06 |
| Emanuel Walton | 00 17 06 |
| Nathaniel Walton | 00 17 06 |
| William Skeppe | 00 17 06 |
| John Anderton | 00 17 06 |
| Alexander Gardiner | 00 17 06 |
| Francis Oxeley | 00 17 06 |
| John Stewarte | 00 17 06 |
| William Nicholls | 00 17 06 |
| William Bragge | 00 17 06 |
| Nathaniel Browne | 00 17 06 |
| George Foster | 00 17 06 |
| John Carter | 00 17 06 |
| Thomas Tinseley | 00 17 06 |
| William Kinge[349] | 00 17 06 |
| Warner Trott | 00 17 06 |
| Ralph Brockes | 00 17 06 |
| John Adams | 00 17 06 |
| Jeffery Cornewell | 00 17 06 |
| William Scrivener | 00 17 06 |
| Randall Stockton | 00 17 06 |
| Cornelius Leaper | 00 17 06 |
| Thomas Farmer | 00 17 06 |
| William Grainger | 00 17 06 |
| Robert Avis | 00 17 06 |
| John Pharrowe | 00 17 06 |
| Thomas Lewes | 00 17 06 |
| Timothy Kimpton | 00 17 06 |
| Edward Sheppard | 00 17 06 |

[348] William Allen of Hoddesdon, gent, High Constable of the Hundreds of Hertford and Braughing, 1643-7 [HALS: QSB2B *f*39d; QSR7 *f*95]

[349] William Kinge, High Constable of the Hundred of Hertford, 1626 [HALS: QSB2A *f*63]

| | |
|---|---|
| Lawrence Cooper | 00 17 06 |
| Edward Smith | 00 17 06 |
| John Tucker | 00 17 06 |
| Ezekiell Ayres | 00 17 06 |
| Samuel Atkinson | 00 17 06 |
| William Fardell | 00 17 06 |
| Walter Lewington | 00 17 06 |
| Jesper Arnold | 00 17 06 |
| Moses Price | 00 17 06 |
| John Palmer | 00 17 06 |
| John Hatton | 00 17 06 |
| Thomas Stratton | 00 17 06 |
| Thomas Austine | 00 17 06 |
| William Fowke | 00 17 06 |
| Phillip Spooner | 00 17 06 |
| John Graye | 00 17 06 |
| David Evans | 00 17 06 |
| Francis Evans | 00 17 06 |
| John Smith | 00 17 06 |
| Thomas Burcher | 00 17 06 |
| George Butts | 00 17 06 |
| John Jacques | 00 17 06 |
| | 143 17 06 |

**[108] TNA: SP28/130 Part II Humphrey Packer's account *ff*40-40d List of payments from the Militia Committee to Captain Moulson's troop, October 1643**

A list of the gentlemen and soldiers under the command of Captain Thomas Moulson payd from the tenth of October to the seaventeenth 1643

| | £ s d |
|---|---|
| Thomas Moulson – Captain | 13 13 00 |
| Symon Ailoffe - Leiutennant | 06 06 00 |
| Robert Fitzwilliams Cornett | 04 14 06 |
| Steven Taylor Quarter Master | 03 03 00 |
| Edward Fairecloth } | |
| Richard Gynne } Corporalls | 03 03 00 |
| Christopher Morecroft } | |
| John Saywell } | |

| | |
|---|---|
| Edward Davis } Trumpetts | 02 02 00 |
| William Kinsman | 00 17 06 |
| Ralph Hardinge | 00 17 06 |
| Richard Alexander | 00 17 06 |
| Edward Harlocke | 00 17 06 |
| Richard Duckins | 00 17 06 |
| Edward Buninge | 00 17 06 |
| Henry Kelley | 00 17 06 |
| Robert Wallis | 00 17 06 |
| Richard Younge | 00 17 06 |
| Augustine Warde | 00 17 06 |
| Thomas Gregory | 00 17 06 |
| Thomas Lodge | 00 17 06 |
| Richard Patman | 00 17 06 |
| Henry Southen | 00 17 06 |
| Edward Mosum | 00 17 06 |
| Richard Trott | 00 17 06 |
| Joseph Hall | 00 17 06 |
| Isacke Rutt | 00 17 06 |
| Edward Clarke | 00 17 06 |
| Samuel With | 00 17 06 |
| Robert Beldinge | 00 17 06 |
| John Heydon | 00 17 06 |
| Richard Roberts | 00 17 06 |
| Samuel Capell | 00 17 06 |
| Richard Wadley | 00 17 06 |
| Gerrard Morecraft | 00 17 06 |
| John Marson | 00 17 06 |
| William Dell | 00 17 06 |
| Nathaniel Heydon | 00 17 06 |
| Thomas Steines | 00 17 06 |
| William Gate | 00 17 06 |
| Charles Booth | 00 17 06 |
| Thomas Betts | 00 17 06 |
| Richard Winter | 00 17 06 |
| Richard Arrys | 00 17 06 |
| Robert Weller | 00 17 06 |
| Thomas North | 00 17 06 |
| Jeames Pharrowe | 00 17 06 |

| | |
|---|---|
| John Thoroughgood | 00 17 06 |
| Maurice Seare | 00 17 06 |
| John Therneham | 00 17 06 |
| Richard Woodhouse | 00 17 06 |
| Richard Grymes | 00 17 06 |
| Thomas May | 00 17 06 |
| Henry Bayly | 00 17 06 |
| Robert Moody | 00 17 06 |
| Richard Durant | 00 17 06 |
| Henry Hudnall | 00 17 06 |
| John Peace | 00 17 06 |
| John Denycombe | 00 17 06 |
| Freeman Norris | 00 17 06 |
| Thomas Laughton | 00 17 06 |
| John Smith | 00 17 06 |
| Christopher Phillips | 00 17 06 |
| William Clarke | 00 17 06 |
| Bartholomew Harvey | 00 17 06 |
| Thomas Smith | 00 17 06 |
| William Pattison | 00 17 06 |
| Henry Hickman | 00 17 06 |
| John Almond | 00 17 06 |
| Henry Beech | 00 17 06 |

**[109] TNA: SP28/232 Account of Colonel Nicholls for mustering and exercising the militia in northeast Hertfordshire, November 1645**

<u>Colonell Nicholls Account</u>
For one days muster and on days exercise at Buntingford being the 18th and the 27th of November 1645

| | £ s d |
|---|---|
| Layston 12 men for 2 days each | 00 16 00 |
| Therfield 17 men | 01 02 00 |
| Buckland 5 men | 00 06 08 |
| Widdiall 5 men | 00 06 08 |
| Barley 12 men | 00 16 00 |
| Brent Pelham 6 men | 00 08 00 |
| Stock Pelham on man | 00 01 04 |
| Royston 14 men | 00 18 04 |
| Hormead Magna 13 men | 00 17 04 |

| | | |
|---|---|---|
| Hormead Parva 6 men | | 00 08 00 |
| Reed 5 men | | 00 06 08 |
| Anstey 13 men | | 00 17 04 |
| Mesden 4 men | | 00 05 04 |
| Nuthamsted 3 men | | 00 04 00 |
| Furnex Pelham 13 men | | 00 17 04 |
| Barkway 10 men | | 00 13 04 |
| | Sum is | *(deleted)* |
| The colonel for 2 days at each meeting | | *(deleted)* |
| Captain Lieutenant for 2 days | | 00 08 00 |
| The ensigne for 2 days | | 00 06 00 |
| The foure sergeants | | 00 06 00 |
| The foure corpralls | | 00 02 08 |
| The marshall 2 days each | | 00 13 04 |
| The warrants careing out | | 00 04 00 |
| The two drummers 2 days each | | 00 04 00 |
| For 128 men for two dayes and for one day on man | | 09 04 00 |
| Sum Totall | | 11 08 08 |
| *(deleted)* | | *(deleted)* |
| For 2 drummes bought of Captain Sherlocke | | 02 10 00 |
| *(deleted)* | Sum | *(deleted)* |
| | | 13 18 08 |

**[110] TNA: SP28/231 Fromabove Dove's account for paying troops, 1644**

| | |
|---|---|
| Fromabove Dove his accounte | |
| The 14th of February 1643 the received of Mr Hickman Tresurer <at> St Allbans | 360 00 00 |
| Of Mr Packer treasurer at Hartford | 540 00 00 |
| Payde at Ware in the presence of the committee to Sir John Norwich[350] Colonell and to his souldiers | 881 02 10 |
| And then left in the hands of Mr John Kinge, Muster maister by the appointment of the Committee sittinge in Hartforde | 018 18 02 |
| | |
| The 29th February receved of Mr Hickman | 299 04 00 |
| The very money I delivered to Mr Gabrill Barber by the Committee's appointment | 299 04 00 |

[350] For Sir John Norwich see Appendix

| | |
|---|---|
| The 6th March 1643 then I received at the hands of John Andrew and William Melsom by the appointment of the Committee sitting at Hartford | 200 00 00 |
| and of Mr Hickman treasurer in St Albans | 160 00 00 |
| Payde by me to Sir John Norwich Collonel to his regiment at Moreton in Bucks. Since the 10th March | 360 01 06 |
| The 22nd March Received of Mr Hickman | 400 00 00 |
| Then of Mr Packer treasurer | 600 00 00 |
| Payd to Mr Leaman[351] at Cambridge treasurer 24th March | 1000 00 00 |
| The 20th July 1644 received of Mr Hickman Tresurer by order of the Committee sitting at St Albans towards my paye as Quarter Master payed | 006 13 00 |
| So the hole warrants out of boath treasurers amounts to | 2565 17 00 |
| And I have payd as abovesaid accordinge to order | 2559 06 06 |
| Ther beinge righte cast up then in my note in my hand towards my charges and payments as presented | 0006 10 06 |

*Per mee Fromabove Dove*

**[111] TNA: SP28/231 Militia Committee Payment to Henry Peach, 9/8/1644**

9 August 1644

Mr Turnor the treasurer is to pay Henrye Peach for his journey 3 dayes carying up Mr Carye and attending the Committee *ix*$^{s}$. More for setting out and carrying money to the Oringe Regiment 4 dayes cometh to *xii*$^{s}$. More for carrying and paying at London 300$^{li}$ – two dayes- *vi*$^{s}$. More you are to pay him for the keeping a mare tenn weeks at *ii*$^{s}$ *vi*$^{d}$ per weeke for publique service cometh to *xxv*s- The totall of all is fiftye two shillings, which you are to pay

£2-12s-0d

*Gabriel Barbor Chairman, William Carter, John Finch, Francis Clerke, William Barbor, Henry Marsh,*[352] *Dannill Nicoll*

[351] William Leman of Northaw, later MP, under treasurer of the Association see Appendix

[352] Henry Marsh of Shenley Esq. was put on local militia and assessment committees from September 1643 to July 1659 [F&R I &II *passim*]

***(Endorsed along left hand edge)*** Received the day and yeare aforesaid of Mr William Turner, treasurer, the summe of 2li.12s for that use aforesaid by mee *Thomas Bevis*

**[112] TNA: SP28/231 William Love's Bill for paying soldiers, 1/7/1644**

The treasurer, Mr Turners required to pay Mr William Love eighty eight pounds out of the Scotch monies which is to cleere Collonell Michells pay who lyeth in siege of Greenland howse, which said 88$^{li}$ you are to repay the account, out of the monies next ~~monies~~ to be received for the Millicia, and for the payment of the said 88$^{li}$ this shalbe your warrant. Hertford 1 July 1644
*Gabriel Barbor Chairman, Thomas Niccolls, William Plomer, Thomas Meade, John Finch, Henry Marsh, Robert Draper*

**[113] TNA: SP28/231 Order to Treasurer Turner from Hertford Committee to pay William Love, 4/11/1644**

November the 4$^{th}$ 1644
Mr Turner Treasurer, you are required to torn over unto William Love, paymaster for the Black and Oringe Regiments, whatt moneys are upon arrears for all the taxes for the militia, except the last tax which is now collectinge, that hee may putt it over to the captaynes in parte of payment for theyr companyes, which summe is, we are informed, is neare five hundred pounds and other money to make it upp five hundred and fotye pounds. We order you to putt over, to the said William Love and take his receipt for it, for so much moneys payd him for that purpose, with which hee shall stand charged uppon his account. Yet neverthelesse, if any of the sayd moneys cannot bee received by the Captaynes to whom hee assignes it but that you disclayme it and returne the order by him to you given to receive it. Then the said William shall agayne returne so much defalced[353] upon his account, and this shall bee your warrant for so doinge. Given under our hands the day above written:
*Gabriel Barbor, Joseph Dalton, Maior, John Wittewronge, William Barbor, Thomas Meade, William Carter, John Finch, William Plomer*

[353] This is probably defalked, i.e. to make a defalcation or reduction, which was a phrase often used when referring to accounts. My thanks are due to Professor John Miller for this interpretation

***(On reverse)*:**Received of William Turner, Treasurer, according to the above committee order by the arrears of taxes and moneys payd to commander and officers, which I have charged upon theyr accounts the summe of five hundred and forty pounds. I say received the 5th of November 1644 in manner aforesaid £540 *Per me William Love*

**[114] TNA: SP28/233 William Love to the Hertford Committee re arrears, 23/3/1645(6)**

Honoured Gentlemen,
The souldyers want of moneys <both in the garrison and in the armyes> doth not onelye haunt and persue mee from place to place, but now is come to the Committee of the Eastern Asosiation, who on Saturday night enjoyned mee to use all diligence to get in the whole 12 moneths tax least our forces (as they seemed to feare) should disband. They allso desired, although I allreadye have borrowed for them £1,200 and have yet repayd scarce £600, to borrow more moneys untill the taxes come in, which, speedilye to effect, it is ordered a short additionall ordinance bee this day drawen, to morrow brought into the howse for the speedye collectinge the arrears of all ordinances in the Asosiation (whereby you may perceive that those who have beene most forward in payments have not onely done best service to the state, but allso to your Countrey). I doubt not but you have, as I desired last Munday, sent out your agents this weeke to the severall townes and that those collectors have brought some good considerable summe to Mr Turner. But whether so or not, yett, the exegencye beinge as it is, I desire you, though you borrow it all, furnish Captain Whitbread with £500 to St Albans will not fayle uppon Tuesday of payinge 300 if not more, who allreadye have payd 600. I my selfe have beene since this week in Essex got £600, which I have payd the firste parte of which I borrowed, must away agayne to morrow to make it up, must also on Thursday be at Berrye for money asigned Bedford thence to pay yours at Newarke uppon Fryday. I must bee at Newport[354] haveinge engaged my selfe to make pay day before Easter, which must onelye bee done with Hartfordshire money, £250 expected from Berrye and what can bee got at Northampton, all much to litle to pay 6 weekes pay, beinge £2460 which is

[354] On 24 April 1645 soldiers in the garrison complained they were not getting paid and were near mutiny. Love came without the expected taxes and Joseph Barbor had signed for Hertfordshire from the Committee of the Garrison about this [HMC 8th Report Duke of Marlborough MSS p7: Committee of the garrison to Sir William Boteler]

expected, but must in great parte bee made up with good wordes and fayr promises for the future.
This new intended ordinance to bringe in arrears will necessarilye occasion to demonstrate what each countye ought to have payd, hath payd and still doe owe to Newport at what time. I shall have oportunytye for the case of our Countye to make use of the two accounts given mee, one by Mr Gardner for Hartford, the other by Mr Hickman for St Albans of moneys payd to Collector Ayloffe which accounts I keepe carefullye. Neither doe I forget what was payd Major Temple by my Lord of Manchesters order the full of all I will put in but am ascertained from some of the howse who wish right well to our Country. Yett all I put in will not pass but what can have any appearance of equity and shall send readye assistance. In breife asure your selves I will not in my spheare bee any wayes wantinge to promote the good of the Countye. Though I must tell you it hath not a litle troubled mee this weeke to heare, since I came to towne, that it should bee reported in our owne Countye, nay in my owne towne, I am clapt by the heeles for couseninge the state. I thanke God I am not onelye readye but have desired to give an account at any time and will justlye balance the account. The author I hope to discover but doubt it will rather fall uppon som beggarlye rascally or rich malignant. But yet howsoever thorough good and bad report until the kingdomes troubles or myselfe end, I shall not pull backe my hand nor doubt to approve my selfe to the state and each of you a faythful servant.
*William Love*
London March 23 1645

**(*On reverse*)**
Hertford 25 *Martii* 1646
It is this day ordered by the Committee that Mr Turner, High Collector, shall pay (accordinge to the contents of Mr Loves letter hereunto belonginge) the summe of fower hundred <and fiftie pounds to Captaine Whitebread> (out of the money that is raised for the guarisons) for the use of the guarison of Newport Pagnall, they beinge nowe in greate want and necessity. And this shall bee your warrant, Signed by us of the Committee the day and yeare abovesaid.
*Gabriel Barbor, William Presiley, Thomas Tooke, Alexander Weld, John Humbarstone*

## Section C The effect of the war on individuals and communities

### Part 1 Effect of free quarter and depredations by soldiers

**[115] TNA: SP28/11 Pt 1 *f*73 Colney Street claims for free quarter (undated 1643-4)**

William Umment of Colney Street quartered Simon Smith being of Captain Reedes Companye in Collonel Thompson's Regiment five weeks £0-12-06
John Hall of Colney Street - (for) George Anderson 13 weeks as above and he receved of the said George 6 Shillings is due 26-6d
John Sutton of same – one week 2/6d
Quartered 2 dragooners under Meldrum[355] 3 nights 2/-
Other losses and charges 3/-
*John Hall* his mark ***X***

**[116] TNA: SP28/11 Pt 1 *f*28 St Stephens Park Ward - John Beech's claim, 1644**

Note for John Beech charge and quarter and los by soldiers
20 October 1643 Colonel Meldrum's 3 men
15 November 1643 Captain Hills troop 2 men
1 March 8 other Colonel Meldrums
2 of Captain Andrews soldiers came 14 February went 6 May £2-10
I lost 4 sheep worth 8/- a peece with the soldiers
Severall times I lent to the Committee at St Albans 40/- witness Edmund Dell[356] and John Field £2

---

[355] Sir John Meldrum, a Scotsman and specialist in military engineering, helped organize the defence of Hull in July 1642 and was successfull in besieging Portsmouth the following month. By 1644 he was in charge of the London Auxiliary regiment previously commanded by Lord Saye and Sele and was sent to attack Newark in February, but Rupert drew royalists from a number of garrisons and defeated him after a furious battle. Meldrum's force surrendered but was allowed to go free having forfeited their arms [Adair, J., *Roundhead General: The campaigns of Sir William Waller* (Stroud, 1997) pp34, 36; Haythornthwaite, *English Civil War*, pp76, 147]

| | |
|---|---|
| When Captain Aylward[357] went to Hitchin he had of me 13/- | |
| towards setting out[358] one soldier | 13/- |
| When Captain Marsh went out 8/- ditto | 8/- |
| William Birchmore[359] and William Eware[360] | 5/- |
| Loss of poultry | £1 |
| Loss a peece[361] worth | 16/- |

**[117] TNA: SP28/11 Pt II *f*160 St Stephens Park Ward - John Hart's claim, (undated 1643-4)**

Note of John Hart's losis and quatering sogars of free quarter as followeth St Stevens parish in parke ward.
Colonell Mederems[362] Draguners under Captaine Mainerd came to quarter in my house with five men and five horse and staid three days

| | |
|---|---|
| For thare own diet | 7/6d |
| For thare horse ottes and hay | 8-0 |

One of Captain Pile's soger John Ouger came to quarter at my house 7 November with 2 horsis and stabled three weekes

| | |
|---|---|
| For his diet and horse ottes and hay | £1-0-0 |

Thomas Paige and his Brother, gentillmen of the life guard[363] came to quarter at my house with three horsis and one man and

---

[356] A John Dell, one of four sons of Robert Dell, had lived in St Albans in 1495, and there were Dells in St Michaels and Radlett in the late 17th century [Flood, S (ed.*) St Albans Wills 1470-1500,* Hertfordshire Record Society Vol IX, (Hertford, 1993) p128; Smith and North, *St Albans*, pp147, 229]

[357] The Aylewards were an extensive local family. A Henry Ayleward of St Stephens died in 1487 leaving sons William and John. John and Nicholas Ayleward had leased the manor of Cell Barnes from Sopwell Nunnery before the reformation and the family had at least three local branches by the 17th century. It is therefore not clear from which branch this Captain Ayleward came [Flood, *St Albans Wills,* p 85; Smith and North, *St Albans 1650-1700*, pp211-3]

[358] 'Setting out' meant equipping a soldier with a uniform, a helmet, possibly other armour and a weapon

[359] Possibly William Birchmore, High Constable of the Hundred of Dacorum in the 1620s, or a relative [HALS: QSB2A *ff*32, 63]

[360] Possibly a descendant of Reginald Ewer, who had lived in 'Halywelstret' in St Albans in 1476 [Flood, *St Albans Wills*, p31]

[361] A peece was a fowling piece or sporting gun

[362] Meldrum's dragoons

[363] The Lifeguard was the regiment of cavalry associated with the senior commander of the parliamentary army acting as his bodyguard

staid 2 dayes for thare diet etc. 6/-
John Rocke gent of the Life guard came to quarter 27 December with toe men and 2 horsis and he and his horsis staid 3 weekes and his man staid ten weekes – for diet etc. £2-18-0
Towe sogers belonging to the London Trained band came to quarter 28 December staid 11 dayes 6/-
William Rye, under my Lord Robert came 4 March staid 7 weekes 10/6
Col Mederams dragooners came and tucke away a fouling peece and one shepe
For fowling peece 10/-
For the sheep 8/-
Paid for Armes and seting forth a Sogar under Captain Alerd 15/-
Under Captain Nash 9/4
Under Captain Noake[364]
Listed a black gelding valued £6
Somme is £8-8-4

Signed *Daniel Manesty* }
*John Ivory*[365] } Commissioners

**[118] TNA: SP28/155 Bushey parish accounts *f*2 claims for free quarter, 1643-1644**

<u>*f*2 The charge of Quateringe</u>
The first of August 1643 came 4 companies of dragoones under the Command of Major Moore, Captain Woolfe, Captain Ewer and Leiutenant Wattson consisting of 150 men and horse and stayed 8 Dayes 60 00 00
The 22nd day of October 1643 came two Regiments of my Lord Generalls and stayed one nighte 25 00 00
The 25th of October 1643 came two troops of my Lord Denbys[366] of

---

[364] Noake was a captain in the Hertfordshire volunteer regiment under Wittewrong at Uxbridge in April and Aylesbury from May to July 1643 [HALS: DE/Lw/O2]
[365] Possibly related to Robert Ivory, four times mayor of St Albans [Smith and North, *St Albans,* p46]
[366] Basil Fielding, second Earl of Denbigh, former courtier and diplomat, fought for parliament at Edgehill, created commander in chief in the north-west midlands in June 1643 but did not reach there until the winter and returned to London in mid July 1644. The horse therefore must have been taken well before this [Anne Hughes, 'Fielding, Basil, second Earl of Denbigh (*c*1608-1675)' N*ewDNB*]

| | |
|---|---|
| 200 men and horse and stayed one day and nighte | 05 00 00 |
| The 6th of November 1643 came Capt. Ewing with 40 men and horse and stayed 4 days | 08 00 00 |
| The 7th of November 1643 came came (*sic*) Capt. Abercrombie with 55 men and horse and stayed 9 weeks | 173 05 00 |
| The 16th of November 1643 came Captain Garner with 54 men and horse and stayed 2 days | 05 08 00 |
| The 23rd November 1643 came Major Hambleton with 56 men and horse and stayed 12 weekes | 133 14 00 |
| February 9th 1643 cam Trooper Robert Pye with 60 men and horse and stayed 3 weeks | 63 00 00 |
| The 8th of March 1643 came Colonel Hamsted with a Regiment of foote of 250 and stayed 7 weeks | 183 15 00 |
| The first of May 1644 Holborne[367] with 500 foote and stayed two dayes | 25 00 00 |
| att 1s 6d per diem for horsemen and 6d per diem for foote | £674 02 00 |

not anie thing for oates.
here is not anie of my Lord of Manchesters

**[119] TNA: SP28/155 Extracts from East Barnet parish return to Mr Foxwist and the Sub-Committee of Accounts *ff*7-8 12/12/1644**

*f*7 It appeares also to us that by one warrant dated 21 November 1643 and under the hands of Charles Fleetwood,[368] John Cocke and Nicholas Skinner, wherein they tearme themselves commissioners to his Excellency, (and upon

[367] Colonel James Holborn was one of the Scots officers commanding parliamentary troops. A fortnight after this claim, he, Colonel John Middleton and others petitioned the Commons. By August he was the Major-General of foot in Waller's army. He distinguished himself at the Battle of Newbury in October and by December he was in the Southwest where he reached Taunton. He was ordered to raise cavalry there, but ended up paying for them himself. He resigned after the passing of the Self Denying Ordinance, possibly because the troops were too Independent in religion for his liking [*CJ* III, pp493-4; IV, pp1-2, 112-3, 179-81; *LJ* VII, pp40-1; Kishlansky, *New Model Army*, pp48-9; Adair, *Roundhead general*, pp203, 220, 231]

[368] Charles Fleetwood, by May 1643, when he was a captain, was empowered to seize the assets from sequestered royalists in the eastern counties. Colonel of a cavalry regiment in the Eastern Association under Manchester, later also in the New Model Army he commanded the horse at Dunbar as Lieutenant-general. He was a friend, then son-in-law of Oliver Cromwell, marrying his widowed daughter Bridget, as his second wife [Toby Barnard, 'Fleetwood, Charles, appointed Lord Fleetwood under the protectorate (*c*1618-1692)' *NewDNB*]

the testimony of diverse of the said towne) 8 Bedds, 6 Boulsters and 15 blanketts were sent out of the said Towne to the Towne of St Albanes for the Earl of Essex Souldiers then there, which bedds, boulsters and blanketts were never restored to the said towne, were prized at £6-19-3d

Freeman Nicholls,[369] it is also averred before us by aforesaid that he had twoe carts taken away at London, one by Mr Jude for the service of Parliament to carry the carriage belonging to Sir William Waller's[370] army; the other taken by Mr Richardson for the army under Colonel Brownes command which were never restored or other satisfaction given him and were worth at least £10

It alsoe appeareth daylie and is notorious amongst us that diverse pretending to bee souldiers and other loose persons come to the inhabitants' houses in a bold and terrifieing way, craveing reliefe, both in meate and money, which the inhabitants have bein, for feare in a manner enferred, to yeild them, and that charge haveing continued for a long tyme hath ben and is an extreame burthen unto them.

Also duringe the time of quarteringe souldiers amongst us, diverse sheepe, swine and poultry have ben taken away by the souldiers, some in the presence of the owners, some by stealth to the very greate burthen of the inhabitants. Alsoe dureing the same tyme diverse gates in the severall grounds of the inhabitants as alsoe their hedges and fences have bein commonly broken, spoiled and carried away by the souldiers and some <more> corne in the strawe and some in the granary hath bein taken and given to horses and spoiled.

And what is as grievous as any, the houses and landes of the inhabitants in these tymes <some> cannot bee lett at all, some cannot bee lett but to excessive abatement of the prices[371] and few tennants *(f8)* are able to pay those rents they take grounds at, whereby the inhabitants are impoverished extreamely.

---

[369] Mr Daniel Nicholl of the town of Barnet was an assessor for the county for the 5th and 20th part in June 1643 and was on Hertfordshire committees from 1643 to 1660 [TNA: SP19/2 *f*23; F&R I&II *passim*]

[370] Sir William Waller was the commander of the second main parliamentary army in the South

[371] i.e. at much reduced rents

Alsoe by coulor of a warrant from Mr White, a minister sent into the parrish to officiate the cure,[372] severall of the inhabitants were required to pay and did pay diverse somes of money over and above their due tythes[373] to the said minister in regard hee officiated there in the winter at which time noe tyeth was due. *W. Greene, Fenton Parsons, Freeman Nicoll*

**[120] TNA: SP28/154 Redbourn parish accounts *f*8 Damages done by soldiers, 1643**

<u>*f*8 The Account of the damages done by souldiers within the parishe of Redborne 1643</u>

| | |
|---|---|
| *In primis* John Dell had 8 sheepe taken away by the Souldiers that quartered at St Albans valued | 03 04 00 |
| Feb. 1644 Thomas Saunders had 16 sheepe taken away by souldiers 14 of them nowe greate with lambe valued at | 09 12 00 |
| Robert Beech had 2 sheepe taken away by Souldeiers valued at | 00 16 00 |
| Jeremy Fynch had a foulinge peece[374] taken away out of his howse by souldiers by violence valued at | 01 00 00 |
| November 1643 John Thewer gent[375] informeth that he sustained losse by souldiers of the City Regiment[376] under Coll Hudson which pulled down soe many of that his house or Inn in Redborne Street being 2 bayes of buildinge to the value of as he sayeth of | 55 00 00 |
| but worth not one quarter soe much | |
| Tymothie Axtill Sustayneth losse by souldiers which tooke from him 3 sheepe and one Lambe which souldeirs quartered at St Albans valued at | 01 10 00 |
| Alsoe they damnified me in my frames? | 00 10 ? |
| Edward Arnott sustayned losse by souldiers which tooke from him one horse prised at | 05 00 00 |
| And alsoe 3 bushells of oates | 00 05 ? |

[372] Serve as minister
[373] Tithes – a tenth of the income of parishioners paid to the minister for himself and the church, normally paid at Easter, but presumably collected once then, and demanded later by the new incumbent
[374] A sporting gun
[375] John Thewer was appointed to the county assessment committee on 31 March 1643 [F&R I, pp117-23]
[376] City of London militia regiment

Richard Kingham sustayned losse by 3 souldiers which he quartered upon free quarter takeinge away his horse that *(torn)* (he has) vowed that he will not have them agayne until he is payed to have them *xs* (0 10 00)
Allin Rawlings sustayned losse by souldiers which tooke away from him 5 sheepe valued at 02 00 00
John Twydall sustayned losse by souldiers that quartered with him upon free quarter which tooke away from him one Byble valued at 00 08 00
Likewise Collonel Hudsons souldiers cutt downe his trees to the value of 01 00 00
John Thewer of Redborne above named informeth that he sustayned losse by having his whole teame of horses taken out of the plowe in the cheefest of seed tyme by William Stepney[377] then constable by warrant from my Lord General as he affirmeth insomuch that with his jorney after them he and his servants for the space of a whole weeke or more the hinderance in his season and his best horse left quite to the value in all of 20 00 00
We think not halfe soe much
Richard Peacocke[378] informeth he had one horse stolen to the value of 00 10 00
1643 Colonel Hudson kept his mayne Cort of Guard at the howse Of Jane Egleton widow 11 weeks as she informeth that she was damnified therby 10 00 00
Alsoe she informeth that some of his souldiers opened her locks and did take from her out of a box in a chamber £8 in money 2 gold rings and a chayne and whistle of silver worth £17 17 00 00
120 00 00

*f8d* Redborn 1643
William Rose informeth that he is damnified by the free quarter of Souldiers and sheepe stolen from him to the value of 18 02 08
William Saunders informeth that some of Collonel Bluer? his souldiers quartering in towne stole from him a Byble and carried away as much of his hay as was worth 04 10 00

[377] A Ralph Stepney had inherited the manor of Lawrence in 1527, Isaac Stepney was a glover and a George Stepney had a house at Street End with seven hearths in 1663 [Munby, *Redbourn*, pp23, 38, 43]
[378] In 1663 Richard Peacocke, (Pocock) the former constable, had a house with seven hearths at Dean End [Munby, *Redbourn*, p38]

He alsoe informeth that Collonel Hudsons Souldiers broke downe his Rayles and cut down his trees to the value of £*v* and that the free quarter of other Souldiers came to £3 3s toto 08 03 00

Bartholomew Bond informeth that some of Collonel Hale[379] his troopers broke open his barne and did take away his oates unthreshed to the value of 00 10 00

And that Major Bofa his troopers brake open his barne 3 several tymes and did take away his oates in strawe and fed and littered their horses throughout to the value of *l*s 02 10 00

And that a Souldier of Capt Man[380] his company stole a sheete from him worth 00 10 00

And that other of his company stole away 2 curtaynes worth *xx*s 01 00 00

And that others of them called for wine and beere as much as came to *x*s and would not pay for it 00 10 00

And that Collonel Hudson for his owne fire burnt him as much wood as came to £*x* and would pay ~~no~~ nothinge for it 10 00 00

And that Collonel Hudson's souldiers cut downe his trees pulled up his gates and pales and spoyled his fences which will not be made good agayne for £*x* 10 00 00

And that some of Collonel Barkleyes regiment pulled up his Pales brake up his ware[381] which flowed[382] meddowes and cut down his trees to the value of 03 00 00

*Item* George Symons informeth that he had 2 sheepe stolen to the value of *xx*s 01 00 00

**[121] TNA: SP28/155 North Mymms parish accounts – Losses to the Parish (undated 1643-4?)**

<u>*f*8 Losses and other burdens to the parish</u>

Mrs Coningsby[383] 4 fat weathers, I ewe, 31 pistoll, breade geese, 10 duckes, 12 hens, 1 port mantle,[384] 10 ackers cut downe and

[379] Colonel Hale probably one of the widespread family of Hales in East Hertfordshire.

[380] This may be Joseph Mann who was empowered by Lord Grey to seize delinquents' horses which caused considerable complaint in Essex [Holmes, *Eastern Association*, p81]

[381] Weir

[382] Flooded

[383] Wife of Sir Thomas Coningsby, imprisoned in The Tower of London

[384] Portmanteau – a case or bag for carrying clothing

| | |
|---|---|
| carryed away | 11 00 00 |
| Mr John Grubbe losses in sheepe | 00 10 00 |
| Henry Paine 1 nagge, 2 sheepe, 30 hens, I platter, 6 napkins, 2 tablecloths, 1 holland[385] apron | 05 00 00 |
| John Dell one mare 9 sheep | 09 10 00 |
| John Redwell a gray nagge and sheepe | 07 10 00 |
| Mr Andrewes Linen and an Axe | 00 11 06 |
| William Alway losse in sheepe | 01 10 00 |
| Henry Canon 3 sheepe kild | 01 15 00 |
| John Gervais 2 sheepe, linen and poultry | 01 10 00 |
| John Roberts 2 Ewes, a fat weather[386] | 01 10 00 |
| John Nichols one sheepe | 00 10 00 |
| Richard Chappell losse in sheepe | 02 00 00 |
| Robert Salter A mare | 03 10 00 |
| John Salter one horse, 13 sheepe, 2 lambs, 2 Bibles and a ewe | 21 03 00 |
| Arthur Hollingsworth Hens, ducks | 00 14 00 |
| Thomas Grigges one mare, 5 sheepe | 05 11 08 |
| Hugh Todde 5 ewes with lambs | 02 12 00 |
| Thomas Pursey, twoe mares, 6 sheepe | 18 00 00 |
| Thomas Marbery 2 Ewes | 01 00 00 |
| Henry Beach Sheepe and lambs | 02 00 00 |
| John Clarke Junior 15 Geese, 5 lambs 4 Hens | 02 00 00 |
| William Francis a mare | 03 00 00 |
| Mrs Pindar 4 Horses valued at | 34 00 00 |

**[122] TNA: SP28/155 Bushey parish accounts – Goods taken, 1643**

*f*4 Goods taken away

| | |
|---|---|
| William Ewer had two horses taken from him by officers under Sir Sammuel Luke one of them sayd his name was John Russell and he took £5 for one horse one of the horses (*sic*) and the other horse was worth £10 | 15 00 00 |

Thomas Marston Junior had one of horses taken away out of his teame as he was going from Bushey to Hempstead in August 1643 by som 20 troopers under Major Bofa for which horse he might have had £13 for which was a great losse to him he

[385] Holland was a type of linen fabric named after the Dutch province

[386] A wether is a castrated ram

| | |
|---|---|
| haveinge nothing but his teame to live upon | 13 00 00 |
| Thomas Nicholls[387] this 15th of March 1643 had one horse taken away by Major Harvey | 06 00 00 |
| William Barley had taken from him by souldiers under my Lord Generall out of his barnes in November 1643 wheat and hay to the value of £5 | 05 00 00 |
| Henry Hickman had taken from him in November 1643 by souldiers under Captain Saltkin two horses and a fouling peece worth £13 | 13 00 00 |
| Samuell Hickman had sheepe taken from him by my Lord Generalls souldiers worth £3 | 03 00 00 |
| | 55 00 00 |

**[123] TNA: SP28/129 Part II Free quarter repayments to parishes and towns, 6/3/1644(5)**

***(Front cover)*** In this booke is the quarter for the Earlle of Manchesters souldyers and at the farder off the booke is the order for my paimentt off itt, so farre as I cann

*f*1r A perfect account what every towne is to have and is allowed for quateringe of the Earle of Manchesters souldiers and for what Captains they are allowed

| Digswell | | Ippolitts | |
|---|---|---|---|
| Captaine Browne | 03 01 04 | Captain Browne | 00 02 08 |
| Captaine Packer[388] | 02 15 04 | Major Alford | 01 05 04 |
| Captain Crowe | 20 11 00 | Major Crawford | 06 02 04 |
| | 26 08 04 | Captain Swallow | 07 04 08 |
| Welwin | | Captain Margery | 02 09 08 |

[387] Thomas Nicholls of Bushey and Watford corresponded with Alban Coxe in 1652 over a dispute with Dr King and William Hickman concerning the assessments for the Liberty of St Albans. He was added to the Militia Committee in 1659 and on the Assessment Committee in 1660 [HALS: Coxe Papers 70559: Nicholls to Coxe 29/1/52; *CJ* VII, p760; F&R II, p1370]

[388] Captain William Packer, later Major, who was one of Cromwell's Ironsides, and became Deputy Major-General for Hertfordshire in 1655 and elected MP for Hertford in Richard Cromwell's Parliament. He and other soldiers bought the manor and palace of Theobalds, which was largely demolished by them to build their own houses. It is possible that he was a relative of Humphrey Packer, or even was the William Packer, carpenter of Hertford, who took on George Welch as an apprentice in 1636. He was a Particular Baptist who turned Theobalds into a Baptist settlement [HALS:, HBR 26 f 46; See C H Firth, 'Packer, William (*fl* 1644-1662)', rev D N Farr, *NewDNB*]

| | | | |
|---|---|---|---|
| Captain Browne | 08 08 00 | Captain Dingly | 03 13 04 |
| Major Crawford[389] | 06 17 10 | | 20 18 00 |
| Captain Packer | 03 15 00 | The Earls Lifeguard | 00 02 08 |
| Captain Pell | 00 02 04 | Lieut-Col Huson[390] | 01 00 06 |
| Captain Crowe | 51 14 00 | Captain Jenkins | 00 18 06 |
| Ditto | 06 03 00 | Captain Rolt | 00 00 10 |
| Lieut.-Col. Montague[391] | 00 04 00 | | |
| | 77 04 02 | | |
| | | Captain Axtell[392] | 00 07 10 |
| | | | 22 09 06 |
| Langly | | Iccleford | |
| Captain Browne | 03 07 08 | Captain Browne | 00 04 00 |
| Major Dodson | 00 04 00 | Ditto | 05 01 04 |
| Lieut-Gen. Cromwell | 00 04 00 | Major Alford | 00 05 04 |
| Colonel Norwich[393] | 00 02 00 | Capt. Ireton[394] | |

[389] Major Crawford, a Scots mercenary soldier, who was appointed third in command of the Eastern Association army in February 1644, was a strong Presbyterian and opposed to the influence of radical sects. His arrest of William Packer (above) for disobeying orders may have been related to their religious differences. This conflict was one of the bones of contention between Cromwell, who defended Packer, and Manchester, who disliked officers of radical religious persuasion [C H Firth, 'Crawford Lawrence (1611-1645)', rev Sean Kelsey, *NewDNB*]

[390] John Hewson served under Essex and Manchester then appointed Lieutenant-Colonel of Pickering's New Model regiment, into which some of the Hertfordshire forces were merged. In December, he succeded Pickering as colonel, Daniel Axtell becoming his lieutenant-colonel, with whom he subsequently fought in Ireland, becoming Governor of Dublin [Christopher Durston, 'Hewson, John, appointed Lord Hewson under the protectorate (*fl* 1630-1660)' *NewDNB*]

[391] Edward Montagu (Mountagu) (1625-1672) later first Earl of Sandwich, cousin to the Earl of Manchester, deputy lieutenant of the Association, fought at Hillsden House in March 1644 with Hertfordshire troops and in the recapture of Lincoln, as well as at the battles of Marston Moor and the second battle of Newbury. He became Governor of Henley 1644-5 and acting major-general in the west. As the MP for Hunts, he was excluded from military command after the Self-Denying Ordinance. He sided with Cromwell against Manchester, later being made an admiral, diplomat and member of the Protectorate Council of State by Cromwell [J.D. Davies, 'Montagu, Edward, first Earl of Sandwich (1625-1672)' *NewDNB*]

[392] For Axtell see Appendix

[393] For Colonel Norwich see Appendix

[394] Henry Ireton, fought at Edgehill, became major in Thornhagh's Nottinghamshire regiment, fought with Cromwell at Gainsborough in July 1643, becoming deputy governor of the Isle of Ely under Cromwell, who became his friend. He became quarter-master general in the Eastern Association army under Manchester and fought at Marston Moor and the second battle of Newbury. He was appointed colonel of a horse regiment in the New Model Army and

| | |
|---|---|
| Captain Griffin | 01 10 00 |
| | 05 08 04 |

Preston

| | |
|---|---|
| Captain Browne | 02 12 00 |
| Captain Dale | 01 15 00 |
| | 04 07 10 |

Willian

| | |
|---|---|
| Captain Browne | 03 05 04 |
| Major Dodson | 04 07 04 |
| Captain Lawrance | 00 14 08 |
| Colonel Norwich | 05 06 00 |
| Major Crawford | 08 10 08 |
| Captain Swallow | 03 18 00 |
| | 26 02 00 |

*f*2v Letchworth

| | |
|---|---|
| Major Disborowe | 05 03 04 |
| Major Crawford | 04 04 08 |
| Captain Swallow | 00 04 08 |
| Captain Gladman | 03 11 04 |
| Lieut.-Gen. Cromwell | 00 03 04 |
| | 13 07 04 |

Weston

| | |
|---|---|
| Major Disborow | 19 15 04 |
| Major Alford | 17 00 00 |
| Colonel Norwich | 07 18 08 |
| Capt Ireton ¼ Master | 05 13 04 |
| Lieut-Col. Whaley | 11 03 04 |
| | 61 10 08 |

Walkerne

| | |
|---|---|
| Major Disborowe | 09 01 08 |
| Captain Crowe | 06 18 00 |
| | 15 19 08 |

| | |
|---|---|
| 1/4r Master | 03 11 04 |
| Captain Margery | 19 18 00 |
| | 29 00 00 |

Hinxworth

| | |
|---|---|
| Captain Browne | 07 07 04 |
| Ditto | 01 10 08 |
| Ditto | 26 07 08 |
| Capt-Lieut. de Jemes | 22 04 04 |
| Captain Ishborne | 00 00 00 |
| | 57 09 04 |

---

commissary-general of horse on the eve of Naseby, where he commanded the cavalry's left wing. He married Cromwell's daughter, Bridget, in 1646 [Ian J Gentles, 'Ireton, Henry (*bap.* 1611, *d.* 1651)', *NewDNB*]

| Lawrance Ayott | |
|---|---|
| Major Disborowe | 05 05 04 |
| Colonel Norwich | 10 15 08 |
| Lieut.-Gen. Cromwell | 01 00 00 |
| Capt.-Lieut. Merrest | 07 11 04 |
| | 24 12 04 |

| Stevenage | |
|---|---|
| Major Disborow | 00 02 08 |
| Captain Horseman | 02 09 00 |
| Colonel Norwich | 29 01 08 |
| Ditto | 09 11 04 |
| Captain Moulson | 21 04 08 |
| Captain Swallow | 04 12 00 |
| Lieut.-Gen. Cromwell | 00 13 04 |
| Captain Berry | 09 14 00 |
| Ditto | 19 01 00 |
| Captain Bethell | 08 18 08 |
| Major Brudnell | 28 16 04 |
| Captain Drury | 09 09 00 |
| Traine of Artillery | 00 14 08 |
| Lieut.-Col. Whaley | 00 09 04 |
| | 135 08 08 |

*f*3r

| Bigrave | |
|---|---|
| Captain le Hunt | 01 10 00 |

| Walington | |
|---|---|
| Captain le Hunt | 06 11 00 |

| Ashwell | |
|---|---|
| Captain Porter | 56 00 00 |
| Ditto | 03 16 04 |
| Captain Lawrance | 04 08 08 |
| Captain Crowe | 09 15 08 |
| Lieut.-Gen. Cromwell | 06 13 04 |
| Ditto | 00 10 08 |
| Capt Ireton ¼ master | 12 14 00 |
| Ditto | 59 18 04 |

| Baldock | |
|---|---|
| Captain Porter | 15 09 04 |
| Captain Horseman | 18 04 00 |
| Captain Lawrance | 00 05 04 |
| Major Dodson | 21 18 00 |
| Ditto | 27 13 08 |
| Lieut.Gen.-Cromwell | 02 08 08 |
| Captain Berry | 00 06 00 |
| Capt Ireton ¼ Master | 08 09 00 |
| Captain Margery | 07 15 00 |
| Captain Bethell | 13 11 04 |
| Captain Evers | 04 07 08 |
| Lieut.-Col. Whaley | 01 04 00 |
| Captain Abbott | 02 18 04 |
| Captain Peapes | 00 00 00 |

| | |
|---|---|
| Ditto | 18 03 00 |
| Ditto | 06 11 00 |
| Captain Margery | 00 15 04 |
| | 179 06 04 |

Westmill

| | |
|---|---|
| Captain Porter | 04 00 04 |

Aston

| | |
|---|---|
| Captain Porter | 04 17 08 |
| Captain Tomlinson | 06 16 08 |
| Captain Selby | 05 14 08 |
| | 17 09 00 |

Yardley

| | |
|---|---|
| Captain Horseman | 05 10 00 |

| | |
|---|---|
| Captain Carter | 02 17 04 |
| Captain Pritchett | 00 16 08 |
| Lieut. Col. Grymes | 01 01 00 |
| Captain Freeman | 00 13 04 |
| Captain Pyott | 01 00 08 |
| Captain Berners | 01 03 00 |
| Captain Southcoates | 04 03 08 |
| Captain Wilkes | 00 13 08 |
| Capt. Lieut de Jammes | 02 12 00 |
| Lieut-Col. Montague | 01 18 00 |
| | 141 09 08 |

Ayott Parva

| | |
|---|---|
| Captain Horseman | 01 04 00 |
| Lieut.-Gen. Cromwell | 05 02 08 |
| Captain Berry | 08 08 08 |
| Captain Hamon | 00 19 00 |
| | 15 14 04 |

*f*4r

Barkhamsted Parva

| | |
|---|---|
| Major Alford | 00 01 04 |
| Major Harrison[395] | 00 10 08 |
| Captain Selby | 02 17 04 |
| Captain Bethell | 16 04 00 |
| | 53 04 00 |

Hatfeild

| | |
|---|---|
| Major Alford | 00 01 00 |

Easenden

| | |
|---|---|
| Major Alford | 26 08 04 |
| Captain Selby | 02 13 04 |
| Captain Bethell | 22 00 04 |
| Ditto | 22 08 00 |
| Ditto | 02 04 08 |
| | 75 14 08 |

Wimondly Parva

| | |
|---|---|
| Captain Lawrance | 00 14 08 |

[395] Thomas Harrison, (*bap*. 1616, *d.* 1660) the regicide, had enlisted in Essex's lifeguard, then joined the Eastern Association army because of its more radical religious viewpoint, where he was a major in Fleetwood's regiment. He fought at Marston Moor, and, in reporting the battle to parliament, praised Cromwell and the Independents at the expense of the Scots' contribution. He joined the New Model Army and fought at Naseby, Langport and the siege of Basing House, where Hertfordshire troops served. After the war it was Harrison's regiment that turned up against orders at Cockbush Field and took part in the Ware Mutiny, though he was not present himself, having helped to draw up the engagement presented to the soldiers there [Ian J Gentles, 'Harrison, Thomas (*bap*. 1616, *d.* 1660)', *NewDNB*; Thomson, A, *The Ware Mutiny 1647: Order restored or revolution defeated*? (Ware, 1996) pp54-8]

| | |
|---|---|
| Lieut Gen Cromwell | 32 01 04 |
| Ditto | 16 13 00 |
| Captain Gladman | 00 11 04 |
| The Earls Life Guard | 01 13 04 |
| Captain Bethell | 01 02 08 |
| Ditto | 09 16 00 |
| Ditto | 27 10 04 |
| Ditto | 02 02 08 |
| Lieut-Col. Whaley | 05 00 04 |
| Captain Pell | 00 07 00 |
| Captain Wade | 00 18 08 |
| Captain Alborne | 13 10 00 |
| Captain Shanke | 02 12 04 |
| Captain Spencely | 01 01 08 |
| Captain Shepheard | 00 03 04 |
| Captain Ashwell | 00 09 04 |
| Captain Barnes | 05 10 00 |
| Colonel Hubbard | 05 18 00 |
| Captain Berry | 04 14 00 |
| Major Knight | 00 16 08 |
| Colonel Palgrave | 00 02 00 |
| | 134 13 06 |

Hertford All Saints

| | |
|---|---|
| Colonel Norwich | 08 17 00 |
| Ditto | 49 03 08 |
| Captain Moulson | 06 16 09 |
| Major Brudnell | 02 03 08 |
| Captain Langridge | 00 00 00 |
| | 67 01 01 |

| | |
|---|---|
| Captain Griffin | 01 16 00 |
| Ditto | 08 00 08 |
| Major Crawford | 02 12 00 |
| Ditto | 04 05 04 |
| Captain Swallow | 01 10 00 |
| Ditto | 02 02 00 |
| Ditto | 02 16 08 |
| Lieut-Col. Grymes | 01 00 00 |
| Lieut-Col. Montague | 00 17 08 |
| Captain Rogers | 00 15 00 |
| | 26 10 00 |

Wimondly Magna

| | |
|---|---|
| Captain Lawrance | 01 12 00 |
| Major Crawford | 05 06 08 |
| Captain Swallow | 02 19 04 |
| Ditto | 06 02 00 |
| Captain Dingley | 13 03 04 |
| | 29 03 04 |

Amwell Magna

| | |
|---|---|
| Colonel Norwich | 03 03 04 |
| Captain Moulson | 02 04 00 |
| | 05 08 04 |

*f*5r

~~Amwell Magna~~

| | |
|---|---|
| ~~Colonel Norwich~~ | ~~03 04 04~~ |
| ~~Captain Moulson~~ | ~~02 04 00~~ |
| | ~~05 08 04~~ |

Hertford St Andrew

| | |
|---|---|
| Colonel Norwich | 04 07 08 |
| Major Harrison | 05 06 08 |

Chesthunt

| | |
|---|---|
| Major Dodson | 02 06 08 |

Tewinge

| | |
|---|---|
| Colonel Norwich | 00 09 04 |
| Captain Crowe | 29 06 08 |
| Major Brudnell | 04 01 04 |

| | |
|---|---|
| | 09 14 04 |
| Hertingfordbury | |
| Colonel Norwich | 28 15 04 |
| Ditto | 09 18 08 |
| Major Harrison | 07 09 04 |
| Ditto | 07 16 00 |
| Captain Bethell | 18 02 00 |
| | 72 01 04 |
| Baiford | |
| Colonel Norwich | 11 02 00 |
| Ditto | 07 01 04 |
| Major Harrison | 07 04 09 |
| Ditto | 15 16 08 |
| Ditto | 18 05 04 |
| Captain Bethell | 07 09 00 |
| Ditto | 20 07 04 |
| | 84 06 04 |
| Ware Intra[396] | |
| Colonel Norwich | 98 07 04 |
| Ditto | 16 06 08 |
| Ditto | 23 04 00 |
| | 137 18 00 |
| Ware Extra[397] | |
| Captain Moulson | 08 16 08 |
| Ditto | 04 00 00 |
| Ditto | 01 11 04 |
| Major Brudnell | 01 00 00 |
| | 15 08 00 |

| | |
|---|---|
| | 33 17 04 |
| Thundridge | |
| Colonel Norwich | 03 17 04 |
| Walden Regis | |
| Captain Lawrance | 50 10 00 |
| Radwell | |
| Captain Crowe | 02 08 00 |
| Major Harrison | 01 14 08 |
| | 04 02 08 |
| Datchworth | |
| Captain Crowe | 03 19 04 |
| Captain Dandy | 11 15 04 |
| Colonel Fleetwood | 06 19 08 |
| | 22 04 04 |
| Standon | |
| Major Dodson | 02 15 00 |

396 Ware Town

397 Ware rural (now Wareside)

*f*6r

| | |
|---|---|
| Reede | |
| Major Dodson | 01 01 04 |
| | |
| Royston | |
| Major Crawford | 02 01 00 |
| | |
| Brickendon | |
| Major Harrison | 14 19 00 |
| Captain Bethell | 05 19 00 |
| | 20 18 00 |
| Watton | |
| Major Harrison | 07 02 00 |
| | |
| Hartford St Johns | |
| Major Harrison | 01 10 08 |
| | |
| Munden Magna | |
| Captain Berry | 05 16 08 |
| | |
| Lilly | |
| Captain Harman | 00 04 00 |
| Captain Clisson | 01 12 08 |
| Captain Catwood | 01 01 10 |
| | 02 18 06 |

| | |
|---|---|
| Barly | |
| Captain Hale | 00 13 04 |
| Captain Done | 00 15 04 |
| Captain Tailor Done | 01 06 08 |
| | |
| Ofley | |
| | |
| Lieut-Col. | |
| to Lieut. Col. Russell | 01 02 04 |
| Major ~~Dodson~~ Russell | 01 09 08 |
| Captain Rance | 01 07 08 |
| A captain to | |
| Colonel Russell | 00 00 00 |
| | 03 19 08 |

*f*6v **(*Written upside down*)** A breviate of the allowances for quarter in the severall townes within the 3 divisions for the Earle of Manchesters souldiers

| | £ s d | | £ s d |
|---|---|---|---|
| Digswell | 26 08 04 | Hatfeild | 134 13 06 |
| Welwin | 77 04 02 | Hertford All Saints | 67 01 01 |
| Langly | 05 08 04 | Easendon | 75 14 08 |
| Preston | 04 07 10 | Wimondly Parva | 26 10 00 |
| Willian | 26 02 00 | Wimondly Magna | 29 03 04 |
| Ippolitts | 22 09 06 | Amwell Magna | 05 08 04 |

[398] Rushden

| | |
|---|---|
| Iccleford | 29 00 00 |
| Hinxworth | 57 09 04 |
| Hitchin | 245 08 04 |
| Pirton | 03 02 08 |
| Gravely cum Chisfield | 34 13 02 |
| Bradfeild | 01 09 00 |
| Cottered | 03 12 00 |
| Risden[398] | 02 07 04 |
| Kimpton | 79 18 00 |
| Bennington | 16 11 00 |
| Knebworth | 32 04 08 |
| Letchworth | 13 07 04 |
| Weston | 61 10 04 |
| Walkerene | 15 19 08 |
| Lawrance Ayott | 24 12 04 |
| Stevenage | 135 08 08 |
| Bigrave | 01 10 00 |
| Wallington | 06 11 00 |
| Ashwell | 179 06 04 |
| Westmill | 04 00 04 |
| Aston | 17 09 00 |
| Baldock | 141 09 08 |
| Yardley | 05 10 00 |
| Ayott Parva | 15 14 04 |
| Barkhamstead Parva | 53 04 00 |
| | 1343 08 08 |

| | |
|---|---|
| Hartford St Andrew | 09 14 04 |
| Hartingfordbury | 72 01 04 |
| Baiford | 84 06 04 |
| Ware Intra | 137 18 00 |
| <paid off: Ware intra | |
| and extra | 136 16 08 |
| The rest not done> | |
| Ware Extra | 15 08 00 |
| Chesthunt | 02 06 08 |
| Tewin | 33 17 04 |
| Thundridge | 03 17 04 |
| Walden Regis | 50 10 00 |
| Radwell | 04 02 08 |
| Datchworth | 22 04 04 |
| Standon | 02 15 00 |
| Reede | 01 01 04 |
| Royston | 02 01 00 |
| <paid | 12 18 08> |
| Brickendon | 20 18 00 |
| Watton | 07 02 00 |
| Hartford St Johns | 01 10 08 |
| Munden Magna | 05 16 08 |
| Lilly | 02 18 06 |
| Barly | 02 15 04 |
| Offley | 03 19 08 |
| Buckland | 03 13 04 |
| | 829 08 09 |
| | 1343 08 09 |
| Summa Totalis | 2172 17 05 |

*f*7r The names of such Captaines as are not of the Earl of Manchesters army and not allowed

| | |
|---|---|
| Captain Aslicew | 08 13 00 |
| Captain Wogun | 03 08 08 |
| A captaine | 01 04 04 |
| Captaine Peapes | 00 17 04 |
| Captain Roult | 00 03 10 |
| | 14 07 02 |

| | |
|---|---|
| Captain Drury | 01 03 04 |
| Captain Isborne | 01 17 04 |
| Captain Lukeman | 02 08 00 |
| Captan Langridge | 03 10 00 |
| | 08 18 08 |
| | 14 07 02 |
| | 23 05 10 |

Whereas there was a peticon preferred to me and the committees of the Assosiacon by the inhabitants of Hartford for the payeing of the severall quarters of the souldiers belongeing to my army as they passed and repassed through the said county. Upon which peticon I referred the examinacon of the billeting of the said souldiers unto the committees of the said county who hath returned the particulars of every captaine with their companies and troopers which amounteth unto the sum of £2175 18s 9d as by the particulars appeareth. Attested under the hands of the committees sittinge at Hartford for the 3 divisions of Hertford and Braughin, Edwinstrey and Odsey and Broadwater and the halfe hundred of Hitchin.

These are therefore to require you forthwith to pay unto Mr William Turner one of the High Collectors for the said county the summe of £2175 18s 9d for the payeinge of the severall inhabitants. And you to charge it upon each officers accompt. And if it shall appeare that any part of this money hath beene unduely charged upon any the said officers or souldiers, then the severall persons soe offendinge within the said townes, parishes and places shall repay back that money to the officer or souldier upon reasonable warneinge. And this shall be your warrante. Dated the 6 March 1644

*Earl Manchester, Isaac Puller, Humphrey Walcott,*[399] *William Harlakenden,*[400] *Comissary generall*

To Gregory Gawsell and William Leman Esquires Treasurers for the Association *Vera Copia Examinat per* I.P.

| | | |
|---|---|---|
| Allowed | £2175 18 09 | |
| Disallowed | 23 05 10 | as abovesaid |
| | £2149 04 07 | |

***(f8 and f9r Blank)***

*f*9v March 13th 1644

Ordered by the Committee that Mr William Turner High Colleckter doe pay to two or three severall persons off the severall townes in thesse three devitions for ther quarter as followeth:

[399] Walcott was the Lincs representative on the Cambridge committee, came from a minor gentry family, and had settled in Boston in the 1630s. He later was returned to the Barebones Parliament for Lincolnshire [Holmes, *Eastern Association,* pp125-6]

[400] Harlackenden was the younger son of a gentry family from Earls Colne, Essex, related to many involved in the New England colonies. Having been to university in Cambridge, he became paymaster to the Essex troops stationed there in 1643, becoming Commissary-General and personal assistant to the Earl of Manchesteer [Holmes, *Eastern Association*, pp128-9]

First, those towns thatt ther quarter comes to more then ther taxes, be paid as farr as ther taxes doth com unto in part off ther quarter. And those that ther taxes are ~~lesse~~ <more> then ther quarter be paid in full, upon condition that wher as Mr William Turner hath nott so mutch mony by fowre hundred pound in his handes as will satisfy all the townes in thesse three devitions for ther above said quarter, they shall repay to the said William Turner whatt ther proportion in the losse shall bee in casse that the committees cannott have the above said £400. And that they allso to whom he shall pay in part shall have ther like proportion in casse the £400 cannott be had. Which we will usse the best meanes we cann for to procure, the remainder of the quarter shall be paid in to the perssons in every parish which received the first partt as in part off payment.
*Joseph Dalton, Maior, Thomas Meade, Garbriel Barbor, Thomas Tooke, Alexander Weld*

***(f10 blank)***
***(On back cover)*** The quarter booke for the Earlle of Manchesters souldyers Examined by the Committee for Accomptes

**[124] TNA: SP28/154 Payments to parishes in the 1650s for free quarter taken by soldiers quartering in the Hundreds of Cashio and Dacorum in the 1640s**

A true and perfect Accompt of monys Paid by William Hickman of St Albans for satisfaction of Soldiers Quartering to the severall Places following Acording to the Order of the 25th February 1653

| | | | | |
|---|---|---|---|---|
| folio 29 | Paid Abbots Langley | 071 | 19 | 10 |
| 30 | paid St Albans fol: 30 61:06:04}150:15:06<br>89:09:02} | 150 | 15 | 06 |
| 36 | paid Aldbury | 042 | 18 | 08 |
| 27 | paid Aldenham | 115 | 00 | 03 |
| 33 | paid Birkamstead | 154 | 10 | 08 |
| 36 | paid Chippen Barnett | 115 | 09 | 03 |
| 38 | paid East Barnett | 173 | 02 | 04 |
| 33 | paid Bovingdon | 034 | 17 | 06 |
| 27 | paid Brantfeild [401] | 020 | 13 | 00 |

[401] Bramfield

| | | | | |
|---|---|---|---|---|
| 28 | paid Bushey | 095 | 10 | 07 |
| 40 | paid Caddington | 018 | 07 | 08 |
| 36 | paid Coddicote | 71 | 04 | 05 |
| 28 | paid Coltshill | 030 | 17 | 06 |
| 38 | paid Flamstead | 145 | 18 | 10 |
| 33 | paid Flaundin | 010 | 11 | 04 |
| 38 | paid Gaddsden magna | 055 | 19 | 03 |
| 40 | paid Gaddsden parva | 066 | 12 | 04 |
| 31 | paid Harpenden | 057 | 03 | 06 |
| 37 | paid Hempstead | 190 | 06 | 00 |
| 27 | pd Ilestrey[402] | 058 | 04 | 02 |
| 39 | paid Kensworth | 036 | 02 | 09 |
| 27 | paid Kings Langly | 071 | 01 | 06 |
| 40 | paid Market Street[403] | 020 | 15 | 04 |
| 41 | paid Long Marston | 065 | 09 | 08 |
| 27 | pd Newenham | 004 | 02 | 10 |
| 26 | paid Northawe | 005 | 12 | 00 |
| 29 | paid Northmims | 349 | 08 | 00 |
| 38 | pd Northchurch | 084 | 01 | 08 |
| 31 | paid Norton | 010 | 17 | 04 |
| 24 | paid Parkewarde | 017 | 01 | 04 |
| 41 | paid Pauls Warden | 002 | 11 | 08 |
| 35 | pd Puttnam | 028 | 05 | 02 |
| 31,35,44 | paid Redbourne | 137 | 07 | 04 |
| 32 | paid Rickmersworth | 041 | 15 | 00 |
| 31 | paid Ridge | 015 | 05 | 08 |
| 34 | paid Sanderidge | 041 | 05 | 02 |
| 28, 37 | paid Shenly | 025 | 08 | 03 |
| 37 | paid Shephall | 004 | 08 | 04 |
| 36 | paid Studham | 014 | 07 | 00 |
| 26 | paid Tittenhanger | 022 | 07 | 00 |
| 33 | paid Tringe | 120 | 09 | 02 |
| 40 | paid Wattford | 169 | 14 | 08 |
| 29 | paid Wiggington | 030 | 00 | 04 |
| 39 | paid Wilsterne | 074 | 17 | 04 |
| 32 | paid Windrerdgecold[404] 25 | 029 | 00 | 09 |

[402] Elstree
[403] Markyate

| 28 | paid Whetthamstead | 076 | 14 | 06 |
|---|---|---|---|---|
| | | 3172 | 13 | 11 |

## Part 2 General effects on individuals and parishes

### [125] TNA: SP28/230 House of Commons order re Wingate arrears, 7/4/1643

*Die Veneris* 7 April 1643
Uppon a petition from divers inhabitants of the County of Hertford presented to the Committee for that County and this day from them exhibited to the House of Commons desiring that the arrears due to Captayne Wingate[405] may be payed. It is this day ordered by the Commons now assembled in Parliament that the arrears of pay due to Captayne Wingate, as Captayne of a troope of horse by him raysed at the command of both houses for the defence of the parliament, bee payed unto Mrs Wingate, or her assignes, out of the monthly colleccons, as shalbe raysed out of the hundreds of Broadwater and Hitchin in the Countie of Herts. and that acquittances, under the hands of the assignes of the said Captayne Wingate, bee allowed to Sir Gilbert Gerrard as soe much money payed by him, and the collectors discharged thereof.
Henry Elsing *Clericus* Parliament and Commons

***(On reverse)*** At the 3 halfe moones on new Fish Streete Hill Thomas Walker
At the Black Talbutt in Watling Streete Jeremiah Whitworth

### [126] TNA: SP28/155 Sandon parish account -John Caesar's claim, 1643

*Imprimis* I gave an horse upon The Propositions which Captaine John Andrewes had; valued at thirty five pound
I paid ~~the money~~ in money to the Therasurer at Hertford, for my fift and twentieth part, fifty pound
I paid twenty five pound for the Advance of our Brethren in Scotland
Captain Hales Leiutenant, and one Wood, a shoo-maker of Hertford with others, broke open my stable in the night, upon the 12th of July 1643 and tooke out <two> bay horses, valued by my neighbours to whom they were

[404] Probably refers to Windridge a hamlet west of St Albans
[405] For Wingate *See* Appendix

well knowen <at> thirty pounds and produced authority for theire action, from the Committee at Hertford and Knights of the Shyre.[406]
Upon the first of August, 1643, Captain Sanderson came to my house with many souldjers, and tooke out my carts bringing in harvest and out of my pastures, nine horses valued at one hundred pounds
Upon the 7th of August 1643, Major Battersby came to my house and tooke two of my coach horses valued forty pounds and both these officers produced their authority from Sir W Waller
After the losse of all these horse, <and those armes which were in my house,> I was commanded by the Committee at Hertford to pay to Sir John Norwicke[407] seventeene pounds, to provide one sufficient horse and armes.
Upon the Reviewe, I was called by the Earl of Manchesters Commissioners at Royston,[408] who upon examination of the premises, with greife for my losses, were pleased to dismiss me.
Thus much 1 will justifie. *John Caesar*

**[127] TNA: SP28/230 Little Wymondley - Eustace Nedham's[409] claim, 9/10/1644**

Wimondley Parva October the 9th 1644
The account of Eustace Nedham Esq. of what mony plate and horse he hathe advanced upon the firste propositions. And what hee hath payd for the fifte and 20 parte. And upon the review by whome and to whome the same was payed by ticotes and apparent proufs. And what monyes hee hath lente to the £3000 for the advance of the Scotes, by whome and to whome it was payed. And what horses and armes hath byn taken from him and by what warrant or pretence. And what mony hath byn given to exscuse or redeme any of them.
15th November 1642 I under writt a white geldinge att Welwin for the Kinge and Parliament sarvis before Sir John Read[410] and Captayne Hale

[406] i.e the two Hertfordshire MPs, Sir William Lytton and Sir Thomas Dacres
[407] Sir John Norwich commander of the county brigade to defend the northern borders from royalist attack
[408] Manchester's commissioners to review the sums paid under the 5th and 20th part met at Royston for those living in the Northern parishes
[409] Nedham had the manor of Wymondley Priory settled on him by his father when he married in 1615 and then bought the Graveley Hall estate in 1637. The family had been in the county since 1536 and held the advowson to Wymondley church. Eustace had been a captain in the militia, hence why he had arms and armour etc. His son George had been admitted to Lincoln's Inn in 1638 when Eustace was described as gent [*VCH Herts* III, pp85-90, 185-91; *Lincoln's Inn Admissions* I, p235]

Commissioners praysed att eaight poundes And was presently commanded upon the parliament sarvis by authoritie from the parish to Wendover and ther was lamed.
4th January 1642 I listed an iron-gray nage att Hartford for the king and parliament sarvis before Mr Carter commissioner praysed att nine poundes this I did upon the propositions, witnes the bookes.[411]
27th February 1643 lente upon the £3000 for the advance of the Scotes twenti pound by ticet payd to Isacke Puller and Williham Turner Treasurer
23rd June 1643 payd twentie poundes upon ticet to the fifte and 20 parte into the handes of Humphrey Packer and Joseph Dalton, maior, wittnes the bookes
25th September 1643 payd five poundes more for the fifte and 20 parte by ticet into the hand of Humphery Packer, Treasurer, and five pounds more was abatted me for the fifte and 20 parte by Mr Barbor and Mr Carter for a horse which my Lord of Denbee did take from me which cost me £v poundes
15th June 1644 payd by ticet into the handes of Mr William Turpin, Treasurer ten poundes for the Review of the fifte and 20 parte
Summa £77 00 00
<u>What horses armes and ammunision hath byn taken from mee</u>
4th of Aprill 1643 Thomas Westwood, Quarter Master under Captayne Salkins of my Lord Grays Regiment, did take too horses, too geldinges from mee for which I refused from the hands of honiste men above £64 Wittnes Robar Willson and Thomas Gater before the committees att Hartford. Besides the same Westwood did take from me a light horse armes with back brest hedpeece with a bener[412] and elbow gauntlett a dragoone and bandoleer, three poundes of gunpoulder and a case of pistalls all worth sevene poundes with out any authoritie but sayd hee was commanded by the committees of Hartford.
20th of Aprill 1643 Thomas Briges, Corporrall under Captayne Crumwell[413] of my Lord Grayes regiment, did take from mee one geldinge one stone horse worthe twentie poundes besides too steele armes,[414] one blacke armes, too gauntlates, one steele cote, one horne cote,[415] one dragonne with bandeleres,

---

[410] Sir John Reade of Brocket Hall, Hatfield (*see* Appendix)
[411] He presumably is here referring to the account books which should have been kept by the officials
[412] A banner or flag
[413] Probably one of the sons of Oliver Cromwell as Oliver had been promoted to Colonel in February 1643 [John Morrill, Cromwell, Oliver (1599-1658)', *NewDNB*]
[414] Arms or armour, either covering the forearm or possibly a whole set of armour
[415] A coat or tunic with pieces of horn sewn into it as light armour

one hedpeece, one pad saddle (all in all) worth £16 and woold shew noe authoritie, witness my curett,[416] Mr John Wood, and all my sarvantes.
20 June 1643 Captayne Robottumes[417] men did take from mee too horses worthe twenty pound after the Ordinance of Parliment was in force that noe man should take any horse without the handes of the Commissary to ther authoritie, but thay woold shew noe authoritie though I demanded. Witnes Mr John Wood, my currett and also my sarvantes. Somme £127 00 00

*Eustace Nedham*

**[128] TNA: SP28/155 Sarratt parish accounts *f*2r - Mr Lane's claim, 1644[418]**

About 10 Jan 43 by Mr Lane himself
Paid by Mr Lane at St Albanes to Mr William Hickman treasurer to the Committee of Hertfordshire for the 5 and 20 parte for Mr Lanes lands there 08 00 00
Laid out for charges rideinge upp and downe aboute his taxes[419] 00 07 08
5 March 43
Lent upon the Ordinance for the Scotts advance and paid to <Mr> Thomas Oxton and Thomas Cowley att St Albanes 05 00 00
Laid out for charges for travellinge about this 00 03 06
Aboute and before 4 March: 43
Paid in the parish of Sarrat for settinge out a light horse charged by the Committee upon the parishe 02 08 00
paid 2 months pay to the Lord Generall 00 13 04
paid then 12 weeks pay to the Earle of Manchester 03 00 00
paid more for drums and feathers[420] for the particular assotiacon of the Countie 00 12 00
paid for quarteringe of soldiers at Rickmansworth beinge a charge raysed by the soldiers upon this parishe by Captain Carmihills troope under Collonel Barie 02 08 00
Paid towards helpe of maymed soldiers hurt in these warres and soldiers widowes and towards makinge of Bulwarks (at St Albans)[421] 00 03 00

[416] curate
[417] Robert Robotham *see* Appendix
[418] This is in the same sources as Document 6 in Secton A
[419] Presumably collecting the tax and going to St Albans to pay it
[420] Feathers were probably emblems for the regiment

<u>10 January 43</u>
Paid Roger Ewer Mr Lanes rent for twoe moneths pay to the Lord Generall 00 12 00
<u>About that tyme</u>
Paid <towards> a charge upon this parishe upon the ordinances of parliament of the 2 September <and> 18 October 43 of £3 6 8d and another charge <of £3> on the parishe for caryeinge of wood to St Albans when the <Lord> Generall lay there.[422] This £3 was charged by warrant from one Joseph Hill the woodward and towards both these, Mr Lane was rated at 18s and paid it. 00 18 00

**[129] HALS: Off Acc 1162 Nos. 981-3 Receipts for taxes paid by Francis Emberton of St Albans (1644)**

**<u>981</u>**
John Briges received of Francis Emberton a shilling for seting out of a dragonnere, layd upon the landes belonging to Santall bones, the land lying by broken X.[423]
**<u>982</u>**
Received the 3rd of Aprill 1644 of Francis Emmerton the some eight and twenty shillings for 4 monthes pay and is for the lands belonging to the poor of St Albones £01-08s-00d
I say received *per* mee *Frances Moyse*

**<u>983</u>**
Received the 5 of Aparill 1644 of Francis Emberton the some of six shillings and is for fowre monthes pay for the landes belonging to the poore of Sant Albones. I say received by me John Herington, gentellman

**[130] TNA: SP28/230 St Stephens - John Marshall's claim, 6/12/1644**

<u>6 December 1644</u>
John Marshall of St Stephens parish in Hartfordsheire his bill of chardges hee hath byn att for what hee advanced upon the propositions, and likewise upon and towards the payment of the hundred thousand pounds for the Scottish

---

[421] The local rate for maimed soldiers and their widows dated from Tudor times. The Bulwarks were defences constructed around St Albans (*see* **67-72)**
[422] When Essex had his winter headquarters in St Albans
[423] I assume this means the broken cross, a St Albans boundary stone

Army, for free quarter taken att his house by souldiers and for other losses as followeth vizt: £ s d[424]

First I lysted and enrolled the sixt of August Anno Domini 1642 one roane geldinge with wall eyes valued by the commissaries att eight pounds as appears by a ticket under their owne hands 8 – 0 – 0

I allsoe payde and delivered to John Warner and Thomas Andrewes Treasurers appointed by the ordinance of parliament to receive all such moneys as should be brought in upon plaine propositions etc., the summe of five poundes as appears by their acquittance dated November the 28th 1642 beinge printed *v* – 0 – 0

I allsoe payde and delivered to Thomas Oxton and Thomas Cowley beinge treasurers for raysinge of money towards the payment of the hundred thousand pounds to bee advanced for the payment of the Scottish Army twentie shillings as appears by their receipt printed and dated the 27th of Januarie 1643 1 – 0 – 0

I allsoe quartered tow of my Lord Generalls <gent'> souldiers beinge of his life Gard their horses, their men and their horses, eleven weekes and others at severall tymes, <some of> whose names appeare in my bill I have already delivered in, and their commanders the summe of which beinge allowed of comes to six pounds tow shillings eight pence 6 – 2 – 8

*Item* I carried for the use of my Lord Generall <halfe a load of hey> when hee quartered last att St Albans worth fifteene shillings beinge still unpaide 0– 15 -0

I allsoe lost five sheepe carried away by the souldiers woth fortie shillings *ii* – 0 – 0

I allsoe had taken out of my house and abroad <goods> by the souldiers worth thirtie shillings 1 – 10 -0

I was chardged parte of an armes which I delieverd to the Committee att St Albans cost mee twelve shillings six pence 0 – 12 -6

*John Marshall*

[424] For some reason this account has been partly written in Roman, partly in Arabic numerals. This is not unusual for this period. It is one of a series written in the same hand for inhabitants of St Stephens Parish

### [131] TNA: SP28/230 St Stephens -Mr Rolfe's claim, 7/12/1644

| St Stevens 7 December 1644 | £ s d |
|---|---|
| Mr Rolfe of St Stevens in Hertfordsheire his bill of chardges as followeth: | |
| I payd and delivered for my fifte and twentieth parte by vertue of an ordinance of parliament to that purpose the summe of fortie shillinges to William Hickman Treasurer as appears by his acquittance printed dated December the 9th 1643 | *ii* – 0 – 0 |
| I quartered Sir William Constable[425] a colonel of a foote regiment, his leiftenant colonel Grimes, his captaine leiftenant and all his officers of his own particular companie, and aboute threescore souldiers of his owne companie, fower saddle horses and as many waggon horses with hay and oates and diet which stood mee in all chardges fower pounds | 4 – 0 – 0 |
| I have quarterd divers severall souldiers both horsemen and footemen and their horses att severall tymes which chardged mee five pounds | *v* – 0 – 0 |
| I have had tymber cutt of from my grounds in St Michaells parish and have lost in wood there and likewise aboute my house and fermes in St Albans, and the outhouses there soe broken and spoiled which cannot be valued lesse than eight pounds. This was done last winter when the army lay att St Albans | 8 – 0 – 0 |
| I had one stoned hogge[426] and poultrie taken away from mee by the souldiers woth twemty shillings | 1 – 0 – 0 |
| *~~Nich Rolfe~~* | |
| Captaine Chichester <under Colonell Middleton> and his leiftenant Captaine, a scothman, entred my house with 60 men the fast day night in Februarie and it was Anno 1642, and tooke away a new pad sadle,[427] a birdinge peece,[428] a pocket pistoll of brasse, and other things to the valew of fower pounds | 4 – 0 – 0 |
| *Nicholas Rolfe* | |

[425] Sir William Constable, Baronet raised a regiment of foot for parliament in 1642, fought at Edgehill and in east Yorkshire from July 1643, was deemed a regicide after his death because he had signed the King's death warrant [David Scott, 'Constable, Sir William, baronet (*bap.* 1590, *d.* 1655)', *NewDNB*]

[426] A non-castrated boar

[427] A soft stuffed saddle without a tree support

[428] A gun for shooting birds

**[132] TNA: SP28/230 St Stephens - William and Ellin Rolfe's claim, 6/12/1644**

December 6th 1644
William Rolfe of St Stevens parish in Hertfordsheire yeoman his bill of moneys parted withall upon the propositions and other chardges as followeth vizt: £ s d
November the 28th 1642 I payde and delivered upon the propositions the summe of fiftie shillings for which I have a receipt printed under the handes of John Warner and Thomas Andrewes treasurers ordained by parliament for that purpose *ii* – 10 -0
I quarterd three troopers and their horses under Captaine Pile belonginge to my Lord Generall wherof tow of them and their horses quarter 9 daies and the other and his horse quartered 4 dayes
I quartered foote souldiers under the command of Colonell Tompson[429] and Leiftenant Colonel Peleolagas: James Bagges a month, Robert Moore, Thomas Payne a weeke.
I quarterd William Aylward, David Marlo, Henry Snellinge under the command of Captaine Dongon of which tow of them staied thirteene dayes and one of them six weekes
The losses I had five sheepe and other thinge by the souldiers fortie shillings *ii* – 0 – 0

*William Rolfe*

December 6th 1644
Allun Rolfe widdowe her bill for what shee advanced upon the Propositions
I payde and delivered the summe of eight poundes accordinge to the propositions ordained for which I have the printed receipt or acquittance under the handes of John Warner and Thomas Andrews printed treasurers appointed for that purpose dated the 28th of November 1642 8 – 0 – 0
*Elen Rolfe*

[429] Colonel George Thompson of the London Trained Bands [Thomson, *NewDNB*]

**[133] TNA: SP28/230 St Stephens - John Edmonds' claim, 6/12/1644**

6 December 1644

John Edmonds of St Stevens parish in Hartfordsheire his bill of money parted withall by him upon the propositions and allsoe for the Kinge and Parliament. Allsoe for free quarter taken att his house by the souldiers and goods taken and losses hee had by them as followeth: £ s d

First I payde for the use of the Kinge and Parliament to Captaine Cox,[430] one of the committee the summe of five pounds as appears <by> a certificate under the hande of Mr Raphe Pemberton another of the saide committee which is dated the nienth of November 1642 *v* – 0 – 0

Secondlie I payde and delivered into the hands of William Hickman, treasurer, upon the propositions the summe of fortie shillings as appears by his acquittance or receipt under his hand beinge printed[431] dated the 13th day of Aprill 1644 *ii* – 0 – 0

I quartered three troopers of Captaine Piles and their horses eleven dayes in November 1643 as my ticket under the quartermasters hande sheweth 1 – 14 - 0

John Euington one of my Lord Generalls life Gard[432] quartered with me tenne weekes and his horse as longe att hey and corne 4 – 0 – 0

*Item* I quartered both horsemen and foote souldiers severall tymes which chardged mee forty shillings and upwards *ii* – 0 – 0

Item I ~~I~~ was chardged with my teame of horses in carriages Seven shillings six pence 0 – 7 – 6

Item one geldinge taken away by three troopers out of the plough from mee the 15th day of Aprill worth five pounds *v* – 0 – 0

*John Edmonds*

**[134] TNA: SP28/232 Petition of Edward Wood to the Committee of Hertford, 21/3/1644(5)**

To the worshipfull Committee of Hertford. The humble petision of Edward Wood, Ensign

---

430 The rank is a mistake as this is Colonel Alban Cox

431 By this stage of the war a number of treasurers are issuing printed receipts for routine payments, the blanks being completed with the individual's details

432 This was probably in the winter of 1643-4 when Essex's troops were quartered in the St Albans area

Humbly sheweth
That whereas your humble petisoner for 5 weekes together night and day was imployed in this county for the disarmeing malignants by the command of his Exellencey and the directions of your worships for wich service never as yett receaved any pay thoughe the service was very painefull and chargeable. Moreover your peticioner have wasted his stocke and runne into debt by continueing Ensigne to Captaine Dawgs the space of a yeare and more without pay exepting that small tyme we weare one service and now being to the greefe of his heart out of imployment in this just cause of King and Parliament and all his kindred that are able to suply his wants. Malignants and disafected persons doth not know a friend under God to make knowne his wants to rather then your worships, who have had soe much experience of his activety and fidelity.
Wherefore your petisioner humbly requireth your worships seriously to consider the premises and to afford him your assistiance in procuring him such releife as your worships in your wisdoms shall thinke fitt
And your poore petisioner as he is bound shall pray

21 March
The committee in consideration of Edward Wood his readynes to act and to obay ther commands, it is ordered that Mr Turner give in way of free gifte *xls* to the said Edward Wood for his scoute service
*Gabriel Barbor, John Barbor, Roger Draper, George Banaster, Joseph Dalton Maior, Thomas Meade, William Carter*

***(Endorsed along the side)*** March 21 1644
Received off William Turner *ii* accordinge to this order forty shillinges} £2
*Per Me Edward Wood*

## Part 3. The victims of war[433]

### [135] TNA: SP28/231 Order re payment to the widdow of Daniel Field,[434] 21/2/1643(4)

*Die Mercurii* February 21st 1643
It is this day ordered by the Committee for the County at Hartford at their generall meeting[435] at Hartford that William Hickman Treasurer for the two hundreds of Cashio and Dacorum upon the receipt hereof pay unto the Widow of Captaine Daniel Feild or such person as shee shall appoint to receive it, the summe of foure score pounds being part of the arrears < of one hundred one pound eleven shillings> due to the said Captaine at his decease, as appears by the Commissaries accounts, which monies so issued out are to be referred to account <until> ~~when~~ the accounts of both treasuries shall be audited, And this shall be his discharge
*Thomas Niccolls Chairman, John Robotham, John King, William Carter, William Dawges, Raphe Pemberton Esq., Thomas Lewins*

***(On reverse)*** Received this 2nd March 1643(4) in full of this order within written to the some of four score pounds for the use of the widdow Feild £80
*Per me William Field*

### [136] TNA: SP28/231 Hertford Committee payment to widow Gill[436] for care of the wounded Daniel Wright, 31/12/1644

31 December 1644
Whereas Danyell Wright, <soldier under the Earle of Manchester>, who was shott and soare wounded in his side and arme, and hath lyen in greate paine in the howse and at the charge of the widow Gill (who is a very poore woman) wee the Committee doe require you Mr Turner to pay unto Joseph Buncker, Constable, towards the discharge of the said widdow for keeping the said soldier $x^s$. Wee say $x^s$.

---

[433] For a recent assessment of the treatment of the sick and widows in neighbouring Essex, see Appleby, D, 'Unnecessary persons? Maimed soldiers and war widows in Essex 1642-1662', *Essex Archaeology and History*, 32, 3rd Ser. (Colchester 2001) pp209-221

[434] For Field see above p xxviii & n73

[435] This was a joint meeting of committeemen form Hertford and St Albans

[436] Gill was the former landlady of the Chequer Inn, Hertford [Information from Alan Greening]

*Gabriel Barbor, Joseph Dalton Maior, William Carter*

*Received by me Joseph Buncker* £0- 10s-0d

**[137] TNA: SP28/230 Hertford Committee order to pay Daniel Wright 12/2/1644(5)**

Mr Turner, treasurer, is requyred to pay unto Daniell Wright who ys a wounded souldier and verie sicke one of my Lord of Manchesters Armye beinge in the keepinge of the widow Gyll the some of tenne shillings out of the moneys seased upon that ordynance of sendinge out 500 foote and a 100 horse. I say tenne shillings this twelfe day of Februarie 1644. *Gabriel Barbor*

Paid this to George Pettett

**[138] TNA: SP28/231 Hertford Committee order re money for sick soldiers, 1/11/1644**

Mr Turner,
Whereas these eight soldiers beinge of the regiment of the Earle of Manchester were att the taken of Linckolne[437] and att the fight att Yorke[438], but beinge sick (so that they could not march) they staide behinde att Huntington from whence they now are goeinge the nearest way to Readinge.[439] These are to authorize you for to distribute unto each of them, out of the treasury, 18d a peece which comes to twelve shillings < to helpe them in ther journeys>. And for you so doeinge this shall be your warrant. Given under our hands this first of November 1644.
*Gabriel Barbor, William Carter, Thomas Meade*
Paid this 12s
You may put it in your accounts for the Earle of Manchesters horse

[437] The taking or recapture of Lincoln by the Eastern Association Armies
[438] Battle of Marston Moor
[439] Hertfordshire troops were sent to the garrison at Reading to protect the Thames valley from the Royalists at Oxford

## Part 4. Political effects of the War

### [139] HALS: QSR6 1643-4 *f*262 Draft petition of the Grand Jury to Quarter Sessions, 8/7/1644

To the right worshipfull the Justices of Peace for the county of Hertford att the generall quarter sessions now holden for the sayd county. The Humble Peticon of the Grand Inquest for the said county on the behalf of themselves and the rest of the inhabitants thereof.

Presenting to your serious consideracions the many vast disbursements by the inhabitants of this county to the much exhausting of theire estates in which we will nott descend to particulars, butt onely in what is beyond the proportion of the rest of the Association; as the many extraordinary taxes and payments imposed upon the sayd county, by virtue of the ordinance for the new militia,[440] which was propounded, solicited and procured withoutt our consent, or knowledge or any publike notice thereof given to the country; as alsoe the heavy pressure of free quarter, butt that which wee desire may bee immediately looked on as most destructive to our estates is the drawing outt of our country all our forces which, besides the unsupportable charge of maintayning them abroade, the very want of theire labour and assistance for the gathering in the fruites of the ground this hay time and harvest will utterly disable us for any further contributions, and indeed of subsistance, haveing in many of our townes[441] where greate store of corne is growing nott the fifth parte of the men that will bee requisite for the inning thereof, and in many places the plough standing still for want of men and many poore men abroad whose wives and children ly upon the charge of the parish in theire absence and by the loss of theire worke in the time of harvest will bee disabled to mainetaine them all the yeare after.
Wee therefore humbly pray that by your assistance some effectual meanes may bee used for the speedy calling home of our men. And that you would bee pleased the knights and burgesses[442] which serve for this county (of whose faithfull endeavours for the good of the county wee are most assured) that they would present these, our greavances, to the house of Parliament and Committee of Both Kingdoms.[443] And wee shall ever pray etc.

---

[440] The Ordinance of 18 December 1643 [F&R I, pp356-8]
[441] Townships or communities
[442] The MPs for the county and the boroughs of Hertford and St Albans
[443] The central executive body running the parliamentary war effort

**[140] TNA: SP16/502 *f*56 Petition of Militia Committee to Committee of Both Kingdoms, 12/7/1644**

To the Committee of Both Kingdoms
The humble petition of the Committee for the Militia of the County of Hertford

Whereas all the three regiments of this countie are at present in actuall service out of the countie the payment wherof amounteth each week to about £1000. The commanders and soldiers daily solicit us for monies, we accordingly send out warrants for the levying and collecting thereof, but monies not coming in proportionablie to our disbursement we have bin constrained for the preventing of the daylie disbanding of our soldiers to borrowe some hundreds of pounds upon our own creditts both to provide ammunicion and to paie our souldiers as also to send out letters to divers able persons to borrow money of them, engaging ourselves for repayment when it is collected, which for a time did bring in some quantities of money to supply our occasions.

But since the publishing of the late ordinance of 5 July,[444] which seems to transferre the power of the militia from the committee to the Lord Lieutenant and deputie lieutenants, little or noe moneys either upon the said letters or other taxes is brought in, either to paie our regiments or enable us to make repayment of what we have borrowed. But contrariwise the ill-affected assemble in great numbers triumphing in the new ordinance and with approbrious speeches villyfieing the committee and commanders (men who will willingly sacrifice their lives for the defence of the Parliament) by us employed.

And upon Munday 8th present at the quarter sessions, three or four of those ill-affected persons caused a peticon[445] in the name of the whole countie to be by the Grand Jury (men not well raised in business of this nature) presented to the bench complayninge of oppression by us for the mainteyninge of the militia, (whereas what we have done hath ben in the command of this Honourable Committee and a deepe sense of the kingdoms necessitie soe requiringe.)

---

[444] The ordinance, which concerned regulating the trained bands in the associated counties, was passed by the House of Lords on 3 July and appeared to give the lieutenancy back its power to control the local militia, only giving the militia committee a supporting role [*LJ* VI, pp613-5; F&R I, pp462-6]

[445] For the grand jury petition see **139** above. This appears to be a move by more conservative elements both locally and in parliament to curb the power of the more radical militia committee

In brief, the maine scope of their endevor is to alienate the affections of the people from the committee for the militia, whereby monies may be withheld, which of necessity must occasion the disbanding of our soldiers, erect the shadow of a militia in stead of a substance and by degrees to make the malignant the major prevailing party, which, when effected, what condition this countie and the residue of the Association will soone be brought unto.

Pray the time limited in their ordinance may be renewed to keep in being so make payment of monies borrowed for maintaining their regiments and to perfect that work wherein they have so far proceeded; and that, in the ordinance to be renewed, those of their committee who seldom attend, and show disaffection to the Parliament cause, may be left out, and those continued in it protected from any oppression through the new ordinance which they may expect in regard of the service they have done.

56.I Four heads showing what the present committee have done for the county in the Parliament interest.

1. The Committee found the countie in an undefensible estate.[446]

2. The countie was dayly in danger of ruine and commissioners of array being appointed commissions to them given the day of execusion?

3. Malignants did arme themselves and combine together did drawe pestilent peticons pretending peace, gathered multitudes of handes to it, sent it to Oxford[447] by such persons as are nowe either in actuall war against the Parliament or for feare there of thence previously justley secured themselves and complices disarmed, which persons soe imployed to Oxford did bringe from thence multitudes of pardons for such as would submit, dispensing them in our countie to whome they pleased, which should have been at the bloudy day as the red thred given by the speyes of Rahab,[448] which hellish plot was alsoe discovered and prevented by those whoe are nowe of the committee for the militia.

---

[446] The committee found the county in an indefensible state, when it was first set up

[447] The ‘accommodation petition’ of January 1643

[448] This is a reference to Rahab the prostitute, who hid the spies of Joshua in Jericho, in the Geneva Bible’s Book of Joshua Chapters 2 and 6. She let them down outside the city walls by a cord out of the window in exchange for the lives of her family, and in Chapter 2 verse 18 they said “Behold when we come into the land, thou shalt bind this line of red thread in the window whereby thou lettest us down.” Whilst the rest of Jericho perished she and her family were saved by the red thread hanging in the window. In the King James’ version of 1611, the word ‘red’ is replaced by ‘scarlet’, but older members of the committee would have been brought up on the Geneva Bible.

Countie now in a posture of defence, malignants quelled and well-affected, armed, able to defend themselves against ill-affected, if their number not increased by the last ordinance

56.II Requisits to be considered by this honourable committee whether two severall militias in this countie of Hertford, at one and the same time, managed by severall persons be profitable to the state or not
If resolved negatively
Then propound a more advantageous way, less chargeable to the countie out of the regiments already by us raised, armed, disciplined and in actuall service, of the (e)affecting of what is intended in the no(e)we ordinance leave to your lordshipps consideracions whether it is convenient to alter the forme of the militia alreadie settled on or whether they may be not destructive one to the other, men of different affections beinge imployed in places of command.[449]

Reasons demonstratinge why the militia should be disposed of as formerly by the committee:
1 Whereas the raisinge of 500 foot and 100 horse accordinge as in the new ordinance is propounded, wilbe an ease to the country, we conceave it will not soe prove except to dissipate and nullifie the 3 regiments already raised, and soe to make an easie entrance for the enemy be an ease to the country for otherwise there wilbe soe much more the want of men, soe much the more money expended as must arme them all, which done they are still rawe and unexperienced souldiers, upon whose valour it is not safe to hazard a countie much lesses a kingdome. But if the ordinance for the militia be renewed and still continued in the hands of the committee we shall within a few dayes, out of our three regiments, drawe the number of 500 able, armed, well-disciplined and approved souldiers for the standinge foot army, and 100 more of the like to be mounted on light horse and dragoones and all to be commanded by men of experience and of approved integritie and yet will not nullifie our 3 regiments, but although for the tyme of harvest they shalbe returned home, to get in the fruits of the earth,[450] yet will we at any time upon an allarum given

[449] The more conservative and radical groups in the county, the former allied with the 'Peace Party' in the Commons, the latter with the 'War Party'
[450] The desertion of the militia to go back to their farms to get the harvest in was a perennial problem for commanders of all kinds, and could have been one reason why the war lasted so long and why the attack on Oxford was so slow in getting going

have them ready to joyne with a standing army for the defence of the associated counties, the citie, parliament and kingdome.
2 Because malignants and persons unconformable to the Parliament have by the endeavoures of the committee bin brought to conformitie to all ordinances of parliament.
3 Because it is to be suspected some plot of dangerous consequence is now hatchinge in our countie, malignants of late beinge growne soe audacious and jocund.
4 Because they threaten to stabb the most active of the committee with approbrious speeches, traduce them and the officers imployed by them.
5 Because they resort in great multitudes to market townes in divers partes of the county to plot and continue their designs, whose frequent congregating themselves at such times and such places complayninge against the committee and their proceedings doe sufficiently demonstrate their hatred to the committee for their works sake.
6 If this committee be unempowered, malignants will soone be rearmed and made capable of not only of defence but offence.
7 Because the committee men formerly well reputed of have by their fidelity to the Parliament put themselves upon the odium of the malignant party of the countie.[451]

**[141] TNA: SP28/232 Correspondence between Gabriel Barbor and Sir Thomas Dacresm re copies of ordinances on spoilers,[452] 25-26/4/1645**

*f1* For Sir Thomas Dacres Knight one of the Knights of the Shire for the Countye of Hartford present this with care

---

[451] A petition from the militia committee was presented to the Commons on 27 July. On that day the Commons read a new ordinance for the second time. This petition, the new ordinance, complaints against the Committee and a petition concerning Gabriel Barbor, were all referred to the committee for reforming the army. On 5 August the committee reported back, and the new draft ordinance was sent to the Lords. This continued the militia committee in power by extending the December 1643 ordinance. They were able to raise up to £300 per week, but their treasurers had to submit quarterly accounts to the lieutenancy and all members had to take the Covenant of June 1643. This appears to have been a carefully worked out compromise [*CJ* III, pp575, 579-81; *LJ* VI, pp664-6]

[452] 'Spoilers' was the term used in early 1645 for Royalists breaking through from Buckinghamshire and spoiling or laying waste land in west Hertfordshire [Thomson, 'Hertfordshire Communities', pp273-4]

*f2* Sir Thomas Dacres: our committee for the millicia doe humblye and earnestly pray you would procure and send us by this bearer 140 of the ordinance here inclosed to be read in every church in our Countie and wee doubt not to cleere our County of the spoilers. Wee expect our messengers retorne by tomorrow morning that the ordinance be read in our market and the rest in every parish church next Lords day. Pray Sir give directions and if they be not allowed us, wee will pay for them. I am your faithfull and humble frend *Gabriel Barbor*
Hartford 25 Aprill 1645 post hast

I pray deliver to your bearer heareof 140 books as is desired for the use of the county of Hartford at the usuall rates for the service of the parliament, he giving you money for them if the other countyes are put to pay, that they be not printed at the charge of the Commonwealth.
Lyonsy House in Westminster 26 Aprill 1645 *Thomas Dacres*

**[142] TNA: SP23/82 *ff* 775-782 The charges against Sir John Boteler,[453] 29/8/1643-12/9/1643**

*f775* 29 August 1643 At the committee of the House of Commons for examinations.[454] The charge against Sir John Butler of Watton in the County of Hertford
Article 1 That hee had a Commission of Array[455] and spake in the defence of it sitting at his owne table saying it was legall and just and indeavoured what in him lay to put the same in execucion.
To this Sir John Butler being examined saieth hee had the Commission about a yeere since, but kept it not a weeke. It was sent to him from Haddam from the Lord Capelle, denyeth the putting it in execucon or indeavouring or intending to do it, and denieth the justifying of it. And saieth because the country did not like it therefore he sent it back to the Kinge.

The Proofe: Dr Peter Smith[456] saieth that about a yeere or 13 months ago being at Sir Peter Salting<s>talls house, Sir Peter tolde him he had received a

[453] For Boteler see Appendix
[454] The Committee which was used to examine or question those suspected of being Royalists
[455] The Commission calling on all in the county to raise forces for the king against the king's enemies

letter from Sir John Butler touchinge the Commission of Array which they had speech of, and he had seen the superscripcion of other letters in the messengers hand requesting other gents to meete at Hartford the Thursday following, this being Monday as he remembereth. So Sir Peter Saltingstall and others met but Sir John Butler met not, as he heared, and Sir Peter Saltingstall tolde him that he conceived those letters did desire them to meete there about that Commission of Array.

*f*776 Captain Robert Tompson,[457] saieth he heard Sir John Butler speake in defence of the Commission of Array but it being about a twelvemonth since he remembreth not what perticuler words he spake; and that he spake in a flighting manner of the militia, but knoweth not in perticuler what words he used. It was at his house after dinner.

Captain Isaac Needham saith he remembreth not that he hearde Sir John Butler at any time speake of the Commisssion of Array, yet divers gents was about it, but Sir John Butler was not there, nor did indeavour to execute it. Saith that, at a sessions, Sir John Butler did speake in disgrace of the militia and said that those that exercised in it were idle fellowes and did that they needed not to do for the countrey had trained men enow to defend it.

Sir John Butler, to this saieth that hee, seeing Captain Nedham and others came insolently into the courte at the sessions, did reprehend him for it, and that was all he did, and said that there were 1500 of the trained band that were sufficient to defend the country without them.

Captain Needham saieth that he was at that time (as he remembreth) ensigne of the volunteers, and that one House was bound over to the sessions by Sir John Watts and that Colonel John Watts,[458] who is now with the Lord Capell, did call this informant and the rest that were with him rogues; and that Sir John Butler did seeme to second him therein, saying, as formerly he hath

[456] Smith was the vicar of Barkway and a member of the Assembly of Divines, a learned preacher who gave a fast-day sermon before parliament on 29 May 1644 [HALS: Hine Collection Vol. 30 Civil War Tracts; F&R I, pp180-4]

[457] Robert Thom(p)son of Watton, younger brother of Maurice and Colonel George [Alan Thomson, 'Thomson, George (*bap.* 1607, *d.*1691)' *NewDNB*]

[458] Sir John Watts of Mardocks remained on the local magistrates' bench and kept a low profile whereas his son, Captain, later Colonel John Watts, became the royalist governor of Chirk Castle, North Wales and was knighted for its defence (*see* Appendix)

saide and when old Sir John Watts and Colonel John Watts had justified the binding over *f* 777 of House, to the sessions, Sir John Butler seemed to second them in it; saying, they were a company of base fellowes and troubled themselves more than they needed. Saieth they were called rogues and rascals in the Dolphin and Crowne in Ware, but this informant heard not these words spoken; and saieth that Sir John Butler did not justifye those words of rogues and rascals, but the binding over of that House, who was bound over for reporting those words of rogues and rascalls as a scandall cast upon them.

Sir John Butler saith that Captain Needham and those that were with him came in an insolent manner and he checked him for it as aforesaid.
<u>Article 2</u> That Sir John Butler went to Oxford under colour of a peticion for peace,[459] and brought from thence the Kings pardon[460] for Hartfordshire upon condicion they should no more assist the Kings enemyes and Sir John caused the same to be publiquely proclaimed he himselfe being present.

To this Sir John Butler saieth that he brought certaine papers from the King sealed up from Oxford about Xmas last, and was tolde there was in it a pardon for Hartfordshire, but what els he knoweth not nor caused any of them to be proclaimed, nor was present when any of them was read, and saieth he brought the papers to St Albans and there he delivered them to the high sheiriffe.[461]

<u>Proofe</u> John Deeman saieth that Mr Ingoldsby[462] said publiquely in the church that his Majestie had granted a gracious pardon; but whether Sir John Butler wished him to do it or no he knoweth not.

---

[459] The accommodation petition of January 1643

[460] A letter of 7 January 1643 reported that the previous day a number of the chief gentlemen of Hertfordshire had presented to His Majesty a brave petition for the King's assistance and protection against the rebels, and a pardon was issued to the inhabitants of Hertford by the King on the same day [*HMC Portland Mss* I, p86; Larkin, *Proclamations*, pp843-4]

[461] Thomas Coningsby, who was later imprisoned as a malignant

[462] William Igoldsby was the previous vicar of Watton at Stone 1641-3, who had been sequestered because in April 1643 he had confessed that he had preached "That those that have taken the Protestation and do fight against the King they were foresworn" and that he had written a book "full of malignant expressions and imputations upon the proceedings in Parliament". This book was a printed sermon in which he had implied that the Oaths of Supremacy and Allegiance and the oath taken under the Protestation committed subjects not to resist their king. The sermon had been printed in 1642 under the authorship of G I and was entitled "*The doctrine of the Church of England, Established by Parliament Against*

Sir John denyeth that he delivered any of the papers (*f778*) to Ingoldsby, nor that he gave any direction about it to him or any body els, but likely he might have somme speech with him about it.

3 Article
That he tolde a tennant of his who is a godly religious man that his house was the randezvous for the Roundheads and tolde him he would ere long breake the route of them, further saying he would burne his house before such a one as he should dwell in it any longer.

Sir John Boteler to this said he remembreth not any such thing but confesseth that there were meetings at the house of one Carter, his tennant, where he was published to be a papist, and that he said that rather then such a fellow should dwell in this house, he would set fire on it, or words to that purpose.

Proofe John Carter saieth that Sir John tolde him that his house was a rendezvouz, and that he would turne this informant out of his house, and said that he would burne it before this informant should dwell in it, for that this informants wife said he was a papist, which he denied.

4 Article That when the churchwardens of the parish according to the ordinance of parliament went to his house to desire him to take the Covenant,[463] Sir John asked them if they meant to be hanged, or to have their houses burned over their heads and said that they were all traitors and forsworne men that tooke it.

Sir John Butler, to this, saieth that Miles, one of the churchwardens, came to him and tolde him that *(f779)* Mr Welles,[464] minister of the parish desired him to come to church to take the Covenant upon Sonday following. Sir John bid the churchwardens tell him he would not come to church so long as the said Wells had any thing to do there, understanding that the said Wells was put in

---

*Disobedience and Wilfull Rebellion.*" Ingoldsby was put in the Fleet prison [Vallance, E, *Revolutionary England and the National Covenant: State oaths, Protestantism and the political nation, 1553-1682*, (Woodbridge, 2005) pp 68, 112; Shaw, W A, *A History of the English church during the Civil Wars and under the Commonwealth 1640-60*, II, (1900) App II, pp308, 310; *CJ* II, p161; III, p36; *LJ* VI, p20]

463 This was the order relating to the taking of the covenant for the new church, for which all officeholders were expected to take an oath, and all inhabitants to subscribe

464 Welles was presumably intruded by parliament once Ingoldsby had been sequestered

by the Parliament and saieth the reason why he did forbeare coming to the church was because he sent him word that he would advise him to forbeare preaching treason and denyeth all the rest of the article.

8th August[465] 1643

Edward Miles churchwarden saieth that upon Friday last was sevenight[466] he went to Sir John Butler to his house and desired him to come to church to take the Covenant on the Sonday following. He asked this informant whether he had taken it, hee answering yes. Sir John said do you think long to have your house burnt over your head, or to be hanged. This informant desiring him not to take it ill at his hands, he being compelled to do it being an officer; he answered, being very hot and angry, that he was not offended with him, but he saide they were forsworne and traitors that tooke it.

John Halfehead,[467] the other churchwarden saieth he heard all the words above menconed spoken, saving that he remembreth not that he heard those last words they were forsworne and traitors that tooke it.

John Deermer saieth that Halfhead tolde him when he was last at London that he heard Sir John Butler speake all the words abovemenconed, saveth *(f780)* the last vizt (forsworne and traitors)

12th September 1643

~~John Halfehead~~ Edward Miles being re-examined said he heard Sir John Butler speake the words as is before deposed, and saith that John Halfehead, his fellow churchwarden, went with him to Sir John Butlers house, and he went into the kitchin and Halfehead stood behinde the walls and heard the words Sir John Butler spake to him for Sir John spake very loude and when this informant came out of the kitchen he found Halfehead in the buttery.

William Plummer saieth that John Halfehead tolde him that he and Miles went to Sir John Butlers about the Covenant, and that Sir John asked Miles if he had taken the Covenant and he said he had. Then Sir <John> said do you longe to have your house fired over your head, or to be hanged and that he

---

[465] Presumably this is a mistake for September

[466] i.e. seven nights or a week ago

[467] The Halfheads were related to the Thomsons of Watton, Robert Thomson's mother being Elizabeth Halfehead. Both families held land as tenants from Sir John Boteler [HALS: DP/118/1/1 Watton Parish Register]

<the said Halfehead> stood behinde him and that Sir John saide that they were all traitors and foresworne men that tooke it and this Halfehead tolde this informant the next morning after the words were spoken.

John Halfehead being re-examined saith that he told Plummer that Miles tolde him the words that Sir John Butler spake.

Thomas Heath saith that he heard Halfehead say he heard Sir John Butler. Sir John was angry, he went into the buttery and saith that Miles and Deerman were present when Halfehead spake the words.

Witness for Sir John Butler
William Trott, servant to Sir John, saieth that *(f781)* Miles and Halfhead came to speake with Sir John and being drinking in the buttery, Sir John came out into the hall, and then this informant called Miles forth, who went to the hall to Sir John above; and this informant went into the buttery and saith that all the whiles Miles was in the hall speaking with Sir John, Halfehead was in the buttery drinking with other sevants. Saith that he heard nothing but about Mr Wells the minister; and that when Miles and Halfehead came into the house they went into the buttery and he went up to call his master, Sir John, and that when Sir John came downe, all the speech was with Miles in the hall and in the entry going into Sir Johns Chamber, which entry is between the hall and the kitchin, and that Sir John and Miles were not in the kitchin together; and saith that this was about sun downe, the day or week he knoweth not but saith that after Sir John, his master, parted with Miles in the entry, he went to bed.

John Okely, servant to Sir John, said when Miles and Halhead came to his master, Sir John, they came first into the buttery, and when Sir John came down out of his chamber into the hall both of them went out of the buttery, both Miles and Halfehad, and Miles went to the end of the hall with Sir John and Halfehead turned back into the buttery and did but go out of the buttery one step and not about and was all the while with this informant till Miles came in to call him.

Sir John Butler saith that Miles was not with him in the kitching.

Edward Miles saith that Sir John spake to him in the kitchin the words in question, and that (*f*782) then he went into the buttery and was called out and spake with Sir John in the hall and that when he went into the kitchen,

Halfehead went with him to the kitchin doore and Sir Johns sonn called Halfehead first.

John Halfehead saith that Sir John Butlers sonn came to him and Miles when they came first into the house and said his father was going to bedd; and that Miles went to Sir John, being then in the kitchen, but he went not into the kitchin, but was a little way in the entry about two steps and returned againe into the buttery. Saith that the son Miles go into the kitchin, and after that Sir John and Miles were in the hall speaking together, this informant went out of the buttery into Sir Johns yard.

<u>5 Article</u> That he slighteth the ordinances of parliament in denying to contribute his parte to the just and necessary assessments as namely that of the £400,000, the Associacion, the monthly payments and such like.

Sir John Butler to this saieth he had paid all and sheweth a certificate from the Committees of Cambridge for association and payment to the value of £200 in money and horse.

<u>6 Article</u> That he keepeth a priest in his house who the last fast day dranke Prince Ruperts[468] health and the Lord Hoptons[469] and said in a taphouse in the towne that the Lord Mayor of London was a pimpe[470] because he locked up St Pauls Church.

Sir John to this saieth he keepeth a chaplain (*f*783) in his house, a learned orthodox and sober man, and he knoweth of no such thing don by him nor doth believe it.

---

[468] Prince Rupert, nephew to Charles I was his most effective cavalry commander [Ian Roy, 'Rupert, Prince and Count Palatine of the Rhine and Duke of Cumberland (1619-1682)' *NewDNB*]

[469] Ralph Hopton, royalist army officer, had married Elizabeth, Lord Capel's aunt, the daughter of Sir Arthur Capel. He secured Cornwall for the King, and although severely injured in July 1643, mananged to defeat the parliamentarians under his friend Waller at the battle of Roundaway Down. However he was later defeated by Waller in Sussex, but was always considered a man of great honour and integrity [Ronald Hutton, 'Hopton, Ralph, Baron Hopton (*bap*. 1596, *d*. 1652)', *NewDNB*]

[470] Pimp had the modern meaning, but also was generally used in the early 17$^{th}$ century to mean a person who ministered to the baser passions or evil designs of others

Simon Michell saieth that he heard one Abbot[471] on a fast day about nine of the clock being at an alehouse with some of Sir John Butlers servants, and there were two healthes drunk Prince Ruperts and the Lord Hoptons, there he left them.

**[143] TNA: SP23/82 *f*771 Sir John Boteler's allegations and answer[472] (undated 1645?)**

Sir John Botelers allegacions and answer to the Committee at Goldsmyths Hall which hee prayeth they please to take to theyre consideraciones reporte accordinglye.
First that hee is indebted to the vallewe of £3000 havinge lately maryed a daughter and hath five children more to provyde for.
2. That his rents are fallen and his landes turned into his handes soe that he looseth £300 yearlye.[473]
3. Free quarter in his house for solldiers which hath consumed allmost all the stocke in his groundes, hee payinge excise for what they eate and drinke.
4. That he hath suffered imprisonment allmost two yeares[474] to the very greate prejudice of his health and losse in his estate.
5. That he hath obeyed all the ordinances of parliament and they have hadd greate assistance from him viz in horse and arms £300 and in ready monyes £1200 at the least.
6. That hee fyndes[475] at this present both men and horses at his owne charge and hath at severall tymes sent to Allisburye, Newport Pagnell, Bedford and Northampton seaven solldiers each tyme and mayntyned them, and lately to Hitchyn eight of his householde servants.

---

[471] Abbott was presumably the chaplain to Sir John, and may well have been a high Anglican or Arminian in belief and practice and therefore hostile to Presbyterians and the covenant. Arminians were assumed by radicals (unjustly) to be the same as Catholics

[472] The date this petition was received was 8 March 1645. He was ordered to be discharged from his imprisonment in The Tower, his delinquency and his sequestration on 25 September 1645. In March 1646 he was allowed to pay the last £500 of his fine in five instalments over five years, However in April 1650 the sequestration was re-imposed as he had neglected to pay the remainder of the fine [*CJ* IV, pp284-8, 471; *CCC*, pp852-3]

[473] The lands, which had been leased out were returned to him, as he could not find tenants, so then lost income from rents.

[474] He was first imprisoned in the Peter House and then in The Tower [ Kingston, *Herts* p130]

[475] i.e. he provides men and horses at his own cost for the parliamentary war effort, particularly the garrisons

7. That he hath not assisted the Kinge with horse, man or moneys which he offers to justifie upon his oath.

And that farther hee submits to the pleasure of the House and prayeth that his offer of £1000 to bee payd by Midsomer at the farthest togeather with his allegacions may be presented, which he hopeth will bee accepted. Howsoever he will endeavour to give <the> honourable House content and that for the recoverye of his health (after soe longe imprisonment) and the procuring such moneys as shall bee imposed upon him he may have libertye to goe to his owne house and bee discharged from his imprisonment.

### [144] TNA: SP28/209B List of Royalist and Catholic delinquents[476] (undated 1643?)

A particular of the names of those who are delinquents and papists within the ordinance of parliament for sequestracions within the Countie of Hartford who hath estates in the same countie
Hertford Delinquents
The Earle of Bedford[477]
The Earle of Carnarvan[478]
The Earl of Dover[479]

---

[476] The date of this list is probably late 1643 as it was after Harrison and Russell had been sequestered, but before Marmaduke Rawdon was knighted by the King in December.

[477] William Russell, first Duke of Bedford, son of the late parliamentarian Francis Russell, fought for Parliament at Edgehill, but defected to the King in August 1643. He held lands in Flaunden, tithes from lands in Hitchin worth £500 p.a. and payments in kind from tenants there worth £200 pa [TNA: SP28/209B Returns of Joseph Hill and Samuel Robbins Collectors for Cashio and Edward Chandler and Edward Heath Collectors for Hitchin; Victor Slater, 'Russell, William first Duke of Bedford (1616-1700)' *NewDNB*]

[478] Robert Dormer, first Earl of Carnarvon, (*c*1610-1643) held extensive estates, mainly at Ascott near Wing, Bucks but also at Studham, then in Hertfordshire. He fought at Edgehill for the King and commanded a regiment of horse at Roundaway Down but died at the first battle of Newbury. The Dormer family had held land on the Bedfordshire border since 1600 [TNA: SP28/209B Return of James Roberts, collector for Dacorum; *VCH Herts* II, p275; Ian Roy, 'Dormer, Robert first Earl of Carnarvon (1610-1643)' *NewDNB;* GEC, *Complete Peerage,* III, pp44-5; Newman, P R, *The Old Service: Royalist regimental colonels and the Civil War*, (Manchester, 1993) pp98, 116, 46-7, 162, 184, 228, 300]

[479] Henry Carey, Lord Dover of Hunsdon, MP for Hertfordshire 1601-14 and active in the Virginia and Guinea Companies 1618 and 1627. He joined the King at Oxford, where he was the nominal commander of an auxiliary regiment of Oxford gentlemen strangers and scholars (the University Regiment), which remained part of the garrison as long as the war lasted. He was also a member of the Council of War 1644-6, having fought as a gentleman volunteer at

The Earle of Monmouth[480]
The Lord Capell[481]
The Lord Dunsmore[482] Guardian to the Lord Butler[483]
Endymion Porter Esq.[484] Guardian to <the> same Lord
Sir Thomas Fanshawe[485]
Sir Symon Fanshawe[486]
Sir John Harrison[487]
Sir John Huett[488]
The Lord Maltravers[489]

---

Edgehill in the Lifeguard. His property in Hunsdon was sequestered by Heath and Chandler, an act which caused problems with his son Lord Rochford, who remained there [Rabb, T K, *Enterprise and Empire: Merchants and Gentry investment 1575-1630*, (Harvard, 1967) p260; Newman, *The Old Service*, p83; Ian Roy, 'The Royalist Army in the First Civil War', Oxford DPhil, 1963, pp63, 190-2)]

480 Robert Carey, second Earl of Monmouth lived at Kenilworth Castle, Warwickshire whilst his mother the dowager countess lived at his house at Moor Park, Rickmansworth. His property there was sequestered by the collectors for Cashio [Crummett, J B 'The Lay Peers in Parliament 1640-1644', University of Manchester PhD Thesis, (1972) p193]

481 Arthur Capel, Baron Hadham, was fighting for the Royalists in the Northwest and Wales, and thus had his estates at Cassiobury, Hadham, Walkern and elsewhere sequestered by the Hertford sequestration Committee (*see* below **149-51** and Appendix)

482 Sir Francis Leigh, ennobled as Lord Dunsmore, later Earl of Chichester, married Audrey Boteler, the eldest daughter of the first Lord Boteler [Huxley G, *Endymion Porter: the life of a courtier 1587-1649*, (1959) p43; Thomas Seccombe,'Leigh, Francis, first Earl of Chichester (d.1653)', revised, Sean Kelsey, *NewDNB*]

483 William, second Lord Boteler of Bramfield, held Hatfield Woodhall and was said to have been an idiot from birth. He was the son of the Duke of Buckingham's sister, who had married the first Lord Boteler [Huxley, *Porter*, pp41-2]

484 Porter, a favourite courtier of Charles I, was married to Lord Boteler's sister Olive, who had converted to Catholicism. He was a monopolist and diplomat but remained a Protestant for political purposes. He fled abroad in 1645 and died virtually a pauper [Ronald G Asch, 'Porter Endymion (1587-1649)', *NewDNB*]

485 Thomas Fanshawe (*see* Appendix)

486 Simon Fanshawe (*see* Appendix)

487 Sir John Harrison (*see* Appendix)

488 Huett held lands in Rickmansworth worth £10 and rents of £30 pa [TNA: SP28/209B Return of Joseph Hill and Samuel Robbins Collectors for Cashio]

489 Either Henry Frederick Howard, 15th Earl of Arundel (1608-1652), or his more illustrious father Thomas, 14th Earl, who were both referred to at different times as Lord Maltravers. This is probably the former, who inherited the courtesy title from his brother in 1624, becoming Baron Mowbray in 1640. A royalist who fought at Edgehill, he was on the council of war at Oxford. However his father had lent £54,000 to the King and parliament confiscated the family estates in 1643, whilst his father was abroad. Had rental income in Edwinstree Hundred of £198pa [TNA: SP28/209B Return of William Gaze and Andrew Hawkes, Collectors for

John Belassis Esq[490]
Thomas Saunders Esq[491]
Marmaduke Roydon Esq[492]
Henry Crumwell Esq[493]
Thomas Offley Esq[494]
Henry Anderson Esq[495]
William Abell late Alderman of London[496]

---

Edwinstree; Gordon Goodwin,'Howard, Henry Frederick, fifteenth Earl of Arundel, fifth Earl of Surrey, and second Earl of Norfolk (1608-1652)' rev J T Peacey, *NewDNB*; R Malcolm Smuts, 'Howard, Thomas, fourteenth Earl of Arundel, fourth Earl of Surrey, and first Earl of Norfolk (1585-1646)', *NewDNB*]

[490] John Bellasyse (1615-89) later Baron Bellasyse, married clandestinely in 1636 Jane Boteler sole heir of Robert Boteler of Watton Woodhall, raised six regiments for the King, and commanded a royalist brigade at Edgehill. His lands worth £259 in Sacombe, £140 in Stevenage and rents in Hertford Hundred worth £238 were sequestered and he was imprisoned by Parliament on four occasions, being put in The Tower where Edward Wingate was allowed to visit him in June 1644. He compounded on the Newcastle Articles for £2,078. He was later involved in the Popish Plot of 1678 and his portrait is in the National Portrait Gallery [TNA: SP28/209B Accounts of John Barre of Hatfield collector for Broadwater Hundred and William Seward for Hertford Hundred; *CJ* III, p519; Newman, *The Old Service,* pp95, 106, 186-7, 215, 229, 239, 281; Henning, *Commons* I, p617; Andrew J Hopper, 'Belasyse, John first Baron Belasyse of Worlaby (*bap.*1615, *d.* 1689) *NewDNB*]

[491] Thomas Saunders, originally of Long Marston, purchased the manor of Beechwood in Flamstead parish in 1628. In 1654 he bought the manor and advowson of Flamstead from Thomas Fanshawe and in 1669 erected almshouses in the Parish. He also held the manor of Puttenham and had land in Redbourn [HALS: D/Z112/T2; *VCH Herts* II, pp193-201, 261-4]

[492] Royden (Rawden) had goods in his house worth £363 [TNA: SP28/209B Account of Edward Heath and Edward Chandler for the Hundred of Hertford]

[493] Crumwell held lands in Studham and Caddington [TNA: SP28/209B Return of James Roberts collector for Dacorum]

[494] Offley was a servant of the King and had goods worth £122 sequestered in Hertford Hundred [TNA: SP28/209B Account of Heath and Chandler]

[495] Sir Henry Anderson (1608-53), of Pendley, Tring, son of Sir Richard Anderson, went to Pembroke College Oxford and Lincoln's Inn. He married firstly Jacomina, daughter of Sir Charles Caesar of Bennington and secondly Mary daughter of Sir William Lytton. JP for the county 1637-41, he was created a Baronet in July 1643 and reportedly fought for the King, which he denied. His property in Broadwater Hundred brought over £300 p.a. rent, was sequestered, and he payed over £2,800 to the sequestrations Committee. Fined over £1,700 he was put in The Tower for non-payment, but pardoned in 1647 [TNA: C231/5 *f*256; SP28/130 Pt II Commisary Book for horses; SP28/209B Account of John Barre; HALS: QSB2A and 2B; Chauncey I, p346; Kingston, *Herts,* pp157-8; GEC *Complete Baronetage,* III, p211; *Al Ox* I, p23]

[496] William Abell (c.1584-c.1655) Alderman of London and master of the Vintner's Company, was responsible, as sheriff, for the violent arrest of the puritan minister Henry Burton, which made him unpopular as did his wine monopoly and he was accused of growing rich illegally.

William Kingesley Gent[497]
Mr Edmunds the parson of Rickmersworth[498]
John Clarke Gent[499]
John Hale Gent [500]
Mr Herbert Thorndike Clerke[501]
Edward Crosbie Gent[502]
George Bromley Gent[503]

---

He was declared a delinquent and arrested in January 1641, a fine of £57,000 being imposed on him. Although released on a pardon, he was later arrested in 1644 for non-payment of tax. Rents from his tenants in Broadwater Hundred were worth over £300 p.a. In 1652 he was living at Hatfield, when he was again imprisoned [TNA: SP28/209B John Barre's Account; Dagmar Friest, 'Abell, William (*b*. *c*1584, *d.* in or after 1655)' *NewDNB*]

[497] William Kingsley of Sarratt held the manors of Roos Hall and Goldingtons before the war. As a Captain he paid £18-15s Decimation Tax in 1656 for an estate there in the right of his wife [TNA: SP28/197 Pt 2 ff6-18; 209B Return of Joseph Hill and Samuel Robbins Collectors for Cashio; *VCH Herts* II, pp438-43]

[498] William Edmonds (c.1592-1667) son of the vicar of Rickmansworth of the same name, educated at Eton, went to Caius College Cambridge, vicar of Rickmansworth until 1644, when he was sequestered and again from 1660 [*Al Cant* Pt 1 Vol II, p87]

[499] Clark(e) held lands in Sleap and Smallford worth £122. He may well have also part inherited Beech Farm, St Peters, from his father. In December 1646 he compounded on the Oxford Articles for bearing arms against Parliament. He was fined over £284, but managed to get £40 rents waived [TNA: SP28/209B Return of Joseph Hill and Samuel Robbins Collectors for Cashio;*CCC*, p1570; *VCH Herts* II, pp412-24;]

[500] John Hale (d.1672) was a younger son of William and Rose Hale of St Pauls Walden, who inherited the manor of Stagenhoe after the deaths of his brothers and his widowed mother [TNA: SP28/209B Return of Joseph Hill and Samuel Robbins Collectors for Cashio; *VCH Herts* II, pp405-11]

[501] Herbert Thorndike (*c*1597-1672), biblical scholar and theologian, was Hebrew Lecturer at Trinity College, Cambridge in 1640 and defended the bishops and the Book of Common Prayer. He became Rector of Barley in 1642, and was defeated for the mastership of Sidney Sussex College in 1643 by puritan opponents, who kidnapped one of his key supporters. He subsequently lost his fellowship at Trinity and his living at Barley but continued to publish controversial scholarly treatises having left Cambridge. His goods were sold at Hertford Castle on 20 October 1644. He regained his posts at the Restoration but resigned from Barley in 1662 and Trinity in 1667 [TNA: SP28/197 Pt 2 *f*62; W B Patterson, 'Thorndike, Herbert (*bap*. 1597? *d*. 1672)', *NewDNB*]

[502] Crosbie held lands in Cashio following his mother's death. He is probably the royalist Major Edward Crosby/ie who lived on Holywell Hill, St Albans after the Restoration. In 1662 he shot dead John Townshend, having violently interrupted a non-conformist meeting near the Abbey. Sir Harbottle Grimston forced the jury at the Old Bailey to reverse their guilty verdict which caused a scandal [TNA: SP28/209B Return of Joseph Hill and Samuel Robbins Collectors for Cashio; Smith and North, *St Albans*, pp6, 100-1, 225]

[503] For Bromley (*see* Appendix)

Richard Newman Clarke[504]
Mr Ewers[505], the Lord Ewers his sonne[506]
Mr William Wroth Esq[507]
Mathewe Bishope of Eely[508]
Thomas Royden Gent[509]
Papists
Christopher Cresakers Moore Esq[510]

---

504 Richard Newman (*c*1589-1663) was educated at St Johns, Cambridge, then became deacon at Peterborough and Rector of Datchworth from 1623, was ejected, but reinstated in 1660. His living was worth £100 [TNA: SP28/209B Account of John Barr; *Al Cant* Pt1, III, p250]

505 Mr Ewers had land in Shenley worth over £300 [TNA: SP28/209B Returns of James Roberts Collector for Dacorum and Joseph Hill and Samuel Robbins Collectors for Cashio]

506 William 4th Lord Eure (*c*1587-1646) had married Lucy the sister of Edward Viscount Campden. His son Ralph died *c*1639. This could be William Eure the 4th Earl's grandson, who became the fifth Earl in 1646. However it was probably the 4th Earl's younger son, Sir William Eure, a Royalist colonel of horse who was killed at Marston Moor [GEC, *Complete Peerage* III, pp293-4]

507 William Wrothe (d. 1677) was the son of William Wrothe (d. 1643). This could be either of them, as they held the manor of Doos in Standon in succession. The total of the goods owned in the Hundred of Braughing came to over £290 [TNA: SP28/209B Return of Edward Chandler and Edward Heath, collectors; *VCH Herts* III, pp347-66]

508 Mathew Wren (1585-1667) was an Arminian much disliked by the Puritans. He had married the widow of Robert Brownrigg and had about 14 children. Active as the Vice Chancellor of Cambridge then successively Bishop of Hereford, Norwich and Ely he vigorously pursued the King's altar policy and attacked puritan worship. Articles of impeachment were drawn up against him in the Commons and he was sent to The Tower at the end of 1642 remaining there for 18 years. Released at the Restoration he was closely involved in the drafting of the 1662 prayerbook. He had rental income from lands in Sleape and Smallford worth £230 p.a. At his death he was very wealthy leaving £100,000 to his four daughters [TNA: SP28/209B Return of Joseph Hill and Samuel Robbins Collectors for Cashio; Nicholas W S. Cranfield, 'Wren, Matthew (1585-1667)' *NewDNB*]

509 Thomas (1622-1666) son of Marmaduke Royden (Rawden) was at Jesus College, Cambridge, then in Portugual, fought for the King at Newbury, fled to Tennerife, then recovered his father's property in the Barbados. He had goods in his father's house worth £28, when it was sequestered. He returned to England in 1662 and retired to Hoddesdon [TNA: SP28/209B Account of Edward Chandler and Edward Heath, collectors in the Hundred of Hertford; *Al Cant* Pt I, III, p424]

510 Christopher Cresacre More (1572-1649), 4th son of Thomas More II, was the great-grandson of Sir Thomas More. He had inherited his father's Hertfordshire estates in 1606. He had three children but his wife Elizabeth died in 1610 and after 1617 he lived at Gobions in North Mymms. In 1629 he settled all his Hertfordshire lands on his son Thomas who married the daughter of Sir Basil Brooke. He is seen as a young man in the More family portrait of 1593 in the National Portrait Gallery on the far right of the picture and he wrote a biography of Sir Thomas More. He died near Hereford in 1649 [*CCC* p2443; Judith H Anderson, 'More (Christopher) Cresacre (1572—1649)', *NewDNB*]

Greene Gent[511]
William Copley Esq[512]
John Newporte Esq[513]
Charles Kemball Esq[514]
James Butler
The widowe Etheringham
The Earle of Clenrickard[515]
The Lady Morely[516]

## Part 6 The Organization of Sequestration

### [145] TNA: SP28/209B Sequestration account (October 1644)

*f*1 A particular account of Edward Heath and Edward Chandler[517] from the 20 of July 1643 untell the 3 of Ocktober 1644 how the appraysing and

[511] This is probably the Thomas Green, a secular priest, who had served as chaplain to the Bendlow family at Brent Hall, near Finchingfield, Essex, who reported on Catholic families in 1635. He was against the meddling in local Catholic affairs by the Jesuits and sent a list of scandals to Rome in April 1635 [Questier, M C, (ed.) *Newsletters from the Caroline court, 1631-1638: Catholicism and the politics of the personal rule*, Camden, 5th Ser. 26, (Cambridge, 2005) pp16, 97, 154, 171, 269-272]
[512] Copley held lands in North Mymms (*see* **146** below)
[513] Newport of the manor of Furneux Pelham had lands in Edwinstree hundred worth £211, rental income of £140 p.a. and goods worth £83. He was an ardent royalist who led all his four sons to fight for the King but died of wounds in 1646. His wife compounded for the property in 1650 [TNA: SP28/209B Return of William Gaze and Andrew Hawkes, Collectors for Edwinstree; *CCC* pp2460-1, 2615, 2663; *VCH Herts* IV, p102]
[514] This may be the brother of John Kemble, the Welsh Catholic priest ordained at Douai in 1625, the latter being a victim of the Popish Plot in 1679. They were the sons of John Kemble and Anne from St Weonards, Herefordshire [W A J Archbold,'Kemble [St John Kemble] (1599-1679)', rev G Bradley, *NewDNB*]
[515] Ulrich Bourke (otherwise de Burgh) Earl of Clanricarde and Viscount Galway (c.1604-1657) was one of the few Roman Catholic Irish nobles who opposed the 1641 rebellion. He was made Lieutenant-General and Commander in chief of the Royalist forces in Connaught. His main estates in Kent worth £29,000 p.a. were sequestered along with his Hertfordshire property [GEC, *Complete Peerage*, III, pp231-2]
[516] Elizabeth Lady Morely, (c.1575-1648) widow of William Parker, Lord Morely and Mounteagle, was the daughter of Sir Thomas Tresham, and sister of Francis Tresham one of the gunpowder plotters. It was the Mounteagle letter to her husband that exposed the plot. She remained Catholic and died at Little Hallingbury, Essex, at the turn of the year 1647-8 [GEC, *Complete Peerage*, IX, pp227-9]
[517] The sequestration collectors for East Hertfordshire

sequestring delinquents estates <and attending of the Committee at Hartford > for theare time, horse hire and expence as followes:

*Imprimis* for 16 dayes a pece att Ware Parke[518] for taking downe and carringe a way the goodes att 2s the day a pece 03 04 00

For our time ~~paid~~ <in> searching and feching away goodes conseled by Mr Buicke 00 03 00

For our time in searching att Ware Park and in the pond and diging in the garden 00 04 00

For searching att William Swancotes and att Mr Cravens[519] <for our time> 00 04 00

For our time in going to Hartford to prayse the goodes that ware found att Mr Buerkes and praysing of the goodes that cam from Mr Bannnesteres 00 06 00

For a jornye to Brocksburn and the apraysing of Mr Osleys goodes for our time and horses 00 10 00

For the Appraysin of Captayn Roydens[520] goodes 01 00 00

For 12 severall jorniss a pece for the setting out of hur 5th peart[521] and stacking a way the goodes and selling of the grase att 4s the pec for our horse time and expences 04 14 00

For our apraysing of the goodes of Sir Petter Saltingstorrre[522] our horse, time and expences 00 18 06

For a jornye to Startford by warrent from the Committee to search for goodes of the Lord Capells which thay had information of that ware thare conceled 00 06 00

11 09 06

*f2* For a jornye to Theballes[523] to search for conceled goodes of Sir Richard Grinses and one tim in bringing of them away lying abrood our time and horse for 2 days 00 19 00

For our ferist jorney to Hiching to give the Earle of Bedfordes

[518] Ware Park the estate of Sir Thomas Fanshawe

[519] Probably Isaac Craven the sequestered cleric from Ware. According to Walker he was imprisoned several times and his widow Mary had to seek relief [Matthews, A G *Walker Revised: being a revisionof John Walker's Sufferings of the English Clergy during the Grand Rebellion 1642-60,* (Oxford, 1948) p198]

[520] Captain Marmaduke Roydon (Rawdon)

[521] The fifth part of the income reserved for the wife and family of delinquents

[522] Sir Peter Saltingstall of Barkway

[523] Theobalds Park at Cheshunt, the former palace of the Stuarts

tennants notis of the sequistration for our time and expences 00 15 00
For a joyney to Kneboth to Sir William Littens[524] for the Apraysing of Sir Thomas Ferns howse goodes 00 15 06
For a second jorneye to to Sir Willyam Lettons to fech a way the goodes our horse and time 00 10 06
For a theird jorney to Sir William Lettones for to demand the treble peart[525] 00 06 06
For our feirst jorney to London about the trebell peart when that the Commettis ded sit a bought it for our time and exspence and horse 01 18 00
For a second jorneye to London a bought the same bissines for our time horse and ~~esp~~ exspence for 3 dayes 01 19 00
For a jorney to Braffin for sequestring and praysing of Sir Richard Stoomers esteat for our horse time and exspence[526] 00 13 00
For a jorney to Anstey to prayse Sir Richard Stoomes estat theire for our time and horse 01 00 00
For a jorney to Anstey hall being sent by the Commettie to take notis in what condishon the goodes war in for our time and exspence 00 10 00
For an nother jorny to Anstyhall to put in Captain Needham[527] for our time and exspence 00 10 00
09 16 06

*f3* For a nother jorney to Ansty hall to fech away the sheepe and hoggses for our horse and time and exspence 00 12 00
For an nother jorney to Anstyhall and from theire to Startford with cattell that ware thare sould for our time horse and exspence for 2 dayes 00 18 06
For a jorney to Uphall[528] to distrayne sum tennants that did

---

[524] The House of Commons had ordered Fanshawe's goods to be sold as early as June 1643 but Sir William Lytton had been added to the Hertford sequestration committee six days before. He then seems to have been instrumental in holding up the sale of his former colleague's goods and possibly concealing some of them at Knebworth, though the committee, set up on 1 January 1644 to investigate, never seems to have reported, perhaps because his fellow MP Sir Thomas Dacres was on the committee [*CJ* III, pp138, 149, 355-6]

[525] Sir Thomas Fern is possibly a shortened form of Fanshawe, who had to pay 1/3 of his income as a penalty under the sequestration legislation.

[526] Sir Richard Stoormer of Braughing and Anstey Hall

[527] Captain Needham of the Hertfordshire Militia

[528] Up Hall between Braughing and Albury

refuse to pay their rent 00 05 00
For a jorny by order of the Commettis to Anstey hall for to sell the corne and cattell for our time horse and exspence 00 12 00
For a jorny to Uphall by order of the Committe for to sell the corn and goodes 00 10 00
For a jorney to Haddam and appraysing of the Lord Capelles goodes being a searvis that noune could bee gotten to undertake for our payens tim and exspence at Startford 02 00 00
For the appraysing of the Lord Caples goodes att Walcorn Parke[529] 01 00 00
For a jornieye to Bayford and apraisinge of the goodes of Sir Simon Fanchor[530] 01 00 00
For an nother jorney to Bayford and the appraising of conceled goodes 00 10 00
For a jorney to Wormley for the finding out of Sir John Moncones[531] tennants 00 08 06
For a jorney to London being ~~war~~ warned up a bought our accounts for our time horse and exspence for 3 days 01 18 00
09 14 00
For the searching out of the goodes of Balls of Sir John Harryson and praysing them 00 10 00
10 04 00

*f4* For a second jorney to London a bought our accounts for our time and exspence 3 dayes 01 16 00
For 2 jorneys to London about Mr Nicoalls[532] for our time and exspence 01 19 00
For distrayning att Mr Bromleys for Mr Belases rent our horse and time 00 06 00
For a nother jorney to prayse Mr Brumlyes goodes 00 04 00
For a nother day in feching away the malt of Mr Bramleys 00 04 00

---

529 Walkern near Stevenage where Capel held property
530 Sir Simon Fanshawe (*see* Appendix)
531 Sir John Monson, of South Carlton and Burton, Lincs, had married Ursula, one of the step-daughters of Sir Richard Lucy, and had land in Broxbourne and Wormley. He was an active Royalist who compounded on the Oxford Articles for £1, 336. He paid £6 10s 6d decimation tax in 1656 and participated in Booth's rising. At the Restoration, as a result of ill-health he retired to Broxbourne [TNA: SP28/197 Pt 2 *f*6; Henning, *Commons* II, p79; Chauncy I, p580]
532 Mr Thomas Nicholls, the tenant of Balls Park, Hertford

| | |
|---|---|
| a gayne for feching away a lode of goodes from Mr Brumlyes and carring them to Hartford | 00 04 00 |
| For a jorney to Mr Rothes[533] and apraysing of the goodes our horse and time | 00 07 00 |
| For a jorney by Edward Heath alowne to the Earle of Dovers abought the sequestring of his estat for horse and time | 00 03 06 |
| For a nother jorney and the apraysing of the Earle of Dovers Estate | 01 00 00 |
| For annother jorney by warrent from the Commettee for the securing of the goodes of the Lord of Rochford[534] our horse and time | 00 08 00 |
| | 06 03 06 |
| *f5* For our time and exspence in attending of the Committee att Hartford from the 20 of July 1643 unto the 4 of October 1642 (sic) being 62 weckes accounting 2 days in a wecke a pece att 2s the day a pece | 24 16 00 |
| The totall summe is | 62 09 00 |

Besid about 20 dayes spent in selling of goods in the castell[535] and in delivering of them out and as many more in making up our accounts all which wee leave to your wisdoumes to consider

This account aproved exammened and allowed by us whouse names are here underwritten Commettes for Sequestration sittinge att Hartford this 10th of October 1644.
*Joseph Dalton, Maior, Gabriel Barbor, Thomas Meade, William Carter, William Dawges*

**[146] TNA: SP28/155 The Information from North Mymms *f6v* Sequestrations of Mr Mores estate, Mr Coningsby and Mr Copleys, 1643-4**

| | £ s d |
|---|---|
| Thomas Pursey paid to Mr Odingsells for Mr Moores goods at Gubbins | 37 07 04 |

---

[533] William Wrothe Esq.
[534] John Lord Rochford, the son of the Earl of Dover
[535] Hertford Castle

| | |
|---|---|
| March 1 1643 Henry Brookshead paid to Mr Odingsells for timber <and of Mr Mores grounds> sold at severall times | 52 10 00 |
| Henry Brookeshead paid John Lownes for timber out of Mr Coningsbys woods | 19 08 00 |
| May 16 1644 William Ircom paid Mr Odingsell for 2/3 of Mr Copleyes goods | 12 03 11 |
| August 7 164~~4~~3 Thomas Pursey accounted with the Committee for Sequestrations at Hartford where hee charged himself with the somme of | 132 01 06 |
| Which sayd somme of £132 -1s-6d hee payd and discharged ~~and paid~~ as appears by acquittance | |
| January 19 1643 Thomas Pursey paid and accounted to Luke Sanders in the behalfe of the committee of sequestrations for Michaelmas quarter last past the somme of | 74 02 06 |
| ~~Aprill 17~~ <May 22> 1644 Thomas Pursey paid and accounted to Nathaniel Hale in the behalfe of the Committee of Sequestrations for one quarter day rent last past the somme of | 74 02 06 |
| May 15 1643 <at the sequestration of Mr Moores>, Thomas Pursey being discharged from having to doe with Mr More's Estate which timber bark (which Mr Odingsells is to account for <to> the sum of | 96 04 08 |
| Besides Barke 1 loade 37 yards, 4 or 5 trees at Burry farme and Likewise was then unpayde by some tennants duringe the time hee was Bayly | |
| All which Mr Odingsell is to account for | |

Mrs Coningsby hath sent a general information unto us concerninge her lands (which were taken away by Sir William Brewertons[536] agents viz. the goods

| | |
|---|---|
| of the first Inventory valued | £800 00 00 |
| of the 2nd inventory valued at | £500 00 00 |
| of Mr Henry Coningsby valued at | £080 00 00 |

The perticilers we hope ere long to informe you off.

[536] Sir William Brereton, Bart. a successful Cheshire estate manager and magistrate, had cleared part of Cheshire and the North Midlands of royalists in 1643, and defeated them again at Nantwich in January 1644. He was rewarded with the right to claim the income from certain sequestered estates [John Morrill, 'Brereton, Sir William, first baronet (1604-1661), *NewDNB*]

**[147] TNA: SP28/209B Inventory of sequestration accounts of the goods of Sir John Harrison from Balls Park, 28/8/1643**

An inventorie of the goods and chattels of Sir John Harrison of Hartford in the county of Hartford taken the eight and twentieth of August 1643

| | £ s d |
|---|---|
| Inprimis in the kitchen 3 potts, 1 kettle, 2 posuettes,[537] 12 peeces of pewter, 4 spitts, a jack and other necessaries in the roome adjoyneinge | 06 00 00 |
| Item in the parlour two tables, 2 carpetts, 9 chaires and stooles, a couch, one paire of andirons,[538] fireshovell and tongs, a little pair of creepers,[539] a backe[540] and 9 cushions | 04 00 00 |
| Item in the studie next adjoyninge, one press,[541] a table, a curtaine and rodd | 01 10 00 |
| Item in the hall one table | 01 10 00 |
| Item in the great parlour 25 chaires and stooles and a couch | 06 10 00 |
| Item in the room next adioyneinge 2 chairs, 4 stooles | 00 10 00 |
| Item in the lodgeinge chamber that goeth to the bell wing, one bedd with furniture, 4 chaires and stoles, and brass andirons | 12 00 00 |
| Item in Sir John's own roome, one bedd with furniture, three chaires and 3 stooles and brass andirons | 11 00 00 |
| Item at the stairs head one table, one trunke and a cubberd | 01 00 00 |
| Item Mistress Anns[542] chamber one bedd with furniture, 3 Chaires and 3 stooles | 04 10 00 |
| Item in the maides chamber, one bedd | 02 10 00 |
| Item in Mistress Margarets[543] Chamber, a bed with furniture and other things | 10 00 00 |
| Item in the corner chamber one bedd, 4 stooles and two chaires | 10 00 00 |
| Item in Mr Sutton's chamber one bedd | 03 00 00 |
| Item in the blew chamber one bedd, a table and carpet | 02 10 00 |
| Item in HAies chamber one bedd | 03 00 00 |
| This side | 79 10 00 |

[537] Possibly pots for warming spicy milk drinks or possets
[538] A pair of horizontal ornamental bars at the side of a fire to support burning wood
[539] A pair of iron dogs placed between the andirons
[540] A tub, probably for holding firewood
[541] A large cupboard for holding clothes, books etc.
[542] Sir John's daughter who married Sir Richard Fanshawe
[543] Sir John's first wife

| | |
|---|---|
| Item in Mr Williams[544] chamber one bedd with furniture, two chaires and 2 stooles | 05 10 00 |
| Item in William Dickinsons chamber one bedstead, 2 chaires, 2 tables and a trunke | 00 04 00 |
| In the servants roome one bedd, 2 quilts | 01-06 00 |
| In the maides chamber, two beds, one chaire, 6 dozen and 8 napkins, 15 towells, 6 pair of pillowbeers,[545] 12 table cloathes flaxen, 18 flaxen cubber[546] and cloathes, 2 dozen and foure newe cloathes, 10 pair of sheets, 5 table cloathes, one quilt, two blankets, two boulsters and 3 cushions | 13 09 08 |
| Item in Mistress Diana Glassopes Chamber one bedd | 02 00 00 |
| Item in the servants roome adjoineinge one bedd with the bedstead | 01 05 00 |
| Item in the dry larder, one cubberd and a table | 00 10 00 |
| Item in the seller 27 hoggs heads[547] and 7 barrelles | 02 07 00 |
| Item the clocke | 01 00 00 |
| Item in the washe house, a furnace, one bucking[548] tubb and two tubs | 03 00 00 |
| Item in the dairy necessary goods | 03 00 00 |
| Item 8 quarters of oates in the garner | 03 10 00 |
| Item the utensells and materials in the brew house | 24 00 00 |
| Item 3 carte-horses | 03 00 00 |
| Item the carte and goods about the houses | 10 00 00 |
| Item xxxiiij fatinge[549] sheepe | 13 12 00 |
| Item xii cowes and a bull | 32 00 00 |
| Item ii heifers | 04 00 00 |
| Item iii calves | 02 00 00 |
| Item a coach and furniture | 03 00 00 |
| Item an elme planke | 00 10 00 |
| The pease reeke | 05 00 00 |
| This side is | 134 04 04 |

544 Sir John's son William, who joined the king at the start of the war and died from wounds in June 1643

545 Possibly an old form of pillow case

546 Unknown but possibly covers made of flax

547 A large barrel or cask for holding wine or other goods

548 A large vat used in steeping or boiling clothes

549 Sheep being fatted up for eating rather than for their wool

| | £ s d |
|---|---|
| Item wheate nowe in the barne 26 acres | 40 00 00 |
| Item the barlie 39 ½ acres | 60 00 00 |
| Item the oates 57 acres | 36 13 04 |
| Item pease 30 acres | 20 00 00 |
| Item rye 25 acres | 24 00 00 |
| Item tares 2 acres | 01 10 00 |
| Item haye 36 acres now in the barne | 20 00 00 |
| Item 260 sheepe | 78 00 00 |
| This side is | 280 03 04 |

The totall of the goods inventoried and appraised is as appeareth 493 17 08

William Saward[550] and Thomas Lashebrooke 17 September 1644

This is a true copie of Sir John Harrisons inventory
*Per me Gabriel Odingsells*

**[148] TNA: SP28/209B An inventory of George Bromley's goods and Sir Thomas Fanshawe's plate sold, 9/12/1644**

An inventory of the goods plate and chattels of George Bromley Gent sould at the Committee of Hertford 9 December 1644
Mr Bromleys
*Imprimis* 4 silver beare bowles, a wyne bowle, a great saulter,
6 frenchen salts, one little salt, a viniger pott, ~~wine flaggones~~
5 spoones, a paire of samplers, a cawdele pott,[551] one tankard,
Two flaggons sould to Mr William Turpin[552] at 4s 10d ½ per
ownce[553] Ownces 176 12 18 00

An inventory *ut supra*[554] 20 November 1644

[550] William Saward (Seward) of Brickendon Green, whose house still stands, was the sequestrations collector for Hertford Hundred, later in trouble for slandering the mayor and chief burgesses of Hertford [TNA SP28/209B Account of William Saward; HALS: HBR9 *ff*194-5; Information from Alan Greening]
[551] A caudle was a sweet spiced warm drink given to visitors or the sick, hence this cup
[552] Turpin was the treasurer for the review of the 5th and 20th part
[553] Silver plate was weighed and sold by the ounce. 16 Ounces = 1 lb weight or c550 grams
[554] Latin for 'as above'

| | |
|---|---|
| Sould the same day of Sir Thomas Fanshawes plate | |
| *Imprimis* one bason was sould unto Thomas Hutchinson of ~~Sawbridgeworth~~ <Bishops Stortford> at 4s 10d ½ per ounce 85 ownces | 20 14 04 |
| *Item* sould to Mr <William> Turpin one silver skellett,[555] 15 plates of silver, one pinte pott or tankard of silver, one porrenger[556] of silver, one guilt cupp and cawcer, 2 silver spoones, one silver handle, one chaffendish[557] of silver, one silver candlestick, 2 silver dishes one silver shuggar box, one greate silver salt, one tumill[558] of silver, one silver bastingsadell,[559] one silver cocke for a cisterne at 4s 10d quadrants[560] per ownce beinge and wayeinge 606 ownces | 147 01 06 |
| | 210 13 10 |
| found in reddy moyneys | 53 04 00 |
| *In toto* | 263 17 10 |

## Part 7. The effects of sequestration

### [149] HALS: M213 Copy of a petition of William Capel[561] to the Sequestration Committee of the House of Commons, c.September 1644

To the Right Honourable Committee of the Lords and Commons for Sequestrations - The Humble Petition of ~~John~~ William Capell Esq.
Sheweth
That whereas by an order, from the Right Honourable the House of Commons to the Committee of Hertford, for the present raysinge of £250 upon the woodes of the Lord Capell in that county, for the widow Meldrum and the widow Cunningham[562], the said Committee did order that 888 pollard trees in

[555] A skillet, a sauce pan or stew-pan
[556] A small basin for soup or porridge
[557] A chafing-dish was a dish for hot water to keep food warm
[558] A tumbler or drinking cup
[559] Presumably a saddle-shaped dish to aid in the basting process of moistening meat
[560] Quarters or farthings
[561] William was the brother of Arthur, Baron Capel of Hadham
[562] The House of Commons had required on 7 August 1644 that the Committee of Hertford order the felling of so much of Capel's woods as would amount to £250 and that £200 would go to Colonel Meldrum's widow, as part of the arrears due to her husband, and the remaining £50 to Colonel Cunningham's widow for the same purpose [*CJ* III, pp581-4]

Hadham Parke[563] and 500 pollard trees in Walkerne[564] should be rooted up for the raysinge of the said money, and did, by letter, send and offer unto your petitioner, to have the <said> trees for the said money and your petitioner, being then in Norfolk upon his especiall occasions and not able to give them in a speedy answer, the said trees were sold by the said Committee att Hertford unto Edward Heath and Edward Chandler. After which, your petitioner's agent agreed with the said Heath and Chandler for the said trees in Hadham Parke and gave him £5 proffit for layinge out of their money two dayes and did then like wise offer them their money for the trees att Walkerne with £5 proffit before they had paid that parte of the £250 to the said widdowes. Which they did then and have since utterly refused, being thereunto enjoined and desired by the said Committee att Hertford, they having received besides £10 which the said widdowes gave them to procure the said £250 for them.

Now for that they have received and beene offered soe much proffit for the layinge outt of their money soe spent and time and benefit will be a coste to the Comonwealth to have soe many trees rooted up and for that the Ferme att Walkerne is lett unto your petitioner by the Committee at Hertford[565] for a certaine rent to be paid to the use of the parliament and that the lopps of the said trees are parte of the profits of which your petitioner shall pay his rent and without which the tenant canot live in that farmehouse for want of firewood, and the rooteinge, cleaninge, coaleinge and carryinge of the said wood will be a greater trespasse and losse to your petitioner as the graser of the said ground and where the said trees did stand.

Your petitioners most humble desire to this honourable committee is that the committee att Hertford may be directed from this board to order the said Heath and Chandler to take and receive the price set upon them by the said committee to make up the aforesaid £250 with the £5 proffit offered unto them the order of the House of Commons being performed to rayse £250 for the said widdowes

And your petitioner shall ever pray etc.

*Vera Copia extractum per me*[566]

*R Vaughan Cleric*

---

[563] The deer park around Hadham Hall at Little Hadham

[564] The Capels had an estate at Walkern

[565] The estates of Lord Capel had been taken over by the Hertford Committee and then leased out to William Capel

[566] Latin for 'A true copy extracted by me'

(***On reverse – in later hand on left***)
Letter from John (sic) Capell respecting sequestration of property AD 1644

(***On reverse in contemporary hand on right***)
Hertford *Saturnii*[567] 14th September 1644
According to an order from the Committee of the Lords and Commons for Sequestrations dated the 6th of September 1644, it hath been moved that Edward Heath and Edward Chandler do accept of a composition[568] from Mr William Capell for the costs in question and they desyre to be excused in respect they have a former bargaine of it. And as touching the other part of the order of the said Committee in obedience to the same, for the said William Capell hath tendered the some of £77- 8s which, with the rest allredy payd, amounteth to two hundred and sixty pounds as payment as agreed. Wee the Committee att Hertford do order that the woods in question be not cutt downe.
*John Barbor,* Registrar Committee
*Copia vera extracta per me Thomas Bevis*[569] *Clericum*

**[150] HALS: M212 *f*1r Draft of letter, William Capel to Arthur Capel c.1646**

Dear brother,

I have made an accounte of whatt monys I have receved, and disbursed since I first undertooke the business;[570] which I desyer you to present unto my Lady.[571] And I can safely protest, I have not with my knowledge concealed or left out unsett downe, any mony that I have receved, and I think I am not mistaken, but have sett down all, and the summes right. I cannot so say for the disbursements, but do thinke I have forgotten to sett downe some in my notes, haveing had so many journeys to ryde, and bussiness to attend.

Your countenances and speeches have been formerly, att some times, such towards mee as I conceve, have geven mee cause to think that there was some jealousy and suspition in your mindes, that I would abuse and deceve you. If it be so, I am very unloveingly and unthankfully dealt with. God is

567 Saturday
568 A lump sum as a composition fee
569 'A true copy extracted by me'. Bevis was the personal clerk to Gabriel Barbor, the chairman of the Hertford Committee
570 The business of being the main tenant of the Capel estates of his brother
571 Lady Capel, wife of Lord Arthur Capel, who remained at Hadham with her family

my wittness my true love to my Lord, with my affection and compassion to my Lady, to be honored for her vertue, and her children in there affliction and distress, made mee to ingage my self in there service, which I have done faythfully, allthough it may be not so sufficiently as you think an other might, and truly I think so to.

But when I first began to undertake your service, you that would willingly have helped and eased mee could not, and some that could and might, would <not.> The feares and cares that have lyen upon mee for them, were more then I ever did take for my self or my other kindred or friends. And you know that I have not refused or spared the labor of my body, but have endured the bitter cold of the winter and the scorching heate of the summer, to travell in there service[572], it may be more then any servant they had would have taken, and att less charge.

Yett do I not looke for or expect any recompense or rewarde, more then a favourable and cheerfull acceptance of my most ernest desyers, and indeavores for there comfort and relief. I shall write no more to trouble you longer, than to acknowledg with all thankfulness Gods goodness that hath inabled mee beyond my strength and abillity to overcome all difficulties, hinderances and discouragements, and to doe that which I have done for them.

And allthough the worst and hardshippe of the worke be I hope paste, he shall be glad of the help and assistance of those that can further him in there service, which he shall continue with a dillagent faythfullness to proceed in and prosecute, untell there pleasures shall be declared to the contrary, who is your loveing brother *William Capell*

**[151] HALS: M212 *ff*2r-2v- Account of William Capel,[573] 1644-5**

*f*2r *column 1* March the 2nd 1645: An account of what rents and monys I have receved, since our Lady Day[574] 1644, when I first began to take the estate of the Lord Capell from the Committees[575] unto the last of December 1645 Receved in mony of the rents att Stebbing[576] from our lady Day

[572] As the main tenant of the Capel estates on behalf of the Sequestration Committee he was expected to collect the rents from the various properties and hand them over to the Committee

[573] William Capel only administered certain of his relatives' lands. Capel lands in Bedfordshire were leased to the Earl of Essex, and after his death, jointly to Edward Hammond of Little Hadham and Mr Thomas Ladds, then to Thomas Rose of Warden [Bell, P, 'Minutes of the Bedfordshire Committee for Sequestrations', Bedfordshire Historical Record Society, Vol 49, (Bedford, 1970) pp81-121]

[574] Lady day was 25 March, one of the traditional days for paying annual or quarterly rent

[575] The Committees of sequestration for Hertfordshire and Essex etc

1644 to Our Lady Day 1645 £635-6-5
Receved in mony of Stebbing rents due att Michaellmas[577] 1645
And payd in before the last of December £113-0-2
Receved att our Lady Day 1645 of the rents then due in Norffolk
besids the 5th part[578] allredy accounted for £39-8-5
Receved agayne att Michaellmas 1645 and here besides the 5th part
allredy accounted for £57-5-3
Receved of Warden rents in Bedfordsheere due att Michaellmas
1645 besides the 5th part allredy accounted for £218-14-0
Recevd of Wattford[579] rents before the last December due at
Michaellmas £100-0-0
Receved from Walkern[580] from Michaellmas 1644 to the last of
December 1645 £544-4-9
Receved of Edward Wood and Barker of Stebbing
£9-9-0
Recevd for loppes of trees sold Norffolk before the last of
December £1-3-0
Receved from Captain Rocke[581] £10-0-0
Recved of Katherine Tinckler and William Kempe £8-0-0
Receved of Henry Wainkford for timber sold £6-0-0
Receved of Robert Nurse for rent Robbetts £1-0-0
Sum totall received before the last of December 1645 £1741-19-10

(***The following crossed through with 2 diagonal lines***)
Of William Ashley for rent receved by him more then he pays to the Collector the last half year now receved by mee but forgotten to be sett downe

(***Sets of random additions and figures as follows***)

| | |
|---|---|
| 3244: 0: 11 | Disbersed £3244-0-11 |
| 2746: 0: 8 | 11-8 0-12-7 |
| 498: 0: 3 | Receved £2738: 0: 8 |
| 3244: 0: 11 | 8: 0: 0 |
| 11 08 | 2746 0 8 |

[576] Stebbing in Essex
[577] Michaelmas Day September 29th another quarter day when rents were due
[578] The fifth part of the income was paid to the wife and family of the royalist
[579] Rents from the Cassiobury estate at Watford
[580] Rents from the estates in Walkern, Hertfordshire
[581] Rocke was a Captain in the Hertfordshire Volunteers and in Wittewronge's regiment

| | |
|---|---|
| Layd out more than receved | 498- 0-3 |
| Sent besids to my Lady | 050- 0-0 |
| In all | 548- 0-3 |
| More payd to William Kempe of Aspell Bonham | 0-11-8 |

*f*2r *column2*

An account of what I have disbursed and payd from our Lady Day 1644 to the last of December 1645

| | £ s d |
|---|---|
| Payd to make up the rent of £449 for the tythes and Quittrents at Wattford in mony to the Committee att St Albons when I passed my accounts | 163 4 9 |
| To the Committee in Essex in part for a years rent ended att our Lady Day 1645 | 402 15 1 |
| To my Lord of Essex[582] | 419 10 0 |
| Layd out in and about Walkern as will appeare in the booke of account where the particulars are sett downe | 986 17 3 |
| Payd to the Collector in Norrfolk at Our Lady Daye 1645 | 40 0 0 |
| Expences out of the rents receved for the Earle of Essex to the last of December | 17 11 8 |
| Payd to my brother Roger, and Mr Henery Scoble[583] that was borrowed of them | 200 0 0 |
| Sum totall disbursed before the last of December 1645 | 2229 18 9 |
| Receved but | 1741 19 10 |
| To make up £2229 18s 9d - must be added | 487 18 11 |
| Oweing to my Lady Wiseman | 100 00 00 |
| To my brother Roger | 30 00 00 |
| To mee | 357 18 11 |
| Payd to Mr Hammond upon bond forgotten to be sett downe before | 32 10 00 |

**(*The following crossed through diagonally*)**

| | |
|---|---|
| Disbursed to the last of July 1646 | 3244 12 7 |
| Receved | 2746 0 8 |
| Layd out more than receved | 498 11 11 |

[582] Following a conference between the Lords and the Commons in May 1643, the Earl of Essex was given income from the Cassiobury estates, as compensation for being the Lord General of the parliamentary forces [*CJ* III, pp59, 83, 89]

[583] Scobel was later appointed to be the Clerk to the House of Commons on 5 January 1649 [*CJ* VI, pp111-2]

| | |
|---|---|
| Lent besids to my Lady | 50 00 00 |

In my account dated August the 7, 1646

| | |
|---|---|
| Disbursed to the last of July 1646 | 3241 15 1 |
| Receved | 2771 10 2 |
| Layd out more than receved | 470 4 11 |
| Lent to my Lady | 50 0 0 |
| | 520 4 11 |

*f2*v *column 1*
An account of whatt hath been receved since the last of December 1645 untill the 26th March 1645

| | |
|---|---|
| Of Stebbing rents receved in mony | 195 0 9 |
| Out of Suffolk[584] receved | 55 2 4 |
| Receved for halfe years rent due from Whitefryers att Christmas last according to Mathews lease | 78 0 0 |
| Receved out of Norffolk | 18 13 2 |
| Receved for wood sold to John Perry of Stebbing | 6 0 0 |
| Receved from Walkern | 223 6 11 |
| Summa Totalis | 576 3 2 |

*f2*v *column 2* An account of whatt hath been disbursed since the last of December to the 26th March 1645

| | |
|---|---|
| Payd to the Earle of Essex February the 24th 1645 | 200 0 0 |
| In Walkern layd out | 46 12 5 |
| In charges expended for the Earle of Essex | 12 18 5 |
| In charges expended for the family | 2 5 2 |
| | 261 16 0 |

***(Along the edge)*** Mr William Capells accounts etc.

584 Capel held extensive lands in Suffolk

**[152] TNA: SP28/255 Thomas Nicholls to Mr Millard,[585] 8/5/1644**

Sir,
I address my selfe unto you my letter (beinge unknowne to anye <other> of the committee of examinations of accounts) to accquaynt you that the Committee of Hartford invited me hither to be one of theyr comittee to assist them in those publike imployments. And because <they> understood that I was destitute of a house and househould nesscessarys (my whole personall estate beinge longe since plundered and my reall estate wholly seized upon by the ennimy), they have accomodated me with the house of Sir John Harrisons and such necessary furniture as are requisite for myselfe and servants I keepe for the managinge of the demeane belonginge to the sayd house which they have comitted to my care and oversight to husband for the best bennifitt to the state. I rendringe the committee an accompt and they giveing me such allowance for my paynes and oversight as they shall thinke fitt. This demayne concistinge most of arable comon feild ground they could not dispose otherwise of it.

I have left ~~to~~ <towards> my destray all charges and to pay all <my> taxes only the corne in the barnes what it was appeareth by the inventory which the solicyter of the committee of sequestrations hath. Fot the cows therein exprest five of them I sold, the monys for foure of them I delivered <to> the solicitor Mr Odingsell, the rest were of necessity to be kept to breed manure for the ground it beinge large and barren, for the most parte.

I imployed two teames for the implements of husbandry and horses they are imploye in that service. For the sheepe what have escaped the rott this wett winter, and the soldiers (some few I kild for the use of the family) are under the sheepheards custody which we must of necessity keepe to fold upon the corne land.

For the houshold stuffe expressed in the inventory, they weare delivered to one of the collectors to be sold by the apoyntment of the committee and desire of the solicitor who sold them and hath the money, except such household stuffe which weare delivered to us for our use (a particular whereof I have in

[585] A Mr Millard had properties in the parishes of St Peter's, Pauls Wharf and St Vedast, Foster Lane, in 1638 that brought in £73 p.a. in rent and may have been the Michael Millard Esq, one of the Captains of the Middlesex Trained Bands, who petitioned the Commons about night watches in November 1641 [*CJ* II, p306; Dale, *Inhabitants*, pp60-1, 179-80]

wrightinge and except some beding and furniture there by me sold, which I charge my self with in my accompt and a sett of chayres and stooles all amounting to the some of about £13 and some few stooles and bedsteedes and tables of small vallew, yett unsold, an old coach.
For the rent I have not medled with the receipts of them untill of late since Lady Day last. The committee haveinge reposed that trust upon me but lately of which as yet I have gott in little under twenty pounds. I am full of publike imployment, the committee haveing chosen me theyr chayreman that my absence is hardly dispenced with. Yett that these gentlemen of your committee will enjoyne me to attend them and doe expect an accompt from me. I shall with a short watinge give them a full and particular acompt such as to which I shall as willingly sweare to as subscribe my name to, that they rest not satisfied that this committee may exception take my acompt. I desyre you to present my respects to them and to acquaynt them that I am ready to apply my selfe to theyr directions. The Earle of Manchester hath betrusted me with his third parte to be accomptable only to him, yett I am ready to yeald an accompt to any that require it. Sir I desire you to do me this frenly office and you shall engage me to be your assured friend to serve you. *Thomas Niccolls*

Hartford 8 May 1644

***(On reverse)***To his much respected fryende Mr Millard at his house in Watling Streete neere Red Lyon Court these be delivered
Mr Niccolls letter to Mr Millard dated the 8th of May 1644

**[153] TNA: SP28/255 Statement by the Hertfordshire. Committee of Sequestrations[586] re Niccolls' account, 7/9/1644**

Reasons why wee cannot allow of the account of Mr Niccolls upon the sequestrations of Balls[587], as it was presented unto us 7th September 1644. As also our exceptions thereunto:
For that Mr Niccolls being possessed of all that was Sir John Harrisons, the goods, the rents, the lands, he giveth not a good account of anie of them.
1 Not of the catell, the number of them sould and remaininge and any mention made of some of them in their kinde, which he was possessed of.

---

[586] The members of this committee were the established county gentry, MPs, and JPs who were more conservative than the Militia Committee chaired by Barbor

[587] The Balls Park estate, Hertford, which Harrison had purchased and constructed a new mansion on between 1638 and 1641

2. Not of the goods, he doth not receite in particuler, what <goods> sould and to whome they were sould and whether accordinge to the ordinance by the candle (which under favour hee observed not) or mention made what goods now remaine.
3. Not of the rents, (1) what is rented, (2) to whom, (3) for what, (4) what received (5) what remaines
4. Not of the quarter of corne ariseinge out of acres of: 26 wheate, 25 rye; 39 1/2 barlie; 57 oates; 30 pease; 02 tares
5. Not of the hay beinge 36 acres made and housed to his hand
6. Not of the profitts of dairie consisting of eleven cows and a bull
7. Not of hopp ground
8. Not of the usual wood beinge about 12 acres felled, not of the lopps and wood sould to Ware a greate quantity
But his account tendered wee conceive to bee (1) confused, (2) obscure, (3) imperfect and miscast, (4) unreasonable.

| | £ s d |
|---|---|
| For that except for some goods which William Saward sould and received by Mr Niccolls appointment which came to | 24 12 01 |
| And for rents received by William Saward | 29 14 02 |
| All the rest being in Mr Niccolls his hands, and at his dispose hath beene soe managed that his receipts come but to | 267 14 09 |
| And his disbursements amount unto | 272 04 02 |

But his disbursements <to> which he discounts beinge most of them (as it appeareth by his accounts) the charges of his wife and children and family. And necessaries for himselfe and them wee allow not.
And desire him to exhibit a more perfect account for that by this account it appears there beinge disbursed by Mr Odingsells for getinge in the corn in

| | |
|---|---|
| harvest 1643 | 37 03 03 |
| And also disbursed by William Saward for seed corne, ploweinge and workmens wages upon the premises the profits of all which accrued to Mr Niccolls | 39 06 09 |
| The Parliaments loss by this sequestration | 21 13 02 |
| Besides taxes unpaide | 63 11 03 |
| and labourers wages unpaid | 31 01 10 |
| | 116 06 03 |

Goods sould }
Rents spent } to an unknown value
Stock impaired 186 17 00
Except a few goods now in the hand

*Thomas Dacres, William Presley, Edward Atkyns,*[588] *W. Lytton, E. Wingate, Thomas Tooke.*

**[154] TNA: SP28/255 Resolution of the Committee of Lords and Commons for Sequestrations re Niccolls' account, 11/9/1644**

11 September 1644 Att the comittee of Lords and Commons for Sequestrations
It is thought fitt and ordered by this committee that it be referred to Mr Prinne[589], Mr Glover, Mr Collins and Mr Stephens on any two of them to peruse Mr Nicholls Accompt and the Committee of Hartfords exceptions thereto and the sayd Mr Nichols answer to there exceptions and to certifie the state thereof to this committee with convenient speed. John Wylde *Vera Copia*

**[155] TNA: SP 28/209B The account of Mr Thomas Niccolls, 1/10/1643-1/09/1644**

*f*1r The account of Mr Thomas Niccolls from the first of October <1643> to the first of September <1644> upon the Sequestracon of Balls being the lands of John Sir (*sic*) Harrison in the County of Hertford

*f*1v A note of the Goods corne and oates which Mr Niccolls chargeth himselfe with rated and valued in the inventory as followeth

| <u>Corne</u> | £ s d |
|---|---|
| Inprimis wheate valued at | 40 00 00 |
| Item rye rated at | 24 00 00 |
| Item barley rated at | 60 00 00 |
| Item peas rated at | <u>20 00 00</u> |
| Harrison admisseth? | 144 00 00 |

Had sowed of the severall grayne (vizt) of wheate and rye 26 bushell, of barley 140 bushell, of peas 126 bushell. Spent in the harvest 10 bushells of rye and 11 quarter of barley for beare the rest he chargeth himselfe with.

| <u>Goods</u> | |
|---|---|
| Received for 25 chayres and stooles and a couch soe valued | 06 00 00 |

[588] For Atkyns (*see* Appendix)

[589] This is William Prynne, the puritan, who had fallen foul of King Charles in the 1630s and been pilloried twice. As an Erastian he opposed the extreme forms of Presbyterianism and Independency [William Lamont, 'Prynne, William (1600-1669)', *NewDNB*]

| | |
|---|---|
| Item received for one old bed, table and carpet soe inventoried valued | 02 10 00 |
| for a clock soe valued | 02 00 00 |
| Received for a bed and furniture of Mistress Ann's[590] chamber soe valued | 04 10 00 |
| Received for an old bed and motheaten covelett and blankitt | 02 00 00 |
| Received for a bed and bolster | 01 17 00 |
| These Mr Nicholls chargeth himself with | 18 17 00 |
| Cattle | |
| Three calves valued at | 02 00 00 |
| Foure cowes sould by Heath and Chaundler Collectors for £9 10s which was <by them> payd Mr Odensell | |
| One cow three pounds one shilling | 03 01 00 |

The two heyfores and the other kine cows and a bull remayne good to the state.
Three cart horses remayne
Sheepe 167 remayne the rest died of the rott[591] and taken by soldiers except 28 or 30 killed in this whole yeare for the family
Oates, tares, hay spent upon <horses and> cattle about the house and upon troopers, except 120 bushells sowed, ~~sould~~ 11 bushell and two load of hay delivered Mr Oddensells,[592] those that are sould charged upon him

*f*2r A note of the catle he found uninventoried
Imprimis <two heyfors>, one bay yonge horse, another white lame mare and three yonge coltes
The yonge bay horse one colt and the two heyfors remayne
The white lame mare and one colt is fetched away by order of the committee of Hartford
The third colte is sold and charged upon account
Parte of a limekill[593] sold to Captayne Wild[594] which he owes for. Sold for £5-10s-00d

| A note of what rents he hath received | £ s d |
|---|---|

[590] Anne Harrison later Anne Fanshawe, the wife of Sir Richard Fanshawe, and the author of the celebrated memoirs
[591] Probably foot rot, a common complaint of sheep on poorly drained ground
[592] Odingsells the county solicitor for sequestrations
[593] Lime kiln
[594] Alexander Weld (Wylde)

| | |
|---|---|
| c[595] Received of John Rosse | 06 00 00 |
| l Received of <deleted> Pipkin | 06 15 00 |
| h Received of Tompkins | 00 08 00 |
| m Received of Dainell | 02 08 00 |
| e Received of Mrs Fisher | 01 07 00 |
| l Received of Simon Browne | 02 00 00 |
| £18 - 18 – 00d | |

| | | |
|---|---|---|
| A Rentall of lands lett by him | | |
| To | William Fisher | 03 00 00 |
| | Davis | 04 00 00 |
| | William Moore | 07 04 00 |
| | Edward Raysin | 01 17 00 |
| | William Fisher and Raysinge | 06 13 00 |
| | Mr Barber[596] which was lett by the committee | 06 00 00 |
| | Lewis | 02 06 06 |
| Downes and field | | 05 08 00 |
| Cooke for grasse in the field | | 00 09 00 |
| Symon Browne | | 03 00 00 |
| William Pryor for the hopyard | | 10 00 00 |
| Henry Chalkely | | 09 00 00 |
| Tompkins for Blewclose meade | | 06 00 00 |
| Rosse the smith for meadowground | | 01 08 00 |
| £67 06s 00d | | |

| | |
|---|---|
| A rental of landes lett by Sir John Harrisson | |
| Thomas Smith[597] | 18 00 00 |
| Pipkin | 24 00 00 |
| Symon Browne | 08 00 00 |
| Sampson Higby | 03 00 00 |
| Tompkins | 01 00 00 |
| Rosse | 50 00 00 |
| Richard Rogers and Thomas Brigg | 18 10 00 |
| William Holland of Little Amwell | 02 00 00 |

---

[595] It is not clear to what these letters in this column refer

[596] Probably Gabriel Barbor, the chairman of the committee

[597] Smith was gaoler and master of the house of correction in Hertford [HALS: QSB2A *ff*220d, 223d]

| | |
|---|---|
| Lowen | 06 00 00 |
| William Fisher | 03 00 00 |
| John Daniell | 06 00 00 |
| Christopher Smith | 80 00 00 |
| Fulkes per a lime kill | 03 00 00 |
| Edward Hamby | 03 00 00 |
| Christopher Barleggs | 03 00 00 |
| John Raymond | 04 00 00 |
| John Flower | 07 15 00 |
| Francis Clarke for tarres | 00 13 ?? |

*f2v* Sowed and inned[598] of all sorts of grayne acres — 160 ~~bushells~~

| Vizt | Acres of |
|---|---|
| Wheate | 27 |
| Mislinge[599] | 03 |
| Rye | 06 |
| Barley | 45 |
| Oates | 35 |
| Tares | 01 |
| Peas | 43 |

The grounds fallowed are: acres — 084
Grounds as River Lea of little worth which are: acres — 200
Pastures grounds acres — 056
Whereof 17 acres are mowed and inned, 6 acres mowed not yet lett. The rest (vizt) 33 was depastured[600] with cowes and heyfors horses etc.
Meadow ground inned: acres — 54
Whereof 18 acres lett, the rest (vizt) 36 acres inned
The totall of all the hay carried home and inned — 53 acres

***(Back cover)***
Mr Nicolls Accompts concerning Sir John Harrisons estate in Hertfordshire which was referred by the Committee of Commons for Sequestrations to Mr

[598] Inned means brought in from the fields and put in store
[599] Meslin was a mixture of wheat and rye grains that were sown and harvested as mixed grain
[600] The animals pastured on the grass, ate it, and therefore it was not available to be cut

Glover, Mr Pym,[601] Mr Stephens and Mr Collins who on 20 September 1644 made a certificate which is here fyled.

## Part 8 The sale of Sequestered and concealed goods

### [156] TNA SP28/209B Concealed goods of Sir John Harrison, 4/6/1644

Goods of Sir John Harrisons found in the barne at Balls 4 June 1644

| | £ s d |
|---|---|
| *Imprimis* In the greate chest 6 course table clothes 2 yards longe | 01 04 00 |
| *Item* 7 fyner table clothes 3 yards longe | 02 02 00 |
| *Item* 6 sidebord clothes of diaper | 00 18 00 |
| *Item* 3 fyne damaske table clothes | 04 10 00 |
| *Item* 2 fine table clothes of damaske | 01 10 00 |
| *Item* five side board clothes of damaske | 02 07 00 |
| *Item* 2 fyne damaske towells at | 00 06 10 |
| *Item* 6 fyne damaske large towells | 01 16 00 |
| *Item* 2 fyne side board clothes | 00 18 00 |
| *Item* 4 diaper table clothes | 01 04 00 |
| *Item* 13 diaper long towells | 02 00 00 |
| *Item* 11 dozen <of> fine damaske napkines | 11 00 00 |
| *Item* 5 dozen of fine diaper napkins | 02 05 00 |
| *Item* 16 dozzen course diaper napkines | 04 16 00 |
| *Item* in the marrage box 5 pairs of Holland sheetes at 14s | 03 10 00 |
| *Item* 5 paire of flaxen sheets at | 02 08 00 |
| *Item* in a flatt box locked: one crimson damaske faice sute for a bedd with a large coverlett of damaske and valance with deep longe fringes and another damaske crimson vallance with frenge, 5 damaske curtaines and a crospeece and 2 other peeces for the head and the testor[602] and 2 layses about all the peeces very rich. | 12 00 00 |
| *Item* one crimson satten suite imbroidered with large fringes of gold and silke, the other taffeta[603] with fringes with 5 satten imbroydered curtens and a large inbroidered satten coverlett with | |

[601] John Pym the leader of the opposition to Charles I in the Long Parliament and in the early years of the war, before his death on 8 December 1643 [Conrad Russell, 'Pym, John (1584–1643)', *NewDNB*]

[602] The tester was either a canopy over the bed or the headboard and its fittings

[603] Taffeta was various fabrics, but probably then a light thin silk

| | |
|---|---|
| gold lace round about | 20 00 00 |
| | 72 07 00 |

*Item* 166 bookes at 4s per peece 66 at ***(Ends here)***

**[157] TNA: SP28/217A Inventory of Sir John Harrison's concealed goods, c.1643-4**

A roll specifyinge what goods of Sir John Harrison were founde in the barne at Balls and sould as herby may appeare videlt

| | |
|---|---|
| *Imprimis* sould to Mr Chandler of Ware a sute of dyaper at | 001 18 00 |
| *Item* more sould to him certaine other dyaper at | 001 10 00 |
| *Item* sould to Mrs Puller junior a sute of dyaper at | 001 11 00 |
| *Item* sould more to her an other sute of dyaper at | 001 10 06 |
| *Item* more sold to her a sute of damaske at | 004 02 00 |
| *Item* more sould to her a sweete bag also a silke pincushion | 002 05 00 |
| *Item* sold to Goodwife Squire of Ware a sute of dyaper at | 001 09 00 |
| *Item* more to her an other sute of dyaper at | 001 07 09 |
| *Item* more sould to her 2 paire of flaxen sheets at | 001 12 00 |
| *Item* sold to Mrs Peck a sute of dyaper at | 001 08 07 |
| *Item* sold more to her an other sute of dyaper at | 001 07 00 |
| *Item* more old to her a sute of damaske at | 004 18 00 |
| *Item* more sold to her all the furniture for a bedd of red damaske at | 011 13 00 |
| *Item* sold to Mrs Nicholls of Hertford one sute of dyaper at | 001 07 00 |
| *Item* sold to Mrs Smith of London a sute of dyaper at | 001 03 00 |
| *Item* sold more to her a sute of damaske at | 003 03 00 |
| *Item* sold more to her an other sute of damaske at | 003 10 00 |
| *Item* sold more to her all furniture to a bed of red satin with tassle of gold lace | 007 15 00 |
| *Item* sold to Mrs Willett a sute of damaske at | 003 13 04 |
| *Item* sold to Mrs Hardwick of Hadham a sute of dyaper at | 001 05 07 |
| *Item* more sold <her> certaine parcels of damaske at | 001 08 00 |
| *Item* sold to Mr Sanders 2 paire of sheets at | 001 10 01 |
| *Item* sold to Mr Heathe a payre of sheets at | 000 15 00 |
| *Item* sold to Mrs Hala payre of sheets at | 000 10 03 |
| *Item* sold to Mrs Overstall 3 payre of sheets at | 002 05 00 |
| *Item* sold to Goodwyfe Clarke of the Wyte Harte one payre of | |

| | | | |
|---|---|---|---|
| sheets at | | | 000 15 05 |
| | (Proved) | Summa | 068 09 07 |
| *Items* sould to (*space*) | Books found at Sir John Harrisons | | 026 00 00 |

| | |
|---|---|
| The totall of Sir Simon Fanshawes goodes sould is | 237 06 09 |
| The totall of Sir John Harrisons goodes sould is | 111 01 08 |
| The totall of this whole rowle is | 353 08 04 |

**[158] TNA: SP28/209B Unfoliated list of concealed goods of Sir Simon Fanshawe, June 1644**

*f*1r Concealed goods found in severall places of Sir Simon Fanshawes June 1644 as follows:
*Inprimis* att James Reas in the chest by the bedd side
2 tapstres[604] carpetts, 2 peeces of tapstre hangeings
1 great pewter flaggon and a pair of bellowes 04 04 00
*Item* in the chest in the howse 4 peeces of tapstry hanging 04 00 00

Att Elizabeth Butts 3 carpetts, one black suite and cloake, stuff[605] dublett and breeches with lace, 2 white stuff peticoats, 2 table cloathes and 1 towell, 2 horse cloathes and velvett side sadle and bridle, a little saddle of vellvett and a leather coveringe 04 07 04

Att Robert Greenes 2 dozen pairs of damasque[606] napkins 1 long damasque tablecloath, sideboard damasque cloth and a towell, 1 blew silke cloake lined with satten, 2 embroydered satten petticoats, 1 suite and a cloake of cloath laid with great broad silver and gold lace, one black sattin plush[607] cloake and a sattin suite, 2 cloakes one of silke stuff another of cloath lyndd with plush, a paire of sleves of a wastcoate and 2 pair of foreboddyes[608] wrought with gould, another wrought wastcoate with gould, one faiced cloth wrought with gould, one pair of

[604] A tapestry carpet was one in which the warp yarn forming the pile was coloured, so as to produce the pattern when woven
[605] 'Stuff' was a particular kind of woollen textile fabric of the time used for clothes
[606] Damask was a twilled linen fabric with designs which showed up by opposite reflections of light from the surface and was used mainly for table linen
[607] Plush was a silk or woollen cloth having a nap softer and longer than that of velvet
[608] The front of a bodice or upper part of a dress

| | |
|---|---|
| silke garters wrought with silver, one other wrought gold wastcoate, 2 wastcoates and a pair of bodies, one white petticoate, 3 white wastcoates, one black wastcoate, 3 linnen veiles of the ladyes and a face cloath and tyffernyes[609] | 34 03 00 |
| Att John Beeremans: 4 diaper tablecloathes, 3 sideboard cloaths and 2 towells and a comeinge[610] lynen cloath, 4 damasque curtaines and valences[611], 5 damasque tablecloaths, sideboard damasque cloth, 2 towells, 3 dozen and 2 diaper nappkins, 3 dozen of damasque nappkins, 4 Hollan[612] towels, 1 table cloth and sideboard cloth, 7damasque nappkins, red vallens with silver fringe 2 little cabinets | 11 14 00 |

***(rest of page damaged and unreadable)***

| | |
|---|---|
| *f1v* Goods found att Widdow Bartens | |
| A suite of hangings containeinge 5 peeces | 12 00 00 |
| 2 peeces of hangeings of a suite | 03 10 00 |
| 3 pieces of greene borderes with needdell worke | 02 10 00 |
| 1 pair of old sheetes | 00 03 00 |
| Att John Biggs att Punsborne a whole suite for a bedd wrought with needlework another whole suite ~~wt~~ wrought with loopes of red, a red coverlet and a wrought coverlett all of needlework | 07 00 00 |
| Summa Totalis | 93 11 04 |

Praysed by *Edward Chandler*, *Edward Heath*

*Memorandum* found att John Deeremans 2 barrells filled with books and evidences which were never praysed

[609] Tiffany was thin transparent silk or gauze muslin for a head-dress or veil

[610] Probably a linen cloth to cover the shoulders while combing the hair to protect the garment worn

[611] A valance was a border of drapery hanging either round the canopy or the frame of a bed

[612] A linen fabric originally from Holland

**[159] TNA: SP28/217A Pt 2.2 Sale of Simon Fanshawe's concealed goods, c.1643-1644**

*Item* a roll specyfyinge what goods of Sir Simon Fanshawe were sold that had bene concealed in diverse places *videlicet*

| | | |
|---|---|---|
| London- *Imprimis* | to Mrs Willet 5 peeces of hangings at | 25 00 00 |
| *Item* | to Mrs Smith 2 peeces of hangings at | 04 08 00 |
| *Item* | to the same Mrs Smith 3 peeces of hangings | 03 12 00 |
| *Item* | to her more one facecloth embroydred with goulderen | 01 06 00 |
| *Item* | more to the same many severall things embroydred | 01 11 00 |
| *Item* | more to her one paire of Holland sheets | 01 12 03 |
| *Item* | more to her the said Mrs Smith 6 peeces of hangings | 12 01 00 |
| Ware | *Item* to Mr Heath 3 peeces of greene embroidree | 03 12 00 |
| | *Item* to the same one redd rugge | 01 08 00 |
| | *Item* more to him one pettycoate and one wastcoate | 01 16 11 |
| | *Item* to Mr Chandler one cloake | 02 00 00 |
| | Mr Chandler one satin pettycoat with gold lace | 02 12 00 |
| To Mr Chandler Saddle and Bridle | | 00 09 06 |
| To Mr Heath Sute and black cloake | | 01 09 00 |
| Rest to Heath | | |

**[160] TNA: SP28/217A Pt 2.2 Inventory of goods of Sir Simon Fanshawe sold at auction in Hertford, October 1643**

A roll specyfinge what goods of Sir Simon Fanshawe were sold at Hertford by the candle[613] by William Saward October 1643 as followeth £ s d

| | |
|---|---|
| *Imprimis* to the wyfe of Michaell Browne a parcel of linen, a flaske, a box, two little baskets, twoe little pare of andyrons, a fyre shovel, tongues, a bason, a ewer of chyna staff at | 00 19 00 |
| *Item* to Susan Walby a parcel of linen, a bedsteede and a cubbat | 00 11 08 |
| *Item* to John Burr and Joseph Wilkinson, a bedsteede, a featherbed, bolster, twoe pillows, 2 blanketts, one rugge, 3 chares, 3 stooles one little table, one pare of bellowes, 2 pair of andirons, one pair of tongues, and one fine shorle | 04 10 00 |

[613] To sell by candle was to sell by auction in which bids are received only so long as a small piece of candle burns

| | |
|---|---|
| *Item* more to them 2 old halfhead bedsteads, 2 old featherbeds, other bedcloathes and one warminge pann at | 02 06 00 |
| *Item* more sold to them a parcel of linen | 01 01 00 |
| *Item* to Thomas Bayley a trunk, a parcel of linen an old ridinge cloth and a basket at | 00 09 04 |
| *Item* to George Smith a parcel of linen a pare of bellowes, a firkin and twoe gall dishes | 00 05 06 |
| *Item* to (blank) a bedsteede, a featherbed, a bolster, 2 pillowes, three blankets and a rugg at | 04 02 0 |
| *Item* to John Thorowgood a little table at | 00 02 00 |
| *Item* to William Brayant 2 old bedsteedes, 2 old featherbeds, with bolsters and blankets, 2 boxes and one 3 legged table at | 05 03 06 |
| *Item* to the widdowe Barton a little table at | 00 02 04 |
| *Item* to James Goodman 2 little tables a trunck and one paire of andyrons at | 00 14 00 |
| *Item* to Goodwyfe Hodges 2 blanketts, a parcel of old hangings some chyna ware and a cuppe | 00 12 08 |
| *Item* to Richard Goodman 5 chares, 3 stooles, one bedsteede with curtaine rodds and valence one chaire, one canopy, 2 stooles, one window curten, and a redd cowche and some chyna ware | 03 17 02 |
| *Item* more sold to him an olde bedsteade, 2 blankets, one featherbed, 2 stooles and 2 cubberd clothes at | 02 10 00 |
| *Item* more to him 3 pillowes and 2 blanketts | 00 10 00 |
| *Item* to Goodwyfe Hills a canopye with the curtens and a sydeborde | 00 05 00 |
| *Item* to Jacob Pickeringe 3 cutens 7 rodds | 00 10 00 |
| *Item* to wife of Michaell Browne a bedsteede with curtens and rodds, Oscavels? chares and 2 stooles at | 03 06 00 |
| *Item* to Francis Clerks wife a bedsteede with curtens and rodds, 2 chares and a stole | 01 07 06 |
| *Item* to Robert Pennyfather 2 velvet stools | 00 03 00 |
| *Item* to Thomas Hills wife 3 chares, one stoole, 2 curtens, one rodd, one olde cubbert cloathe, and one pare of andirons at | 00 12 06 |
| *Item* to William Byrde one half-headed bedsteedeone bed and bolster and blankets | 00 02 00 |
| *Item* to Smiths wife an olde truncke, a curten, a wheele, and a ruyned stoole | 00 03 06 |
| *Item* to Joseph Pryor a little table | 00 03 06 |
| *Item* to William Pryor one olde chest, one truncke, 2 curten and | |

rodds and one old paynted cloth at 00 12 08
*Item* to Henry Pett one drawinge table, one truncke one tub and 3 chyna dishes at 01 05 04
*Item* to Joseph Wilkinson 2 chamber potts, and one basket 00 03 04
*Item* to a chapwoman an old screene cloth, one windowe curtain, one sheet and one old blanket 00 12 08
*Item* to severall persons 8 dozen of trenchers a firkin and a searre 00 05 00
*Item* to Susan Walbye a pare of curtens, an old truncke, a box, a tubb, a kenell 00 08 06
*Item* to William Lyon warminge pann and a dozen of trenchers 00 04 00
*Item* to Mr Hale pare of tables 00 02 06
*Item* to Nicholas Lamm a bedsteede, an old press, and a halfheaded bedsteede 00 08 00
*Item* to Francis Clarke a safe, a glass shelf, 4 hogsheads and a turning vat 01 02 00
*Item* to William Byrde a little table and a pare of tongues at 00 05 00
*Item* to Uffatt of Ware a boultinge mill and a table at 01 02 00
*Item* to Edward Chandler 3 brass panns, 3 kettles, 4 skillets, 2 scumers, 2 ladles, 2 big open kettles, 2 dripping pans, 7 spitts, a pare of jacks, one jack with the weights and chayne, one yron pott one fryinge pan, one warminge pann, choppinge knives, one cleaver, one pouldringe trough and one pouldringe tubb at 04 16 04
*Item* to John Strange a table and a frame at 00 07 00
*Item* to Gabriell Hardinge, a bedsteede at 00 08 00
*Item* to Goodwyfe Dyer a halfheaded bedsteede, one bed, one bolster with blanketts, one rugg and one quilt at 02 00 00
*Item* to Mr Herres 4 pillowes at 00 08 00
*Item* to John Hollan 2 featherbedds, one bolster, one pillowe, 3 blanketts, one rugg and one quilt 05 15 09
*Item* to goodwife Dyer one bolster and 2 pillowes at 00 13 00
*Item* to Goodwyfe<?> 3 blanketts and an old quilt at 00 07 00
*Item* to Goodwyfe Hollan one bolster and 2 pillowes at 00 11 00
*Item* to Gabriell Hardinge one featherbed and one bolster at 03 19 03
*Item* to Goodwyfe Peacock one old feather bedd and 2 blanketts 01 05 04
*Item* to William Gardiner one featherbed and one bolster at 01 12 09
*Item* to Samuel Goodman one featherbed and one bolster 02 04 06
*Item* to Gabriel Hardinge one featherbed and one bolster 01 16 08
*Item* to Thomas Heath a featherbed and 2 blankets at 01 17 04
*Item* to William Heathes wife one bolster and 2 pillowes at 00 14 00

| | |
|---|---|
| *Item* to Thomas Cramphorne a bedsteede, a featherbed, one bolster, blanketts, a rugg and a chare at | 02 10 00 |
| *Item* to him more a rugg, a coverlet and 4 blanketts | 00 17 00 |
| *Item* sold a drawinge press and boxes with other things | 00 13 00 |
| *Item* to Christopher Bareleggs a flockbed and blankets at | 01 00 00 |
| *Item* to the widdowe Dane a halfheaded bedstead & a canopy at | 00 04 00 |
| *Item* to John Frank one mare color sorrel at | 01 00 00 |
| *Item* to Mr Odersell 2 blanketts and one pare of sheets at | 00 05 00 |
| *Item* to Captain Neeham one cowche and 5 chayres at | 02 10 00 |
| *Item* to Edward Heath 53lb of pewter at 9d per lb | 01 19 09 |
| *Item* to him more 3 pare of brass andirons at | 03 12 00 |
| *Item* to Mrs Smith a rounde table at | 00 15 00 |
| *Item* sold more 2 square tables and an <yron> ~~rounde~~ and yron at | 00 15 00 |
| *Item* sold the greate round table and the hanging press at | 01 17 00 |
| *Item* sold diverse small things to divers persons at | 01 03 00 |
| *Item* sold of rounde woode and blacke 14 loads at 7s per loade, 6 loads of faggots at 6s per loade and 10 loads of brushe faggott at 2s per loade | 07 14 00 |
| *Item* sold 12 loades and 20 foote of tymber at £1-10s per loade | 12 08 00 |
| The somme of the goods inventoried | 130 13 08 |
| The somme of the goods sold (proved) | 111 07 04 |
| The somme of the goods unsold | 19 06 04 |

**[161] TNA: SP28/217A Part 2.2 Item 2 Goods of Sir John Harrison[614] sold by Auction, October 1643**

A roll specifying what goods of Sir John Harrison were sold at Hertford by the candle by William Saward, October 1643

| | |
|---|---|
| *Item* Sold to Goodwyfe Downes[615] of Hertford one dimity sute for a bed wrought with colours, 4 stools covers and 2 chairs at | 002 00 00 |
| *Item* to William Gardner one paire of brass yrons at | 000 10 00 |
| *Item* to Mrs Puller Junior[616] 4 windowe cushions | 001 00 00 |
| *Item* to Mr Peck 5 chayres and 2 little cushions at | 001 07 00 |
| *Item* to Goodwyfe Downes one paire of valences at | 010 02 00 |

[614] For Harrison see Appendix
[615] Probably the wife of Hezekiah Downes, blacksmith
[616] The wife of Isaac Puller (*see* Appendix)

| | |
|---|---|
| *Item* to Goodwyfe Dyer 2 sutes of bed curtaines at | 000 15 00 |
| *Item* to Goodwyfe West one old greene carpet at | 000 05 00 |
| *Item* to John Saward towe old coverlets and one curtaine | 000 05 00 |
| *Item* to diverse women 4 quilts at | 001 00 00 |
| *Item* to John Porter one quilt at | 000 03 06 |
| *Item* to Goodwyfe Grove one yellow rugg & 3 blanketts at | 001 05 00 |
| *Item* to Thomas Kinge 3 featherbedds, 3 bolsters & 3 pillowes at | 004 06 03 |
| *Item* to Goodwyfe Archer one <old> feather bed, one bolster one pillowe, one yellow rugg and 3 blanketts at | 001 18 06 |
| *Item* sold to Goodwyfe Haynes one old fether bed, 2 blanketts and an old red rugg at | 001 02 06 |
| *Item* sold to severall persons 10 paire of sheets at | 001 05 00 |
| *Item* sold 6 cubbert clothes to severall persons at | 000 07 00 |
| *Item* sold 17 table cloathes to severall persons at | 000 19 06 |
| *Item* to Goodwyfe Downes 17 towells at | 000 12 00 |
| *Item* to severall persons sold 17 napkins | 000 03 00 |
| *Item* sold to severall persons 6 dyaper towels | 000 02 00 |
| *Item* sold to severall persons 16 dyaper table clothes at | 001 16 06 |
| *Item* sold 4 dozen and 5 dyaper napkins to severall persons at | 010 16 08 |
| *Item* to goodwife Dyer 5 pillowebeers at | 000 09 00 |
| *Item* to Mrs Puller Junior 4 chaires, one stole, one paire of andyrons, one fyer shovel, one paire of tongues and 2 close stooles at | 000 15 00 |
| *Item* more to her one payre of little brass andyrons, 4 stooles, 2 chayres, 2 paire breeches and a paire of brass scales | 001 02 00 |
| Summa | 024 12 01 |

**[162] TNA: SP28/231 Memorandum of sale of Sir Richard Stormer's sequestered goods, 10/12/1644**

<u>Anstey Hall - Solde to Captain Needhame</u>[617]

| | £ s d |
|---|---|
| 4 Horses att £16 | 16 00 00 |
| Grass 13 Akeres att 16s the Akeres | 10 08 00 |
| Wheate and Barleye 76 Akeres att 40s the Aker | 152 00 00 |
| Peas and oates 77 Akeres att 20s the Akeres | 77 00 00 |

[617] Needham was the tenant put in by the committee to run the estate. He had been a Captain in the local militia in the 1630s

| | |
|---|---|
| Horse harnis | 01 00 00 |
| 3 Cowes 2 Bullockes and a bull | 12 00 00 |
| | 268 08 00 |
| | |
| 27 Dry sheepe[618] att 5s piece and 15 Croplers[619] att (5s)? | 11 15 00 |
| 2 souse and a bore[620] | 01 05 00 |
| 2 sous att | 00 13 04 |
| 4 souse att | 10 00 00 |
| 10 August 1644 | 291 01 04 |

It is this day ordered by the committee of sequestrracyennes nowe sittinge at Hertforde that the corne and goodes of Sir Richarde Stormer, nowe solde by Edward Heathe and Edward Chandler to Captain Isaack Needhame and Captaine Thomas Heathe, is allowed to stand, sale is confirmed by this committee.

**[163] TNA: SP23/77 *ff* 83-5 Letter from Alban Cox and William Carter to the Committee for Compounding re Thomas Coningsby's estate at North Mymms, 1649(50)**

*f*83 Accordinge to an order of this honourable committee of the 9th March 1649, wee whose names are hereunto subscribed beeinge the twoe next Justices of the Peace in the countie of, where the Mannor of Northmymms beeinge the estate of Mr Coningsby in the peticon named, doth lye, have considered of the particulars menconed in the said peticon, and examined the truth thereof, And upon vewe and examinacon of the decays of the howses, and buildings, and the distruccon of the woods, and other the spoiles committed and done upon the said Mannor of Nothmimmes, Wee doe finde that the mannor howse is much decayed in the leade and gutters about the said howse, which doe lett in the water ~~upon~~ everye raine upon the seeleinges and brickworke of the said howse, which thereby is much decayed.
As allsoe wee finde the howse much out of repaire in the tileinge, ~~and~~ lathinge, glaseinge and waleinge of the said howse, and in the copeinge of the ~~of the~~ brickwales about the said howse, which to bee sett, in good repaire wee

[618] Young ewes not yet producing milk
[619] Young castrated rams
[620] Pigs i.e. 2 sows and a boar

doe conceave will cost neere fiftie pounds or thereabouts, but if not timely repaired, may cost a farr greater some to repaire the same;
Wee likewise finde that a farme howse, parcel of the said (*f*84) mannor of Northmimmes, formerly by lease demised unto John Dell, dated the tenth of Aprill in the yeare of our Lord God 1639, for fifteen yeares from our Ladye daye 1638, whoe was bound by the covenants of the said lease to repair the same, is allsoe verye much out of repaire and in decaye, which to sett in good repaire may cost (as wee conceave) about fortie pound more or thereabouts, as allsoe the tenant quittinge the possession and caringe of the croppe and soile out of the yards contrarye to covenants, and since by the destruction of the fireboote[621] wee <finde and> are are credibly informed that the said farme is worse by twentie pounds a yeare to bee let;
Wee likewise finde that the bruehowse and the wellhowse thereunto adioyneinge (in possession, and not in lease) are likewise verye much out of repaire and will cost (as wee conceave) about twentie pounds to sett in good repaire; Wee likewise finde the gates, posts and railes about the hop garden, and the yards adioineinge to the said brewhowse, all pulled upp and taken away, most of them, as we are informed, togeather with much of the bricke, from of the brickwales, about the said mannor howse, by unruly and disorderly people liveinge thereabouts, whoe findeinge not one constant (*f*85) liveinge thereupon or that had any care of the preservation of the said estate, tooke the bouldnes to take and carrye away the same.

Wee are allsoe, upon examinacon credibly informed that all other the farme howses of the said Mannor (beeinge many) are extreamely fallen to decaye by reason the tenants have not beene suffered to have anye timber for repaires; Wee finde further that the coppices and underwoods are all felled, that are worth the fellinge or fitt for fuell, twoe or three acres of which, wee finde upon examinacon to have beene felled since the order of the 26th of February 1649 of restraint of fellinge any more woods annexed to the said peticon;
And that most of the pollards and husbands for to supplie the said Mannor with fireboote are lopped and taken awaye and disposed of by the tenants holdinge the same in sequestracon; As allsoe about 100 of the bodies of the pollards (and severall other timber trees) soe that there is not left for reasonable fireboote for the said Mannor necessarye to bee spent thereupon

[621] Fireboot, or fire bote, was the right of a tenant to take fire-wood from the landlord's estate, or the wood so gathered

for one yeare; And last of all wee finde that the springes,[622] beeinge not kept (*f86*) with sufficient fenceinge are spoiled and eaten upp by the cattell of the inhabitants dwellinge thereabouts, whoe daylie thrust in theire cattell into the said springs and underwoods lately felled; All which wee humbly certifie unto your honours and leave unto your most most judicious and grave consideration
*Alban Coxe William Carter*

***(On reverse fold)*** To the Right Honourable the Committee for compounding for delinquents estates
(***At right angles***) Mr Coningsby papers

## 9. The effect on sequestered clerics

### [164] HALS: 46349 Sequestration Order to Edward Jude, 14/11/1643

To Mr Jude, minister of Hunsdon
By virtue of an order of the Commons House of Parliament appointing us or any five of us to take examinations touching scandalous ministers, these are to will and require you, if you desire to have the witnesses against you examined in your presence, to make your personall appearance before us at the Bell in Hartford[623] on Friday next by nine in the morning, then and there to heare what hath been or shall be testified against you. Hereof you are not to faile at your perill. Given at Hartford the 14th of November 1643
*Joseph Dalton Maior, William Prestley, Gabriel Barbor, Alexandar Weld, Thomas Meade, William Carter*

### [165] HALS: 46350 Articles against Edward Jude, 6/10/1643

A true copie of the Articles exhibited to the Committee at Hartford against Edward Jude of Hunsdon Clerke, October. 6. 1642.

1. That he is addicted to scandalous lying and hath averred falshoods with deep and solemne oaths and protestations.

---

[622] A spring was a copse or wood consisting of young trees springing up naturally from the base or stools of old ones
[623] The Bell Inn, now the Salisbury Arms, Fore Street, Hertford

2. That he hath not onely attempted the chastities of one or more women, but also hath committed the act of adultery and uncleanenes.
3. That in his preaching he hath uttered words tending to the justification of the popish religion.
4. That in his preaching he hath vilified the Parliament and spoken contemptuously of their proceedings.
5. That he or his agents for him by indirect meanes have indeavoured to corrupt or take off the testimonies of such as freely and voluntarily have testified the truth against him, and hath threatened to article against such as have spoken their knowledge of him.
6. That he hath made use of persons of evill name and repute, and of scandalous conversation to be witnesses in his behalfe. *L Saunders Clericus*[624]

You are required to bring in your answer in writing to these articles on Thursday next, being the nineteenth of this instant October. *L Saunders Clericus*

**[166] HALS: 46351 The draft answer of Edward Jude, (undated 1643?)**

*f*1r The answer of Edward Jude parson of Hunsdon to the articles given in against him
1. It is ~~here~~ confessed by me that in Auguste now a yeare synce there cam three of my neighbours, to know what I would give ore doe towards the parlament war; unto whom I answered, what sad news is this, I hard of late that the kinge by proclamation ore sum other waye had sent to know what ~~they~~ his subjects would doe for ~~them~~ him. One of them replyed, what speake you of the kinge he is nothinge but words. I ~~unto whom I replyed~~ reproved him saying it becam not us to speake unreverentlye of our kinge. I ame angrye with you. Soe desiringe them to ~~carrye~~ limit the damidge, to carrye themselves like weaned children and not to medell with things that weare too high for them. I parted with them sainge unto two of them you are welcome, but unto the thirde (who in my judgment did forget himselfe in speakinge of his majesty, I saide I can hardlye bid you welcome as well as I love you. They did <not> saye to me what will you lend upon the propossicions of parlament neither did I denye to lend. ~~but take time to consider of it~~ These weare not officers, but inferior men. But when the constable cam to me, my

[624] The clerk to the Hertford Sequestrations Committee

answer was, that I was redye and willinge to doe any thinge that was in my power. I desired to be excused for not waiteinge upon them that daye, ~~by reson I~~ by reson I had ministerial occasions.[625] The answer was well accepted as he reported to me, and will upon ~~his~~ oath affirme it, and my redinesse at all times, night and daye, to do my service amd make my payments unto the Parlament, noe man in parish more forward, there is not any collector but will affirme the like. I never lent ore sent monye ore aide to the kinge.

2. I answer, I never refused to read anye order, ~~that came to me if I had it I received by it~~ declaration set forth by parlament if I had but the high constables warrant for the doeinge of it ore the readinge of any thinge commanded by him, as the constable will testifye. I denye not but the churchwardens did once call upon me to reade sum thinge ~~followinge me from church~~, of whom I demanded who would have it read, they answer, the neighbours. I requested to know what neighbours, which they denyed to tell me. ~~upon~~ I replyed I praye God make us wise to walke betwixt the kinge and the parlament. I hard him <not> saye that I was commanded by the Committee, then should I have ~~donne~~ read it; when I never refused any commandes by the high constable, neither doe I remember any thinge commanded in this kind but by the high constable. I denye not but I might saye to one of the churchwardens that wheras there are many things that are affirmed to cum from the parlament which do not, therfore my care shall be to have them sent unto me by a commande <from> ~~of~~ the high constable ore from others; although I doe not remember it.

3.4.5 I answer that I never saide any such things against the parlament nor ever had it in my thoughts ~~to~~ that the parlament should drive awaye the kinge, neither did I heare that the basse of the Cittye should laye hand of the kings coach, but from inferioures ~~but~~ without indangering him, and that he had at White Hall (*f*1v) a courte of garde ore the like to kepe off the common multitude.

6. I answer that I was soe farre from diswadinge any man from assistinge the parlament, that I perswaded them that cam to advise with me, as one says it to associates and Edward Eliot to take the covenants.[626]

---

[625] i.e. he had ecclesiastical or pastoral duties to perform

[626] The clerk who took the minutes left a space in the narrative here so it does not make sense

7. I answer that, the parlament having sat longe and the Lord had not given such a blessinge to there procedings as was expected, the kinge and parlament commanded a daye of publique humiliasion.[627] In my sermon I had an alusion unto Samson, that great deliverer, who when his locks were cutt off thought to doe as in former tmes, but could not et.[628] For a more full answer I shall produce my notes and to clere that other branch of the acusation, which is that I should compare the parlament to a man that had received poyson: for it was at that time, I made use of that comparison, as it apeares by my notes.

8. I answer I never refused to deface the crucifix, nor to have any popish pictures[629] taken downe. I am confident that I never observed anye peece of a crucifix to be there but synce we received the command, and longe synce, I have requested my neighboures that the painted glasse, which is in the windowe next the pulpit, might be ~~altered~~ changed, for it was a wronge to my sight, and there is not any but in that windowe, but the reson why these were not taken downe at that time was my Lord of Dover[630] sent down word that ~~that~~ he would spedely cum and se them defaced, that the coate armes might be preserved for the pew is belonginge to his house. I deny not but I did aske the churchwardens who should glase it, for the church ~~lye~~ lay ruinous, for want of paneinge and glaseing.

9. I answer that I never said any such thinge, neither did I ever heare what number compleat a parlament, neither doe I thinke that the major parte is with the kinge.

10. I answer I never said any thinge conserninge the death of the Earle of Straffoard, neither did I ever knowe anye man have soe honorable, ~~and~~ a triale.

11. I answer that I never saide any thinge conscerninge my Lord of Essex, and the miserye ~~at Bran~~ that sett out at Branfort.[631] I never soe much as hard that

[627] A day of public humiliation was when everyone in the country was encouraged to go to church to confess their sins collectively and seek guidance from God

[628] The shortened form of etc

[629] Pictures of saints in mediaeval stained glass windows were considered idolatrous by Puritans and therefore Catholic or Popish. Many had been removed since 1640

[630] Henry Carey, Lord Dover, owner of Hunsdon House, who joined the King at Oxford

[631] Brentford, which the Royalists attacked after Edgehill, to be then turned back at Turnham Green

my Lord was there but billetinge from souldiers there <they> weare unexpectedly cutt off.

12. I answer, I never discouraged volunteers from exercisinge and for the Commission of Array and until of late I never hard off it, and I never saide if that weare read then all things should be settled.

13. I answer, for the Covenant, I did all things that was commanded me, I publiquelye read it, and attended upon it, diverse dayes and apoynted a daye to perfecte it, but was sent for by warrant to attend this honourable committe.

*f*2r 14. I answer that I did not refuse to associate, the constable shewinge me the warrant. We did not conceive by the warrant that ~~I was~~ it had anye reference unto me at all, for the word clergye was not in this as in the former, and I adviseinge with a minister that cam out of Essex where they had associated, he affirmed the constable never asked ~~*illeg*~~ upon him. But I leift monye in his hands that searve in my armes that upon all occasions he might goe for the ~~ff~~ safitye of the Countyes as a volunteer, as he did

**[167] HALS: 46352 Evidence at the examination of Edward Jude (undated 1643?)**

Wheras there is an article exhibited agaynst Mr Jude of Hunsden, wherein he is accused to be addicted to scandalous lyinge, and averringe falshoods with oathes and daungerous protestacions viz: that in March or Aprill last, the troopers cominge to him and demandinge a horse and … (*space*), which horse he denyed to be with him, affirminge with manye oathes and protestacions that his sonne was gonne with him by eight of the clock that morninge to Cambr(idge).

To which he answereth that the said troopers never demanded anye horse of him, as appeareth by the tenstimonye of his 2 menservants who were all the while present. As also by ther owne search, it not beinge probable that they should seeke for a horse in chambers, clossets and in bedds. He also further answeareth that his sonne was not nor had not bin with him halfe a yeare before. But the said troopers asked indeede for his sonns man, and for him they made that diligent ~~sear~~ search, but he was gone by eight of the clock that morning towards Cambr(idge). He further confesseth that when the troopers were gone from his howse and returninge suddainelye agayne upon the informacion of some neighbors that the said Mr Jude had horses in a stable,

they then came and demanded a horse, which he presentlye tooke the keyes and shewed them where he was, but towld them indeede that he was lame and unfit to stirr, which appeared so to be, by the troopers owne confession, sayinge to Mr Judes man, that it was a lame horse indeede, so sore ridden that he was unfytt for their use, yet tooke him away not withstandinge. ~~And later the said horse was sent home lame and over ridden by troopers appears by a ticket and~~ it appeareth further by the testimony of his servants one of which <beinge his boys man> hath served with him 3 years and the other, his howsehold servant, hath lived with him 13 yeares and neither of them in all the time ever heard Mr Jude use anye sutch or like oathes as are expressed in the said article agaynst him. But that he hath oftne heretofore, and especiallye in these late troublesome times, charged his said servants, that they should not tell a lye, thowgh it were to the savinge of his whole estate, which they are readye to affirme uppon their oathes.
*Edward Allices,* the mark *X* of Richard Waterman

It is further testifyed by James Sprat and his wife that the troopers retorninge back agayne and sayinge that Mr Jude denyde the horse, wee heard Mr Jude say to the troopers, yee demanded of mee my sonnes man and not the horse and that then the said James Sprat and his wife sawe Mr Jude go presentlye to the stable with the troopers shewinge them where the horse was, himselfe opining the dore.
The marke of James *X* Sprat, the marke of Joane *X* Sprat

***(On reverse)*** A testimony concerning the horse

### [168] HALS: 46353 Certificate from the constables of Hunsdon (undated 1643?)

These are to certifye by vertue of a warrant sent unto us, constables of Hunsdon, for armes and 20s a man to be delivered by him that found the man, the parlament promisinge with all convenient speede that the mony should be paide backe againe, we cumminge to our minister Edwarde Jude, he with all redinesse rose up and delivered both his armes and the monye to my fellowe constable which serveth in his armes that warrant beared date October 24th 1642. Likewise calleinge upon our minister by vertue of an other warrant sent unto us to know what he would doe for the defence of his majesties person and parlament bareinge date January 2nd 1642 as more larglye apeare in that warrant. He returned this answer by me which I delivered that he was redye

to doe anye service for the good of the Kinge and Countye that was in his power which without any acception[632] was well taken and this I ame redye to affirme upon my oath. Cutbert *X* Wharlye Constable
The Commissioners were Mr Barbor and Mr Packer of Hertford with sum others

**[169] HALS: 46354 Order re the Sequestration of Hunsdon Rectory, 1/6/1644**

We the committee of the House of Commons in Parliament concerninge plundered ministers June 1st Anno Domini 1644.
Whereas the rectory of the parish church of Hunsdon in the County of Hertford was by order of the Committee sequestered from Edward Jude for severall great misdemeanours proved against him to the use of Robert Garret, a godly and orthodox divine, and the Right Honourable John Lord Rochford[633] hath sithence[634] moved this committee that in regard hee liveth in the said towne and that the advowson of the said rectory descendeth to him, hee may (be) given liberty to commend to this committee a minister to have the benefit of the said sequestracion, and this committee hath thereupon, for the satisfaction of his lordship and for the quiet of the said parish, and the preventing of all strife and difference that is or may arise betweene or among the said parishioners, removed the said Mr Garret to another place. And the said John Lord Rochford hath since commended to this committee *inter alia* William Thomas, Master of Arts, a godly and orthodox divine, to have the benefit of the said sequestration.
It is therefore this day ordered by the said committee, that the said rectory and the profits thereof, shall from henceforth bee and stand sequestered from the said Edward Jude, to the use of the said William Thomas, who is hereby appointed and required forthwith to officiate the said cure[635] as Rector, and preach diligently to the parishioners of the said parish in the said church, and shall have for his paines therein, the parsonage house and gelebelandes[636] and all the tithes, rents, duties[637] and profits whatsoever of the said rectory till further order shall bee taken in the premises and all arrears of tithes and

---

[632] Exception
[633] Son of Lord Dover (*see* Appendix)
[634] Since then
[635] Carry out all the spiritual duties associated with the post
[636] Glebe or church lands attached to the rectory, rent from which went to the rector
[637] Dues

profits fallen and become payable since the said sequestration (the charges of service of the said cure and taxes assessed thereupon first deducted). And all person and persons are required quietly to permit the said Mr Thomas to officiate the said cure and to enter, possess and enjoy the said house and glebelands and to have, receive and take, to his owne use, all the tithes, rents, duties and profits whatsoever of the said rectory, as they will answere the contrary at their perill. *John White*

# APPENDIX

## BIOGRAPHIES OF KEY INDIVIDUALS

The brief biographies below are designed to give an idea of some of the key individuals in the county during the period. Details of other individuals appear as footnotes to the text and those in bold are elsewhere in these biographies. References to sources appear in square brackets.

**Atkyns, Edward, Kt. (1587-1669)** was the third son of Richard Atkyns of Hempstead, Gloucs, a Judge in North Wales, by Eleanor, daughter of Thomas Marsh of Waresby, Hunts. He went to Queens' College Oxford and Lincoln's Inn, was called to the bar in 1613, and to the Bench in 1630 becoming a Sergeant at Law in 1640 and Steward of the Borough of Hertford in 1644, following the imprisonment of **John Keeling.** In 1633 he had defended the Feofees for Impropriations in the struggle of puritan gentry to place ministers in livings in defiance of Archbishop Laud. He was also a local JP from 1631, was appointed to the County Committees for Defence, Assessment, Sequestrations and for the Eastern Association in 1643 and a key member, and sometimes chairman of the Sub-Committee of Accounts for Hertfordshire from 1644. In 1645 the Commons appointed him a Baron of the Exchequer, having been nominated for the post by the King in 1640. In 1646 he became one of the Commissioners of the Great Seal and in 1654 was appointed to the High Court of Justice.

He was associated with the ruling county elite through his first marriage to Ursula the daughter of **Sir Thomas Dacres**, and through his third marriage to "The Widow Goulstone", presumably the widow of John Goulston, another local JP. He bought and sold local property, purchasing Wickham Hall in Bishops Stortford and Little Hadham in 1629 then sold it to **Arthur Capel** in 1633. In 1649 he bought, with Sir Richard Lucy, Abbotsbury Manor, Barley, and in 1661 bought four manors for £5000 in Albury from Robert Hale. In 1661 he was living at Aldebury where his house was rated for 11 hearths. In 1666 he purchased Affledwick Manor (Beauchamps) from John Taylor and Richard Goulston, thus extending his landholdings to Layston, Anstey, Great Hormead and Wyddial. He was described by Chauncy as "a grave and learned judge, a most just and charitable man". His sons, Robert and Edward were both sent to the puritan Sidney Sussex College, Cambridge, and became MPs [TNA: C231/5 *f*64; E179/248/23 *f*77; HALS: 39770; F&R I, pp119, 170, 231, 294; Chauncy, I, p294; *VCH Herts, III*, p302; *IV*, pp38, 54; Calder, I M, *Activities of the Puritan Faction of the Church of England 1625-1633,* (1957) pp xxii, 64, 91, 96, 97; Henning, *Commons* I, p564; Prest, W R, *The Rise of the Barristers: A social history of the English Bar, 1590-1640* (Oxford, 1986) Appendix E, p341]

**Barbor, Gabriel, Mr. (1576-1649)** was the son of William Barber of London and was married to Elizabeth, daughter of John Gray of Wichford in the Isle of Ely. He was an active overseas merchant, being a director of both the Bermuda Company in 1615 and the Virginia Company in 1616, and a member of the East India Company in 1622 and the Providence Island Company in 1630. He was elected one of the Assistants of the Borough of Hertford in 1621, Chief Burgess in 1634 and Mayor in 1635, becoming an active borough JP 1644-8. He was a Puritan activist and a member of the Feofees for Impropriations and endowed the vicarage of All Saints and St Johns Hertford with the impropriate tithes of the Liberty of Brickendon. He may also have tried to unite the Rectory of St Andrews with All Saints, the feoffees having received it from Sir William Soame in 1626. He was responsible for appointing the radical millennial preacher, John Archer, to the vicarage of All Saints in 1640. He was described by Holmes as "the most active Parliamentarian in the County and an extreme Independent". He was also a London property developer and owner of houses in Drury Lane, Covent Garden and St Giles in the fields, as well as in Hertford. He had paid £2 out of the £55 Ship Money for Hertford in 1637. He invested in property in Ireland when he purchased 260 acres in Leinster in the 1650s. He became Chairman of most of the Hertford wartime committees, being particularly associated with the committee for the volunteers that became the radical militia committee. His son Gabriel became a physician in Norwich, his son John, active in the local volunteers and militia, and Joseph a cornet in the regiment of Colonel Norwich. One of his daughters married **Isaac Puller,** another active local Puritan [HALS: HBR46 *f*907; TNA: PROB11 84 Fairfax; F&R, pp119, 170, 231, 289, 294, 356, 539, 622, 638, 967, 1084, 1238; *Vis Herts*, 1634; Chauncy I, pp492-3; Cussans, *Hertford Vol* pp57, 87; *VCH Herts* III, p150; Seaver, P S, *The Puritan Lectureships: The politics of religious dissent 1560-1662*, (Stanford Calif. 1970) p251; Holmes, *The Eastern Association,* p125; Rabb, T K, *Enterprise and Empire: merchant and gentry investment 1575-1630* (Harvard, 1967) p240.

**Beaumont, William Mr. (d. 1661)** was admitted into Lincoln's Inn at the request of Erasmus Earle, law reader, on 6 August 1639. He was added to the Assessment Committee on 31 March 1643 and became the High Constable of

Dacorum in 1644. On other committees from 1649, by the 1650s he was a JP in both the county and liberty. He held the lands of Redbourn Priory and the advowson to the rectory of Studham. He also acquired a watermill in Redbourn in 1655 [TNA: C139/13/4 *f*43d; HALS: QSB2B *f*45d; DP/93/5/2 *f*66; *VCH Hert.* II, pp280, 368; F&R, I, p119; II, p36; *Lincoln's Inn Admissions*, I, p239, Munby, *Redbourn*, p15]

**Boteler, John, Kt (1587-1653)** of Watton Woodhall, which he inherited on the death of his brother Robert in 1622, was a cousin of Lord Boteler of Hatfield Woodhall. He was knighted in 1625, when he represented the county in Parliament, having married Anne the daughter of Sir Richard Spencer of Offley. He had six children, sons Sir Philip and John and at least one daughter. He became sheriff in 1630 and was an active JP from 1635 to 1643, when he was forced out and accused of being a royalist. He had been sent a Commission of Array by the King, consulted various colleagues and spoke out against the local volunteers exercising under the Militia Ordinance at the Hertford sessions. As a result he was declared a malignant and put in the Peterhouse in London, being promised release on payment of a £2000 fine, which was probably the annual income of his property. However he was again overheard attacking MPs and was put in The Tower, eventually being released in 1645, though his failure to pay off the instalments on his fine led to further sequestration [Bodleian Library: Microfilm of Tanner Ms 64 *f*121; *CJ* III, p674; Kingston, *Herts,* p130; Cussans, *Herts (Broadwater*), p170]

**Bromley, George, Mr (fl. 1627-1663)** son of a London haberdasher, and citizen of London, lived at Waterford Hall and held the manors of Stapleford and Westmill and various lands in Ware in 1629. He had refused to pay the forced loan in 1627, and on refusing to pay Ship Money he had goods seized but then he rescued them back again. However by 1642 he was a royalist and was accused of helping **Thomas Fanshawe** of fraudulently conveying property, and of preventing a tenant from paying rent. In 1646 he was listed as of Ware Westmill and he and his wife Margaret, the daughter and heir of William Reeve, had had at least five sons, George in 1625, William, Jonathan, Thomas and then Edward in 1635, sending the eldest to the Inner Temple. In 1663 he paid tax on 11 Hearths [TNA: E179/248/23 *f*113r; SP16/400 *f*130; Trinity College Library: Box 44 (VI) 7 No 99 Terrier of Ware Rectory; HALS: DP/116/1/1 Ware Parish Register; *Inner Temple*, p324; Chauncy I, pp411, 530; *CCC,* p847; Cussans, *Hertford*, p161]

# APPENDIX

**Capel(l), Arthur, first Baron Capel of Hadham (1604-1649)** royalist commander and politician, son of Sir Henry, inherited the Capel estates at Hadham, Hertfordshire and elsewhere and, through his wife, the Morrison estates at Cassiobury, Watford, becoming one of the richest men in England with land in ten counties. Despite, as MP for Hertford, criticising the king in 1640, he was granted a peerage and became a royalist commander, fighting at Edgehill in the king's lifeguard and was appointed the lieutenant-general of north Wales and the northwest. His lack of military experience was a disaster and he was outmanoeuvred by the parliamentarian forces. He spent large amounts of his own money losing areas under his command and was replaced. On 30 April 1643 his sequestered estates in Hertfordshire were granted to the Earl of Essex. He went into exile with the Prince of Wales and returning in 1647, retrieved his estates, but lost them again when he engaged for the royalists in the second civil war and was captured after the siege of Colchester, put on trial and executed [Skeet, F J A, 'Arthur Lord Capell, Baron Hadham 1604-49', *East Herts Archaeological Transactions*, III, Pt III (1907) pp312-335; Hazell, M, *Fidelity and Fortitude: Lord Capell his regiments and the English Civil War,* (Leigh on Sea, 1987); Ronald Hutton, 'Capel, Arthur, first Baron Capel of Hadham (1604-1649)' *NewDNB*]

**Cecil, Charles, Viscount Cranborne, (1619-1660)** first son of **William, 2nd Earl of Salisbury**, JP in St Albans in 1640 and elected to both the Short and Long Parliaments for Hertford Borough, which he represented from 1640 to 1653. He was created Lord-Lieutenant after his father's return from York in 1642 being only 23 at the time. However he was rather slow in putting the Militia Ordinance into effect, and though active for a time locally, being nominated to most local committees, he returned to parliamentary duties. He seems to have been hampered by a spendthrift wife who ran up large debts and, being Lord Lieutenant of Dorset and nominated to Wiltshire committees, would have been more concerned to recover the Cranborne estates from the royalists. He died before his father, his eldest son succeeding to the earldom [Keeler, M F, *The Long Parliament 1640-41: A Biographical study of its members,* (Philadelphia, 1954) p130 (henceforth *Members*)]

**Cecil, Robert (c1621-c1680)** Second son of **William 2nd Earl of Salisbury,** elected to the Long Parliament for his father's pocket borough of Old Sarum, he ceased to sit after Pride's Purge but returned briefly as MP in 1659. He replaced Endymion Porter as the captain of the 500 strong trained bands in St Martins in the Fields in January 1642, as Porter was thought to be a Catholic.

Appointed to a number of local Hertfordshire committees, on which he occasionally served, he was also put on a number of parliamentary committees including that dealing with the Uxbridge garrison in March 1644, where some Hertfordshire troops were based [*CJ,* III, p434, Keeler, *Members* p130; Coates, Jones and Snow (eds) *Private Journals of the Long Parliament*, (Yale, 1982) pp143, 150-1, 155]

**Cecil, William, second Earl of Salisbury (1591-1668** ) inherited all the Salisbury estates at Hatfield, Cheshunt, Queen Hoo Hall etc. in Hertfordshire, and the Cranborne estates in Wiltshire etc. from his father, Robert Cecil, on the latter's death in 1612. Although appointed a Privy Councillor in the 1630s, he never gained major office and being a moderate Puritan was unsure whether to side with the King in 1642. Persuaded by his son in law, the Earl of Northumberland, to return to Hatfield from York, he remained under suspicion, and, though on early local committees, was eased out by the more radical elements. His sons **Charles, Viscount Cranborne**, and **Robert Cecil** became MPs for Hertford and Old Sarum in 1640 under Salisbury's influence. Charles replaced his father as the Parliamentarian Lord Lieutenant for Hertfordshire. The earl's loyalty was later recognized when he was appointed to the committee of Both Kingdoms in February 1644. He sat in the Rump as a recruiter MP for King's Lynn, became a member of the Council of State, even becoming its president. He organized local syndicates which won most Hertfordshire seats in the Protectorate Parliaments, but was denied entry to Parliament in 1656. He made his peace with Charles II at the Restoration and attended his coronation. Hatfield House was assessed for 97 hearths in 1663, and Salisbury's house Quixwood at Clothall, which he had acquired in 1617, for 44 hearths [TNA: E179/248/23 *ff*24, 65; *CJ* III, *395*; Lionel M Munby, *Early Stuart Household Accounts*, Hertfordshire Record Society Vol II, (Hertford, 1986) p v; G D Owen, 'Cecil, William, second Earl of Salisbury (1591-1668)*, NewDNB*]

**Chester, Edward, Kt,** (*c*1590-1664) was the son of Sir Robert Chester, former senior JP (died 1641), who had lived at Cockenhatch, Barkway until his death, having settled Royston Manor on Edward. Edward was at Christs College Cambridge in 1606 and at the Middle Temple in 1609. He was put on the County Commission of the Peace by the King on 15 July 1642, and was knighted in 1643, presumably to try and win him over to the royalist cause. His mother was the daughter of Sir Henry Capell, and he married in May 1642, as his second wife, when he was 50, Ann the 22 year old daughter of Sir

Peter Saltonstall. His first wife, whom he had married in 1615, had been Catherine daughter of John Stone Esq sergeant at Law of London. His brothers Granado and Robert were the Rectors of Broadwater and Stevenage respectively. He is likely to have had royalist sympathies but kept his head down during the interregnum. His son Edward inherited all the Chester properties including Nuthampstead and the Saltonstall estates through his mother [TNA: C231/5 *ff*330-1; *VCH Herts* III, p261; *Herts Vis*, p40; Chauncy I, pp182, 205, 211; Foster, *Marriage Licences*, p272]

**Combe, Toby, Esq, (1586-1669)**, was the second son of Francis Combe (*b.* 1558) of the Bury, Hemel Hempstead, farmer of the great tithes of the former monastery of Bonhommes at Ashridge, and younger brother of Francis Combe (*b.*1583), who died in 1641, Toby inheriting part of the Manor of Hemel Hempstead. He had been an assessor for ship money in Cheddington, Bucks in the 1630s. He was appointed to assessment, sequestrations and the volunteers committees, and acted as treasurer for a number of taxes in the western hundreds of the County. High Sheriff in 1649, he was also appointed to assessment committees 1648-60. He left a common place book in which, at over the age of 80, he recounted his early life. He had been at Oxford and not liking to go into the church became the manager of his father's estates, doubling the rents. He included a scathing attack on his elder brother's behaviour, second marriage and debts that Toby had to pay off. He also included a diatribe against his own son Francis, for his extravagant living. He claimed the war cost him over £2000 and he had to sell land and houses in Hemel Hempstead to pay his way. However he also held back about £100 allocated in his brother's will for setting up a school at Watford [HALS: D/Z16/Z1; DP/47/1/2 Hemel Hempstead Parish Register*;* F&R 1, pp119, 170, 356, 1112; II, p 36, 300, 468, 665, 1070, 1370; Bonsey, C G and Jenkins, J G, (eds) *Ship Money papers and Richard Grenville's Note-book*, Buckinghamshire Record Society, 13, (Welwyn Garden City, 1965) pp36-7; *VCH Herts* I, p220; Brenda Burr, 'The Combe family of Hemel Hempstead', *Herts Past and Present*, 3rd Ser No 5 (Spring 2005) pp14-19]

**Coningsby, Thomas, Kt, (1591-1654)** was the 2nd son of Sir Ralph Coningsby, married Martha, daughter of William Button of Alton, Hants and succeeded to the manor of North Mymms in 1625, having previously lived at East Barnet. A vigorous Ship Money sheriff who employed his own collectors, he was petitioned against in 1640, despite being elected as MP for St Albans in April, though defeated in the elections to the Long Parliament by

Sir John Jennings who had opposed him. Reappointed sheriff by the King in November 1642, he tried to implement the commission of array in St Albans in January 1643, and was arrested by Cromwell who was travelling from London to Cambridge. Imprisoned in Ely House, his lands were sequestered and his high handed attitude at a House of Commons committee of investigation led him to be put in The Tower. Although a composition fee for his delinquency was agreed in 1645, he could not pay it and was kept in prison. He died on 1 October 1654, his son, Henry the translator, recovered the family estates, but sold most of them in 1658 retiring to Wold Hall, Shenley, with his mother [*CJ* III, pp523, 674; IV, 72; Alderman H M, 'Sir Thomas Coningsby of North Mymms', *Hertfordshire Countryside,* 10, No 39 (1955) p108; Elizabethanne Boran, 'Coningsby, Sir Harry (*fl.* 1633–1665)', *NewDNB;* Kingston, *Herts* pp4, 8, 14, 15, 31]

**Cowley, Thomas, Mr. (*d.*1673)** mercer and draper, was Mayor of St Albans in 1639, 1650 and 1661, holding office in the town for more than 40 years and helping to obtain a new mace for it under the commonwealth. He was the county treasurer for the Decimation Tax in 1656 and was put on the St Albans Assessment Committee in 1657 and 1660. He and his wife Joan (*d.* 1688) had a son Abraham, also a mercer and draper, in business with his father, and a son Thomas, also mayor. It was alleged in 1661 that the father put his sword on for the first time in 20 years in 1642 to encourage the people to fight against the king. He had a large house in the High Street and by his death was living next to the Corner Tavern, in the Vintry, which had been extended at the end of the 16th century and was taxed for 11 hearths in 1663. He also owned property in St Peter's Street and St Stephen's parish as well as the Antelope Inn in Church Street. At the restoration he was regarded as a member of the 'Phanatique party' for his support of Nathaniel Partridge, removed from the Abbey church [TNA: SP28/197 Pt 2 *ff*6-18; F&R II, pp1070, 1370; Chauncy II, pp301, 303; Smith and North, *St Albans*, pp14, 47, 66-7, 101, 109-110, 204]

**Cox(e), Alban, Esq, (c1600-1665) o**f Beamonds (Beaumonts) outside St Albans, heir of Sir Richard Coxe, Master of the Household under the previous three monarchs. In 1636 he had been appointed Master of the King's Stables in St Albans and was a Colonel in the local militia. He was ordered by Parliament to train the St Albans volunteer troop of horse in August 1642 and became an active Committee man, using the buildings in the Great Court of the Abbey as his HQ when he commanded the county volunteer horse, which was used to prevent incursions by royalists. He helped round them up after Naseby, then sided with the New Model Army against Parliament in 1647. His company was attached to Colonel Fortescue's Regiment of foot and John Cox was its lieutenant. It engaged for Ireland, but is unlikely he went. He was the recruiter MP for St Albans in 1649, and, although appointed governor of Guernsey by Fairfax in the October, he spent a long time organizing supplies and troops in Dorset into the winter and returned after a few months and went with Cromwell to Scotland. By 1652 he was back in St Albans, acting as a JP in the Liberty, but quarrelled with **Dr John King**. He was returned to both Protectorate Parliaments for St Albans and was a Colonel under the New Militia in 1655. His second election in 1656 was contested by **Richard Jennings** who accused him of using force, but Coxe petitioned against Jennings' 'false information' and went on to oppose the 'Other House' in 1657 and to sit in Richard Cromwell's parliament. Identified as a Cromwellian, he was defeated in the elections to the Convention Parliament in 1660 by **William Foxwist**, and unsuccessfully challenged the result. He was assessed in Sleape and Smallford in 1663 for ten hearths. His son Thomas married Elizabeth, a daughter of the prominent Cowley family, and his other son, a daughter of the Aylewards, also active in the militia, and members of St Peter's parish [BL: Add Mss 11,315 *ff*2-13d; University of Reading Archives: HERT5/1/1 Alban Cox papers 1621-1660; HALS: Cox Papers 70536-70578; Bodleian Library: Microfilm of Tanner Ms 58 *f*65; *CJ* II, pp712-3; IV, pp77-9; *LJ* V, pp288-93; VII, pp273-5; Henning, *Commons* I, p271]

**Dacres, Thomas, Kt, (1587-1668)** was a magistrate, deputy-lieutenant and MP for Hertfordshire, the eldest surviving son of Sir Thomas Dacres of Cheshunt, and Frances Pigot. Sheriff in 1615, knighted in 1617, he had fought abroad in the early 1620s. He was elected MP for the county in 1626, 1628 and 1641, when he replaced **Lord Capel**, and was again MP for Higham Ferrers in 1660. He was active in pursuing the war in 1642 and served on numerous committees in Parliament and the county during the war and worked in the Commons in getting compensation for soldiers' widows and orphans. A Presbyterian, he was a peace party man by 1644, was excluded in 1648 and survived the Restoration, when his extensive estates in a number of counties and London were valued at least £1000 p.a. He married Martha, daughter of Thomas Elmes of Lilford, Northamptonshire, his sister Elizabeth married Richard Hale of Tewin and his sister Ursula married **Sir Edward Atkins**. Of his 13 children, his first son of the same name, whom he outlived, became an active local JP 1646-9, sitting on committees in Hertfordshire and

Bedfordshire as well as becoming MP for Callington. His third son, Edward, who had been a captain in the local militia, bought Bedwell Place, Essendon in 1648 and married Arabella the widow of Henry Atkyns. His sixth son, Arthur Dacres (1624-78) became a noted Physician at St Bartholomew's Hospital [HALS: Fremantle Mss F409-10; Keeler, *Members,*pp150-1; Henning, *Commons*, I, pp337-8; II, 184-5; Holmes, *Eastern Association*, pp183-4; Underdown, *Prides Purge*, pp151, 371; Norman Moore, 'Dacres, Arthur (*bap.* 1624, d.1678)' rev. Patrick Wallis, *NewDNB*]

**Dove, Fromabove, (fl.1629-1648).** Dove was a dyer in St Albans who had been made a Borough Assistant in 1629. He had taken on Robert Longe, the son of a Dunstable inn holder, as his apprentice in 1632 and was also involved in renting out the toll on the market. That same year he and others accused John Wells, the postmaster of St Albans, of impressing their horses for the post corruptly in order to procure a bribe for their release and he refused to pay Ship Money in 1638. He was used in a number of roles in the war in the financial administration of the western half of the shire, including being the quartermaster responsible for the transportation of pay from the treasurers to the local troops and to Cambridge for the Association troops. His name suggests that he was the son of puritan parents who welcomed his arrival with joy [TNA: SP16/399 *f*81; HALS: StABR P1/S1/168 Mr Ivory's mayoral account; 286 *f*6v, Book of Apprenticeship enrolments; *CSPD 1631-33,* pp257; Chauncy, II, p304]

**Draper, Robert, gent, (fl.1643-8)** of Hitchin, was added to the Hertford Committee in October, 1643 and was on the Militia Committee in December. He was active in organizing local forces in the north of the county in the summer of 1645. He had a house with orchard and gardens called the Stonehouse in Bancroft and other lands in Hitchin and Ippollitts. He was the father of George Draper, Steward of Hitchin Manor, who drew up the Hitchin Survey of 1676 [Howlett, B (ed), *Survey of the Royal Manor of Hitchin, 1676,* Hertfordshire Record Society Vol 16, (Hertford, 2000) pp1, 79, 86; *LJ,* VI, pp257, 342-3]

**Eure (Ewer), Henry, Esq (fl, 1621-1648)** of Watford, had been required to pay £10 under the forced loan in 1625. He was the younger son of Thomas Ewer of the Lea, Watford (*d*. 1627). He had been a JP for the Liberty before 1627, was removed (possibly because he refused to pay the loan) and then restored in April that year, when he also succeeded to the Manor of Bushey.

He, Abel and Jonathan Ewer had bought the estate of Hillside (Waterlands with Doggets) in 1621 from Roger Glover, the estate lying in the three parishes of Ridge, Shenley and Aldenham. By 1634 he was living at The Lea, Watford, where his father had lived in 1625, Abel and another Thomas were living at Shenley, and a William Ewer at Bushey. In 1637 he settled on his son, also Henry, of South Mymms, and on Joan his wife, the daughter of Randall Marsh of Hendon, the manor of Meriden, Watford and property in Bushey. He was still acting as a JP in July 1648 [TNA: C231/4 *f*222r; HALS: 11307-8, 11310, 11643, 72325; QSB2A *f*89d; *VCH Herts* II, pp324 n, 390, 459, 462; *Hert Vis*, pp51, 52]

**Fanshawe, Simon, Esq. (c.1600-1680)** was the middle son of the three surviving sons of Sir Henry Fansahwe of Ware Park, Hertford, being baptized in St Mary's Ware on 23 April 1604. He trained as a lawyer but was described by his sister in law, Anne, as "more of a libertine than any one of his family". He probably fought at Edgehill and Brentford for the King. He had married Katherine Walter in Bengeo church, 5 weeks after her wealthy husband, Knighton Ferrers, had died in 1640. After being knighted in 1641 and having been a taxation Commissioner in May 1642, they moved with the rest of the family to Oxford, where she died in 1643, leaving Simon to look after her 8 year old daughter, Catherine Ferrers, by her previous marriage. He put her in the care of his sister Alice. Returning to fight under Sir Richard Willis, he subsequently became Lieutenant-General to Sir Charles Lucas at Marston Moor. His property was sequestered and the contents of his house and concealed goods sold at auction. After surrendering and compounding under the Newark articles in August 1646 and having given security, he was allowed a pass to go into France for a month to visit his sick brother **Thomas Fanshawe.** He managed his insane brother John's estate, and is reputed to have arranged the marriage between his step-daughter Catherine and his nephew Thomas (1632-74), the son of his brother of the same name in April 1648. He later became involved in the Sealed Knot conspiracies of the late 1650s hoping to involve **Sir John Watts** and Sir John Gore in an uprising, but survived to the Restoration [HALS: DP/116/1/1 Ware Parish Register; LZ777- 204/100E -Colin Field 'The Wicked lady of Markyate-Studies and Documents', (Typed manuscript 1979); Cambridge University Library: Ec.3.30; Underdown D, *Royalist Conspiracy*, pp189-90, 250, 269; *LJ* VIII, p460; Loftis, J (ed), *The memoirs of Anne Lady Halkett and Ann Lady Fanshawe*, (Oxford, 1979) p106; Barbara White, 'Ferrers, Catherine (1634–1660)', *NewDNB*]

# APPENDIX

**Fanshawe, Thomas, first Viscount Fanshawe of Dromore (1596-1665)** was the eldest son of Sir Henry Fanshawe, who inherited his government post as Remembrancer of the Exchequer and the Ware Park estate at Hertford, becoming MP for the Borough for all parliaments 1624-41. He was suspected of preparing arms for the royalist cause and his estates were raided before the war started. In 1642 he was expelled from Parliament, left the county and fought at Edgehill for the King, and was one of his advisers, lending him money on the security of his forests. Towards the end of the conflict he joined the Prince of Wales and helped him escape to the Scillies. His estates were sequestered early on and the bailiffs even drained his pond looking for hidden arms and money and he compounded for his property in 1648 for a fine of £1300. He returned to Ware Park until arrested for royalist plotting in 1659. He was given an Irish peerage at the Restoration, but most of his estates were sold off to pay debts. He married twice, firstly Anne, the daughter of Sir Giles Alington of Horseheath, Cambridgeshire by Dorothy Cecil daughter of the Earl of Exeter and secondly Elizabeth, daughter of Sir William Cockayne. He was assessed for 26 Hearths in 1663. His younger brother, Sir Richard, baptized in St Mary's, Ware on 23 June 1611, was poet, and secretary for war to the Prince of Wales, and, after composition, joined Charles II, but was taken prisoner after the Battle of Worcester in 1651, released on grounds of ill health and lived briefly in Bengeo and in the Friary (now the Priory), Ware. His wife was Anne Harrison, the daughter of **Sir John Harrison** of Balls Park Hertford, the author of the famous memoirs. After the Restoration he became ambassador to Spain [TNA: E179/248/23 *f*113r; HALS: DP/116/1/1 Ware Parish Register; Loftis, J (ed) *The memoirs of Anne Lady Halkett and Ann Lady Fanshawe, (*Oxford, 1979) pp133-7; Sybil M Jack, 'Fanshawe, Thomas, first Viscount Fanshawe of Dromore (1596-1665)' *NewDNB*; Lionel M Munby, 'Sir Richard Fanshawe (1608-66) and his family', *Hertfordshire Past and Present*, No 3, 1962/3, pp2-13; Peter Davidson, 'Fanshawe, Sir Richard, first Baronet (1608-1666)' *NewDNB*]

**Foxwist, William, Esq, (c.1610-1673)** was the third but first surviving son of Richard Foxwist of Caernavon who married Mary the daughter of John Pemberton, grocer of London and St Albans. Called to the bar in 1636, despite being behind with his ship money payments in 1638, he was put on the Commission of Array by the King for Caernarvon in 1642 but appointed Recorder of St Albans in 1645 a post he held until 1661. As such, he presided over the borough's civil Court of Record. As the chairman of the Hertfordshire Sub-committee of Accounts, he played a key role in auditing the wartime expenditure. He also became a JP for both the county and Liberty of St Albans and sat on assessment committees after 1647. He was MP for Caernarvon in 1647, playing a minor role on a number of committees, and though purged a year later sat in protectorate parliaments for Welsh seats and returned as MP for St Albans against **Alban Coxe** in the 1660 Convention Parliament. He lived in a large house on St Peter's Street and was assessed for 12 hearths in 1663 [TNA: SP16/399 *f*81; *CJ* V, pp97, 134, 142, 168, 195, 236, 382-3; Clutterbuck, *Herts* I, pp51, 53; Henning, *Commons* II, p360]

**Gardiner, William (c1614-1691)** a Hertford draper, had been elected a borough assistant in 1639, and became a chief burgess of the borough in 1644, and mayor in 1648 and again in 1656. When the freeman's list was drawn up in 1648 he had diversified to become a grocer. He had been an apprentice to Thomas Bromhall, whose step-daughter, Mary Stone, he had married in 1636. He became a captain in the militia before the civil war, supplying coats etc. for local troops during the conflict. He had presented the petition to parliament in March 1642 on behalf of All Saints parish to replace Humphrey Tabor by Abraham Puller as vicar. Whilst mayor he paid a parliamentarian, Captain Stewart, to take his men out of Hertford, to be quartered elsewhere. He sat on local assessment committees 1649-57. Although he took the oath under the Corporations Act, he was removed as Chief Burgess in 1662. After a lengthy case in the Court of King's Bench, he won the right to be re-instated in 1674.

From his first wife, he had William and Mary, two children, who died in infancy, and 3 more: Samuel, John and Susan. His first wife died in 1668 and he married Joan (Johanna) Hales in 1672. In 1641 he had a servant, Susan Saxe, and was assessed for £10 in the poll tax. He employed Thomas Barnes, either as an apprentice or clerk, and in 1650 he took on as an apprentice, Henry Rainsford, the son of the rector of Tewin. In 1663 he was taxed for 12 hearths and acted as appraiser for deceased goods in 1664 and 1671. However by 1676 he was in severe debt, had given up his trade, sold his house and was in prison, being forced to resign again as Chief Burgess. However before his death he seems to have recovered some wealth and property and to have been partially rehabilitated [TNA: E179/248/23 *f*121; HALS: HBR20 *ff*422d-3; 25/6; 26 *f*59; *CJ* II, p488; Chauncy, I, p491; F&R II, pp300, 665, 1070; Adams, *Hertford Wills*, pp63, 88; Alan Greening, 'The Draper's Tale', *Hertford and Ware Local History Society Journal*, (Hertford, 2005) pp3-14]

# APPENDIX

**Garrard, John, 2nd Baronet (c1612-86)** was the son and grandson of Lord Mayors of London, whose father had bought Lamer Park, Wheathampstead and whose wives Elizabeth Barkham, and Jane Lambarde (nee Lowe) were daughters of former Lord Mayors. His son, the second Baronet, married Jane Lambarde's daughter, Jane, a year or so after her mother had married his father. The first Baronet died a year later in 1637, having been a senior magistrate and deputy lieutenant. The second Baronet became a deputy lieutenant in August 1642 and commanded a militia regiment at the start of the war, and was appointed parliamentary sheriff of the county 1643-5 following the removal of **Sir Thomas Coningsby** the royalist. Kingston claimed that Garrard's regiment was disbanded for lack of pay, but he seems to have led his regiment into Newport Pagnell Garrison in November 1643 and under Major-General Browne in 1644. He was appointed to most local parliamentary committees in the 1640s, but was not a regular attendee, presumably because of his military duties. His stepmother lived at Bride Hall, the property being described in the Garrard Mss in 1617 and his estate at the Restoration was valued at £750 p.a. [HALS: Garrard Mss 27235-7; D/EB2102/T14; GEC, *Complete Baronetge* I, pp188-9; Henning, *Commons* II, p373; Kingston, *Herts*, p52; F&R, I, *passim*]

**Harrison, John, Kt, (1589-1669),** customs farmer and 17$^{th}$ century equivalent of a modern multi-millionaire, he had purchased the Hertford Priory estate and built the Balls Park mansion by 1640. In 1640 he made a loan of £50,000 to the crown to help pay for the Bishops' War. He had been placed in the house of Sir John Wostenholme by the first Earl of Salisbury and given a minor post in the customs, which he had built into a privatized customs collecting empire, as well as having interest in the Virginia and East India companies and an alum business. He had also, in 1616, married Margaret Fanshawe, a member of the Derby branch of the Fanshawes, living with the Wostenholmes at Barking, and they had three sons, John, William and Abraham, as well as two daughters, one Anne, who was to marry Richard Fanshawe of Ware Park. After his first wife's death in 1640 he married Mary Shadbolt of Ardley and had two more children Richard and another daughter. Having failed to get a repayment of his loan, and when the customs farmers were attacked in Parliament, and having obtained a knighthood in 1641, he joined his daughter Anne and her new husband at Oxford. As a result his property in several eastern counties was sequestered in August 1643, the contents of Balls Park being sold by auction. Originally from Lancashire, he sat as MP for Scarborough in 1628, probably with Buckingham's support, and for Lancaster in 1640 and again from 1661-9. Of his sons, he outlived the first three, disinheriting John for his support of parliament, losing William in 1643 from injury, and allowing Abraham to be a working goldsmith in London. Harrison returned to Balls Park where he was assessed for 31 hearths in 1663. His son Richard lived at South Mymms until his mother's death, when he moved into Balls Park [TNA: E179/248/123 *f*117; Henning, *Commons* II, p501; Robert Ashton, *The crown and the money market 1603-1640,* (Oxford, 1960) pp86-7, 98, 101-5, 108, 110-12, 176; Keeler, *Members*, pp205-6; Gruenfelder,J K, *Influence in early Stuart elections 1604-1640* (Ohio, 1981) pp102, 141-2, 187; *VCH Herts* III, pp412-3; Mander, R P, 'The Harrisons of Balls Park', *Hertfordshire Countryside,* 19, No 75, (1964) pp106-7]

**Hickman, William, (died c1677),** became a Borough Assistant in St Albans in 1624 and later the Treasurer of the Hundreds of Cashio and Dacorum for the St Albans Committees. As such he was a key link in the financial administration of the war in the western half of the county. He was a prosperous ironmonger in the town, associated with the Pemberton and other puritan families. He survived the Restoration and in 1663, and was living in a house in St Peters Street being assessed for eight hearths. His second wife was the daughter of Sir Jeremy Whichcot, Baronet of Hendon. By the 1670s he had accumulated property in Spicer Street, Dagnall Lane and School Lane, St Albans [TNA: 179/248/23 *f*153; Chauncy II, p304; Smith and North, *St Albans*, pp98, 152, 172-3, 234]

**Jennings, Richard, Esq, (1619-68)** of Sandridge was the eldest surviving son of the 22 children of Sir John Jennings, MP for St Albans until his death on 5 August 1642. Richard succeeded his father as MP and as Deputy-Lieutenant, and the following year married Frances Thornhurst, daughter of Lady Lister by her first husband, and coheir with her sister Barbara of her father's property in Agnes Court, Kent. He was appointed to a number of committees in 1643, but was never very active, becoming a JP in 1644, serving on the bench until 1648 and again from 1658. He was also one of the visitors of St Albans School. Sometime in late 1645 or January 1646 he and his wife were captured by royalists from Farringdon and he was later exchanged for Sir Thomas Weston. Excluded in 1648 he was elected MP again to the Convention and Cavalier Parliaments. He had two sons and three daughters and was the father of Sarah, later Duchess of Marlborough and the builder of Blenheim Palace. He was assessed for 24 hearths in Holywell Ward, St

Albans in 1663 [TNA: E179/248/23 *f*148; HALS: QSB2B *f*49d; *CJ* IV, pp410. 413; *CSPD 1645-7*, p313; Foster, *Marriage Licences*, p760; Henning, *Commons* II, pp649-50; Chauncy II, pp294, 400; *VCH Herts* II, pp64, 433; James Falkner, 'Churchill, Sarah, Duchess of Marlborough (1660–1744)' *NewDNB*]

**Keeling, John, (1607-71)** Son of John Keeling, a member of the Inner Temple and a lawyer in the forest courts, had been born in Hertford, where his father held ten properties and his wife, Martha, was the daughter of Sir Thomas, the Bedford branch of the Boteler family, where he also had property. Admitted to the Inner Temple in 1624, called to the bench in 1632, he served as the Borough Steward 1637-44. In 1637 his father paid £2 and he himself £1 of the £55 ship money levied on Hertford and in 1641, £5 and £3 in lands respectively towards the subsidy, both being thought capable of spending £100 p.a. in the poll tax. He was imprisoned from February 1643 because of his conflict with the local militia at the Hertford sessions, having refused to take *The Protestation* and having been declared a disturber of the peace in the county by parliament. He was probably released sometime after August 1644, when he was replaced by **Edward Atkyns** as Steward of Hertford borough, and does not seem to have returned to Hertford. It was his house to which the turnpike in Hertford was attached. After the Restoration he became a sergeant at law in 1660, MP for Bedford in the Cavalier parliament, and chief justice of the King's Bench in 1665, having been council for the crown at the trial of two of the regicides and being described as a bigoted Anglican. Three of his six children, all born in All Saints, survived infancy [HALS: HBR46 *ff*907, 924, 933; *CJ* II, p951; Anon, *Masters of the Bench of the Hon. Society of the Inner Temple 1450-1883 and Masters of the Temple 1540-1803,* (1883) p39; Eric Stockdale, 'Sir John Kelyng, Chief Justice of the King's Bench' *Bedfordshire Historical Record Society, Miscellanea*, 59, (1980) pp43-47; Stuart Handley, 'Kelyng, Sir John (*bap*.1607, *d*.1671)' *NewDNB*]

**King, John, MD, (1605-166?)** is not to be confused with the man of the same name, who had been baptized in the Dutch Church at Austin Friars in London as *Joannes Regius*, the son of Johannes Regius, in 1614. Whilst the latter was studying at Leyden in the mid 1630s, the other practised in both St Albans and Hertford, where he took on a pauper apprentice, Jeremy Stoughton, in July 1636, when **Gabriel Barbor** was Mayor, being paid 5/- towards his clothes. Some of the authorities cited below confuse the two. His father, John Le Roy, had moved to England from France in 1572 and then changed his name to King. Dr King married, as his second wife, Elizabeth (1611–1661/2), youngest daughter of Barnes Roberts of Willesden, Middlesex, sending his son John (1639-77) to St Albans school, Eton and Queens', Cambridge. It is therefore uncertain where and when he trained, but as a young man in 1630, he was already being referred to as "John Kinge, Doctor of Phisicke", when he had been assaulted by George Lewis, a grocer from Whethampstead. By the 1640s he was clearly well established in St Albans, whereas his namesake practised in London. Having delayed or refused to pay ship money in 1638, he was one of the four men into whose care the magazine at St Albans was given in August 1642, and, with the capture of the local MP, Edward Wingate, and the imprisonment of the mayor, William New, he became a key political figure in St Albans, sometimes acting as a link between the borough and the county, and sometimes between the St Albans Committee and Parliament. He became the chairman of the St Albans Standing Committee, being nominated to numerous local committees from 1643 to 1660, as well as serving as a Borough Burgess and as a JP in the Liberty of St Albans from 1645-60 and in the county from 1652. His clerk also worked for the Mayor of St Albans on some occasions and he was involved in the poor rate assessment of 1655 for the Abbey parish. Living latterly in Spicer Street, St Albans, he died from jaundice sometime after 1660. His son, of the same name, became knighted as the solicitor–general to the Duke of York, after the Restoration [TNA: C193/13/4 *f*43d; SP16/399 *f*81; HALS: QSB2A *f*125d; HBR20, *f*141; SAM 1/1/171 Account of Ralph Pollard Mayor 1647-8; 173 Account of John Simpson Mayor 1648-9; 311, Poor rates Overseers accounts 1655-72; 294, List of burgesses; Kingston, *Herts,* p154; Munk, W, *The roll of the Royal College of Physicians of London* I, (London 1878) p246; Roach, J M, *A directory of English Country Physicians 1603-43*, (London, 1962) p105; F&R, I&II *passim;* Smith and North, *St Albans,* pp19, 165; Birken, W, 'Dr John King 1614-1681 and Dr Assurerus Regemorter (1615-1650) brethren in the Dutch Church and in the College of Physicians of London, with added references to other "Dutch" congregants in the Royal College, Dr Baldwin Hamey and Dr George Ent', *Medical History* (1976) 20(3) pp276-95; Stuart Handley, 'King, Sir John (1639–1677)', *NewDNB*]

**Leman, William, (c1600-1667)** born in Beccles, Suffolk, was a successful city merchant, nephew and principal heir of Sir John Leman, former Lord Mayor of London, from whom he inherited lands in Warboys, Cambridgeshire and estates worth £4,000 p.a. in 1632, the year he purchased the estate at

Northaw, Hertfordshire. He had been put on the Liberty of St Albans Bench and was appointed sheriff 1635-6, and deputy Lieutenant in 1642, becoming one of Hertford representatives on the Eastern Association Committee at Cambridge and one of its treasurers in 1643. He was involved in recruiting and maintaining the New Model Army and levying the Scots assessment. An Independent in religion, he became a recruiter MP for Hertford in 1645, replacing **Sir Thomas Fanshawe** the royalist. He served on many parliamentary committees on military matters and was appointed treasurer of the army in 1650 and a member of the Council of State in 1651. Appointed to many local committees in Hertfordshire, Cambridgeshire and Middlesex, he was an active rumper, cooperating with Londoners with commercial interests. He retired to Northaw during the Protectorate, was MP again in 1659, and surviving the Restoration, was made a baronet in 1665 [GEC, *Complete Baronetage* IV, p7; Greaves, R L, and Zaller, R E, (eds) *The biographical dictionary of British radicals in the 17th century,* 3 Vols, (1981-4) p184; Worden, B, *The Rump Parliament,* (Cambridge, 1971) pp30-31; Yule, G, *The Independents in the English Civil War*, (Cambridge, 1958) p106; Brunton, D, and Pennington, D H, *Members of the Long Parliament*; (1954) pp119-20; Holmes, *Eastern Association*, pp127-8]

**Love, William, (fl. 1623-?)** draper, born Aynho, Northamptonshire, had held a house in 1629 with a garden and orchard in Baldock Street, Ware. He and his first wife, Mary, had a son William, and a daughter Mary baptized in 1623 and by his second wife, Esther, had a second son John in 1633. A militia committee member, he was a key figure in the financial administration of the county, acting as paymaster to the local volunteer regiments and travelling around East Anglia and the northern home counties to pay the local troops as well as liaising with parliament on behalf of the local committee. He also acted as muster master at one stage. He uncovered peculation by Captain James Pinckney in relation to the Newport Pagnell garrison and gained a reputation for honesty and probity, which not all the unpaid soldiers shared. His son William was MP for London at the time of the Restoration [Trinity College Library: Box 44 (VI) 7 No 99, Terrier of Ware Rectory; HALS: DP/116/1/1 Ware Parish Register; Tibbutt, *Luke's Letters, passim*]

**Lytton, Rowland, Kt, (c1615-1674)** was the son and heir of **Sir William Lytton** MP and Anne daughter and heir of Stephen Slaney. He had been at Hertford Grammar School, Sidney Sussex, Cambridge and the Inner Temple and then travelled abroad. He married firstly Judith (*d.* 1659) daughter and heir of Thomas Edwards, mercer of London in 1638, by whom he had 2 sons and 2 daughters, and secondly Rebecca, daughter and co-heir of Thomas Chapman, draper of London and Wormley, by whom he had one daughter. He was put on the Commission for the New Model Army and its Assessment Committee in 1645 and was a JP for the county and the Liberty from 1656 as well as MP for the county in 1656, 1659 and 1660. Sheriff 1662 and deputy-lieutenant from 1670, he was also active in the Stevenage Almshouse charity [HALS: Lytton Mss 23378; Ashby, *The Hellard Almshouses,* pp11-14; Henning, *Commons* II, pp785-6]

**Lytton, William, Kt, (1586-1660)** son of Sir Rowland Lytton of Knebworth and Anne daughter of Oliver St John, had been a boyhood friend of **William 2nd Earl of Salisbury** and travelled widely with him. He married, firstly Anne Slaney, and secondly Ruth Barrington, sister of Sir Thomas Barrington, and was related to **Sir Samuel Luke,** so was closely connected to key opposition leaders to Charles I, he himself leading the opposition to Ship Money in the shire. He also held property in Letchworth, Welwyn, Datchworth, Codicote, Hitchin and Stevenage, leased land in Bedfordshire and had considerable influence within the north and centre of the county. He was exercising local militia companies in 1615, served his turn as sheriff in 1625, and by 1629 was JP in the Liberty and the county and deputy-lieutenant. He was MP for Hertfordshire in 1624, 1628 and for the Short and Long Parliaments and was on numerous important committees. In Parliament he presented the various petitions on behalf of the county. He was part of the abortive parliamentary peace delegation to the King in January 1643 and helped William Capel secure the tenancy of his brother's property. He also came under suspicion of concealing some of **Sir Thomas Fanshawe's** goods. He became a member of the peace party, and was excluded at Pride's Purge. He indicated in his will he wanted to be buried according to the Book of Common Prayer, but "without funeral pomp", but was probably a Presbyterian in belief [HALS: Lytton Mss 22881, 23451; *CJ* III, p355; Keeler, *Members*, p263; Underdown, *Pride's Purge*, p152; Cliffe, J T, *Puritans in conflict: The Puritan gentry during and after the Civil Wars* (1988) p73; Holmes, *Eastern Association*, pp288-9]

**Mead(e), Thomas, Esq** (*fl.* 1629- c1658) of Ware, was farmer of the parsonage and tithes of Thundridge and one of the county treasurers. He leased the lands of the rectory manor that belonged to Trinity College, Cambridge and by 1629 had recently constructed one large house in Crib

Street, where five had previously stood, with a garden and orchard, and had various lands on the outskirts of the town. He and his wife Susan had a son Thomas in 1623 and a son Nicholas in 1626. He was on the commission for raising the subscriptions under the propositions in November 1642 and served on numerous local committees 1643 -58. In 1648 he was ordered to pay 5 years arrears to the poor rate of Thundridge. He was buried at Ware on 7 November 1658 [HALS: QSB2B *ff*85, 86d, 98; DP/116/1/1 & 2 Ware Parish Registers; Trinity College Library: Box 44 (VI) 7 Nos 99, 100, 101 Terriers of Ware Rectory, Priors Wood and Glebe land; *CJ* II, p853; F&R I&II, *passim*]

**Nicholls, Thomas, (b. 1596)** of Boycott, Salop, was the son of John Nicholls, draper of Shrewsbury by his wife Anne daughter of David Heylyn. He was educated at Shrewsbury School, Queens' Cambridge and Gray's Inn, and in 1626 had married Mary, daughter and co-heir of John Kynaston of Marton, Salop. They had three sons and four daughters. He became bailiff of Shrewsbury in 1636, alderman in 1638 and was added to the commission of the peace for both Shropshire and Montgomery before the war. He was the step-cousin of **Isaac Puller.** He and his cousin were the main beneficiaries in 1631 of the will of his uncle, Rowland Heylyn. However in October 1642 his estate was plundered by the Royalists, who burnt his writings, spoilt his house and sold his furnace. In a humble petition to the Lords he said that he had been completely stripped of his landed inheritance worth £900 p.a. as well as his personal possessions and had no subsistence for his wife and seven children. He moved to Hertford, obtained the lease of the Balls Park estate from the Hertford Sequestrations Committee, got onto the local militia committee and commanded a local militia regiment. When Shrewsbury fell to the Parliamentarians, Nicholls returned to rescue his property and was re-instated as Alderman in 1645. He was named in the first Presbyterian classis for Shrewsbury in 1647, so was probably a Presbyterian. He was however purged from the Shropshire bench in 1653, perhaps as being too moderate, hence why he stood as MP in Hertford in 1654 in the **Earl of Salisbury's** syndicate. He also had land in Ireland and New England. He sent his son Timothy to Gray's Inn in 1658 [TNA: Prob 11/161/23; C193/13/4; 231/6/271; *LJ* VI, pp673-4; *Gray's Inn Admissions*, p285; *Trans Salop Arch and Nat Hist So.* (Ser 2) vii p251; Information from Miss Reid IHR]

**Norwich, John, Kt and Baronet (1613-1661)** son and heir of Sir Simon Norwich of Brampton, Northamptonshire had been educated at Oundle School and had married firstly, Anne daughter of Sir Roger Smith of Edmundthorp,

Leics, by whom he had 4 sons and three daughters, and secondly after 1650, Mary, daughter of Sir Henry Atkyns of Cheshunt. He was appointed by an ordinance for raising horse in the Eastern Association of 23 July 1643, to be in charge of a brigade of horse from the counties of Bedfordshire, Buckinghamshire, Northamptonshire, and Hertfordshire to defend them against royalist infiltrators [F&R I, p215] (GEC, *Complete Baronetage* II, p110)

**Packer, Humphrey, Senior (fl 1635- b. 1662)** There were two Humphrey Packers, father and son, who were active in the war effort. The father was a wealthy Puritan brewer in Ware, who is usually referred to in the 1640s as Mr or Senior, the younger usually as Junior. The father had obtained the freehold of Place House, the former royal manor house, and was owner of the Cross Keys Inn in the Market Place and considerable freehold and copyhold property. He was in conflict with his elder son, Edward, over this in the mid 1630s, as well as being indicted for selling barrels of beer to unlicensed alehouse keepers. He was active in defending the previous Vicar of Ware, Charles Chauncy, against the successful attempts of **Sir Thomas Fanshawe** to remove him from office. Packer Senior was the Hertford Committee treasurer for numerous wartime funds. The son was assessed for 8 hearths in 1663, the year after his father's death. The younger son of Humphrey and his wife Alice, Humphrey Junior, was baptized in St Mary's, Ware in 1621, and became a collector and treasurer later in the war. This Humphrey Packer, himself had a son Humphrey 24 years later in 1645 [TNA: E179/248/23 *f*113r; HALS: DP/116/1/1 & 2 Ware Parish Registers; Rowe V, 'Place House, Ware, in the seventeenth century', *Hertfordshire's Past*, No 15 (Autumn 1983) pp17-22; Hunt, *The History of Ware*, pp101, 123]

**Pemberton, Ralph Esq (*d.*1645)** was the second son of Roger Pemberton the founder of the St Peter's Street Almshouses in St Albans. He had been one of the county treasurers and Chief Burgess in 1624 then Mayor of St Albans in 1627–8, when he was allowed an additional £32 p.a. because of "greater charges, troubles, losses and expenses" attached to the office and mayor again in 1638. He married Frances, daughter of Francis Kempe and sent his sons to St Albans grammar school. He died in 1645 having served on the St Albans Committees, leaving property in Northchurch, St Michaels, St Stephens. His son Francis, who was educated at Cambridge, was knighted in 1675 and became a controversial Chief Justice of the King's Bench [HALS: QSB2A *f*210d; William Brigg (ed) *The Herts Geneaologist and Antiquary*, III,

(Harpenden, 1899) p243; Smith and North, *St Albans*, pp109, 161; Chauncy II, pp301, 303; Paul D Halliday, 'Pemberton, Sir Francis (*bap.* 1624, *d.* 1697)' *NewDNB*]

**Pennyfather, John (fl. 1630-45)** a Hertford borough assistant in 1645, was the son of a cordwainer (shoemaker) of the same name. He had been apprenticed to Richard Law, cordwainer of Hoddesdon, who had died, completing his apprenticeship with John Tailer of Hertford in 1632. He then took on an apprentice of his own in 1636. As one of the town constables in 1638 he had been assaulted by Thomas Barker, the coachman to **Sir John Boteler** in Mr Scant's Inn (then the Bell, now the Salisbury Arms). He was in conflict with Dr Lindell, the surrogate to Sir John Lambe, in the Commissary Court held at the Sun Inn, Hitchin, on 9 May 1639. He had asked what the judge thought of the Scots. Lindell replied they were rebellious traitors, to which Pennyfather said "You shall answer for these words at the last day", for which he was put in Hertford gaol. Taken before **Sir William Lytton**, who informed the Privy Council, which instructed him to take a bond from Pennyfather and release him. On 19 March 1642 he had presented a petition to parliament on behalf of the parishioners of All Saints, Hertford, requesting the removal of the cleric Humphrey Tabor and his replacement by Abraham Puller. He was later licensed to seize horses by Lord General Essex, but, indicted for an offence, was released by order of Parliament. He was also responsible for supplying Hertfordshire troops in Reading garrison with horses, and became a borough assistant in 1645 [TNA: SP16/420 *f*138; 138/1; 421/85; HALS: HBR17, No 251; 25 *f*6; 26 *ff*46, 154; *CJ* II, p486, III p2; Chauncy, I, p493; Information from Alan Greening]

**Pr(i)es(t)ley, William Esq (c.1594-1664)** of Wildhill, Essendon, was a county JP from 1634 to 1649 and sheriff in 1634. He was nominated as a deputy-lieutenant in June though the king tried to remove him as a JP in July 1642. He married firstly Hester, daughter of Sir John Gore of London, by whom he had four children, all of whom died in his lifetime. He married secondly, Frances Harris, widow of John Harris of Chepstead, Kent, and the daughter of the Hertfordshire. MP, **Sir Thomas Dacres.** His surviving son Thomas was born in 1647, the year he became a recruiter MP for St Mawes in Cornwall. He sided with the Parliament against the local committee and the army in 1648 and was excluded at Prides Purge [TNA: C231/5 *f*539-1; *CJ* II, p602; Chauncy I, p546; *VCH Herts* III, p459; Underdown, *Prides Purge,* p383]

**Puller, Isaac, Esq (fl. 1627-1663)** was the son of the Hertford town lecturer, Abraham Puller and his wife Margery, and son-in-law of the chairman of the Hertford committees, **Gabriel Barbour.** He was the step -cousin **of Thomas Nicholls** of Shrewsbury, and his own son, also Isaac, entered Shrewsbury School in 1627. He inherited land in Middlesex from Rowland Heyleyn, his step-uncle, in 1631. In 1637 he paid 10/- Ship Money in Hertford, and by 1641 in the Poll Tax he was reckoned able to spend £50 p.a. In July of the same year his goods were rated at £3 for the subsidy. He was ordered by parliament in the summer of 1642 to train the Hertford Volunteers and was put on the Sequestrations Committee for the county in 1643. He rose to the rank of Lieutenant-Colonel in the local militia. He became an assistant, then a chief burgess, of the borough in 1644, Mayor in 1647, and was elected the borough JP on the death of Barbor in 1648. By this date he had 5 children, Timothy, Elizabeth, Isaac, Hanna and Rebecca, who were left £100 that year by their grandfather Abraham in his will. He was an active JP for the county 1649-60. He was elected as the single borough MP for Hertford in the 1654 and '56 Protectorate Parliaments and in 1659 joint MP with William Packer in the restored Rump. He was seen as a radical Independent in politics and religion and refused the oath of subscription under the Corporation Act in 1662. He was assessed for 11 hearths in Saint Andrews, Hertford in 1663 [TNA: E179/248/23 *f*121; Will of Abraham Puller 91 Essex; HALS: HBR20 *ff* 422d-3; 25 *f*6; 30 *f*18; 46, *ff*907, 924, 933; Chauncy, pp402-3; Holmes, *Eastern Association,* pp125-6; Turnor L, *History of the ancient town and borough of Hertford*, (Hertford, 1830) pp141-3; Information from Miss Reid]

**Reade, John, Kt, (1616-1694),** of Brocket Hall, Hatfield, was the 4th, but 2nd surviving son of Sir Thomas Reade, of Dunster, Oxfordshire by Mary, 5th daughter and co-heir of Sir John Brockett of Brockett Hall. He was admitted to Lincoln's Inn in 1632, knighted on 12 March 1642 and became a Baronet 4 days later, though his honours were not recognized. He was active as a commissary for the purchase of horses in the early days of the war. He later became a Cromwellian Baronet, having been Sheriff for the county the year earlier, but failed to become elected to the 1654 Parliament as part of the **Earl of Salisbury's** syndicate, probably because of his unsavoury reputation. He was reputed to have kept a mistress, Susanna Style, who died in 1657, whom he encouraged to insult his wife. Pardoned at the Restoration, he took a second wife, Lady Alismon, in 1663 and served again as sheriff in 1673 [*Complete Baronetage* II, pp164-5]

**Robotham, John, Esq, (fl. 1614-1657)** of St Albans had been a JP in the town and liberty of St Albans since the 1630s, his father having migrated south from York. He was put on the local committee in February 1643 and served on both county and liberty committees until 1649. He had married Penelope, daughter of William Pichford of Lee Brockhurst, Salop, and his sister Grace had married the Bishop of London's Commissary, James Rolfe. John's sons were **Robert (b.1614)** and William. John was named in 1638 as a chief person in St Albans who had refused to pay Ship Money through unnecessary delays. He had inherited the Manor of Newland Squillers, which the family had purchased through service to three Tudor monarchs. He also owned the Cock Inn in Cock Lane, now Hatfield Road [TNA: SP16/376 *f*128; 399 *f*81; Smith and North, *St Albans*, pp4, 161, 191; *Herts Vis*, p87; *CJ* II, p714; F&R I&II, *passim*; *VCH Herts* II, p412]

**Robotham, Robert, Esq**, **(1614-98)** of St Albans, son of John (above), admitted to Gray's Inn in 1632, he had refused to pay the £1 Ship Money levied on him in 1636 and was a captain in the local militia. He rose to the rank of major and later formed part of Thomas Sheffield's regiment that was destined for Ireland, though there is no proof he ever went there. He was put on the Hertfordshire Assessment Committees in 1657 and 1660, becoming a JP the same year, serving in both the County and Liberty in the next three reigns. His house was assessed for 12 hearths in 1663. At the Restoration he returned to the Anglican Communion and was a key member of St Peter's church, taking over the pew vacated by Sir Harry Coningsby, and handing it on to Dr Impie in 1666. As lord of the manor, he was an important member of the local vestry, signing the Churchwardens Accounts in 1651, but he had his will witnessed by two local non-conformists and he later sold the manor of Newland Squillers to the Jennings family [TNA: C193/12/3 *f*47; 220/9/4 *f*38; E179/248/23 *f*153; HALS: DP/93/5/2 *f*58; Bodleian Library: Microfilm of Tanner Ms 58 *f*65; Smith and North, *St Albans,* pp63, 75, 83, 100, 108, 161; F&R II, pp1070, 1370; Foster, *Grays Inn Admissions*, p196; Chauncy II, p307]

**Titus, Silius, (1623-1704)** Son of a Bushey landowner and soap boiler of the same name, who rented Tylers farm in Bushey from Henry Ewer and had property in London worth £180 p.a. The son obtained a captaincy in the parliamentary army under Colonel Ayloffe, rather than joining his fellow Presbyterian lawyers in Essex's lifeguard. He was employed by the Hertfordshire Committee firstly with a foot regiment then with the cavalry.

He was present at the siege of Donnington Castle and brought the news of Cornet Joyce's seizure of the King at Holmby, for which he was awarded £50, but his letters indicate a loss of enthusiasm. He was won over to the royalist cause after his contact with the King again on the Isle of Wight, where he attempted to allow the king to escape. He got to Holland but returned in 1649 to become involved in a Presbyterian plot against the Rump. He escaped again to France and went with Charles II to Scotland in 1650. He was involved in various royalist missions, and after the restoration became a Hertfordshire MP, JP and deputy-lieutenant [Henning, *Commons*, III, pp570-4; Carlson, L H, 'A history of the Presbyterian party from Prides Purge to the dissolution of the Long Parliament', *Church History* XI, (1942) pp83-122; Alan Marshall, 'Titus, Silius (1622/3-1704)', *NewDNB*]

**Turner, William, Gent. (fl.1639-1663)** was a grocer of Hertford, who became a Borough Assistant in 1639 and Chief Burgess in 1644. On 1 June 1642 he had complained to the Commons about the activities of the mayor and **Mr Keeling**, who had tried to intimidate those who had been carrying out military exercises under the militia ordinance. As foreman of the grand jury he had argued there was no case to be heard. He was active throughout the civil war as the main treasurer for the Hertford Committees, carrying out their instructions, ensuring that the local people were paid for work done for the war effort, and keeping their receipts, which were then passed on to the local sub-committee of accounts, which, following scrutiny, sent them up to the parliamentary committee for taking the accounts of the Kingdom at Westminster. He became Mayor of Hertford in 1646, 1653, and 1657, and in 1654 was responsible for organizing the elections in Hertford to the first Protectorate parliament. In 1657 he was still the treasurer for the militia for the three north and eastern hundreds. He was unanimously elected mayor again following the death of Mr Lawrence the incumbent in March 1659, but was removed as burgess in 1662, being assessed for 6 hearths in Saint Andrews, Hertford in 1663 [TNA: E179/248/23 *f*121; HALS: HBR20, *ff*332-9, 422-3; 25, *f*6; 30 *ff*5, 22; QSB3 *ff*59d-60; Chauncy, I, pp491-2]

**Washington, Adam, Colonel (1604-1665)** of Brent Pelham, the son of Adam Washington, citizen and mercer of City of London Esq, attended Merchant Taylors' School and Queen's College, Oxford, being admitted to Lincoln's Inn in 1624 and called to the bar in 1632. He was the commander of one of the Regiments of Hertfordshire volunteers and gave early on to the parliamentary cause under the Propositions. He was put on the assessment committee in February 1643 and in 1649, was appointed treasurer for maimed soldiers in 1650, a JP in 1650 and 1656, was on the local Committee for scandalous ministers in 1654 and a commissioner for treason trials in 1656. He appears to have been a radical Independent in religion, and allegedly attacked the Presbyterian Divine, Thomas Edwards, after a sermon he gave in Christchurch, Newgate Street in London, on the grounds he had misinterpreted the parable of the tares. He married Elizabeth, the daughter of Francis Floyer, and had bought the Beeches estate in Brent Pelham about 1640. He retired to his estates in 1660 and had 10 surviving children [TNA: C193/13/3 *ff*30-31; 6 *f*41; HALS: QSB2B *f* 106; F&R I, pp91-2; II, pp35, 971, 1039-40; Edwards, T, *Grangreana,* (Exeter, 1977) p174; Walne, P, 'The honest-hearted Colonel Washington of Brent Pelham who didn't emigrate', *Herts Countryside*, 35, No 259, (Nov 1980) pp39-42; *Al Ox* IV, p1578; *VCH Herts* IV, pp95, 97]

**Wingate, Edward, Esq, (c1606-54)** was the son of William (Edward) Wingate of Lockleys, Welwyn, and Margaret, the daughter of Peter Taverner of Hexton. He married Mary, daughter of Ralph Alway of Cannons, Shenley, whose estates in Shenley, Ridge she inherited. Edward later sold these estates in 1653 for £3,200. Edward's sister Frances married Eustace Needham of Wymondly. Edward had been a local JP in the late 1630s, was probably already a captain in the local militia and was elected MP for St Albans to the Long Parliament, where he was not particularly active, except on committees concerned with religious matters, but was on the committee preparing the militia bill. In April 1642 he presented a petition about laypersons preaching and scandalous ministers and was probably a conservative Presbyterian but was a teller for the supporters of the Propositions. Once the war had started, he commanded a troop against the royalists at Worcester, had an argument with his fellow commanders, as he wanted to proceed more cautiously at Powick Bridge, but was captured and incarcerated at Oxford, Parliament seeking his exchange with a royalist from November. His wife presented a petition for his release on the last day of 1642, which only gradually bore fruit, parliament granting her arrears from his pay in April 1643. However his Shenley property was threatened by local people exploiting his absence and aiming to 'lay all of the said grounds common', an early example of 'digger' activity. However he was successfully exchanged within a month and was back in the house to take the covenant in June [*CJ* II, pp54, 212, 515, 691, 842, 891-2, 909, 935, 965; III, pp33; 94, 120; Keeler, *Members*, pp396-7; Burne, A H, and Young, P, *The Great Civil War*, (1959) pp18-21]

**Wittewronge, John, Kt, (1618-1693)** was the son of a successful Dutch immigrant brewer in London whose mother bought him the Rothamsted estate at Harpenden. He had three wives, the third being Katharine, daughter of Maurice Thomson of Watton at Stone. In August 1642 he became a deputy-lieutenant for Hertfordshire and a Captain of the Militia Trained bands of the Hundreds of Cashio and Dacorum. Appointed Colonel of the first Hertfordshire volunteer regiment in 1643, he was sent firstly to Uxbridge to run the garrison at Aylesbury. He later served on the St Albans Standing Committee and was elected as MP for the County in the Protectorate Parliaments. He made his peace with Charles II at the Restoration and subsequently was made a baronet. He spent his retirement cultivating exotic fruit and vegetables, anticipating the later agricultural work at Rothamsted. [His weather diary has been published in this series: Harcourt Williams M, and Stevenson J (eds) *Observations of weather: The weather diary of Sir John Wittewronge of Rothamsted 1684-89* ,Hertford Record Society, Vol XV (Hertford, 1999). His papers are in HALS: DE/Lw series, papers of the Lawes-Wittewronge families]

# Bibliography

1 Pamphlets and Newssheets in the British Library
a) Manuscripts
Lansdowne MSS 255 *f*5
Add Mss 40630 Capel Estate Papers *ff*131, 134-41
b) Pamphlets
E84 (39), Anon, The Humble Petition of the Inhabitants of the County of Hertford to His Majesty, (London, undated)
E115 (7) Anon, *A Perfect Diurnall of the proceedings in the county of Hartford from Tuesday the 15 of August to the 29* (London, 1642)
E118/13 Anon, *Exceeding joyfull news from Derby. Also the taking of Sir John Watson neer Hertford,* (London, 1642)
669 *f*5, *Humble Petition of the inhabitants of Watford*, (1 July 1642)
c) Newssheets
E53 [21] *Mercurius Civicus* 18
E53 [24] *The True Informer*, 37
E54 [21] *Mercurius Civicus,* 19
E73 [8] *The Parliament Scout* 18
E74 [16] *The Scottish Dove*
E74 [21] *The True Informer*, 7
E75 [3] *Certain Informations*
E76 [22] *Kingdom's Weekly Post*, 3
E77 [8] *The Compleate Intelligencer and Resolver*, 5
E77 [23] *The Parliament Scout,* 23
E85 [15] *Kingdom's Weekly Intelligencer*, 3
E249 [17] *Perfect Diurnall*, 54

2 Other sources in The National Archives
a) Chancery:
C139/13/6 *ff*4d, 41d
C193/13/3 *ff*30-31; 13/4 *f*43d
C231/5 *ff*231, *ff*220v, 256, 330-1, 374, 406, 468, 485, 530-1
b) Exchequer:
E179/248/23 *ff*12, 24, 29, 48, 113r, 121
c) State Papers:
SP16/376 *f*106; 395 *f*111; 399 *f*81;
SP19/2 *f*23;

SP20/1 *ff*153, 232-5
SP28/130 Pt II, Commissary book for horses; 197 Pt 2 ff 6-18, 22-3, 62
SP28/209B Accounts of John Barre of Hatfield collector for Broadwater William Seward for Hertford Hundred, Heath and Chandler for Braughing Hundred , James Roberts for Dacorum, William Gaze and Andrew Hawkes for Cashio
Probate (230 Fines)

3 Other archives
Bodleian Library: Microfilm of Tanner Mss 60 *ff*101, 138, 140; 64 *f*121
Trinity College Cambridge Library: Box 44 (VI) 7 No 99
Cambridge University Library: Ec.3.30 27 Taxation of the Hundreds of Herts May 1642
Dacorum Borough Council: Hemel Hempstead Bailiwick Minute Book, I

4 Hertfordshire Archives and Local Studies (HALS)
a) Estate and personal Papers:
Caledon Mss DE/Cd/F46 Diary of Ralph Freeman
Capel Mss 10602; M9, M212-213
Cassiobury Mss 8745 *ff*68-75, 85, 139-41
Garrard Mss 27235-7
Halsey Papers 12877; Coxe letters 70536-70577
Wittewrong Mss DE/Lw/O2; DE/Lw/Z22/11
b) Hertford Borough Records (HBR):
HBR20 *ff*170v, 175r, 195v, 181, 207d, 211r, 223, 422d-3; 25 *f*6; 26 *ff*40, 49, 51, 52, 75, 174, 207d; 46 *ff*907, 908, 933]
c) St Albans Borough Records:
Off Acc 1162
d) Parish Records:
DP/3/12/1 Aldenham Parish Register
DP/116/1/1 Ware Parish Register
DP/118/1/1 Watton Parish Register
DP/93/5/2 *ff*73d, 96 St Peter's St Albans Churchwardens' Accounts
DP/71/5/2 Little Munden parish account book
e) Quarter sessions Records:
QSB2A, 2B, 3 Quarter Sessions Books
QSMB2 Quarter Sessions Minute Book
QSR 5-7 Quarter Sessions Rolls
f) Miscellaneous:

28529-31; 37693; 46349-54; 78660
D/Z55/O2
f) Local Studies Collection:
Hine Collection Vol 30 Civil War Tracts

5 Printed Primary Sources and Calendars

Adams, B, (ed) *Lifestyle and culture in Hertford: Wills and inventories for the parishes of All Saints and St Andrew, 1660-1725*, Hertfordshire Record Society, 13 (Hertford, 1997)
Anon, *The Journals of the House of Commons 1625-1666*, Vols II-VIII of series (1803)
Anon, *The Journals of the House of Lords 1628-1666*, Vols IV-XI of series (nd)
Anon, *Masters of the Bench of the Hon Society of the Inner Temple 1450-1883 and Masters of the Temple 1540-1803,* (1883)
Anon, *Students admitted to the Inner Temple 1547-1660*, (1877)
Anon, *The Records of the Honourable Society of Lincoln's Inn, I, Admissions 1420-1799* (1896)
Anon *Statutes of the Realm,* V, (1628-80) (1819)
Ashby, M (ed) *The Hellard Almshouses and other Stevenage Charities, 1482-2005,* Hertfordshire Record Society, 21 (Hertford, 2005)
Bell, P, 'Minutes of the Bedfordshire Committee for Sequestrations', Bedfordshire Historical Record Society, *Miscellanea,* 49, (Bedford, 1970)
Bonsey, C G, and Jenkins, J G, (eds.) *Ship Money papers and Richard Grenville's Note-book*, Buckinghamshire Record Society, 13, (Welwyn Garden City, 1965)
Bray, W (ed) *Diary and correspondence of John Evelyn*, (c1919)
Coates, Jones and Snow (eds) *Private Journals of the Long Parliament*, (Yale, 1982)
Dale, T C, (ed) *The Inhabitants of London in 1638,* (2 Vols) (1931)
Dyfnalt-Owen, G, (ed) *HMC Salisbury (Cecil) Mss* Vols XXII (1971) XXIV (1976)
Edwards, T, *Gangreana,* (Exeter, 1977)
Falvey, H and Hindle, S (eds) '*This little commonwealth': Layston parish memorandum book, 1607-c1650 and 1704-c1747*, Hertfordshire Record Society, 19 (Hertford, 2003)
Firth, C H, and Rait, R S (eds) *Acts and Ordinances of the Interregnum 1643-1660,* 3 Vols (1911)

Flood, S, (ed) *St Albans Wills 1470-1500,* Hertfordshire Record Society, 9, (Hertford, 1993)
Foster, J, (ed) *London Marriage Licences 1521-1869* (1887)
Foster, J, (ed) *Register of Admissions to Gray's Inn, 1521-1889* (1889)
Green, M A E (ed) *Calendar of the Proceedings of the Committee of Compounding 1643-1660*, 5 Vols (1889)
Harcourt Williams M, and Stevenson J (eds) *Observations of weather: The weather diary of Sir John Wittewronge of Rothamsted 1684-89,* Hertfordshire Record Society, 15 (Hertford, 1999)
Howlett, B (ed.), *Survey of the Royal Manor of Hitchin, 1676,* Hertfordshire Record Society, 16, (Hertford, 2000)
*HMC Portland Mss* I,
*HMC 7th Report* Appendix Verney Papers,
*HMC 8th Report Duke of Manchester Mss*
*HMC 8th Report Duke of Marlborough Mss*
*HMC Various Collections VII*
King, A J, (ed) *Muster Books for North and East Hertfordshire1508-1605,* Hertfordshire Record Society, 12 (Hertford, 1996)
Larkin, J, (ed) *Stuart Royal Proclamations Vol. II: Royal proclamations of King Charles I, 1625-1646,* (Oxford, 1983)
Loftis, J, (ed) *The memoirs of Anne Lady Halkett and Ann lady Fanshawe*, (Oxford, 1979)
Munby, L M, (ed) *Early Stuart Household Accounts*, Hertfordshire Record Society, 2 (Hertford, 1986)
Philip, I G, (ed) *Journal of Sir Samuel Luke, Vol. III,* Oxfordshire Record Society, XXXIII (Banbury, 1953)
Questier, M C, (ed) *Newsletters from the Caroline court, 1631-1638: Catholicism and the politics of the personal rule*, Camden, 5th Ser 26, (Cambridge, 2005)
Rowe, A, *Garden Making and the Freman Family: A memoir of Hamels 1713-1733*, Hertfordshire Record Society, 17 (Hertford, 2001)
Tibbutt, H G, (ed) *The Letter Book of Sir Samuel Luke 1644-1645,* Bedfordshire Record Society XLII (Bedford, 1963)

6 Secondary Sources

Adair J, *Roundhead General*, (Stroud, 1997)
Alderman H M, 'Sir Thomas Coningsby of North Mimms', *Hertfordshire Countryside,* 10, No 39 (1955)
Antrobus, J J, *Bishops Hatfield*, (Hatfield, 1912)

# BIBLIOGRAPHY


Appleby, D, 'Unnecessary persons? Maimed soldiers and war widows in Essex 1642-1662', *Essex Archaeology and History*, 32, 3rd Ser (Colchester 2001) pp209-221

Ashton, R, *The crown and the money market 1603-1640,* (Oxford, 1960)

Ashton, R, 'From Cavalier to Roundhead Tyranny, 1642-5' in Morrill, J, (ed) *Reactions to the English Civil War 1642-9*, (1982) pp195-7

Aylmer, G, *The King's Servants: The civil service of Charles I, 1624-1642*, (1961)

Aylmer, G E and Morrill, J S, *The Civil Wars and Interregnum,* (1980)

Beaven, A B, *The Aldermen of the City of London,* 2 Vols (1908-13)

Bell, P, 'Minutes of the Bedfordshire Committee for Sequestrations', Bedfordshire Historical Record Society, Vol 49, (Bedford, 1970)

Bennett M, *Historical dictionary of the British and Irish Wars 1637-1660*, (London, 2000)

Bennett, M, *The Civil Wars experienced: Britain and Ireland 1635-1661*, (2000)

Birken, W, 'Dr John King 1614-1681 and Dr Assurerus Regemorter (1615-1650) brethren in the Dutch Church and in the College of Physicians of London, with added references to other "Dutch" congregants in the Royal College, Dr Baldwin Hamey and Dr George Ent', *Medical History* (1976) 20(3) pp276-95

Boynton, L, *The Elizabethan Militia 1558-1638*, (1967)

Braddick, M J, *The nerves of state: Taxation and financing of the English State, 1558-1714,* (Manchester, 1996)

Bray, M, 'The Watford lecturer and his house'*, Hertfordshire's Past*, No 6 (Spring 1979)

Brigg, W, (ed) *The Herts. Genealogist and Antiquary*, III, (Harpenden, 1899)

Broad, J P F, 'The Verneys and the sequestrators in the civil wars 1642-56, *Records of Buckinghamshire,* 27, (Aylesbury, 1985)

Brunton, D, and Pennington, D H, *Members of the Long Parliament*; (1954)

Burne, A H, and Young, P, *The Great Civil War*, (1959)

Burr, B, 'The Combe family of Hemel Hempstead', *Herts Past and Present*, 3rd Ser No 5 (Spring 2005)

Bushby, D, *Wormley in Hertfordshire* (London, 1954)

Calder, I M, *Activities of the Puritan Faction of the Church of England 1625-1633,* (1957

Cannan, E, *The history of local rates in England in relation to the proper distribution of the burden of taxation,* (2nd ed 1912)

# BIBLIOGRAPHY


Carlson, L H, 'A history of the Presbyterian party from Prides Purge to the dissolution of the Long Parliament', *Church History* XI, (1942) pp83-122

Carlton, C, *Going to the wars: The experience of the British Civil Wars, 1638-1651*, (1994)

Chauncy, H, *Historical Antiquities of Hertfordshire*, 2 Vols (2nd ed Bishops Stortford, 1826)

Chenevix Trench, J, 'The houses of Coleshill: the social anatomy of a seventeenth century village', *Records of Buckinghamshire,* Vol XXV (Aylesbury, 1983) pp61-109

Cliffe, J T, *Puritans in conflict: The Puritan gentry during and after the Civil Wars* (1988)

Clutterbuck, R, *The History and Antiquities of the County of Hertford*, 3 Vols (1815-27)

Cockayne, G E, (ed) *Complete Baronetage,* 5 Vols (Exeter, 1900-6)

Cressy, D, *England on edge: Crisis and Revolution 1640-1642*, (Oxford, 2006)

Cussans, J E, *History of Hertfordshire*, 3 Vols (1870-81)

Daniell, H C N, 'Popes Manor Essendon with a note on Edlins', *East Herts Archeological Society Transactions*, VII, pp148-60 (1924);

Davies, G, 'The Parliamentary army under the Earl of Essex 1642-5', *EHR*, 49, No 193 (Jan 1934)

Edwards, P R, 'The supply of horses to the Parliamentarian and Royalist armies in the English Civil War', *Historical Research*, LXVIII, 165, (Feb 1995) pp49-66

Everitt, A, *Suffolk and the Great Rebellion1640-1660,* Suffolk Record Society Publications, 3 (Ipswich, 1960)

Everitt A, *The Community of Kent and the Great rebellion 1640-1660*, (Leicester, 1966)

Fletcher, A, *A county Community in peace and war: Sussex 1600-1660*, (1975)

Gibbs, V, (ed) *Complete Peerage*, 12 Vols (1910-59)

Greaves, R L, and Zaller, R E, (eds) *The biographical dictionary of British radicals in the 17th century,* 3 Vols (1981-4)

Greening, A, 'Needful and necessary men?': Hertford Borough Freemen 1640-1715', in Jones-Baker, D, (ed) *Hertfordshire in History: papers presented to Lionel Munby*, (Hertford, 1991)

Greening, A, 'Much ado about tippling', *Hertford and Ware Local History Society Journal* (Hertford, 2004) pp3-8

Greening, A, 'The Draper's Tale', *Hertford and Ware Local History Society Journal*, (Hertford, 2005)
Greening, A, 'Inside Information', *Hertford and Ware Local History Society Journal*, (Hertford, 2005)
Gruenfelder, J K, *Influence in early Stuart elections* 1604-1640 (Ohio, 1981)
Haythornthwaite, P J, *The English Civil War 1642-1651: An illustrated military history* (1994)
Hazell, M, *Fidelity and Fortitude: Lord Capell his regiments and the English Civil War,* (Leigh on Sea, 1987)
Hennessy, G, *Novum Repertorium Ecclesiasticum Parochiale Londinense* (1898)
Henning, B, (ed) *The History of Parliament: The House of Commons 1660-1690*, 3 Vols (1983)
Holmes, C*, The Eastern Association in the English Civil War*, (Cambridge, 1974)
Hughes, A, *Politics, Society and Civil War in Warwickshire 1620-60,* (Cambridge, 1987)
Hunt, E M, *The History of Ware*, (2nd ed, Ware, 1986)
Hutton, R, *The Royalist War Effort 1642-1646*, (2nd ed, 1999)
Huxley, G, *Endymion Porter: the life of a courtier 1587-1649*, (1959)
Jones-Baker, D, (ed) *Hertfordshire in History: papers presented to Lionel Munby*, (Hertford, 1991)
Keeler, M F, *The Long Parliament 1640-41: A Biographical study of its members,* (Philadelphia, 1954)
Kennedy, W, *English Taxation 1640-1799: An essay on policy and opinion,* (1913 Reprint 1964)
Kingston, A, *Hertfordshire during the Civil War and Long Parliament*, (1910)
Kishlansky, M, *The rise of the New Model Army,* (Cambridge 1983)
Lamb, G, 'Aylesbury in the Civil War', *Records of Buckinghamshire,* 41, (Aylesbury, 2001) pp183-9
Lindley, K, *Popular Politics and Religion in Civil War London* (Aldershot, 1997)
Mander, R P, 'The Harrisons of Balls Park', *Hertfordshire Countryside,* I9, No 75, (1964) pp106-7
Matthews, A G, *Walker Revised: being a revision of John Walker's Sufferings of the English Clergy during the Grand Rebellion1642-60,* (Oxford, 1948)
Melia S S, *The Battle of Newburn Ford 1640*, (Newcastle, undated)
Morrill, J, *Cheshire, 1630-1660: County government and society during the English Revolution,* (Oxford, 1974)

# BIBLIOGRAPHY


Morrill, J, (ed) *Reactions to the English Civil War*, (London 1982)
Munby, L M, (ed) *The Story of Redbourn,* (Letchworth, 1962)
Munby, L M, 'Sir Richard Fanshawe (1608-66) and his family', *Hertfordshire's Past and Present*, 3, 1962/3, pp2-13
Munby, L M, *Hertfordshire Population Statistics 1563-1801*, (Hitchin, 1964)
Munk, W, *The roll of the Royal College of Physicians of London*, I, (London, 1878)
Newman, P R, *The Old Service: Royalist regimental colonels and the Civil War*, (Manchester, 1993)
O'Riordan M, 'Popular exploitation of enemy estates in the English Revolution, *History*, 78, 253, (June, 1993)
Page W, (ed) *The Victoria County History of the Counties of England, A History of Hertfordshire*, 4 Vols (1908-12)
Pearl, V, *London and the outbreak of the Puritan Revolution,* (Oxford, 1961)
Pennington D H, and Roots, I A, *The Committee at Stafford 1643-5*, (Manchester, 1957)
Pennington, D, 'The War and the People' in Morrill, J, (ed) *Reactions to the English Civil War*, (London 1982
Porter, S, *Destruction in the English Civil Wars* (Stroud, 1994)
Porter, S, (ed) *London and the Civil War* (Basingstoke, 1996)
Prest, W R, *The Rise of the Barristers: A social history of the English Bar, 1590-1640* (Oxford, 1986)
Questier, M, Newsletters
Rabb, T K, *Enterprise and Empire: Merchants and Gentry investment 1575-1630*, (Harvard, 1967)
Roach, J M, *A directory of English Country Physicians 1603-43*, (London, 1962)
Roundell, H, 'The garrison of Newport Pagnell during the civil wars, (Pt 1) *Records of Buckinghamshire,* Vol II, 5, (Aylesbury, 1861)
Rowe, V, *The first Hertford Quakers*, (Hertford, 1970)
Rowe V, 'Place House, Ware, in the seventeenth century', *Hertfordshire's Past*, 15 (Autumn, 1983) pp17-22
Seaver, P S, *The Puritan Lectureships: The politics of religious dissent 1560-1662*, (Stanford Calif. 1970)
Shaw, W A, *A History of the English church during the Civil Wars and under the Commonwealth 1640-60*, II, (1900)
Smith J T, and North, M A, (eds.) *St Albans 1570-1700: A thoroughfare town and its people,* (Hatfield, 2003)
Seymour, W, *Battles in Britain and their political background*, Vol 2, (1975)

Shaw, W A, *A History of the English church during the Civil Wars and under the Commonwealth 1640-60*, II, (1900)
Skeet, F J A, 'Arthur Lord Capell, Baron Hadham 1604-49', *East Herts Archaeological Transactions*, III, Pt III (1907) pp312-335
Stockdale, E, 'Sir John Kelyng, Chief Justice of the King's Bench' *Bedfordshire Historical Record Society, Miscellanea*, 59, (1980) pp43-47
Thomson, A, *The Ware Mutiny: Order restored or Revolution defeated?* (Ware, 1996)
Toms, E, *The Story of St Albans* (Rev ed Luton, 1975)
Turnor, L, *History of the ancient town and borough of Hertford*, (Hertford, 1830)
Underdown, D, *Pride's Purge: Politics in the Puritan Revolution*, (1971)
Urwick, W, *Nonconformity in Hertfordshire,* (1884)
Vallance, E, *Revolutionary England and the National Covenant: State oaths, Protestantism and the political nation, 1553-1682*, (Woodbridge, 2005)
Venn, J, and J A, (eds.) *Alumni Cantabrigiensis to 1900,* Part I, 4 Vols (Cambridge, 1922-7)
Walne, P, 'The honest-hearted Colonel Washington of Brent Pelham who didn't emigrate', *Hertfordshire Countryside*, 35, No 259, (Nov 1980) pp39-42
Watts, M, *The Dissenters,* 2 vols (Oxford, 1978, 1995)
Worden, B, *The Rump Parliament,* (Cambridge, 1971)
Wyatt, G H, 'Financing the civil war', *Records of Buckinghamshire,* 18, (Aylesbury, 1970) pp427-36
Yule, G, *The Independents in the English Civil War*, (Cambridge, 1958)
*A History of the County of Middlesex,* Vol 4 (1971)

Unpublished works:
Crummett, J B 'The Lay Peers in Parliament 1640-1644', University of Manchester PhD Thesis, (1972)
Pegram, A W, 'Descriptive list of Title Deeds of Wormley Manor', HALS Typed Ms (1962)
Roy I, 'The Royalist Army in the First Civil War', Oxford DPhil, Thesis, (1963)
Thomson, A, 'Hertfordshire communities and central-local relations *c*1625-1665' University of London PhD Thesis, (1988)

# THE HERTFORDSHIRE RECORD SOCIETY

The Hertfordshire Record Society exists to make Hertfordshire's historical records of all kinds more readily available to the general reader. Since 1985 a regular series of texts has been published.



Membership enquiries and orders for previous publications to the Hon. Treasurer, 190 Lonsdale Road, Stevenage, Herts SG1 5EX

Annual Subscription (2007-2008) £17.50

Previous publications:

I: *Tudor Churchwardens' Accounts*. Edited by Anthony Palmer (1985) O/P

II: *Early Stuart Household Accounts*. Edited by Lionel M Munby (1986) O/P

III: *'A Professional Hertfordshire Tramp' John Edwin Cussans, Historian of Hertfordshire*. Edited by Audrey Deacon and Peter Walne (1987) O/P

IV: *The Salisbury-Balfour Correspondence, 1869-1892*. Edited by Robin Harcourt Williams (1988) O/P

V: *The Parish Register & Tithing Book of Thomas Hassall of Amwell* [Registers 1599-1657; Tithing Book 1633-35]. Edited by Stephen G Doree (1989) Price £6.00

VI: *Cheshunt College: The Early Years*. Edited by Edwin Welch (1990) O/P

VII: *St Albans Quarter Sessions Rolls, 1784-1820*. Edited by David Dean (1991) O/P

VIII: *The Accounts of Thomas Green, 1742-1790*. Edited by Gillian Sheldrick (1992) Price £6.00

IX: *St Albans Wills, 1471-1500*. Edited by Susan Flood (1993) O/P

# HERTFORDSHIRE RECORD SOCIETY

X: *Early Churchwardens' Accounts of Bishops Stortford, 1431-1538.* Edited by Stephen G Doree (1994) Price £6.00

XI: *Religion in Hertfordshire, 1847-1851.* Edited by Judith Burg (1995) Price £6.00

XII: *Muster Books for North & East Hertfordshire, 1580-1605.* Edited by Ann J King (1996) Price £6.00

XIII: *Lifestyle & Culture in Hertford: Wills and Inventories, 1660-1725.* Edited by Beverly Adams (1997) Price £6.00

XIV: *Hertfordshire Lay Subsidy Rolls, 1307 and 1334.* Edited by Janice Brooker and Susan Flood, with an introduction by Dr Mark Bailey (1998) Price £18.50 (£15.00)

XV: *'Observations of Weather' The Weather Diary of Sir John Wittewronge of Rothamsted, 1684-1689.* Edited by Margaret Harcourt Williams and John Stevenson (1999) Price £19.00 (£15.00)

XVI: *Survey of the Royal Manor of Hitchin, c1676.* Edited by Bridget Howlett (2000) Price £18.75 (£15.00)

XVII: *Garden-Making and the Freeman family A Memoir of Hamels, 1713-1733.* Edited by Anne Rowe (2001) Price £18.50 (£15.00)

XVIII: *Two Nineteenth Century Hertfordshire Diaries, 1822-1849.* Edited by Judith Knight and Susan Flood (2002) Price £19.50 (£15.00)

XIX: *"This little commonwealth": Layston parish memorandum book, 1607-c1650 & 1704-c1747.* Edited by Heather Falvey and Steve Hindle (2003) Price £21.00 (£15.00)

XX: *Julian Grenfell, soldier and poet: letters and diaries, 1910-1915.* Edited by Kate Thompson (2004) Price £22.00 (£15.00)

XXI: *The Hellard Almshouses and other Stevenage Charities, 1482-2005.* Edited by Margaret Ashby (2005) Price £21.00 (£1500)

XXII: *A Victorian Teenager's Diary: the Diary of Lady Adela Capel of Cassiobury, 1841-1842.* Edited by Marian Strachan (2006) Price £17.50 (£15.00)

Maps:

*The County of Hertford From Actual Survey by A Bryant In the Years 1820 and 1821* (2003)  £7.50

*A Topographical Map of Hartford-Shire* by Andrew Dury and John Andrews, 1766 (2004)  £9.50

For more information visit www.hrsociety.org.uk

# INDEX OF NAMES

The following abbreviations have been used: Abr Abraham; Ald Alderman; And Andrew; Ant Anthony; Aug Augustine; Bar Bartholomew; Ben Benjamin; Bt Baronet, Capt Captain; Cat Catherine; Chas Charles; Chris Christopher; Col Colonel; Dan Daniel; Dav David; Dot Dorothy; E Earl; Edm Edmund; Edw Edward; Eliz Elizabeth; Fra Francis; Gab Gabriel; Geo George; Goody Goodwife; Hen Henry; Hum Humphrey; Jas James; Jer Jeremy or Jeremiah; Jn John; Jon Jonathan; Jnr Junior; Jo Joseph; Kat Katherine; Kt Knight; Lieut Lieutenant; Maj Major; Gen General; Marg Margaret; Mic Michael; Mo Moses; Nat Nathaniel; Oli Oliver; Phil Philip; Ral Ralph; Ran Randolph; Ric Richard; Rob Robert; Row Rowland; Sam Samuel; Sim Simon; Snr Senior; Ste Stephen; Su Susan or Suzanne; Tho Thomas; Tim Timothy; Walt Walter; Wid Widow; Wm William

Numbers in **bold** refer to the numbers of individual documents, in Roman to the pages in the Introduction and in *italics* to the pages in the Appendix. n=footnote and nn=footnotes

# INDEX OF NAMES

# INDEX OF NAMES

# INDEX OF NAMES

# INDEX OF NAMES

# INDEX OF NAMES

# INDEX OF PLACES AND SUBJECTS

Numbers in **bold** refer to the numbers of individual documents, in Roman to the pages in the Introduction and in *italics* to the pages in the Appendix. n=footnote nn=footnotes

# INDEX OF PLACES AND SUBJECTS

# INDEX OF PLACES AND SUBJECTS

# INDEX OF PLACES AND SUBJECTS

# INDEX OF PLACES AND SUBJECTS

# INDEX OF PLACES AND SUBJECTS

# INDEX OF PLACES AND SUBJECTS

# INDEX OF PLACES AND SUBJECTS

# INDEX OF PLACES AND SUBJECTS

# INDEX OF PLACES AND SUBJECTS

# INDEX OF PLACES AND SUBJECTS

A
B
C
D
G
K
P
A Cowe Bridge
B Old Croße
C S. Andrews
D The mill
E S. Nicolas
G S. Maries
H Hony lane
K Back stret
L Highe stret
M Alhallowes
N Castle stret
P West stret